Japonisme Comes to America

JAPONISME COMES

HARRY N. ABRAMS, INC., PUBLISHERS, NEW YORK

In association with The Jane Voorhees Zimmerli Art Museum, Rutgers, The State University of New Jersey

TO AMERICA

THE JAPANESE IMPACT ON THE GRAPHIC ARTS 1876–1925

Julia Meech and
Gabriel P. Weisberg

The exhibition and publication have been supported by
generous grants from:
Brother Industries, Ltd./Brother International Corporation
Yoshiro Yasui, President of BIL, and
Tomomasa Yasui, President of BIC,
as well as from
The Japan Foundation

Funding has been made possible in part by the New Jersey State
Council on the Arts/Department of State

Editor: Phyllis Freeman
Designer: Dana Sloan

Library of Congress Cataloging-in-Publication Data
Meech-Pekarik, Julia.
Japonisme comes to America: the Japanese impact on the graphic arts
1876–1925 / Julia Meech, Gabriel P. Weisberg
p. 256 cm. 22.5 x 24.5
Exhibition catalog.
Includes bibliographical references.
ISBN 0–8109–3501–5
1. Art, American — Japanese influences — Exhibitions. 2. Art,
Modern — 19th century — United States — Japanese influences —
Exhibitions. 3. Art, Modern — 20th century — United States — Japanese
influences — Exhibitions. I. Weisberg, Gabriel P. II. The Jane
Voorhees Zimmerli Art Museum. III. Title.
N6510.M44 1990
760′.0973′07474942 — dc20 90-64
CIP

Published in 1990 by Harry N. Abrams, Incorporated, New York

A Times Mirror Company
Printed and bound in Japan

Exhibition itinerary:
Nelson-Atkins Museum of Art, Kansas City:
July 22–September 2, 1990

The Jane Voorhees Zimmerli Art Museum, Rutgers,
The State University of New Jersey, New Brunswick:
September 16–November 18, 1990

The Setagaya Museum, Tokyo:
December 20, 1990–January 20, 1991

Title page: Arthur Wesley Dow, *Moonrise,* c. 1910. Color woodcut.
Private collection, photograph courtesy of the Worcester Art Museum

CONTENTS

INTRODUCTION

Japonisme Comes to America: The Japanese Impact on the Graphic Arts, 1876–1925, is a sequel to the 1975 exhibition *Japonisme: The Japanese Influence on French Art, 1854–1910,* organized by the Zimmerli Art Museum (then called University Art Gallery), The Cleveland Museum of Art, and The Walters Art Gallery. Over the ensuing fifteen years much research and a number of important exhibitions have resulted in substantially greater knowledge and a more general awareness of Japan's pervasive effect on the style, content, technique, and philosophy of the arts in Europe and the United States since 1854. It was that year that Commodore Matthew C. Perry and his American fleet of "Black Ships," with a show of force, convinced Japan to sign diplomatic agreements with the United States. With the opening of Yokohama in 1859, Japan, its art, and its culture became more readily accessible and intelligible to the West for the first time in almost two hundred fifty years. This was, of course, to have a major impact on the world—politically, economically, and artistically.

The term "Japonisme" was coined in 1872 by the French collector and art critic Philippe Burty to define the taste for things Japanese, and it is most often associated with nineteenth-century European art, and French art in particular. This relationship has been reinforced by the concentration of exhibitions and monographs on Japonisme, dealing with the work of such immensely popular artists as Monet, Manet, Degas,

Gauguin, Toulouse-Lautrec, and the American expatriates Whistler and Cassatt. Most notable among recent work on European Japonisme in general are: *Japonisme in Art,* the publication of the 1979 international symposium in Tokyo which also accompanied a major traveling exhibition in Japan; Siegfried Wichmann's *Japonisme: The Japanese Influence on Western Art in the 19th and 20th Centuries,* published in Germany in 1980 and in England and the United States in 1981; the series of *Reports* published (primarily in Japanese) in Tokyo since 1981 by The Society for the Study of Japonisme; *Le Japonisme,* an exhibition and publication organized by the Musée d'Orsay, Paris, and the National Museum of Western Art, Tokyo, in 1988; and Gabriel and Yvonne Weisberg's extensive Japonisme bibliography published in 1990. However, one of the earliest and most comprehensive studies of Japonisme is not about European art but about American: Clay Lancaster's 1963 book, *The Japanese Influence in America.* Lancaster discusses Japonisme as it relates to painting and prints but concentrates mostly on the decorative arts and architecture.

It is not a coincidence that of the Americans working in the United States at the turn of the century, the two today probably most associated with Japanese aesthetics, Louis Comfort Tiffany and Frank Lloyd Wright, are also leading figures in the American Arts and Crafts movement. Indeed, unlike Europe, where there is a balance of Japanese influence between the decorative arts and painting, in the United States Japonisme plays a more dominant role within the decorative arts. Subsequent to Lancaster's publication, exhibitions have approached the study of the Japanese influence on American art as one aspect of a larger investigation into the Arts and Crafts and Aesthetic movements. Most recently the history of American ceramics and Japonisme was the entire focus of an exhibition and publication by the Everson Museum at Syracuse, New York.

Beginning with an 1886 watercolor by John La Farge and ending with a 1925 woodblock print by Bertha Lum, *Japonisme Comes to America* is an exhibition of works on paper — prints, posters, watercolors, drawings, and photographs — by American graphic artists inspired by Japan. Most of these artists were printmakers who became fascinated with the craft of ukiyo-e woodblock prints as well as with the medium's illustrative potential — so much so that a number traveled to Japan to learn the technical secrets from native carvers and printers. Other artists attracted by the exotic appeal of the Orient went to Japan to record its people and landscape, while American poster artists, following the lead of Europeans, assimilated Japanese aesthetics as a more powerful means to transmit commercial messages in a two-dimensional format.

Japanese art presented to Americans a new aesthetics — an aesthetics, however, which was also combined with craft and function. It was this combination that was most often attractive to American graphic artists who became not only some of Japanese art's most dedicated practitioners but also Japonisme's most ardent advocates.

Japonisme Comes to America combines the diverse talents of Dr. Gabriel P. Weisberg and Dr. Julia Meech in an in-depth study of the fascinating history of America's early intellectual and visual encounters with Japanese art, either directly or by means of European intermediaries. In so doing it also illuminates the tremendous effects that Japanese art, and specifically ukiyo-e woodblock prints, had upon American graphic arts at the turn of the century. With his strong background in European Japonisme, Dr. Weisberg maps the French, British, and American routes by which Japanese aesthetics was brought to the attention of Americans, beginning with the 1876 Philadelphia Centennial Exhibition and continuing through the 1893 Chicago World's Columbian Exposition. After discussing the aesthetic results of the travels to Japan of John La Farge and Robert Blum, Dr. Weisberg concentrates on two artists — the British-born Louis John Rhead and the American William Bradley — whose works exemplify the American poster movement's involvement with Japonisme. The illustrative views of Japan by La Farge and Blum, among the earliest American artists to travel to Japan, represent the basic nineteenth-century curiosity for all things Japanese; while the decorative poster designs of Rhead, Bradley, and Arthur Wesley Dow reveal the assimilation in America, as in Europe, of Japanese motifs and compositions within the context of the modernist, abstract tendencies of Art Nouveau.

Julia Meech has served as the principal organizer of this exhibition and publication; as a scholar and connoisseur of Japanese art, in particular, Dr. Meech brings to her investigation precise knowledge of the early American travelers to Japan and collectors of Japanese art, William Sturgis Bigelow, Ernest Fenollosa, and Edward Sylvester Morse, as well as the special role of Chicagoans Charles J. Morse, Frederick W. Gookin, Clarence Buckingham, and Frank Lloyd Wright in the establishment of collections of Japanese prints and in the dissemination of information on Japanese art. She also reveals the educational significance of the writings of artists Dow and Henry Bowie — the former work for its role in the Arts and Crafts movement and the latter for American comprehension of Japanese artistic concepts. In addition, she discusses Japanese printmaking techniques, and Meiji period printers, carvers, and art societies as they relate specifically to those Americans who traveled and worked in Japan, such as Helen Hyde, Bertha Lum, and Dow. Finally, Dr. Meech suggests the importance of Japanese aesthetics to American photography at the turn of the century.

The purpose of the Zimmerli Art Museum's International Center for Japonisme is to investigate the mutual cultural and artistic influences between Japan and the West. I am grateful to Julia Meech and Gabriel Weisberg for taking on this particular project and, in so doing, adding greatly to our knowledge of the Japanese/American artistic relationship. Thanks to the enthusiasm for Japonisme on the part of Marc Wilson and Seiji Oshima, Directors, respectively, of The Nelson-Atkins Museum in Kansas City and The Setagaya Museum in Tokyo, this exhibition is able to travel beyond New Jersey and reach an expanded audience within the two countries to which the theme most directly pertains.

Barbara Trelstad, Registrar, and Ellen Lynch, Assistant Registrar at the Zimmerli Art Museum deserve special recognition for their wide-ranging assistance with many details of organization. We are also grateful to Joan Mirviss for a careful reading of one portion of the manuscript.

It has been a pleasure to co-publish *Japonisme Comes to America* with Abrams and especially to work with its editor, Phyllis Freeman. The quality of the publication has been greatly enhanced by her steadfast direction and interest. Thanks are due also to her assistant, Rebecca Tucker.

The exhibition and catalogue have been supported by a generous grant from the Japan Foundation. It is, however, the consideration and willing participation of the numerous lenders—private individuals and public institutions—that have made this project possible. Finally, a great debt of thanks is owed, specifically, to the following individuals for their assistance on this project: Sylvia Ragsdale; Mary Ryan, Mary Ryan Gallery, New York; Robert O. Muller; Gala Chamberlain and Daniel Lienau, Annex Gallery, Santa Rosa; Roberta Huber, Paragon Book Gallery; David Acton, Worcester Art Museum; Barbara Wright and Frank J. Dowd, Jr.; Robert Ravicz; Roy Pedersen; Miwa Kai, Columbia University; John Koza and John Grimes, The Peabody Museum of Salem; Margot Galacar, Ipswich Historical Society; Peter Morse; Hirakawa Sukehiro and Hiraishi Noriko, The University of Tokyo; William Green; Frances Pepper Tarson; Jane Oliver; Beverley Denenberg, Denenberg Fine Arts, San Francisco; Karin Breuer, Judith Eurich, and Maxine Rosston, The Fine Arts Museums of San Francisco, Achenbach Foundation for Graphic Arts; Gioia and Mitchell Brock, Tokyo; Lawrence Fong and Claudia Fischer, Museum of Art, University of Oregon, Eugene; Phillip Nalbone, Yorkville Total Fitness; Takako Sato, Daiwa Securities, New York; Mariko Sato, Tokyo; Satō Dōshin and Yamanashi Emiko, Tokyo

National Research Institute of Cultural Properties; Hosono Masanobu, Yamatane Art Museum, Tokyo; Yamaguchi Seiichi, Saitama University; Taguchi Eiichi, Tokyo University of Fine Arts; Iwakiri Shinichirō, Tokyo; Roberta Waddell and Robert Rainwater, New York Public Library; Doreen Bolger, Colta Ives, David Kiehl, and Ellen Handy, The Metropolitan Museum of Art; Kirstin L. Spangenberg, The Cincinnati Art Museum; Mary Baskett, Cincinnati; Elizabeth Harris, National Museum of American History, Smithsonian Institution; A. V. Griffiths, The British Museum; Steven F. Savitt, The University of British Columbia; John R. Gonzales, California State Library; David Caplan; Martha Severens, Portland Museum of Art; Frederick Moffat, University of Tennessee; Andrew Terry Keats; Richard Campbell and Robert D. Jacobsen, Minneapolis Institute of Arts; Clifford Ackley, Barbara Shapiro, and Nancy Rich, Museum of Fine Arts, Boston

Phillip Dennis Cate, Director
The Jane Voorhees Zimmerli Art Museum

NOTE TO THE READER

Japanese personal names appear in Japanese style, surname first, except in the case of individuals living in or writing for the West who have chosen to adopt the Western order.

Gabriel P. Weisberg

JAPONISME: THE COMMERCIALIZATION OF AN OPPORTUNITY

"Japan seems to be the *terra incognita* that now the busy world desires to know more about; and anything related to that country is interesting."[1] When this appeared in the Philadelphia periodical *The Friend* on April 19, 1851, American awareness of Japan and its culture was still in its infancy. Commodore Matthew C. Perry's opening of Japan to the West a few years later aroused something approaching infatuation with the country, but American understanding of Japanese art and society was slow in coming. When the Japanese government presented to Perry on behalf of the people and president of the United States a number of lacquers, porcelains, fabrics, fans, and books, Americans in general underestimated their artistic value. Only a few of the pieces were placed on public display,[2] in the White House and elsewhere in Washington. Few could imagine that these objects of exquisite craftmanship, with their refined sensibility and taste, would gradually affect the American sense of artistry. However, once stimulated by Japonisme, America began to compete with continental Europe to collect Japanese objects and to assimilate Japanese aesthetic concepts. By the late 1880s, this had encouraged new levels of Western inventiveness, and American designers, printmakers, and artists such as John La Farge enthusiastically reacted to the thousands of ukiyo-e prints and decorative arts that had been imported from Japan.

Curiously, during the 1860s, when both France and, to a lesser degree, England were experiencing the first phase of their passion for Japanese objects, America enjoyed only a brief initial period of "Japan Fever."[3] Part of this early attention was sparked by the Japanese dignitaries who came to the United States to ratify a trade and friendship treaty. In Washington, they met with President Buchanan, toured the nation's capital, attended balls held in their honor, and had their pictures taken by eminent photographers to document for an American audience what the Japanese actually looked like (fig. 1). Several members of the Japanese legation visited key American cities, where they encountered curious natives. Walt Whitman wrote a short poem to commemorate the legation's arrival in New York City. Joining in this popular celebration, some Americans (such as P. T. Barnum, with his American Museum) put Japanese artifacts on display. Yet they had only a momentary interest, which proved shallow. Ultimately, the Japanese arrival in America was unfortunately timed. The Civil War soon tore the country apart, and the visit was lost in the press of more urgent events.

In the years immediately after the Civil War, few Americans were interested in the Far East and in things aesthetic. First the nation had to be restored. Not until much later in the century were Americans able to capitalize on their initial farsightedness in opening Japan to Western commerce and innovations. Instead of exploiting their lead, Americans came to learn more about the value of Japanese creativity, not from the Japanese themselves but from the ways other Western countries assimilated Japanese aesthetics.

At first, the United States became familiar with Japanese culture and artifacts through French and English reports and collections. As the taste for Japonisme spread, America soon competed with European countries for the best goods. It was not until well after the Philadelphia Centennial Exhibition of 1876, however, that Japonisme swept the United States and reached a broad public audience. Spurred by the activities of French and

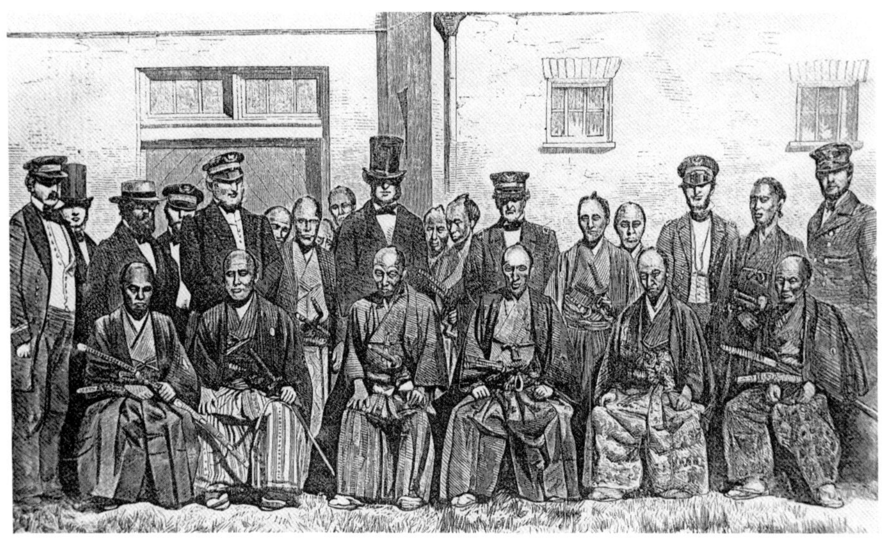

1. *The Japanese Embassy and Their Attendants.* Engraving (from a photograph by Mathew Brady). From *Harper's Weekly,* June 23, 1860

English promoters and industrialists, appreciation of Japanese art encompassed both its own aesthetic merits and its effect on the Industrial Revolution.

Through examples of individual objects on view at the Philadelphia Centennial, Americans could see for themselves how European industrialists were responding to Japanese motifs in ceramics and other decorative art pieces. Once convinced of the works' validity and direction, Americans became even more willing to use Japanese motifs in their own works.

By the late 1880s and 1890s, Japonisme reached a crescendo in the United States and Europe, and many people traveled to Japan to learn more about the country. Not only were commercial ties cemented and private American collections enriched, but the popular craze also continued to grow as Japanese objects became increasingly available. A larger segment of the American public obtained a more accurate glimpse into the unfamiliar territory of Japan through photography, journals, and periodicals. By 1900 so many books and articles had been published on the Far East that few with any interest in culture could have remained totally oblivious to the seduction of Japanese civilization.

Awareness of Japan was so widespread in Western nations by the end of the nineteenth century that it is difficult to disentangle the multileveled strands of influence. Since Japonisme was in itself a complex phenomenon, it is not surprising that the movement's evolution did not follow a single, linear path. Similarly, to think that the American passion for Japanese culture emerged solely from a direct relationship between the two countries is to miss a crucial point. What elevated Japonisme to a truly worldwide status were commercial negotiations (sometimes among several nations), trade agreements, and political machinations and pressures, combined with the personal energy of two generations of entrepreneurs.

Since the United States was the last Western bastion untouched by Japonisme, many — including the Japanese — saw it as a country that could be spurred to new levels of curiosity that could in turn encourage new markets and greater consumption. The numerous implications of this story are worth examining at length, for through Japonisme, America reacted to change, commercialization, and "new" inspiration in the world of the visual arts.

The Fair: The Philadelphia Centennial and Japonisme

The Philadelphia Centennial Exhibition, held during the summer of 1876, provided Americans with their first opportunity to examine a large collection of Japanese objects and artifacts. The exhibit, composed of wood objects, ceramics, glass, and textiles, attracted large crowds and led to an avalanche of articles and illustrations in periodicals such as *Harper's Weekly.* Unusual pieces of furniture and silk fabrics attested to the high level of Far Eastern craftsmanship and technical ingenuity (fig. 3). In addition, sculpture, painting, and architectural designs were shown. A bazaar built as an example of Japanese architecture mesmerized American builders because of the skill in its wood construction.[4] What was not displayed in 1876, however, is also worth noting. Only a few commercially produced photographs of Kyoto were shown, although the vogue for photographs of Japan would reach fever pitch during the late 1880s and 1890s, when visitors to the Far East returned with souvenir albums and hundreds of miniature *carte de visite* images of theatrical performers (fig. 2) and courtesans. More significantly, at no site at the fairground was acknowledgment given to the importance of the Japanese print tradition, a heritage that was already igniting the passionate interest of numerous Europeans. Works on paper, which exerted a lasting impact on American art and craftsmanship later in the century, were totally absent from the fair's halls, even though they were already available in New York and Boston from dealers — albeit not in huge quantities.

Among the objects exhibited by French manufacturers were a number of porcelains (and possibly some faience pieces) that revealed decorators' growing interest in Oriental and specifically Japanese motifs. Although this tendency had been well established throughout France since the mid-1860s — manufacturers in Bordeaux had already contributed designs in the Japanese style — the fact that French manufacturers presented such pieces as part of their official installation in America demonstrated their willingness to turn to the topical and timely as a way to revitalize their lagging industry.[5] The exhibition of such works in Philadelphia, under the aegis of major manufacturers from Limoges, sparked several illustrated articles in the American press. These ceramic pieces stood at the vanguard of what could be accomplished via Japonisme. Only a short while later, other examples of Japonisme-influenced objects became known in the United States, which eventually stimulated a taste for Japonisme in all areas of the visual arts. What began slowly in Philadelphia gathered momentum as promoters of Japanese objects, especially prints, found America to be an area ripe for cultivation.

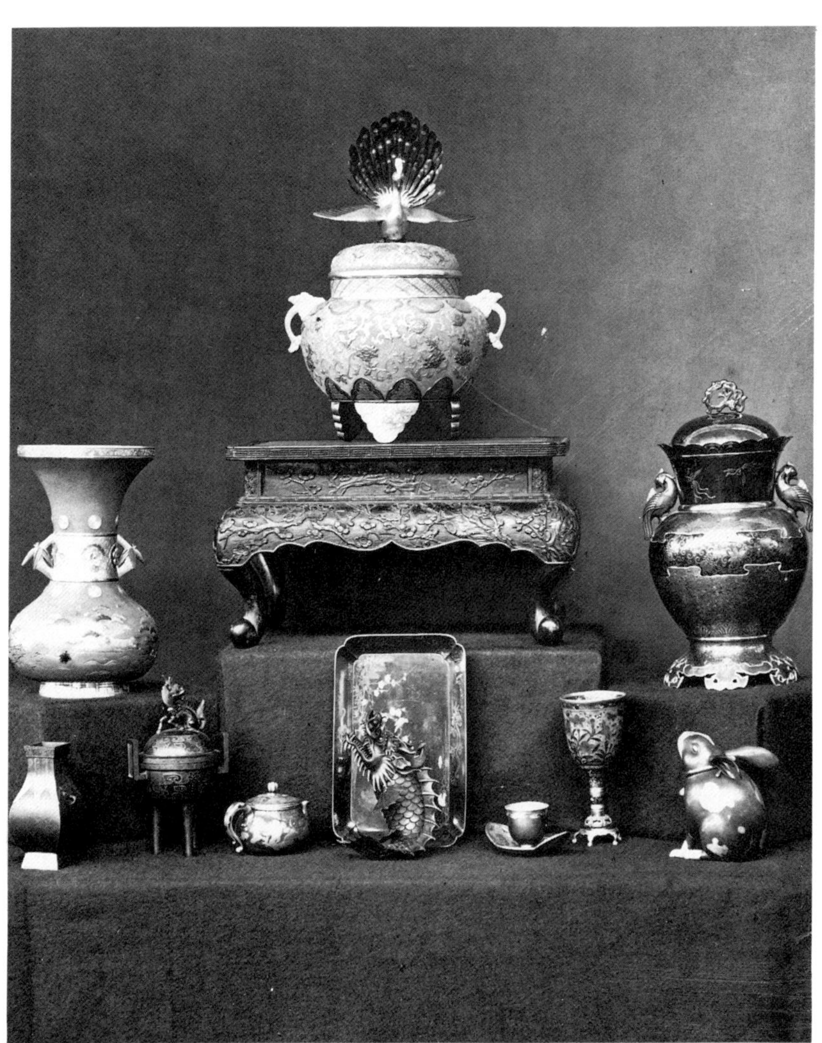

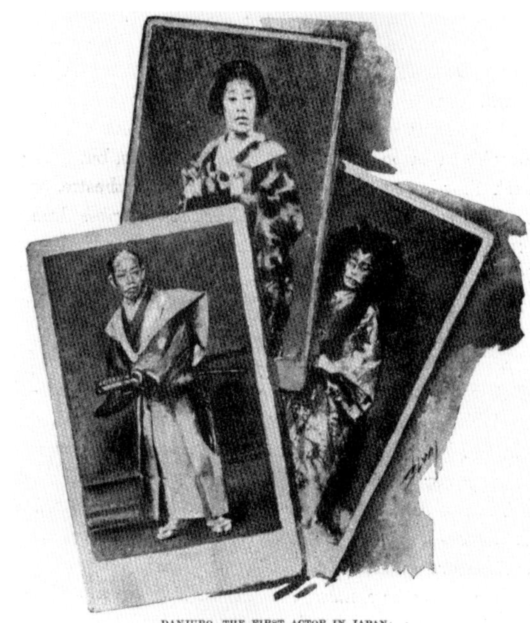

DANJURO, THE FIRST ACTOR IN JAPAN.
In the "Forty-seven Rônins" and other characters.

2. *Danjuro, the First Actor in Japan.* Page from Edwin Arnold, *Japonica,* 1892

3. *Bronze and Lacquer Work in the Japanese Section, Centennial Exhibition.* Engraving. From *Harper's Weekly,* August 12, 1876

French Travelers and Promoters in the United States

Representatives from many areas of the French business and artistic communities traveled to Philadelphia during the course of the Centennial Exhibition to see their objects *in situ.* The fact that some of these visitors were native-born Americans who had established themselves in Limoges made their presence in the United States more timely and welcome.[6] The Haviland firm, which had had a shop in New York since 1855, fostered development of Japanese motifs by some of the leading artistic exponents of Japonisme in France, such as the printmaker Félix Bracquemond. Consequently, the Haviland pieces were among the best known and most frequently studied examples of Japonisme on view in Philadelphia. In addition, the Havilands were becoming recognized as major collectors of Japanese objects, including ukiyo-e — popular woodcut prints of actors, courtesans, and scenic locations. (Charles Haviland amassed an extensive collection of prints and decorative art objects that many could have visited in France.) This not only helped to develop the Havilands' appreciation of the Japanese aesthetic, it also made them extremely sensitive to how the Japonisme craze could be promoted on an international scale. The presence of Japanese-inspired Haviland pieces, among them examples from the "Service Parisien," designed in 1876 by Félix Bracquemond in a blend of Impressionism and Japonisme (fig. 4), greatly encouraged American firms and collectors to accept and utilize Japonisme as a way to keep their own holdings up to date.

In the years immediately after the Centennial the taste for things Japanese continued to spread. Commercial magnates, whose goals were both consumer oriented and aesthetic, further diffused this interest, as did the presence in America of several active French art dealers and others who promoted Japonisme. Exhibits and auctions of Japanese and Japanese-inspired art were organized in key cities on the East Coast, as well as elsewhere in the country, and critics were enlisted to write about

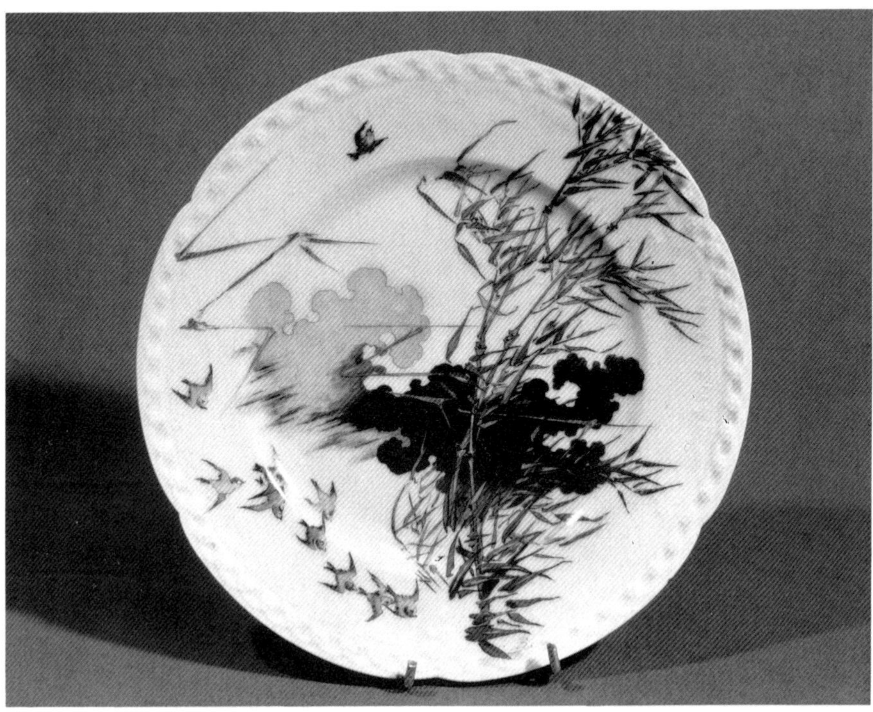

4. Félix Bracquemond. Plate from the "Service Parisien," Haviland and Company, 1876. Courtesy Haviland and Company, Limoges

them in daily newspapers. All this helped to attract the middle-class American to these "new" objects. Additionally, French dealers and collectors who positioned themselves as experts in the United States began to draw American visitors—particularly in conjunction with the 1878 Exposition Universelle—to their headquarters in Paris. There, in the mecca of artistic taste, many Americans whose own awareness of Japanese quality was not very far advanced hoped to secure objects for their collections back home.

Japanese art objects were available in many locations throughout Paris in the 1870s and 1880s. Small illustrated books, often produced for the Western export trade, were found at the Bon Marché, the symbol of the modish department store that made objects easily attainable by all.[7] Some objects came from specialty shops that offered gifts and curios to visitors, while higher quality works were sold through increasingly well-established Paris dealers, such as the dominant Siegfried Bing (1838–1905). In fact, Bing became one of the most powerful figures in diffusing

Japanese art and the taste for Japonisme. He capitalized on the craze in Paris by opening several of his own shops in the early 1880s, and he sold Japanese objects in America.[8]

Under the tutelage of dealers such as Bing, another significant change in Japonisme emerged. By the 1880s, ukiyo-e prints replaced the decorative arts as the primary means of collecting and appreciating Japanese art in France. Exhibitions were held to focus attention on the major Japanese printmakers, and by 1883, Louis Gonse, in his monumental book *L'Art Japonais,* provided a detailed history of their lives and works. Through French persistence in collecting and selling these prints, Americans gradually expanded their boundaries and came to know the works of Utamaro, Kiyonaga, and Hokusai.

The French Art Dealer in America

Some years after Siegfried Bing's first trip to Japan (1880–81), he came to recognize that America offered a large untapped market. Since he had stockpiled innumerable Japanese objects in Parisian storerooms — objects he had obtained from direct negotiations with Japanese dealers and collectors as well as from manufacturing firms that concentrated on the export trade — Bing was well prepared to cultivate the American market, and he did so energetically. Bing's ties with America were further documented when the collector Edward S. Morse visited him in Paris in 1883.[9]

Despite the widespread belief that Bing's ties with the United States were linked solely to the appearance of his pamphlet *La Culture Artistique en Amérique* (1894), his involvement with the American promotion of Japanese art actually began in April 1887, when he was listed as selling Oriental objects through Moore's Art Galleries at 290 Fifth Avenue.[10] Most significantly, the preliminary viewing of objects took place in "the rooms of S. Bing, 220 Fifth Avenue on April 25th," which reveals that he had by then established himself and his firm in the sprawling metropolis.[11] Apparently he was also willing to join with an American auctioneer in order to dispose of pieces from his large holdings in France. Advertisements in *The Evening Post* (on April 21) and in the *New York Commercial Advertiser* (on April 23), suggest that Bing and Moore heavily promoted the sale to bring it to the attention of a broad public. Both the catalogue and flyer noted that the sale included "some rare and antique porcelains, superb bronzes, exquisite lacquers, remarkable jades, crystals and hard stones."[12] Bing was obviously sponsoring all types of Orientalia, although the aesthetic value of the pieces was not always apparent in the escalating atmosphere of rampant promotionalism.

Nowhere, however, in this documentation of Bing's early activities in America is there any indication that he was selling Japanese prints. Most likely he was merely trying to capitalize on the growing general awareness of Japan and of Japanese artifacts of a type that had already been most publicly and privately displayed (for example, in 1881 at the Boston Museum of Fine Arts by William Sturgis Bigelow, who exhibited prints he had collected in Paris) following their initial showing at the Centennial Exhibition. Curiously, Bing carried out the auction arrangements without traveling to the United States. Through intermediaries, he was able to distribute objects from France throughout America without straying from his gallery on the rue Chauchat.

This 1887 sale, which was later to prove crucial to the course of Japonisme in America, was reviewed in *The New York Times.* The more trade-oriented *Art Amateur* reflected public taste, and indicated little enthusiasm by buyers; the reviewer noted that "the Bing auction sale at Moore's afforded golden opportunities for embryonic collectors of Japanese bronzes and Chinese and Japanese porcelains. The first two days the goods were almost given away." He added that attendance was low and that the auctioneer was somewhat parochial in ability. He ended by noting that "the advantage of selling an excellent lot of Oriental goods, with the guarantee of a house like Bing, was wholly thrown away."[13]

This sale underscored issues that required resolution if Japonisme was to advance commercially. The sheer quantity of available objects may simply have overwhelmed Bing's potential American consumers. Further, even though some Americans did not want to pay high prices for all the objects, it appears that some pieces with more substantial aesthetic value were reserved for later in the sale. This suggests that despite America's awareness of Japanese art, Bing still had a considerable amount of educating to do before his customers would not be intimidated by the wide selection of Japanese works or by the hefty prices of significant objects. Through his American minions, Bing had to coax his overseas audience toward a more profound appreciation of Oriental art before he could capitalize on the American market. By working with consumers at a deliberately low level, Bing planned to lead them toward acquiring higher quality pieces in the future.

The following April Bing held a second sale. This time he focused on Philadelphia, which was still entranced with the Japanese art exhibited there in 1876. He organized an auction with Davis and Harvey's Art Galleries, located on Chestnut Street in the bustling city's center.[14] As before, the sale included Chinese and Japanese porcelains, faience, pottery, bronzes, enamels, ivories, lacquers, carvings, silk, embroideries, and some furniture; prints were again excluded. Through this sale of works presumably sent from Paris, Bing strengthened his American network. Supervising the sale was John Getz, who now represented Bing's firm in New York after a career as a designer with Herter Brothers. Getz's personal interest in interior decoration may have led him to encourage wealthy customers to utilize all types of Japanese artifacts as a way to modernize and enliven their homes.

With Getz at work, Bing's firm organized an even larger public auction in New York. This sale, which was held late in November of 1888 and saw a wide range of clients purchase 1,334 objects, was actually held in Bing's own showrooms under the supervision of a Fifth Avenue auction house.[15] The French dealer's decision to conduct the sale in his own quarters not only intimates that his firm was doing exceedingly well but also that American appreciation of Japanese objects — including more expensive items — was increasing.

Bing's personal advancement of Japanese art in America continued into the next decade. When he finally traveled to the United States, in 1894, he expanded his contacts by joining The American Art Galleries in New York in the promotion and sale of Chinese and Japanese objects.[16] Similar to his earlier American sales, this one was widely advertised in the daily press, including *The Evening Post,* the *New York Tribune,* and the *Sun,* which noted that Bing had set a high standard for himself. Some writers who previewed the sale mentioned that the quality of objects Bing was selling was improving. Others who saw the spread of Japonisme in a rather commercial light remained skeptical about the entire venture. Such an attitude, compounded by his own interest in increasing public awareness of Japanese art and culture, led Bing to publish *Le Japon Artistique.*

Artistic Japan and Its Impact

While Bing was actively promoting the sale of all types of Japanese objects in America through public auction, his Paris shop on the rue Chauchat was becoming a recognized mecca for the international promulgation of Japonisme; it attracted artists, collectors, and investors from all over the world. At this moment Bing launched his lavish *Artistic Japan.* This well-produced periodical (the grandfather of today's magazines devoted to the visual arts) utilized the most modern reproduction techniques so that the readers of *Artistic Japan* would be able to see as well as read about exquisite Japanese objects.

The thirty-six issues of *Artistic Japan* — it appeared monthly between mid-1888 and mid-1891 — reached an extremely broad audience since it was printed in French, German, and English. The richly illustrated periodical (fig. 5) reached knowledgeable collectors who were already enthusiastic about Japanese art, as well as wealthy members of the middle class who were eager to add Japanese art to their personal collections or who wanted to decorate their homes with Oriental objects. For each issue Bing selected superb examples of Japanese art based on his knowledge of European holdings. He was either selling other featured objects, or they were safely ensconced in his own private collection, which was housed in his apartment on the rue Vézelay in Paris. Thus in effect, *Artistic Japan* was both self-serving for Bing (after all, he had invested his own money in it) and useful for the promotion of Japonisme. Indeed, the journal's international character paralleled the breadth of the movement in general and allowed *Artistic Japan* to emerge as one of the most visible and popular manifestations of Japonisme.

The magazine offered a far-ranging display of Japanese art — including reproductions of Japanese prints — as well as a valuable visual reference for artists as diverse as the painter Vincent van Gogh, the jeweler Lucien Falize, and the textile designer and entrepreneur Arthur Lasenby Liberty. Its timely essays were written by the day's leading Japonistes, who brought insight and enthusiasm to the cause of Japanese art and culture. In effect, *Artistic Japan* was transformed into an educational tool for the international Japoniste movement.[17] In June 1888, the *Japan Weekly Mail* of Tokyo noted that the periodical was helping to "disseminate the love of Japanese art objects in Europe." The writer could have added the United States, since the magazine was widely advertised in American newspapers and periodicals. It was also sold at Bing's rooms on Fifth Avenue and at Brentano's bookstore in New York. Such widespread availability allowed

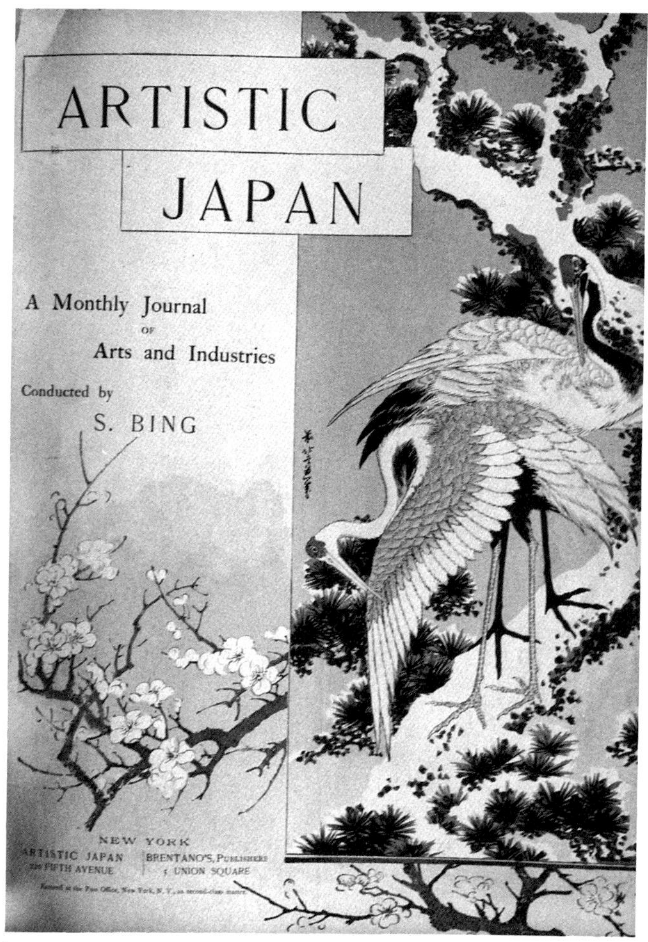

5. *Artistic Japan.* Cover, 1, No. 2 (July 1888)

an American audience to compare the ideas introduced in the journal with the actual objects Bing and his assistants had on display in their New York shop.

Comments on Bing's achievement emanated from numerous countries, as reviewers in England, France, Germany, Scandinavia, and the United States marveled at what he had accomplished in such a short period of time. An American reviewer in *The Critic* of December 4, 1889, wrote that

> Artistic Japan *maintains the high degree of excellence attained in its first numbers. . . . M. Bing writes on the origin of painting gathered from history, and*

writers have, evidently, had generous assistance from native Japanese experts. In each number there are a dozen or more designs in decorative art which we cannot well imagine a good designer in any branch of ornamental industry doing without. We rank this periodical among the highest class of art journals.[18]

No matter what the individual issue's contents or its authors, *Artistic Japan* continued to provoke comment.

In the domain of general interest in Japanese art and culture, the magazine had no peers. It provided an overview of several areas of creativity by examining decorative design and the major printmakers who had influenced artists in the West. More significantly, however, the magazine was seen to demonstrate Bing's personal involvement with word and image: text and design worked in unison through Bing's collaboration with his printer, Gillot. The reader's eye was continually engaged as he read the informative articles. (This type of text and page design may have been of considerable value to the latent American poster movement, as artists involved in this tendency would have known *Artistic Japan* from its inception.)

While the precise range of readership in any one country is not known, it seems that Bing and his collaborators anticipated a large run. They also realized that readers' enthusiasm would wane if articles were too long or if topics were repeated in subsequent issues. Thus from the beginning, *Artistic Japan* was envisioned as a finite publication. Once fundamental concepts had been presented and stressed, Bing determined that the journal would cease. That point was reached at a crucial moment in the appreciation of the art and culture of Japan, just prior to large exhibitions of Japanese art and ukiyo-e prints in the 1890s. For this reason the magazine may be considered not only a Japoniste propaganda vehicle, but also a means of whetting the public's appetite for items that were still available for collecting *chez* Bing.

Bing in America: Japanese Prints Arrive

Once *Artistic Japan* had finished its mission of educating and popularizing, Bing redirected his energies toward disseminating textiles and ceramics from Japan. His trip to the United States in 1894 — ostensibly as an art critic — was intended to promote Japanese art and to organize two sale exhibitions of Japanese prints in America.

Most notable among the other reasons that impelled Bing to journey to the United States was his burgeoning interest in America's own decorative art and how it was influencing designers in Europe. In addition, Bing was troubled by the results of the Chicago Fair of 1893, when Japanese prints had first been presented at a major public exhibition. He still wanted to see Japanese art fully accepted and purchased in America, not only for personal monetary reasons but also for its role in enlivening interiors and revitalizing design. So while he visited American designers from February 12 until he returned to France on April 7, Bing attended to the business of promoting Japanese art.[19]

Bing planned to introduce Japanese art to the United States through the use of the traveling exhibition, a method that had proved successful in Europe. Building on the growing interest in Japanese printmakers, Bing drew objects from the stock of his shop (and possibly from his own personal collection) to develop a show of 290 works ranging in date from 1608 to 1850 by some of the leading ukiyo-e masters. The exhibition and its extensive catalogue were entitled *Japanese Engraving: Old Prints in Color Collected by S. Bing, Paris* (fig. 6) and was first shown at The American Art Galleries in New York in March 1894.[20] In his catalogue introduction, Bing gave the impression that one of the major sponsors and connoisseurs of Japanese art (meaning himself) had decided to educate Americans in the area of prints.

A reviewer for *The Critic* observed that the "exhibition of prints should be of great interest to all who care about the possibilities of color

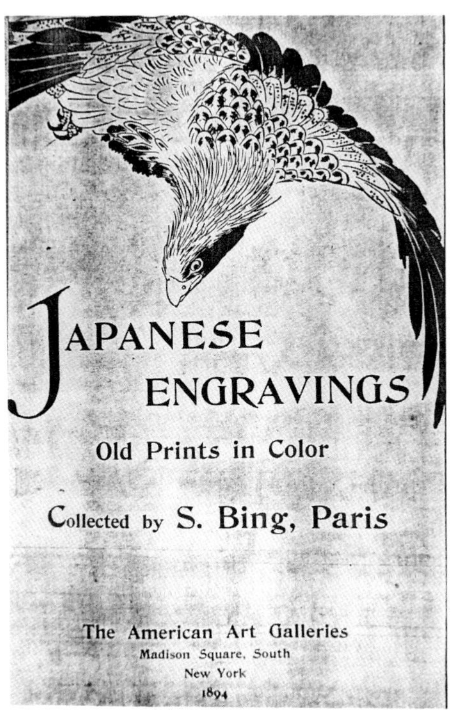

6. The 1894 Japanese Print Exhibition Catalogue at The American Art Galleries, in New York. Cover, 1894

printing, for no more artistic work has ever been done . . . than that produced by the popular school of Japanese art."[21] The show's success in New York inspired Bing to search for other East Coast cities where he might be able to sell more prints. He tried to have the works shown at the Pennsylvania Academy of the Fine Arts in Philadelphia, which had asked him to contribute pieces to its own exhibition of Japanese objects. Although he was able to provide them with textiles, it proved too late and too complicated to include the prints. Nevertheless, Bing soon found another location for his exhibition—Boston.

In April 1894, Bing sent several hundred Japanese prints to the Museum of Fine Arts in Boston, where his friend Ernest Fenollosa, another staunch advocate of Japanese art, was curator of Oriental art. The exhibition of prints was well received by the Boston press, with one critic effusively commenting that the collection was both quite definitive and a "magnificent" display of works that covered the history of Japanese printmaking.[22] Bing did not neglect other types of Japanese objects at this time. A large number of his Japanese textile samples were eventually housed in the Metropolitan Museum of Art, where they promoted Japanese art in still another medium. Other works were acquired by public institutions, so pieces could be studied by connoisseurs and lay visitors alike.

Much as other dealers were beginning to do in the United States in order to introduce the American public to Japanese creativity, Bing relied on the assistance of his colleagues, such as Fenollosa in Boston, and the success of the various Japanese exhibitions at the World's Columbian Exposition in Chicago in 1893.[23]

The Second Fair: Chicago, 1893

Even though Bing did not arrive in the United States in time for the Chicago fair, a strong French contingent did attend and saw numerous

Japanese objects. Undoubtedly they visited the Japanese installation and compared their own interest in Oriental art with what Americans were now experiencing. Quite obviously the Japanese government made its presentations in Chicago with enthusiasm and dedication. It seemed determined to feature only objects of the highest technical quality, perhaps to dispel any association with the somewhat shoddy goods that had been inundating the West, and especially the United States, as part of the country's heavy export trade.

The most significant part of the Japanese installations were the products of "artistic skill,"[24] whose installation required extensive space. (Many more objects were originally anticipated than ultimately were displayed.) Exhibitions of Japanese works were found throughout the fair: in the Palace of Fine Arts, the Horticultural Building, and the Forestry Building, and along the Midway, where a bazaar and a teahouse were constructed (fig. 7).

Among the most ambitious and impressive installations was the Hōōden, or Phoenix Hall (fig. 8), on the Wooded Island in Jackson Park. It consisted of three different types of buildings, each representing a different period in Japanese architecture. The furnishings included screen and wall paintings produced by Japan's leading artists from the Tokyo School of Fine Arts (Tokyo bijutsu gakkō) faculty, such as Kano Tomonobu and Hashimoto Gahō (see Meech, page 111). Since the buildings were widely commented on in the press and were reproduced in a series of engravings, many visitors may have come to the fair to study the sophisticated Japanese architecture that was influencing American designers and architects.[25]

Another Japanese exhibit was a teahouse, which such distinguished American Japonistes as John La Farge and Ernest Fenollosa visited.[26] Other items in the fine-arts pavilion included exquisite hanging scrolls, smaller decorative art objects, and according to the reviewer for *The Critic*, Japanese prints. The actual nature of the prints is in question. The

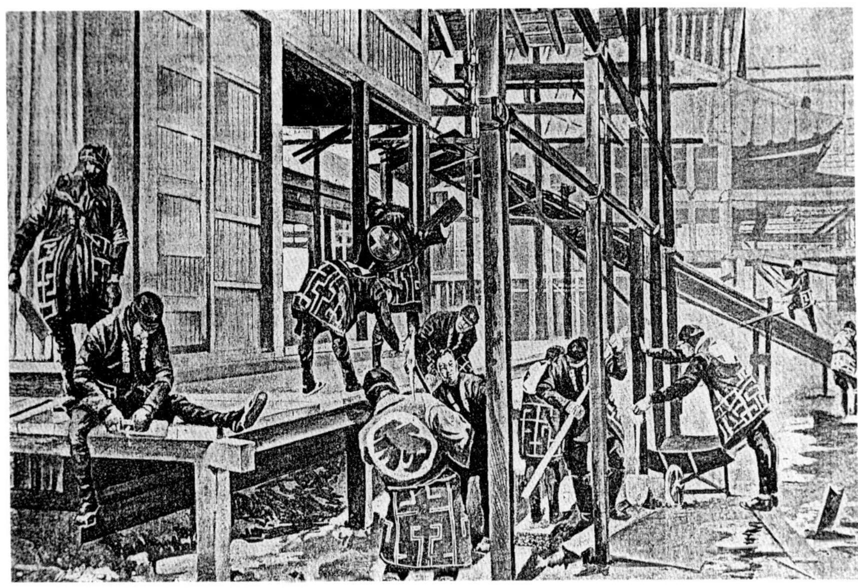

7. *At Work on the Japanese Building — Columbian Exposition, Chicago.* Engraving. From *Harper's Weekly,* March 18, 1893

8. *Hōōden (Phoenix Hall) — Columbian Exposition, Chicago.* Engraving. From *Harper's Weekly,* June 3, 1893

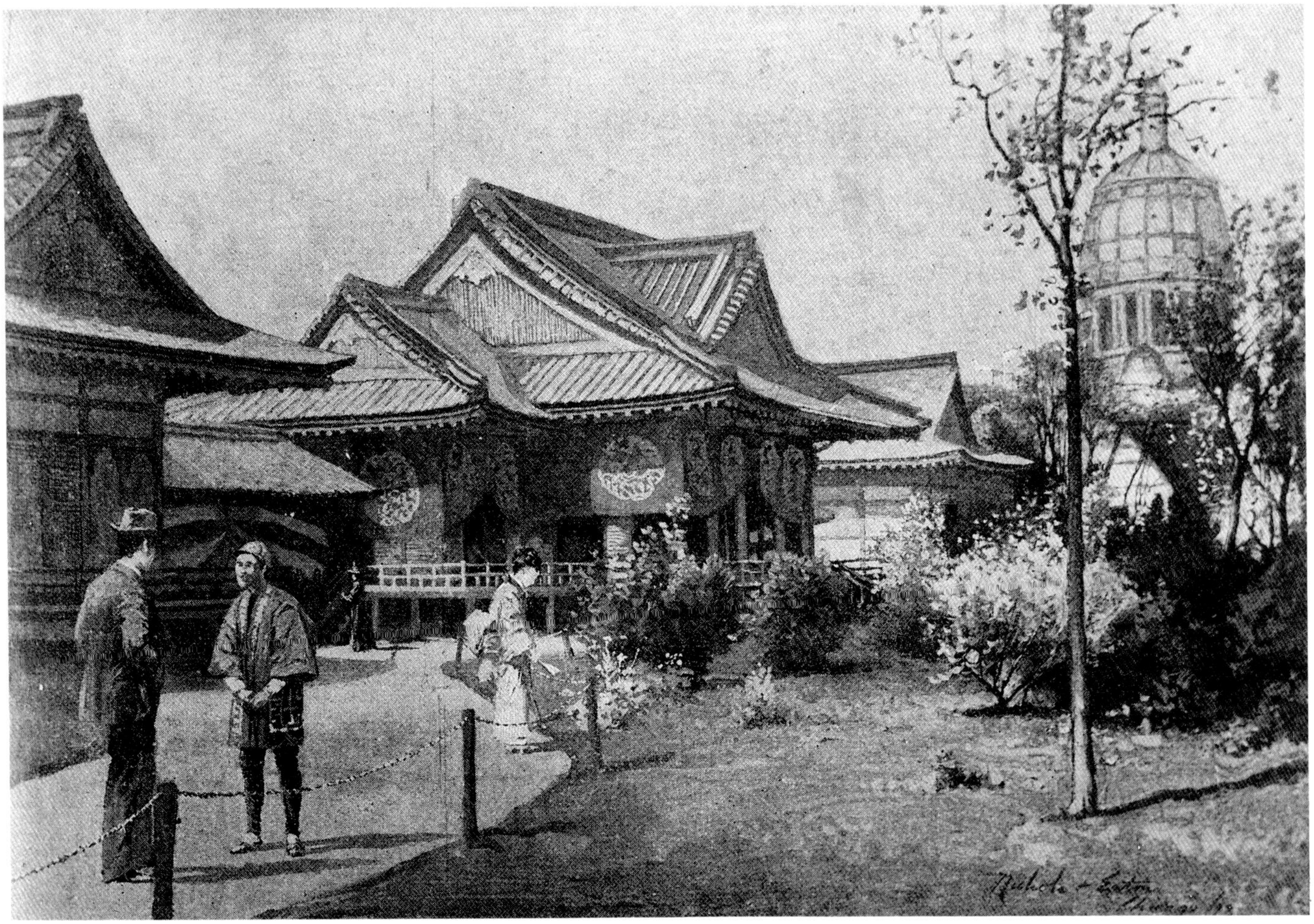

reviewer noted that "the perfection of Japanese lithography is shown by an exhibit of the one hundred and seventeen process prints required for the reproduction of a drawing in color by one of the old masters. The gradations between them are so fine as to be almost imperceptible, but the final result could not be well surpassed."[27] Without further documentation on the prints shown, and in light of the mention of "lithography" (surely an error on the critic's part), it is not clear whether this exhibition of prints was actually a historical display of ukiyo-e prints or more of a technical presentation. The apparent focus on the technique of prints — at a major public fair — significantly inflected the course of future artistic interchange between the United States and Japan.

Undoubtedly, these Japanese installations were intended to secure closer communication between America and the Far East. The Japanese obviously spared no expense in creating objects for the exposition, which was in turn appreciated by thousands of American visitors. With this Japanese presence in the Midwest, Japonisme received an additional boost.

Further French Contacts in the Name of Japonisme

Following the Chicago fair, French art dealers and artists increased their ties with the United States by urging American collectors to appreciate and buy Japanese art. American artists traveled to Paris to meet the major art dealers of the period, including Siegfried Bing and his primary competitor in the 1890s, Hayashi Tadamasa (1853–1906; fig. 9). Hayashi, regarded as one of the most knowledgeable connoisseurs of his day,

had arrived in France in 1878 as a foreign language interpreter for the Japanese corporation charged with managing its country's participation in the Paris Exposition Universelle that year. Determined to make a career for himself in Europe, he stayed on to dispose of the remaining stock, worked for several Japanese trading companies, and

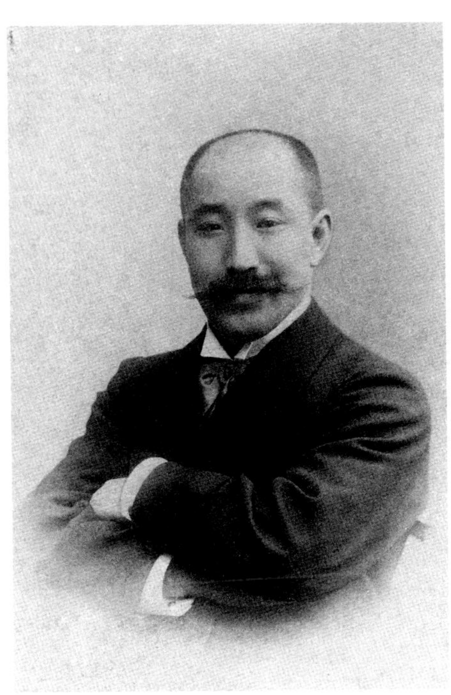

9. Hayashi Tadamasa, in 1896, at age forty-three. Photograph. Courtesy Jōzuka Taketoshi

then in 1884 went into partnership with Wakai Kensaburō, his former employer and a man trained in the antique trade. During the next few years Hayashi traveled widely in China, Europe, and America cultivating clients for Chinese porcelains as well as for Japanese lacquer, bronzes, and prints. From about 1889, when he established himself in sole proprietorship as a merchant of prints, until 1900, when he ceased his commercial activities, he imported 160,000 prints and nearly 10,000 illustrated printed books. He did business from a handsome apartment on the rue de la Victoire.[28]

Budding American entrepreneurs (such as Charles Freer) who had considerable personal wealth to spend on Japanese art made the acquaintance of Bing and Hayashi, among other dealers, and invited them to send objects for possible inclusion in their collections.[29] The prolific painter J. Alden Weir, like many others, purchased Japanese objects directly from Hayashi and Bing, either by mail from Paris or from the latter's New York salesroom. Other American collectors, including the Havemeyers, enlarged their holdings in a similar way during this same time.[30]

While not solely motivated by Japonisme, this artistic interchange between France and the United States was one means by which cultural awareness of the Far East was disseminated and improved. Accordingly, artists throughout America were stimulated by the craze for Japanese art and by the fact that appreciation for Japanese work was due in large part to the influence French designers and dealers had on molding creative energies across the Atlantic Ocean.

The English Response to Japan

French enthusiasm for Japanese art and culture generally has been deemed most pervasive on the European continent, yet the English response to Japonisme was extensive and positive. Since 1862, when Japanese art objects were presented at the London International Exhibition, English artists, collectors, and connoisseurs had become increasingly familiar with Japanese artifacts and aesthetics, and this eventually influenced the creation of artistic pieces in Britain. Concurrently, more and more writings about Japanese art were published. During the mid-1860s, John Leighton published an important and widely read pamphlet on Japanese art in which he proposed aesthetic principles for Western artists. Members of the Pre-Raphaelite circle, such as William Rossetti in 1863, prepared articles that discussed the value of Japanese art. Japonisme also spread in England through James McNeill Whistler, the peripatetic American expatriate whose own fascination with Japanese art began in Paris studios and stores. When he brought his paintings and prints to England, not only did he help to diffuse interest in Japanese art, but his own works also demonstrated how Japanese motifs could be utilized. Whistler's role in English appreciation of Japanese art and in exemplifying the ways in which it could complement European design culminated in his work on the Peacock Room for Frederick Leyland.

At the same time as these early enthusiasms for Japan, impressive articles on Japanese art were published in the widely read British periodical *The Art Journal.* This periodical influenced American audiences, who had ready access to it, especially since English authors and collectors were more likely than their French counterparts to present Japonisme's ideas effectively.

Many of the early articles in *The Art Journal* by writers such as James Jackson Jarves, extolled Japanese "fidelity to nature" and even managed to compare the Japanese to Americans. Jarves found that members of both nations similarly appreciated wit and enjoyed broad, almost slapstick humor.[31] Some of these essays inspired a close assessment of Japanese illustrated books. In his second article, in 1871, Jarves recognized that these books, which were "intelligible to everyone," were used most fully to reach and instruct the multitude in Japan. In fact, he argued that

Westerners would gain considerable insight into Japanese history, myths, legends, and customs if they carefully read and appreciated these print albums.[32]

By the mid-1870s, articles appeared by Sir Rutherford Alcock (1809–1897), the first British consul in Japan and a career diplomat who was quite knowledgeable about events and personalities in the Far East.[33] Aware of the decorative elements in Japanese art that could be used in the West, he helped to formulate a collection of objects from the Far East that could be shown in Great Britain. He saw the decorative arts as being no less serious or important than painting or sculpture. Indeed, his writings were in the forefront in stressing the essential harmony of all the arts. Fundamental to the visual arts after 1870, this concept took root in Europe as well as in the United States by the early 1890s. In a series of articles published in *The Art Journal* in 1878, Alcock emphasized that the Japanese tended to use "limited light and shade." Often the flatness of their forms and lack of modeling dominated the image. These qualities became important to European and American printmakers and poster designers as they increasingly simplified shapes in order to communicate their message more directly.

Coinciding with the appearance of Alcock's articles in widely circulated periodicals was an English series of lavishly illustrated books — or catalogues of contemporary collections — that found an appreciative audience in the United States. Publications such as G. A. Audsley and J. L. Bowes's *The Keramic Art of Japan* (1875) examined a variety of pieces, which were illustrated in excellent reproductions. Other volumes that accentuated travel to Japan also served as extensive guides to the country's art and culture, including a study by Alcock on *Art and Industries in Japan* (1878). Throughout these writings, authors hoped that Japan would retain its sense of purity in design, which in the West was deemed of considerable strength.

Another figure crucial in the dissemination of Japonisme in the United

States was Christopher Dresser (1834–1904). First exposed to Japanese art at the International Exhibition of 1862, in London, Dresser journeyed to the Philadelphia Centennial of 1876. Already a vocal force in the applied arts and the burgeoning design reform movement, Dresser also traveled to Japan. His account of the trip, *Japan: Its Architecture, Art and Art Manufactories* (1882), for decades remained one of the most accurate accounts of life in the Far East. Through his understanding of Japanese art Dresser emphasized a flattened, stylized treatment of natural forms; his writings in American art periodicals such as the *Art Amateur* forged a further awareness of Japan throughout Great Britain and the United States.

The availability of these publications within the United States added to the impressive body of literature that analyzed the pertinent issues of Japanese art and its accompanying cult of appreciation, which some English critics, à la Philippe Burty, called Japonisme.[34] During the 1870s, the translation into English of significant French articles on this growing fad stoked English awareness of this essentially European phenomenon.[35]

English Dealers and Their Exhibitions

The increasing amount of written material on Japanese art and culture coincided with dealers' growing willingness to promote art objects, as well as curios, to the evolving market and eager consumers in Great Britain. Following the Philadelphia Centennial Exhibition, Americans also became more cosmopolitan in their outlook, and if they were not always ready to venture to Japan, their frequent excursions to London (and Paris) continued to tempt them with Japanese art. American collections of Japanese art expanded with regularity the more English dealers championed objects in their London salesrooms or on their business trips to the United States.

One of the primary promoters in London was the dealer and entrepreneur Arthur Lasenby Liberty (1843–1917), who opened India House in 1875. This later became Liberty and Company, which specialized in the production of textiles and objects in an Art Nouveau style.[36] After a trip to Japan in 1889, he reported on his travels to the Royal Society of Arts and published his statements in a comprehensive and widely read article. Liberty's interest in Japanese aesthetics led him to incorporate Oriental motifs into the English designs that were created by the artisans he employed. His shop, which became a major force in disseminating Japanese taste in London, attracted international clients, including Americans, who actively sought out English works produced under the banner of Japonisme.

Central to understanding Japanese art in England were exhibitions organized by the dominant Fine Art Society, a limited liability company with no standing members, and held in their gallery on New Bond Street. In 1888 an extensive presentation of all types of Japanese art objects, from lacquer ware to embroideries, was organized by English and French supporters of Japonisme. Contributors to the exhibition included Dr. William Anderson (who had formed a sizable collection of Japanese objects in the 1870s), writers and collectors Thomas Cutler and Ernest Hart; Marcus Huish (the managing director of the Fine Art Society), the Australian painter Mortimer Menpes, and Siegfried Bing. Well received by the daily press, the exhibition attracted many visitors, who came to be further educated on aspects of Japanese art.[37] Two years later the Fine Art Society assembled a major show of prints by Hokusai, which aroused interest in his work just when worldwide attention was being directed to the history and significance of the Japanese print.[38]

During the early 1890s, these same dealers and promoters continued to write about their experiences in Japan. In June of 1890, Liberty contributed a lengthy article on "The Industrial Arts and Manufactures of Japan" to the *Journal of the Society of Arts.* He complimented the

Japanese for their genius and high level of creativity in woodwork, ceramics, enamels, metalwork, and embroidery. Special emphasis was placed on "the variety of purposes for which paper is used in Japan."[39]

Japanesque versus Japonisme

The booming London market for Japanese goods, as well as the perspicacity of some English collectors and critics, led to the formulation of a new term to meet the growing craze for all things Japanese. "Japanesque" was coined in the 1880s and used by some, especially Marcus Huish of the Fine Art Society, to suggest an English branch of the Japonisme phenomenon.[40] Since influential French dealers such as Bing and Hayashi either had agents working for them in the United States during the 1880s, or they journeyed across the ocean to promote Japanese art themselves, it was natural for Americans to use the French term, and this separation of terms seemed quite logical to some dealers in Great Britain.

Since English dealers did not set up sales channels on American soil — though a few came to the United States to promote Japonisme — American clients were obliged to make their own contacts with major Japanesque dealers or salesrooms in London. Since who worked with whom cannot be documented with certainty, the nature of the English impact on the full promotion of American Japonisme remains imprecise. It is clear, however, that both British and French businessmen and entrepreneurs came to view America as a fertile region where fortunes could be made if the "natives" could be encouraged to acquire Japanese objects. Thus, the United States became the logical locale for the nurturing of Japonisme.

Julia Meech

COLLECTING JAPANESE ART IN AMERICA

When Japan was forced to emerge from several centuries of self-imposed isolation in the mid-nineteenth century, government officials enlarged the little fishing village of Yokohama, eighteen miles southwest of Edo (now Tokyo), as a treaty port for the residence of foreigners. Commercial treaties with America, England, Russia, the Netherlands, and France lured many young entrepreneurs from the West. Although their freedom to travel was strictly circumscribed (it was many years before Westerners could live in Tokyo), visitors found that Japanese merchants were ready for them from the moment the port opened for business in July of 1859. A Japanese print artist documented scenes of the life-style of the foreign community in 1863 with a glimpse into a street-front shop selling fancy lacquer boxes: the Japanese vendor has cleverly thought to provide his Western clients (perhaps art dealers) with a comfortable chair (fig. 10). American visitors were among the featured subjects of Japanese woodblock prints as early as 1860: foreigners—Western women in particular—were as novel to the Japanese as the Japanese were to us. Our curiosity about each other was mutual from the beginning.

As the demand for Japanese merchandise grew in the West, the new government that took power at the beginning of the Meiji era (1868–1912) sent its artisans overseas to study the market and learn modern techniques. Their products, often more Victorian than Japanese, were

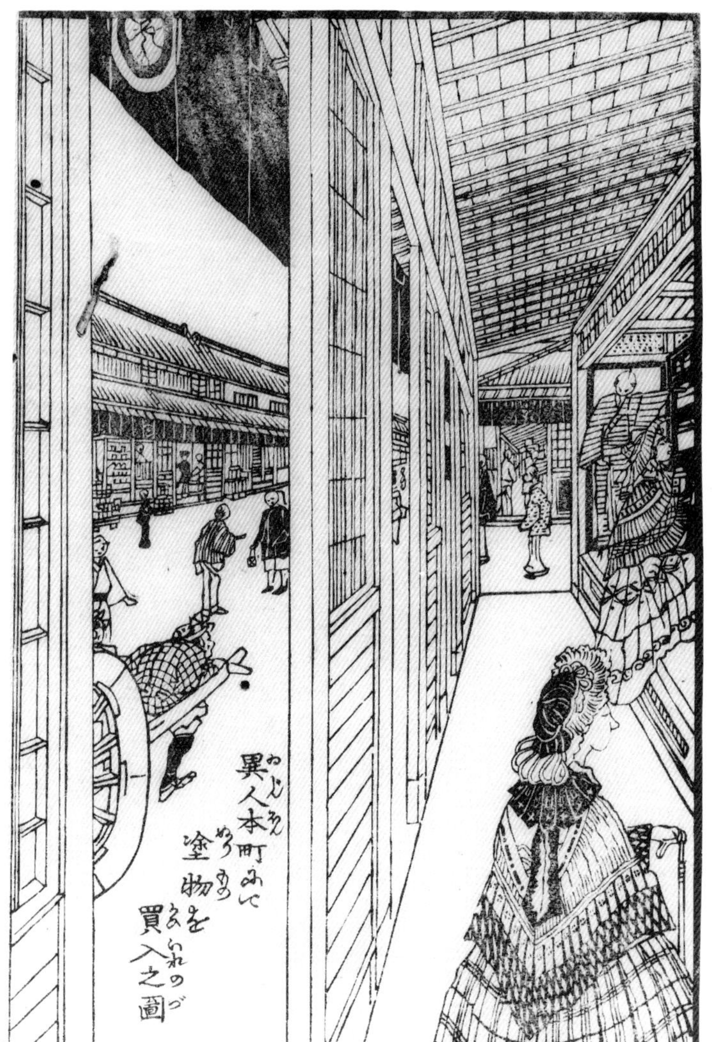

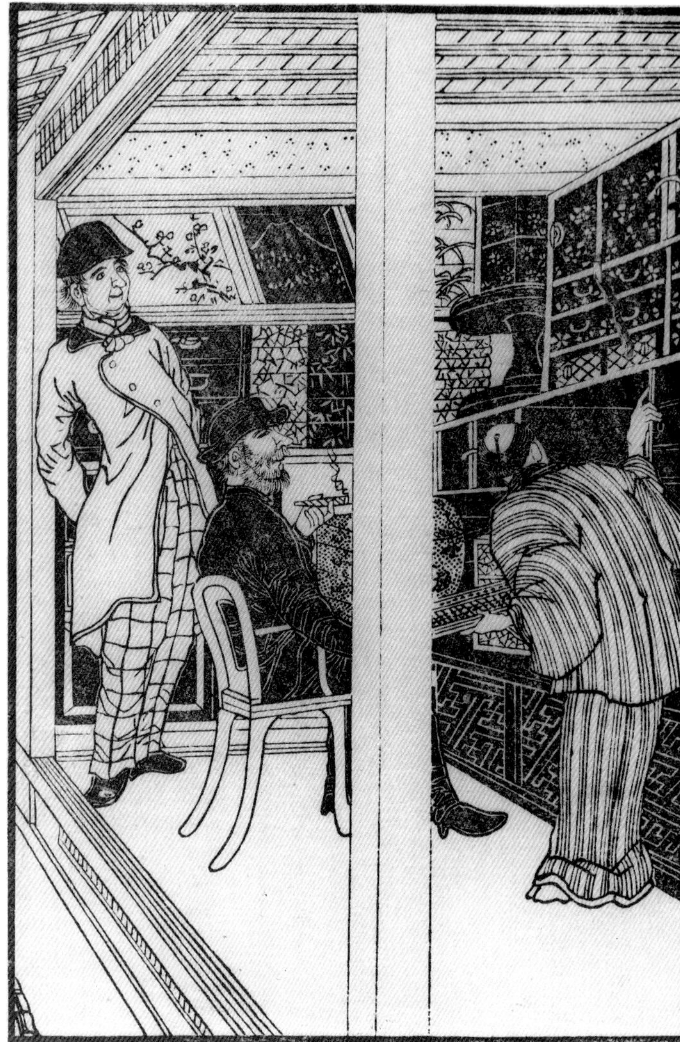

10. Hashimoto (Gountei) Sadahide (1807–c. 1878), *Foreigners Buying Lacquer in Honchō.* From *Record of Things Seen and Heard at the Open Port of Yokohama,* 1, 1863. Woodblock printed book. Lawrence and Bessie Weinberg Collection

then exported to international expositions, where they found immediate favor (in part because they looked so familiar), thereby earning foreign currency needed to finance the industrialization of Meiji Japan. By the 1880s professional dealers and export-import firms moved into the market, and soon Japanese art could be purchased not only in Paris and London but also in Boston, New York, Chicago, San Francisco, and elsewhere, often from vendors who were fairly knowledgeable. With the Museum of Fine Arts in Boston leading the way in this country, Asian art could be seen in permanent public displays as well. Auction houses entered the picture in the 1890s, and soon huge collections were amassed, by artists and connoisseur-collectors alike, each stimulating the other in the still small and ingrown world of Oriental art. Although the tide is now turning, Japanese art has never brought such high prices on the world art market as it did in the early twentieth century (judged in terms of the relative value of the dollar at that time).

Why the vogue for Japanese art (and Japonisme) in America at the turn of the century? Most important, because it was new, which is to say "exotic."[41] In addition, at the instigation of influential interior decorators such as Louis Comfort Tiffany (1848–1933) in New York, it came to be fashionable; people with money were buying it, setting the trend. Tiffany's artists and craftsmen were eclectic in combining decorative styles of many countries, freely mixing European and Japanese aesthetic features. At a time when crafts in general were held in high esteem, the Orient was a fresh discovery. The Vanderbilts and Havemeyers were conspicuous collectors of Oriental art (as well as everything else) and they bought in quantity. Cognoscenti and acknowledged tastemakers in the art-decoration movement, they delighted in choosing a different cultural theme for each room in their Fifth Avenue homes — a Chinese reception room, a Japanese sitting room, an English Renaissance hall, for example. Japan was surely only a peripheral interest for the Havemeyers, whose real passion was Old Master and contemporary paintings. They were in the mainstream of Japonisme and the Aesthetic movement, however, when they hired Tiffany and his associate Samuel Colman (1832–1920), a New York landscape painter, to decorate the interior of their house in 1890. (Both Tiffany and Colman were serious collectors of Japanese decorative arts.) The library ceiling was a mosaic of colorful swatches of Nō robes, and the oak walls were stained to an olive green, imitating the color of a favorite lacquer panel by Ritsuō.[42]

Wealthy museum trustees such as Howard Mansfield (1849–1938) in New York encouraged their institutions to build public collections. Mansfield, a Yale-educated lawyer, served as both trustee and treasurer of the Metropolitan Museum of Art, and acted as its de facto curator of Asian art until a specialist was appointed in 1915 (fig. 11). His collection of more than 300 outstanding Japanese woodblock prints, as well as fine lacquer, painting, pottery, sword guards, and textiles, was acquired by the Metropolitan in 1936. Like so many others of his generation, he came to Japanese art through his first love, Whistler. He had one of the most comprehensive private collections of Whistler etchings and lithographs in America, an interest he shared with businessman Charles Lang Freer (1854–1919), who later purchased Whistler's Peacock Room for his Detroit mansion. A member of the Grolier Club, Mansfield gave the well-publicized Ladies' Day lecture in 1896 (fig. 14) on the occasion of the print exhibition organized by the Japanese entrepreneur-collector Shugio Hiromichi (1853–1927; fig. 12). Shugio, the distinguished Oxford-educated director of the First Japan Manufacturing and Trading Company, purveyors of Japanese porcelain and parasols on Broadway, was a knowledgeable print collector who introduced New Yorkers to the beauties of Japanese woodblock prints and illustrated books. One of the earliest members of the Grolier Club (along with Freer, La Farge, Tiffany, and Havemeyer), he staged the city's first major ukiyo-e exhibition there in 1889 and lectured on the subject well before theer were any noteworthy local collections.[43]

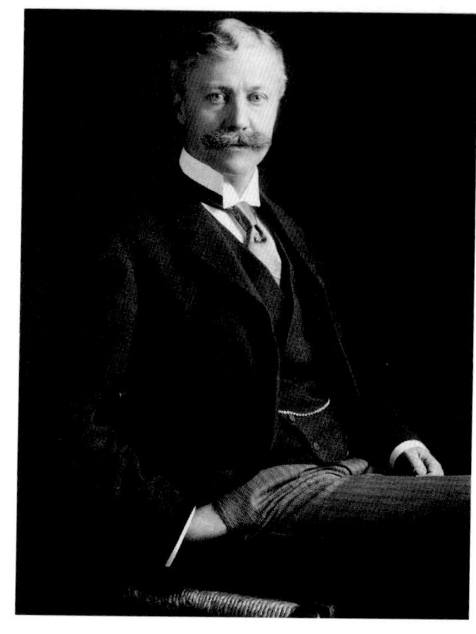

11. Howard Mansfield, 1909. Photograph. The Metropolitan Museum of Art Archives, New York

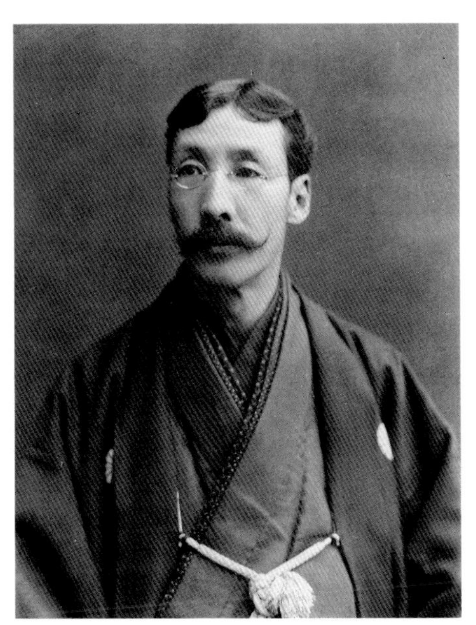

12. Shugio Hiromichi in New York, c. 1884. Photograph. Grolier Club, New York

Charles Freer's own world-famous collection of Asian art, which he bequeathed to the Smithsonian Institution, started with a handful of Japanese prints purchased at a gallery in New York City in 1894. Freer made his first trip to Japan in 1895 and soon assembled a substantial group of 400 prints, primarily works by Katsushika Hokusai (1760–1849) and Utagawa Hiroshige (1797–1858).

New York philanthropist Charles Stewart Smith (1832–1909), who made his fortune in the dry-goods business, was a founder and trustee of the Metropolitan Museum. He spent his honeymoon with his third wife in Japan in 1892, and celebrated by shipping home 1,700 ukiyo-e prints destined for the New York Public Library, as well as 522 Japanese ceramics, which he presented to the Metropolitan.

The triumvirate of Edward Sylvester Morse (1838–1925), William Sturgis Bigelow (1850–1926), and Ernest Francisco Fenollosa (1853–1908) were the apostles of Japanese culture in Boston. Morse, a Harvard-trained zoologist, spent only a little more than two and a half years in Japan, between 1877 and 1879, and again in 1882–83, but he made excellent use of his time. He taught Darwinian evolutionary theory at Tokyo University and initiated the first scientific excavations of prehistoric shell mounds. Soon his interest turned to ceramics and he began systematically to assemble a huge selection of prehistoric and nineteenth-century examples. He sold his personal collection of more than 5,000 ceramics to the Museum of Fine Arts, in Boston, where he held the title Keeper of Japanese Pottery from 1892 until his death. He also assembled an encyclopedic collection of ethnological materials — Japanese folk arts, painting, photography, and textiles, among other things — for the Peabody Museum of Salem, of which he was director from 1880 until 1916 (and director emeritus thereafter). A prolific lecturer and researcher with broad-ranging interests, he wrote and illustrated two influential books, *Japanese Homes and Their Surroundings* (1886) and *Japan Day by Day* (1918), as

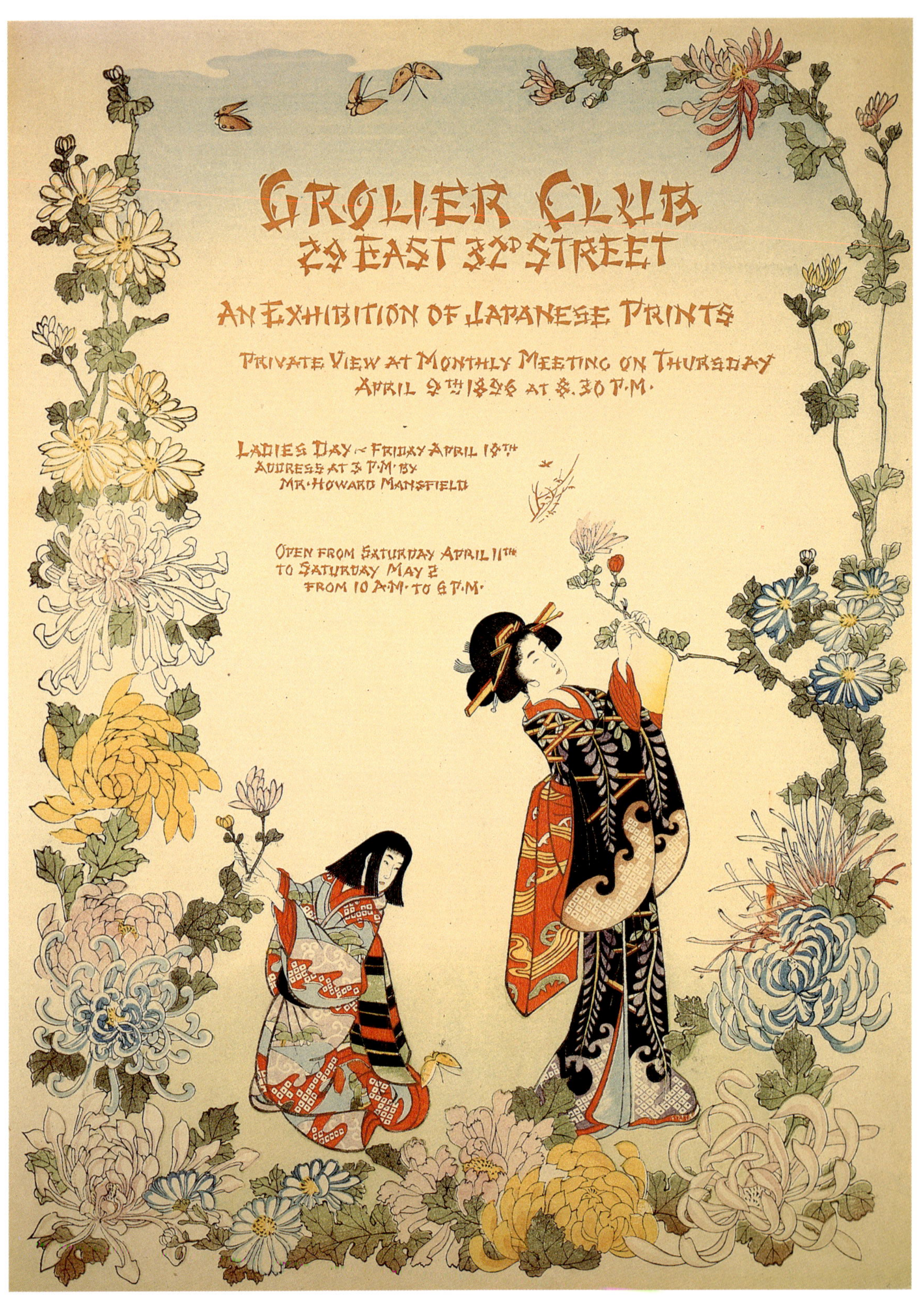
GROLIER CLUB
29 EAST 32D STREET
AN EXHIBITION OF JAPANESE PRINTS
PRIVATE VIEW AT MONTHLY MEETING ON THURSDAY
APRIL 9TH 1896 AT 8.30 P.M.
LADIES DAY ~ FRIDAY APRIL 10TH
ADDRESS AT 3 P.M. BY
MR. HOWARD MANSFIELD
OPEN FROM SATURDAY APRIL 11TH
TO SATURDAY MAY 2
FROM 10 A.M. TO 6 P.M.

well as numerous articles.[44] The book illustrations were taken from the pen and pencil sketches of Japanese life and artifacts he made in his diary (fig. 15).

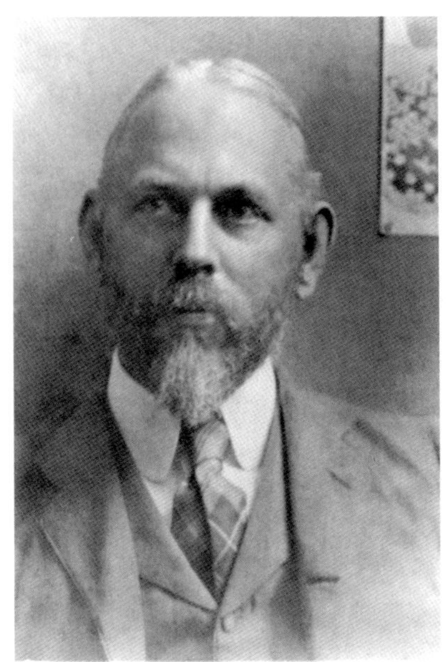

13. Ernest F. Fenollosa, c. 1900. Photograph. Museum of Fine Arts, Boston

There is no question that Ernest F. Fenollosa must be singled out for his key role in educating the public to a higher understanding of Japanese art through public lectures and publications. In memoirs and letters, collectors and artists from Louisine Havemeyer to Arthur Wesley Dow reveal how proud they were to have met or worked with him, praising him as the preeminent authority on Oriental art. After graduating from Harvard, Fenollosa (fig. 13) studied painting for a year at the newly opened art school of the Museum of Fine Arts in Boston; with an introduction from Morse, he went to Japan in 1878 at the invitation of the Japanese government to teach philosophy at Tokyo University. He intended also to proselyte Western oil painting, at which he was himself adept and to which so many young Japanese were attracted at the time. The next year, however, he attended a lecture on Japanese art given by William Anderson (1842–1900), a Scottish professor of anatomy and surgery at the Imperial Naval Academy in Tokyo. The 3,000 Japanese and Chinese paintings purchased by Anderson during his six years in Tokyo came to the British Museum in 1882, and were catalogued in a lavish publication written by Anderson himself in 1886.[45] Fenollosa's exposure to Anderson completely changed his own focus; he, too, became a passionate collector of the traditional arts of Japan, a personal sponsor of several struggling artists such as Kano Hōgai (1828–88) and Hashimoto Gahō (1835–1908), exponents of modern painting "in the Japanese style," now known as *Nihonga* (literally, "Japanese painting"), and an outspoken advocate of an East-West synthesis in the arts — Eastern spirituality and Western technology. He now perceived Western-style oil painting (and Western influence in general) as inimical to the survival of traditional Japanese art and advocated instead a bold new *Nihonga,* an updated style

14. Poster for *An Exhibition of Japanese Prints,* 1896. Grolier Club, New York

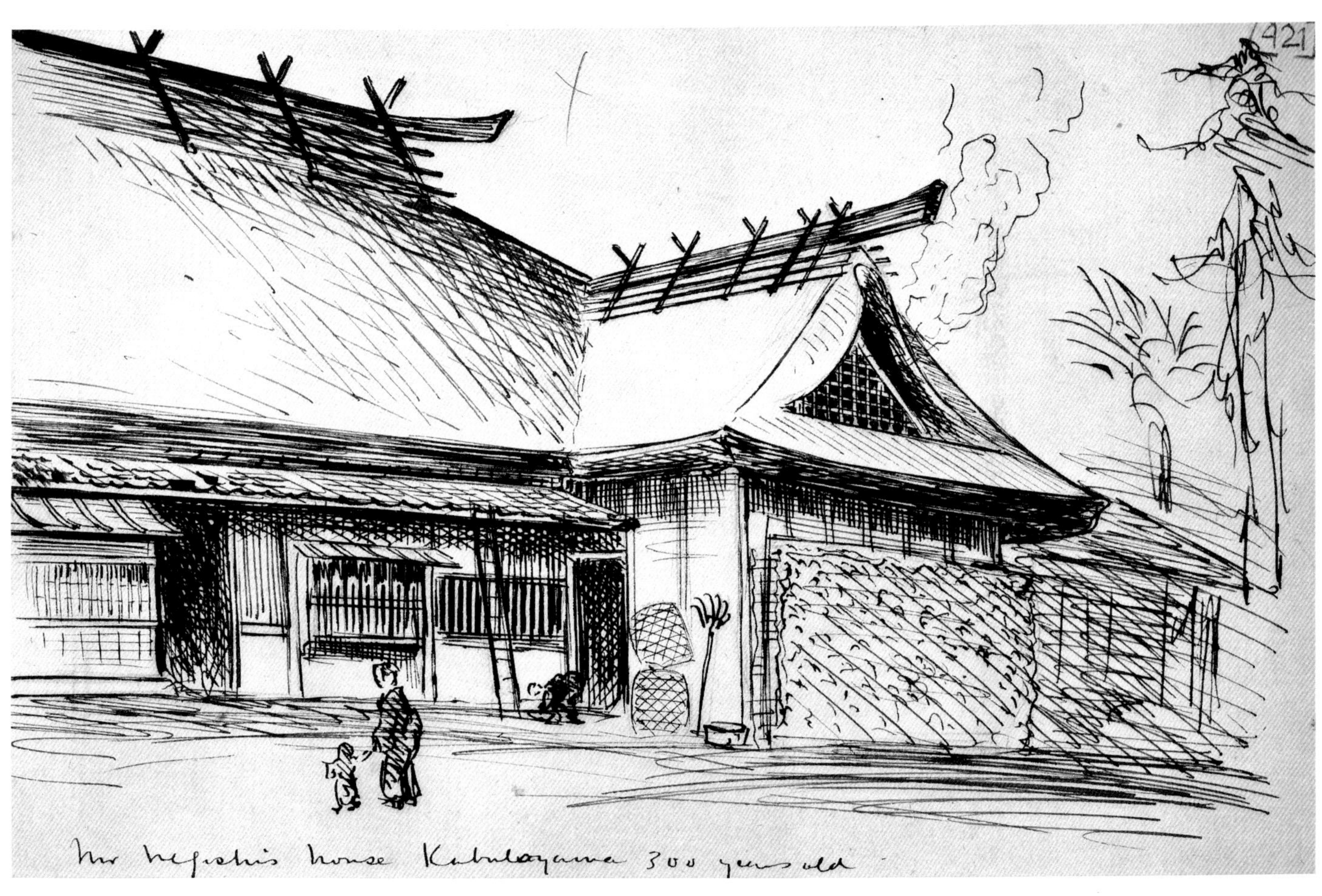

15. Edward Sylvester Morse, *Mr. Negishi's 300-Year-Old House, Kabutoyama,* 1878. Pen and ink sketch from journal. Courtesy Peabody Museum of Salem

of ink painting incorporating Western modes of expression such as chiaroscuro and atmospheric perspective. The result was a generation of Japanese artists working in a hybrid style combining something of the Sesshū and Kano school methods of ink painting with modern Western techniques.

Around 1887, the year after Fenollosa and his protégé, Okakura Kakuzō (1862–1913), returned from a one-year official tour of Europe and America studying modern methods of art education on behalf of the Meiji government, Fenollosa turned his eyes particularly toward ukiyo-e; presumably he had been impressed by the strong interest in this subject in the West. Perhaps Fenollosa was something of an opportunist as well. His articles on the history of ukiyo-e were serialized in the new Western-style art journal *Kokka,* beginning with the first issue in 1890. Ukiyo-e were featured in most exhibitions that he subsequently organized for the Museum of Fine Arts, where he served as first curator of the Japanese department from 1890 through 1895, and they were the focus of the catalogues he wrote starting in 1898 for his good friend and business partner, Kobayashi Bunshichi (1864–1923).[46] Kobayashi, a wealthy young print dealer and vendor of old books, opened a shop in the Asakusa district of Tokyo around 1887. He is described as handsome, and he spoke English, a big asset in his dealings with foreigners.

Fenollosa worked closely with Kobayashi as a consultant and catalogue author after he was forced to leave the Museum of Fine Arts. (The circumstances of his divorce and remarriage to his young assistant in the museum led to his abrupt departure and virtual exile from Boston, still a very conservative city in those days.) The 440 ukiyo-e prints he catalogued for the Ketcham Gallery in New York for a sale exhibition in January 1896 (and for which his friend Arthur Wesley Dow designed the poster) contained material from Kobayashi (fig. 16).[47] Fenollosa's commercial ventures were necessitated by difficulties over alimony payment and child support. He was back in Japan on and off through

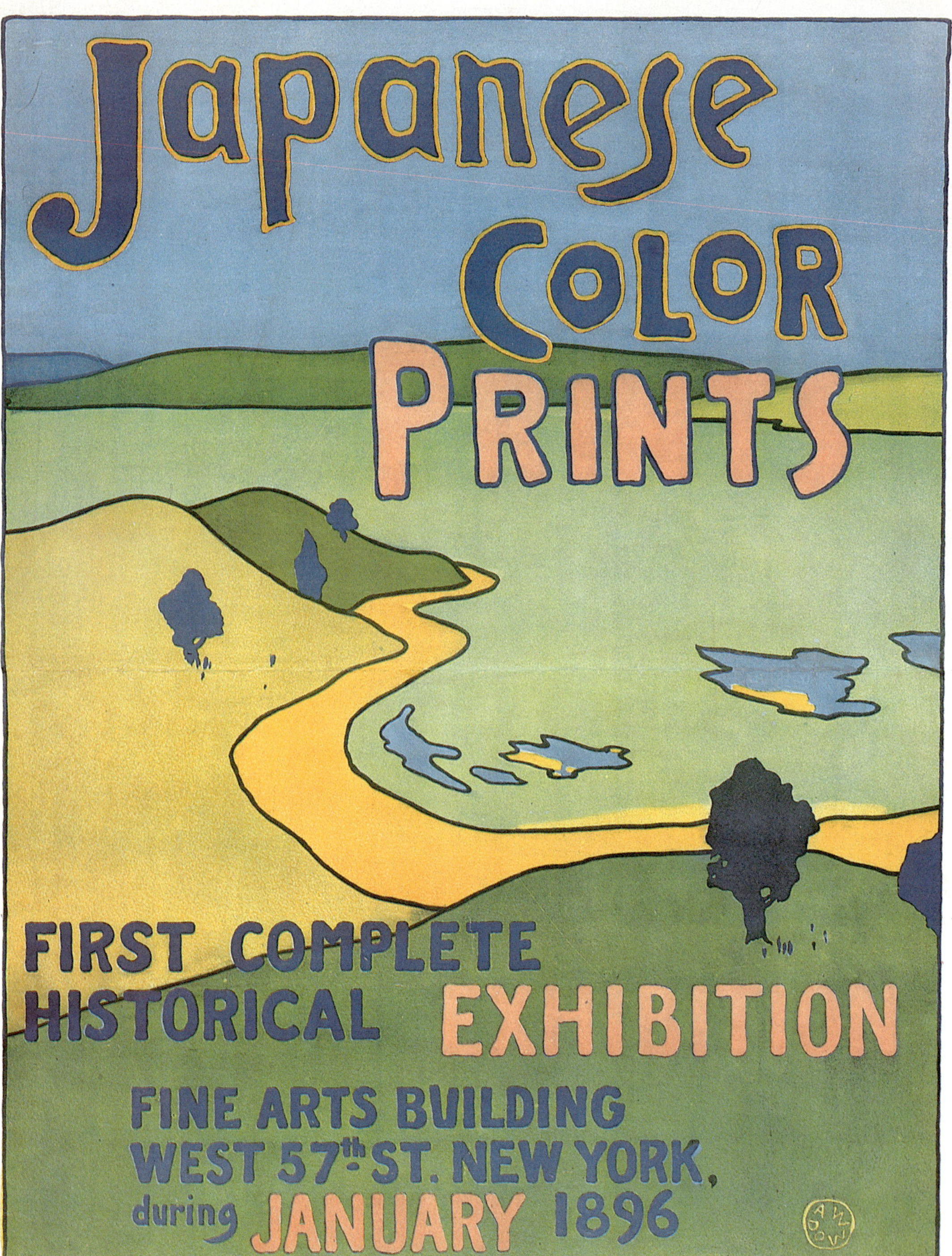
Japanese
Color
Prints
FIRST COMPLETE
HISTORICAL EXHIBITION
FINE ARTS BUILDING
WEST 57th ST. NEW YORK,
during JANUARY 1896

1901 teaching English, studying Buddhism, and writing his important study, *An Outline of the History of Ukiyo-ye,* published by Kobayashi in 1901 with twenty full-size woodblock-printed color facsimiles. Kobayashi opened a branch office in San Francisco, perhaps as early as 1898, when he came to America to visit Charles Freer in Detroit. By 1902 he had a branch in Yokohama, and was making annual pilgrimages to America.

Fenollosa formed a comprehensive collection of Japanese painting, most of which he sold to Bostonian Charles G. Weld in 1886 with the understanding that it would enter the Museum of Fine Arts as the Fenollosa-Weld collection. The world-famous thirteenth-century handscroll *Night Attack on the Sanjō Palace* is the best known of his finds. A teacher and critic active in both Japan and America, he had a cross-cultural role as disseminator that gives him unique importance: he contributed to the appreciation of Japanese art in both countries.

Harvard graduate William Sturgis Bigelow, born of a famous surgeon and a daughter of a wealthy China-trade merchant, studied medicine in Paris with Louis Pasteur in the 1870s and developed a connoisseur's taste for art. He returned to Boston with enough Japanese art, mostly bronzes and lacquers purchased from Siegfried Bing, to sponsor an exhibition of several hundred items at the Museum of Fine Arts in 1881. A sensitive, troubled man suffering from intense feelings of guilt and paralysis of the will occasioned by his inability to live up to the unreasonable goals set by his authoritarian father, he fled to Japan in 1882 and remained for seven years. A convert (like Fenollosa) to esoteric Buddhism, Bigelow found that his experience in Japan served him as a serious and satisfying spiritual pilgrimage (fig. 17).

16. Arthur Wesley Dow, poster for the exhibition *Japanese Color Prints,* January 1896. Lithograph. Solomon and Julia Engel Collection, Rare Book and Manuscript Library, Columbia University, New York

It was enthusiastic lectures by Edward Sylvester Morse that had awakened Bigelow's desire to visit Japan; the two men set off from Boston together in 1882 and, joining up with Fenollosa, traveled widely through Japan. The three Americans would arrive at a small country inn,

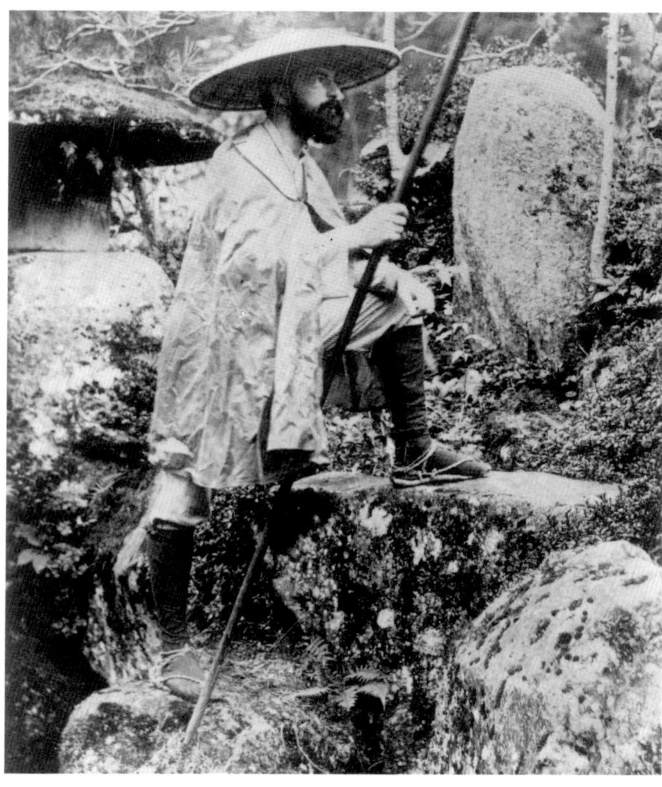

17. William Sturgis Bigelow in Japan, 1880s. Photograph. Museum of Fine Arts, Boston

descend on the local shops, and await the arrival the next morning of eager dealers bearing works of art of all kinds. With their unmatched combination of expertise, connoisseurship, and money (Morse was sponsored by the Peabody Museum and Bigelow had vast personal wealth), they were pioneers as serious collectors of Japanese art. Fenollosa had entrée to temple storehouses and private collections as a representative of the Japanese government empowered to make inventories and register "treasures," sorting the good from the bad.

In 1911, Bigelow officially presented the Boston Museum of Fine Arts, of which he was a trustee, with the collection he had deposited there in 1889. The gift included nearly 15,000 Japanese and Chinese works of art (of which 3,600 were paintings), as well as some 40,000 ukiyo-e prints, the fruits of his years of collaboration with Fenollosa in Japan.[48]

As was described by Gabriel Weisberg in his essay, dealers in Europe (Bing and Hayashi Tadamasa, for example), Japan, and America were

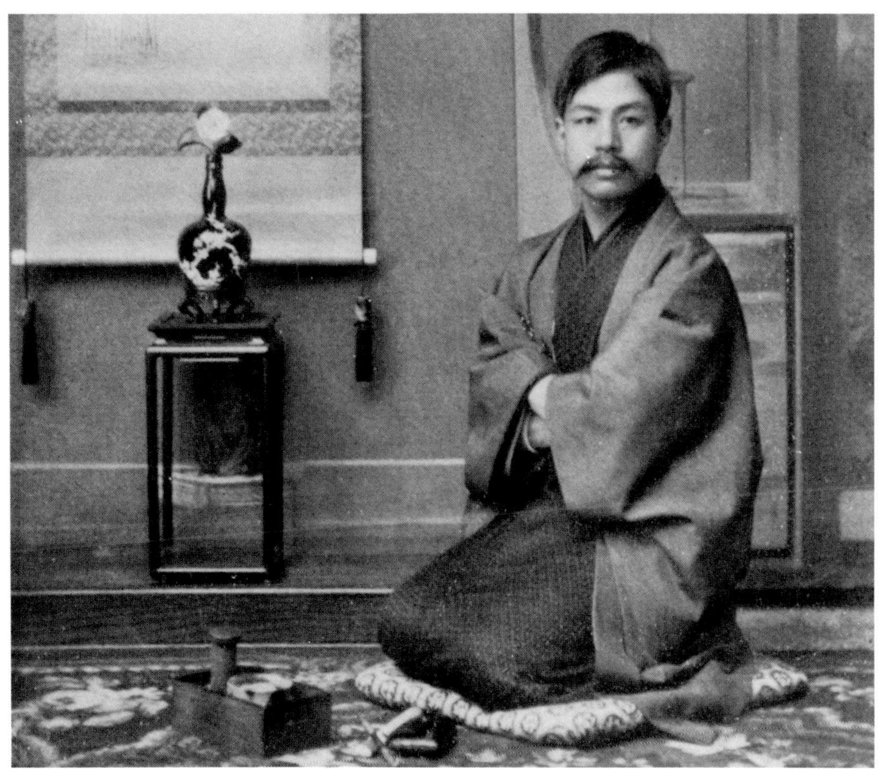

18. Matsuki Bunkio in Japan, 1898. Photograph

instrumental in finding, exhibiting, and publicizing Oriental art. Charles Stewart Smith had purchased his prints and porcelains from an Englishman, Captain Frank Brinkley (1841–1912), active in Japan since the 1860s as a journalist, author, and military adviser to the Japanese government, and eventually as an influential dealer, knowledgeable about everything from samurai to ceramics. He even wrote the official guide to the Japan pavilion at the World's Columbian Exposition in 1893.

Here in America one of the first resident Japanese art dealers was Matsuki Bunkio (1867–1934; fig. 18), whose family were art appraisers. His early education included initiation into the Nichiren sect of Buddhism, schooling in the English language, and a two-year study period as a teenager in Shanghai and Peking. In 1888, he sailed for Salem, Massachusetts, with an introduction to Edward S. Morse, and graduated from Salem High School four years later. He took an American wife, and opened a gallery on Boylston Street in Boston. By

1898 he had begun annual auctions of Japanese art in Boston, New York, and Philadelphia, culminating in the sale of the estate of Arthur Wesley Dow in 1923. A clever salesman, Matsuki was an immaculate dresser, and presented himself in his auction catalogues as a "collector." It is fascinating to learn that as early as 1895 he loaned nearly forty battle triptychs, woodblock prints depicting the Sino-Japanese War of 1894–95, to an exhibition of art posters in Boston.[49] The Japanese prints, which are essentially examples of the art of propaganda showing modern Japan in a very good light (and the Chinese as backward and cowardly), were identified as posters. Seen thus as the art of the common people, they were compared with the everyday themes associated with Western art posters. Thanks to the enterprising young Matsuki, posters by Chéret, Régamey, Toulouse-Lautrec, Grasset, Mucha, and Beardsley hung side by side not only with American posters by Bradley, Rhead, Penfield, Prendergast, and Dow, but with contemporary Japanese woodcuts by artists such as Kiyochika, Gekkō, and Ginkō.

By the turn of the century a trip to Japan, whether a honeymoon, business trip, or just plain adventure, was increasingly common for Americans. On the one hand Japan had proved itself a modern nation in 1894 by going to war against China on the Korean Peninsula and winning easily. In 1904, taking on Russia, a Western nation, it was again victorious on the battlefront, and cemented its credibility as an impressive world power in the eyes of all Americans. On the other hand, Japan retained a mysterious allure by virtue of having been closed to the outside world for two and a half centuries. For many artists, whether Vincent van Gogh or Frank Lloyd Wright, Japan (or the idea of Japan) remained an exotic place of refuge and escape from the decadence and disillusionment spawned by the Industrial Revolution.

American artists were, of course, open to fresh influences from any source, whether painted screens and scrolls, enamels, textiles, fans, or photographs. More often than not, however, it was prints that had a significant impact. Certainly, prints were more readily available than any other Japanese art form, whether on the open market or in popular publications ranging from homemaker's magazines to exhibition catalogues. Fenollosa wrote in 1901 that ukiyo-e is

> *by no means the oldest, the most profound, the most spiritual, or even the most decorative of the Japanese arts. In the classified total of achievements it plays almost an inconspicuous part. . . . And yet it is probably that branch by which Japanese art is most widely known and appreciated in the West today. . . . It is the accessible number of the specimens of Ukiyo-ye that keeps the interest so fresh.*[50]

Most important, however, the medium itself (a multiple art form) related technically and functionally most directly to the graphic art concerns of Western artists. Indeed, while the Japanese print offered new aesthetic options it also reinforced two basic tenets of the Arts and Crafts movement in America. First, that art should be available to the masses, and second, that functional objects including posters and book illustrations should be artfully designed. The movement began in Britain, where it was associated with the activities of John Ruskin and William Morris, with the goal of improving — and simplifying — the way in which objects were made. A movement of renewal and reform in the decorative arts, it was a powerful reaction against the dehumanization of the Industrial Revolution. In America, the Arts and Crafts movement encompasses the four decades that followed the Philadelphia Centennial, reaching its zenith between 1890 and 1910. Japanese art was one of the most important influences underlying the Arts and Crafts. Young artists and designers viewing Japanese art at international exhibitions were inspired by the simplicity of Japanese wares and drew on them for their cult of beauty in everyday objects.

In Japan prints were popular in appeal with a broad-based audience of townsmen whose favorite images were those of actors and courtesans in the entertainment quarters, the *ukiyo,* or floating world of pleasure. (The word *ukiyo-e* means "picture of the floating world.") As restless Japanese travelers began to move up and down the Tōkaidō Road, famous scenic spots became subjects for prints that could be purchased as souvenirs of a visit. Today the visitor to Kyoto would have his photo taken instead. The printers were extremely skillful: in the nineteenth century it was not uncommon for one man to produce a thousand impressions a day. Generally editions were small, but one or two of the most popular landscape series by Hiroshige are thought to have been printed in editions of tens of thousands. Impressions were never numbered, however (nor were prints signed individually, as they are in the West), so the exact quantities are difficult to determine. The wealthy Japanese collector could acquire an original painting of a courtesan or kabuki actor mounted as a hanging scroll, but the man in the street had to be satisfied with a print.

The great majority of prints have disappeared in fires, earthquakes, or through neglect, but the fact that many are preserved in nearly pristine condition suggests that they were carefully stored in portfolios by their Japanese owners or pasted in albums. There were also limited luxury editions of prints called *surimono* (literally, "printed things"), commissioned by connoisseurs and private clubs, but most woodcuts were purchased for their topical, documentary interest, rather than as works of art. Consequently, there was no show of concern when first Europeans and then Americans began to purchase them in ever increasing quantities, to the extent that today the largest and best collections of ukiyo-e are found in the West. Describing the situation as it existed at the turn of the century, Oliver Statler wrote that

> *such a "popular art" always carries a stigma in its own country. Foreigners, untroubled by background associations, see it fresh and on its own merits, but it is only natural that many art-conscious Japanese, intensely proud of their nation's painting and sculpture, should regard* ukiyoe *as something on the outer fringe of artistic respectability.*[51]

Gabriel P. Weisberg

SOWING JAPONISME ON AMERICAN SOIL

John La Farge

Long before he actually traveled to the Far East, John La Farge (1835–1910) had been collecting Japanese art. During the 1850s he had trained in France. By his return to the United States in 1857, he most certainly would have been aware of the general interest in the China trade and the Far East that permeated New England. His 1860 marriage to Margaret Perry, granddaughter of Commodore Matthew Perry, undoubtedly enhanced his interest in the Orient.[52] Japanese tendencies in some of his early works, especially his flower paintings, have been noted. La Farge has also been credited with fostering an early admiration of Japanese art within the United States.[53] Yet only when La Farge traveled to Tokyo in 1886 was he able to make literal transcriptions of Japan.

Some writers today have noted that La Farge did not examine actual Japanese artworks *in situ* and that he failed to appreciate some of the best work of the time.[54] Others have seen his commitment to Japan as being part of a larger naturalistic tradition of compiling extensive data through field notes.[55] (His watercolor of the *Daibutsu, Kamakura* of 1886 could be viewed in this way.) Undoubtedly, La Farge and other members of his circle, including the writer Henry Adams and the collector W. S. Bigelow, photographed important sites and monuments. These photographs — most of which have disappeared — were intended to

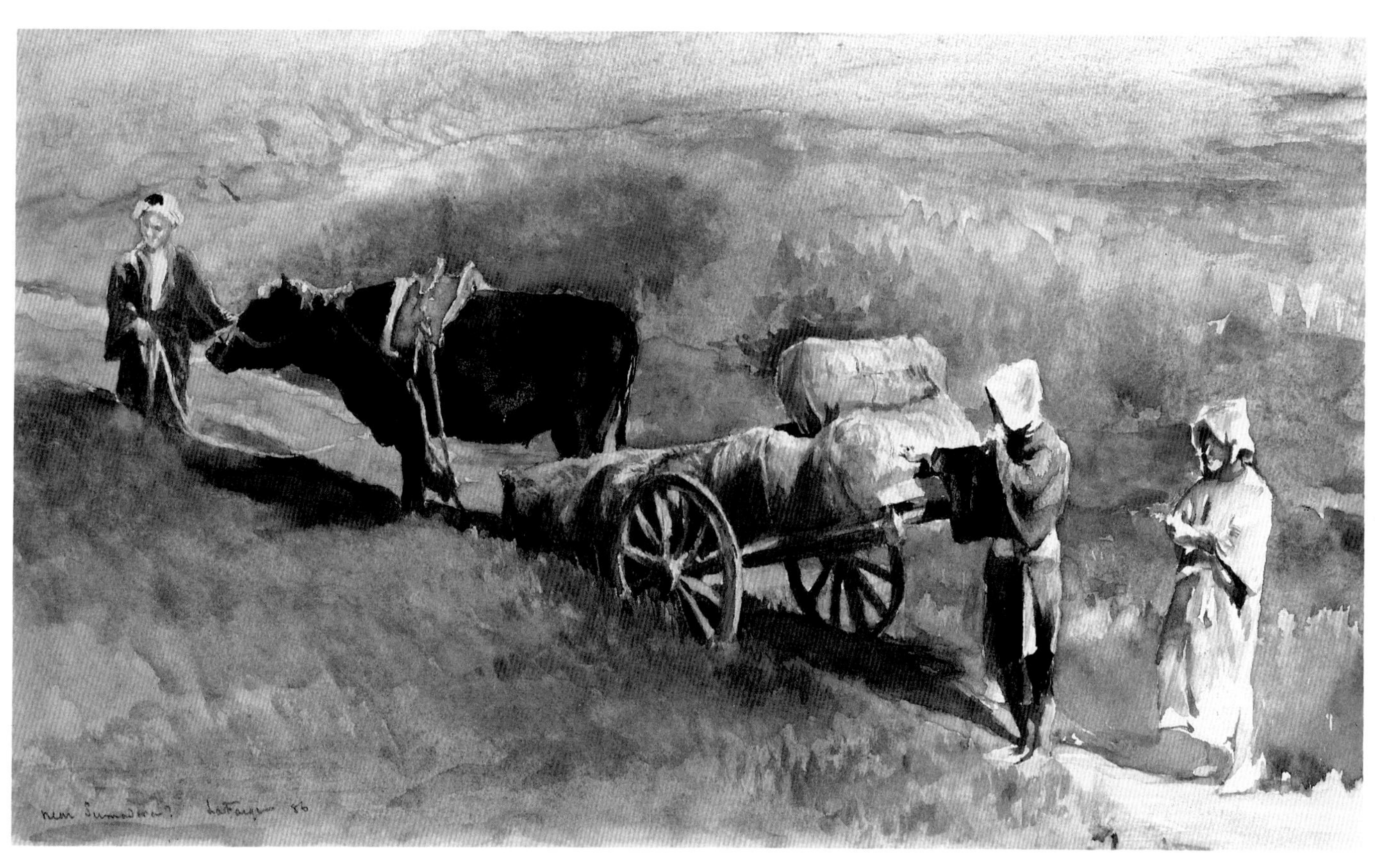

19. John La Farge, *Japanese Peasants,* 1886.
Watercolor. Museum of Fine Arts,
Boston. Bigelow Collection

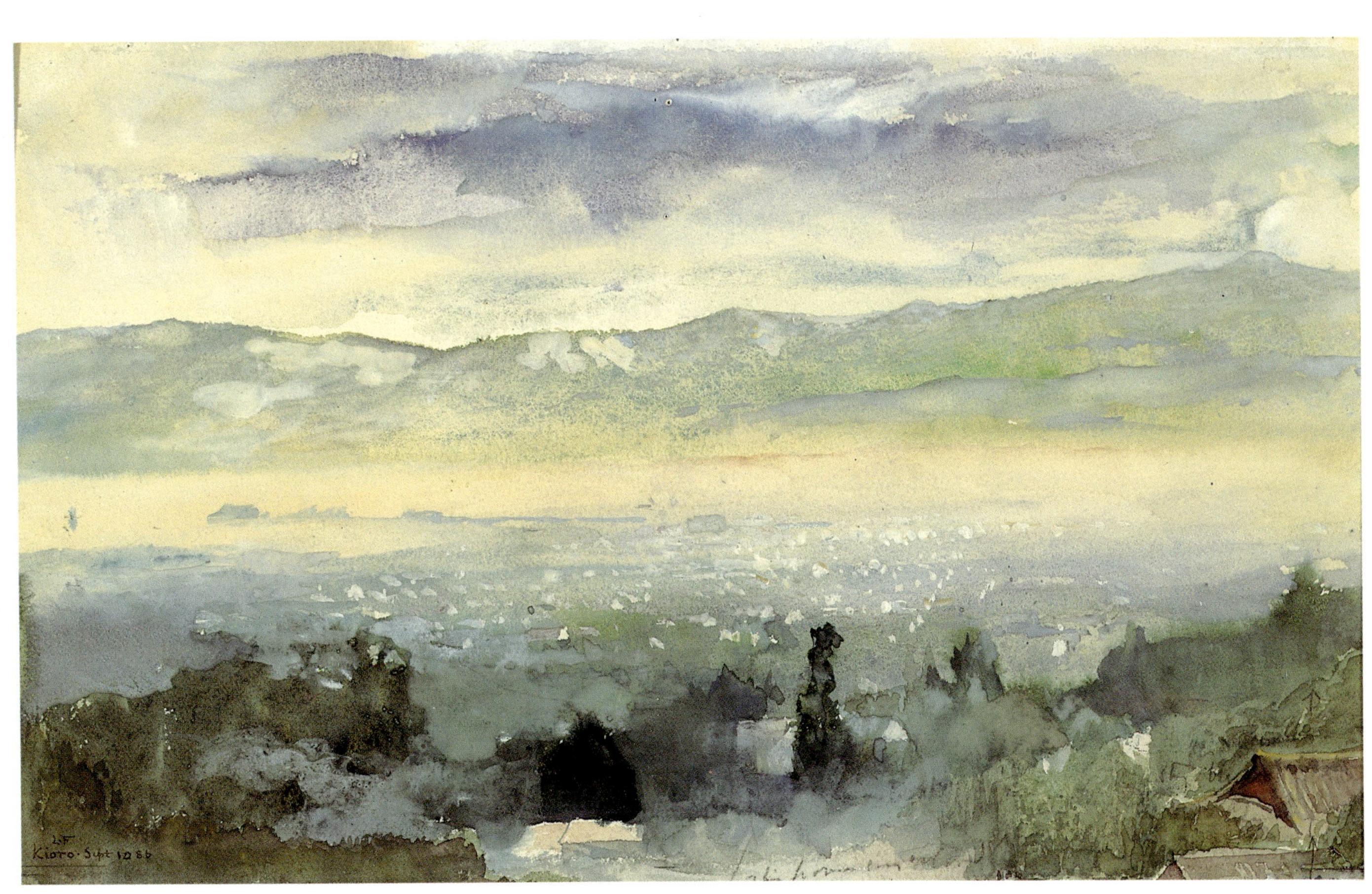

20. John La Farge, *Sunrise in Fog over Kyoto,* 1886. Watercolor. The Currier Gallery of Art, Manchester, NH. Gift of Clement S. Houghton

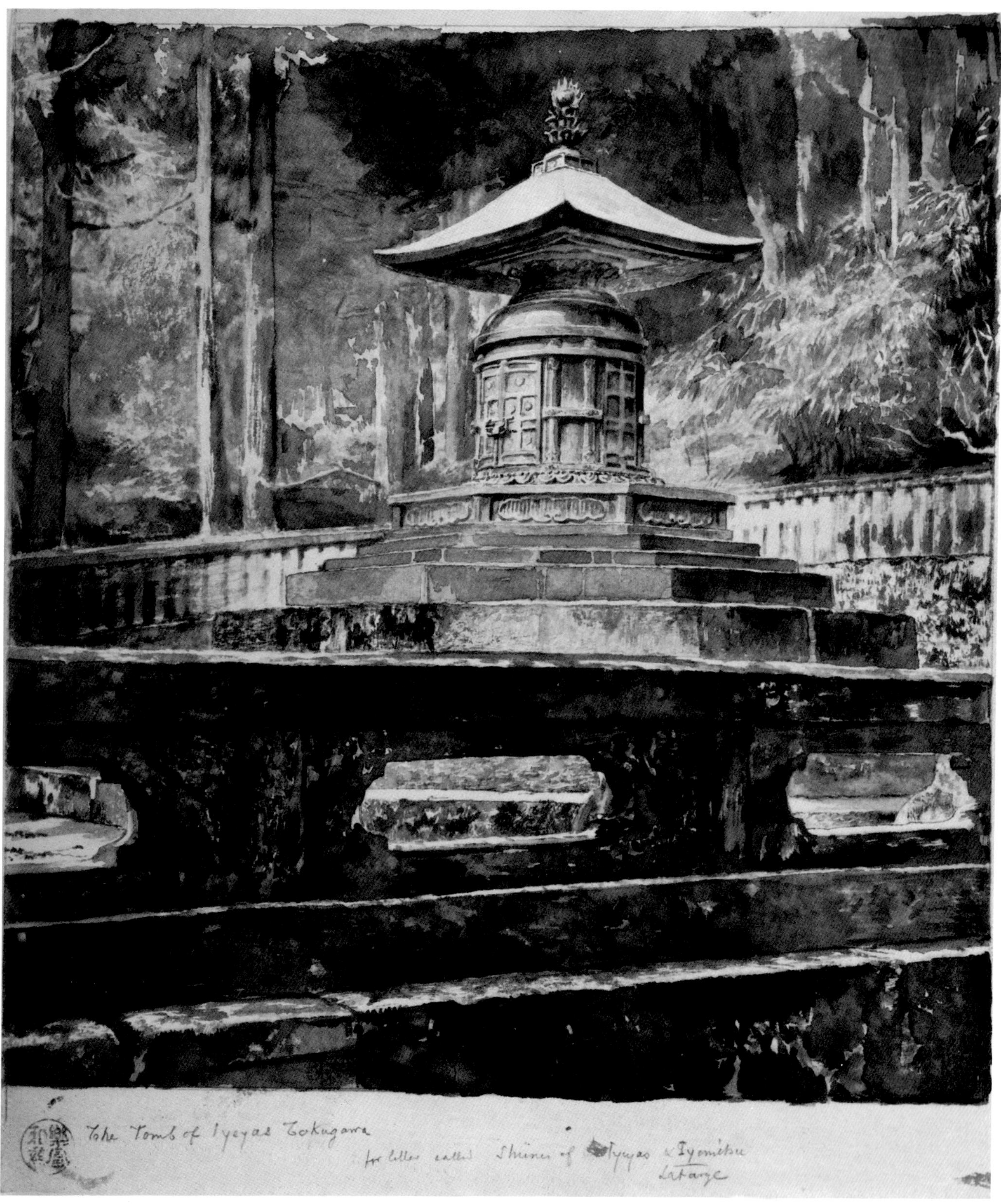
The Tomb of Iyeyas Tokugawa
for letters called Shrines of Iyeyas & Iyemitsu
LaFarge

21. John La Farge, *Tomb of Ieyasu at Nikkō,* c. 1886. Watercolor. The Metropolitan Museum of Art, New York

function much like a reporter's notepad, which would later provide the artist or writer with accurate *aide-mémoire* to trigger reactions to a scene. They might also have served as models from which La Farge could recreate his impressions of a scene with a degree of detachment.[56] Those works on paper and watercolors (fig. 19) that he completed while under the spell of Japan have been characterized as being too "dry" in atmosphere or technique.[57] Critics of La Farge's aesthetic approach have overlooked the well-established tradition—found on both sides of the Atlantic—of using photographs as one basis for recreating naturalistic impressions of the countryside. By working from photographs (although how often he did this is unknown), La Farge utilized a major technological marvel and a modern technique to heighten the accuracy of his work. He also helped place his fascination with Japan within the context of the way other exotic countries were being documented by writers and artists.

At the same time, however, some of La Farge's studies on paper could have been created only from on-site observation. These sketches, frequently of a sunrise over the city of Kyoto (fig. 20), imply that La Farge recorded his sensations during the tranquil moments of the day. This practice, with its concomitant intense romantic subjectivity, reinforces the notion that there were several aspects to the artist's works on paper. When La Farge exhibited his exotic watercolors during the 1890s, he also considered these works to be accurate records of his travels, which is another way to look at them. Watercolors from the 1890s, ten years after his visit to Japan, reveal a far more personal and suggestive side that was seemingly inspired by stories by the popular Japoniste writer Lafcadio Hearn.[58]

Similar to the way Morse used his drawings to illustrate his books, La Farge incorporated some of his own watercolors into his 1896 book, *An Artist's Letters from Japan.*[59] One such work was his study of the tomb of Tokugawa Ieyasu (1543–1616; fig. 21). The watercolor, in photograph-

22. Anonymous, Japanese, *Tomb of Ieyasu at Nikkō,* c. 1880. Photograph. Morse Collection. Courtesy Peabody Museum of Salem

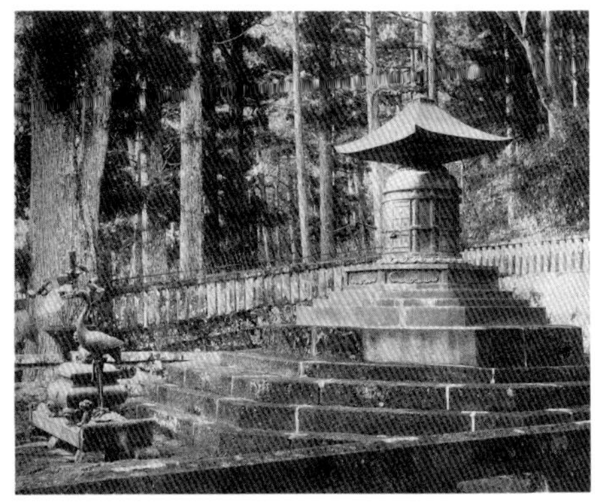

like tones of beige and gray, is related to a large Japanese photograph in the Morse Collection (fig. 22). La Farge's personal character seal in the lower left corner further links him with Japan.

La Farge's works were destined to serve more than his own needs as a creative artist. Rather, he satisfied the curiosity of a public mesmerized by the growing importance of Japan and its domination of the world scene.

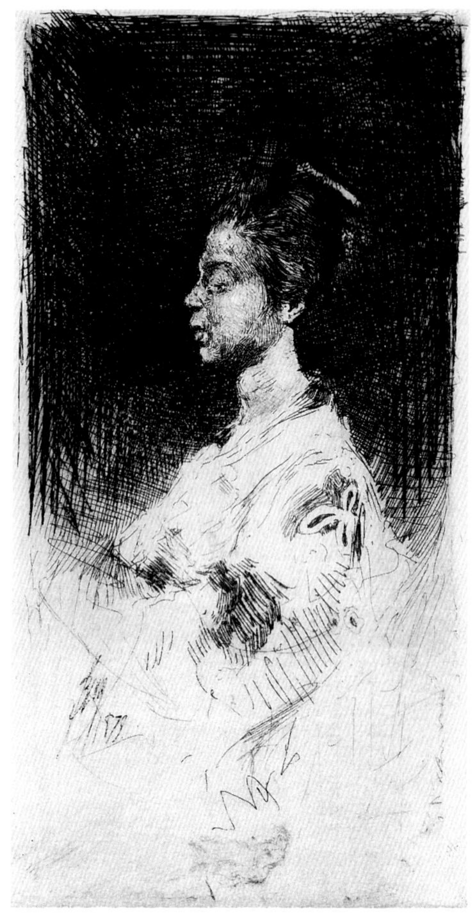

23. Robert Blum, *Head of a Girl,* 1879. Etching. Cincinnati Art Museum, Gift of Henrietta Haller

Robert Blum

In response to Japan's growing significance as an international force beginning to modernize itself under the influence of the West, Charles Scribner and Sons, major literary patrons of the day, decided in 1890 to publish, in their widely distributed *Scribner's Magazine,* a series of popular articles by the distinguished British journalist and Orientalist Sir Edwin Arnold. (These examinations of life and customs in Japan appeared as a book in 1892.)[60] Realizing that if readers were to follow Arnold's discussions, illustrations based on actual observations were needed, they enlisted the services of the well-respected painter Robert Blum (1857–1903).

By 1890, Blum had regularly participated in group exhibitions in New York and had displayed a sympathy toward Japanese themes in some of his early etchings that may have been completed shortly after the Philadelphia Centennial of 1876 (fig. 23). These small etchings recall certain vignette studies by Whistler, who had already shown extensive interest in Japanese sources in his paintings and in some of his prints. As Blum evolved artistically, he became aware of Whistler's contributions.[61] He also maintained an interest in things Japanese by collecting photographs of Japanese objects that had been exhibited at the Philadelphia Centennial.[62] One sign of Blum's willingness to be drawn into the activities surrounding Japanese artifacts and culture was his eagerness to travel to the Far East. When *Scribner's* contacted him to go

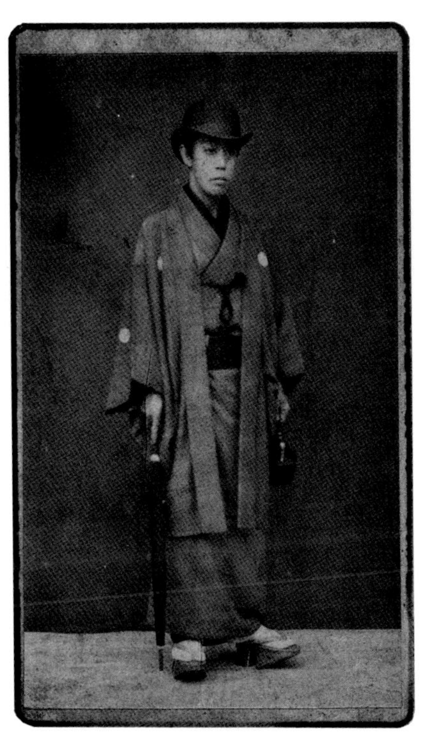

24. Anonymous, *Standing Man with Bowler Hat,* undated. Albumen print on *carte de visite.* Cincinnati Art Museum, Gift of Henrietta Haller. Former collection Robert Blum

to Japan on extremely short notice, Blum quickly accepted the offer.

Blum was accompanied on the trip by Shugio Hiromichi of the First Japanese Manufacturing and Trading Company (see page 44).[63] Upon arriving in Japan, on June 6, 1890, Shugio introduced Blum to numerous influential people, including Hayashi Tadamasa.[64] Shugio also made sure that Blum gained immediate entrance into the artistic circles of Tokyo by introducing him to Watanabe Kōki, president of the Meiji Fine Arts Society and of Tokyo Imperial University.[65] As a result Blum served as a juror for the Third National Industrial Exhibition in the spring of 1890, where he judged a series of Western-style paintings by Japanese artists. Opposition to including "Western-style" paintings, however, produced a schism in the Japanese art world.[66] While Blum's reactions to the works he judged are not known, the fact that these objects were exhibited at all suggests a step toward a "new art for a new age."

While in Tokyo, Blum met Ernest Fenollosa, which he noted in his diary:

Called on Mr. Fenollosa this morning and found him to be a most delightful man. He is just on the verge of departure for America (to take charge of the Museum in Boston) and I was delighted to meet in him a man that appreciates Japanese art in a serious way. He will no doubt do a lot of good in America as he takes probably the finest collection of art in the country with him.[67]

Through these connections with dealers and connoisseurs who were seriously involved with Japanese art and culture, Blum, like many others, actively established a pattern of exchanging ideas with a small circle of colleagues developing his own interest in collecting objects. He often wandered the streets of Tokyo, stopping to purchase woodcarvings, kimonos, inrō, and lacquer boxes.[68] During his stay in Japan, Blum also assembled a collection of eighteenth- and nineteenth-century Japanese prints that included impressions by Hokusai, Hiroshige, and Keisai Eisen (1790–1848; figs. 25 and 26).

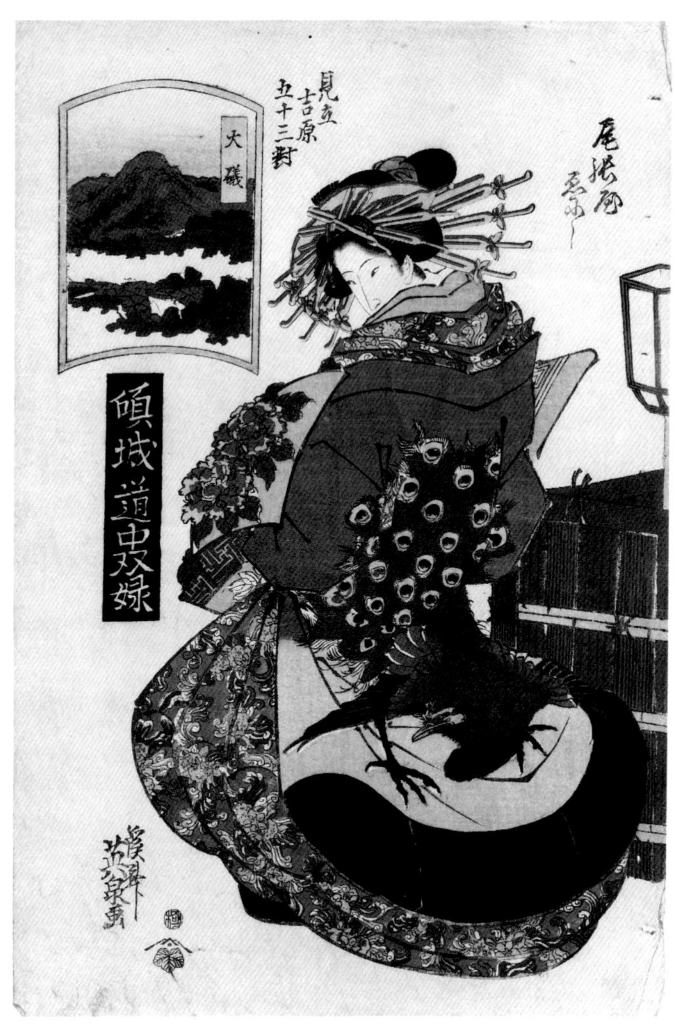

25. Keisai Eisen (1790–1848), *Oisō Enishi of the Owari Establishment,* undated. Color woodcut. Cincinnati Art Museum, Gift of Henrietta Haller

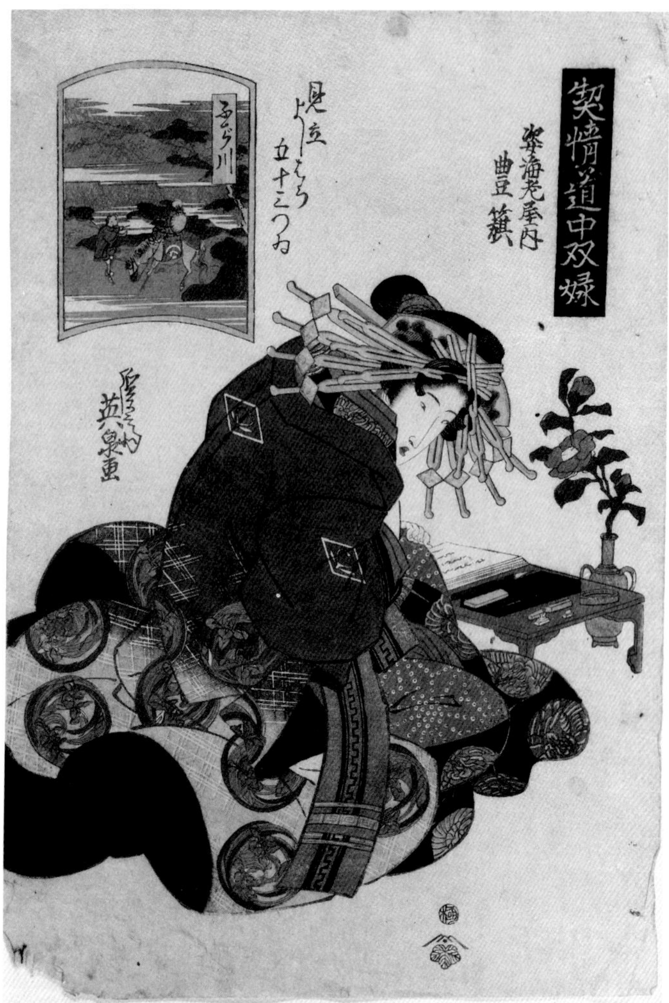

26. Keisai Eisen, *Fujikawa Toyohata of the Sugatabei Establishment,* undated. Color woodcut. Cincinnati Art Museum, Gift of Henrietta Haller

In his earliest days in Japan, Blum lived in the rather confining quarters of the Tsukiji Hotel, where many Westerners stayed, but he tried to get permission to live wherever he wished. Initially he failed to win this concession from the Japanese government, which carefully monitored the movements of all foreigners, but Blum did move more freely than most by developing the ruse that he was actually employed by the Japanese.[69] By August 1890, Blum had rented a house not far from his original hotel; its upstairs rooms gave him enough space in which to work.

Blum also amassed a collection of photographs (fig. 24) that he either purchased or had taken himself to which he could turn as accurate references when he was once again in the United States. Such images proved useful when, following the success of the Arnold series, Blum was asked by *Scribner's* to illustrate articles that were to be based on his own experiences in Japan.[70] These photographs were useful field documents to Blum even if he did not know the name of a particular performer or other sitter.

In addition he recorded his reactions to street scenes in his personal diary and sketchbooks. With a small portable camera he captured the sights along the Ginza and in the city's outlying districts. Occasionally his photographs seem totally spontaneous; figures and rickshaws look like fleeting ghosts. In others the artist took more time to compose the image, although his fresh response to children is both beguiling and without affectation.

At first, Blum's major preoccupation in Japan was to complete the drawings and watercolors that would complement Arnold's texts. Many of these watercolors, such as those of performing dancers (fig. 27) or the side streets of Tokyo, were done from direct observation. His visits to workers' quarters and temple compounds (fig. 28) resulted in a series of exquisite watercolors that demonstrated his highly realistic style and his skills as a draftsman.

27. Robert Blum, *Figure in Red,* undated. Watercolor over graphite. Cincinnati Art Museum, Gift of Henrietta Haller

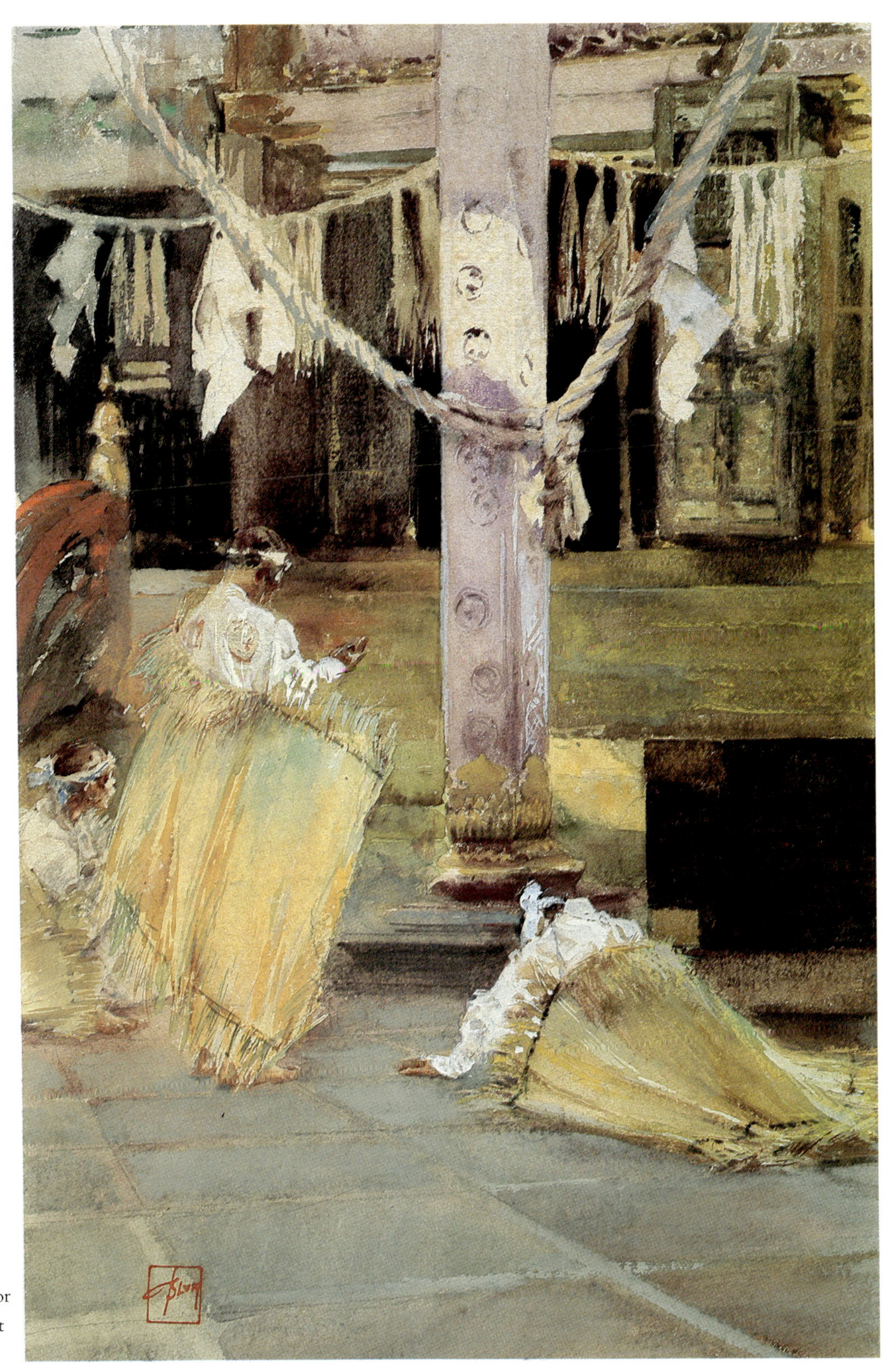

28. Robert Blum, *At Prayer, Temple Interior, Nikkō*, c. 1890–92. Watercolor over traces of pencil. Cincinnati Art Museum, Gift of Henrietta Haller

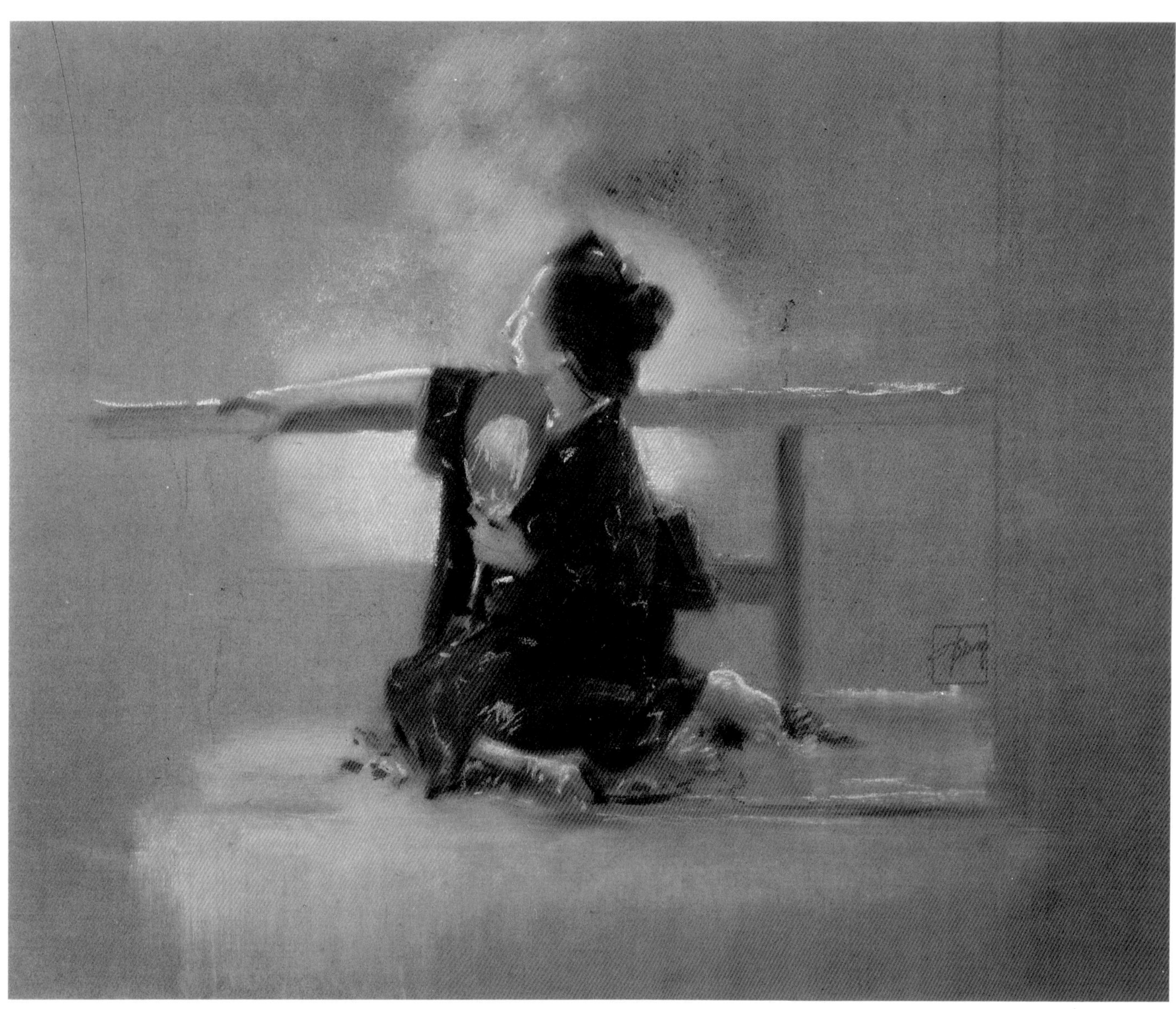

29. Robert Blum, *Japanese Girl,* undated. Pastel on sandpaper. Cincinnati Art Museum, Gift of Henrietta Haller

While in Tokyo, Blum posed (fig. 29) and photographed models in the quarters of Shugio and others for later reference. Whether he used these photographs to create an exact transcription of model and environment remains unknown, but they certainly enabled him to heighten his expressiveness.[71]

Blum's use of photography as one aspect of his creative methods remains haunted by conflicting viewpoints. Like many other European and American artists of the period, Blum often tried to hide the fact that he referred to photographs. As he later advised pupils at the Art Students League in New York, "it is not exact imitation of the model that is desirable, but a representation of the model as it appears in your mind; otherwise photography could do all the work for us."[72] He upheld this attitude on art and the use of photography for a long period of time. Contradictions set in, however, upon close scrutiny of the drawings with which he illustrated the articles that *Scribner's* had asked him to prepare on his own trip to Japan.

For these illustrations Blum developed an unusual working method. The images reproduced in *Scribner's Magazine* were drawings that he had ostensibly completed in Japan. On closer examination and after his photographic materials have been carefully reassembled, however, it is clear that Blum's drawings and watercolors were often direct transcriptions of photographs he had taken. Compare the vignette of a boatman docking his sampan beneath a ship to his photograph of the same subject (figs. 30 and 31). When Blum gave the title of "The Unconventional in Wearing Apparel" to a sketch of a naked child in the street, his ultimate source was most likely two photographs. (The figure behind the child is not found in the same photo that the artist used for the young boy [figs. 32 and 33]).[73]

Blum also relied on photographs for scenes of shops of umbrella or lantern makers, and there are numerous other examples of his use of photographic materials as documentation for his illustrations. Even the

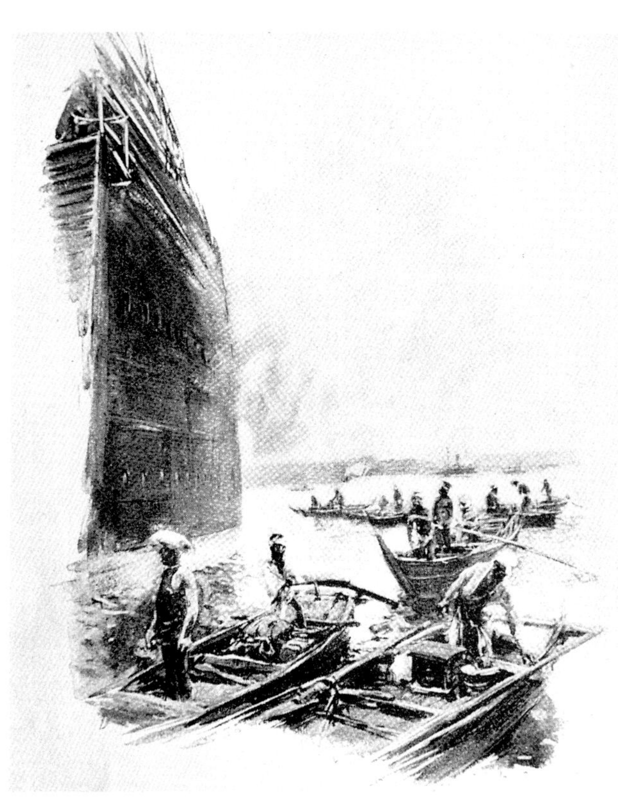

30. Robert Blum, *The Sampans.* From *Scribner's Magazine,* April 1893

31. Robert Blum, attr., *Sampans,* c. 1890–92. Photograph. Cincinnati Art Museum, Gift of Henrietta Haller

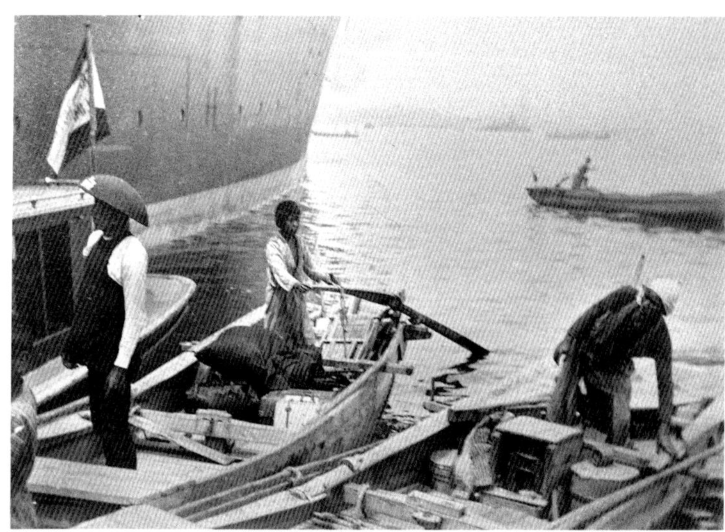

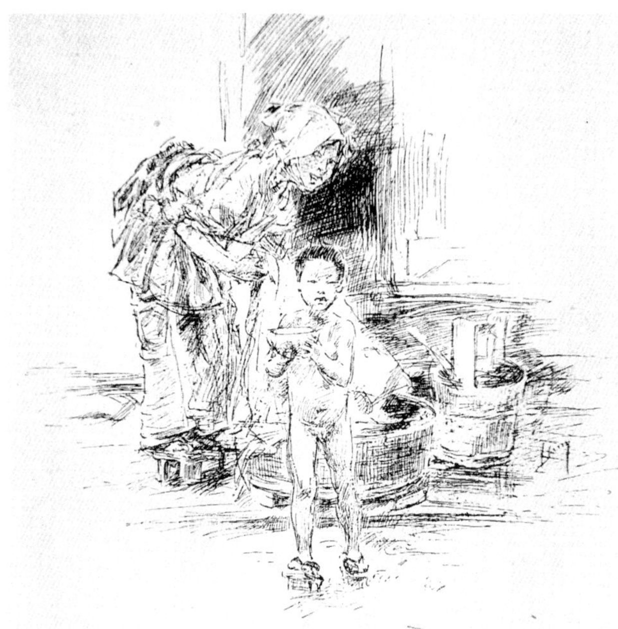

32. Robert Blum, *The Unconventional in Wearing Apparel.* From *Scribner's Magazine,* April 1893

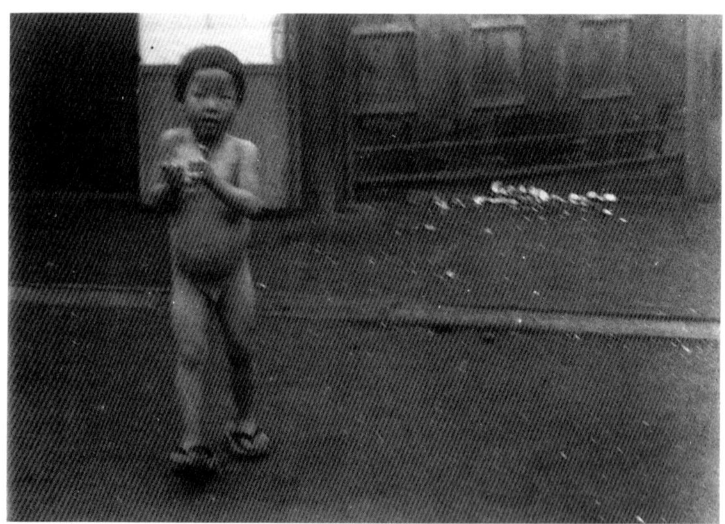

33. Robert Blum, *Nude Boy,* 1890–92. Albumen print. Cincinnati Art Museum, Gift of Henrietta Haller

most casual of references in his drawings, for instance, to workers pulling carts, apparently derived from photographs that he took. Although other images convey the impression of being produced on location, the existence of photographs showing ships becalmed or the interiors of temple compounds raises lingering questions as to whether Blum completed many of his studies, including his watercolors, from observation, as we have been led to believe, or if indeed he allowed photographs to do the work for him. Some of his later watercolors tend to idealize young Japanese women (almost reincarnating a Pre-Raphaelite ideal), while his paintings sentimentalize many of his impressions of Tokyo in order to reach a wide popular audience.

Nevertheless, in preparation for his return to the United States in August 1892, Blum was apparently willing to go to great lengths to have materials from which he could construct illustrations and paintings. In fact, a close analysis of Blum's stay in Japan suggests that he was eagerly pulling together disparate documentation and evidence that he would be able to use in a wide variety of images. Blum apparently wanted an impression of freshness and spontaneity even if his works were not direct sketches. Since the "unposed" study was then prized in European painting, Blum hoped to evoke this effect through his somewhat secretive use of photography. Thus, he manipulated reality to create the impression that he was bringing Westerners a heightened awareness of what the people, countryside, and cities of Japan actually looked like in the early 1890s. And, curiously, he manipulated elements from his Japanese stay to recompose Japonisme according to Western artistic conventions.

Other American Responses to Japan in the 1890s

Inspired by strengthening ties with the Far East, American interest in Japan and its people continued to accelerate during the 1890s. Many articles that appeared in the popular press were illustrated with photographs, engravings, and reproductions of watercolors. In addition to Arnold's articles in *Scribner's,* he published a series entitled "Japan Revisited" in *The Cosmopolitan,* complete with some of his own watercolors. (This suggests that Arnold, like Blum, referred to his watercolors when they were needed for later publications in the United States.) Looser in technique than Blum's studies, these spontaneous impressions recall the time-honored artistic tradition of filling notebooks with small sketches done on the scene, much the way Barbizon painters had created earlier in the century. Arnold's articles are also filled with documentary information. They focus fully on the activities and homes of the commoners in an effort to make Japan more accessible to the broad base of the American public.[74]

Coinciding with the proliferation of reporting about Japan was a continued appreciation of Japanese objects and ukiyo-e prints. The study of Japanese prints attracted new adherents in the United States, due to significant exhibitions that were held in Eastern cities and the return of prominent collectors with their prized possessions. Among the print exhibitions of the late 1880s was one largely drawn from the collection of Shugio Hiromichi, which was shown at the Grolier Club in New York.[75] Reviewed on April 13, 1889, in *The Critic,* the exhibition helped to draw attention to Japanese prints. Interest in organizing other exhibitions of Japanese prints received further impetus in 1894, when Ernest Fenollosa arranged the large-scale presentation at the Museum of Fine Arts in Boston that included prints borrowed from Siegfried Bing.

Fascination with Japanese color prints, especially with the ways in which Japanese artists had used flat areas of tone and two-dimensional rhythmic patterns, was reinforced by New York exhibitions in 1896.[76] One presentation in January 1896 boasted a most effective poster that had been designed by Arthur Wesley Dow (1857–1922), thus revealing how Japanese designs were strongly affecting the thinking of American graphic artists. This poster (fig. 16), more than others of the period, heralded the impact of Japanese art, particularly of its color prints.

A second extensive exhibition of Japanese prints was organized by Shugio Hiromichi for the Grolier Club in April of 1896 (see also Meech, page 44). A wide range of printmakers was represented, including Harunobu, Shunsho, Kiyonaga, Eishi, Utamaro, Hokusai, and Hiroshige.[77] Drawn from the collections of New York painters Samuel Colman and J. Alden Weir, as well as Chicago connoisseur Frederick W. Gookin, and others, the exhibition received detailed comment in *The Critic*.[78] The supportive review noted that the selection of pieces had been made with "uncommon taste and discretion," which allowed an uncommon opportunity for study.

Along with these independent exhibitions of Japanese prints were frequent comparisons of French and American posters. By contrasting these works, exhibition organizers and critics could allude to Japanese art as being one of the primary influences on the emergence of this art form on both sides of the Atlantic. A case in point occurred in November 1890, when the Grolier Club exhibited posters by Jules Chéret (1836–1932), Eugène Grasset (1841–1917), and Adolphe Willette (1857–1926) next to American examples. Both *The Art Amateur* and *The Critic* covered the show; the reviewer for the former noted that the "French affect the Japanese and rely on broad splashes of color and angular outlines for their effect."[79] Other exhibitions of French posters, including one in 1896 in the Meyer Brothers' gallery in New York, further demonstrated how Americans and Europeans were simultaneously elevating the status of the poster, for all countries recognized the Japanese print's achievement of colorful, flat effects.[80]

American posters were also being shown in Paris at the first Salon of Art Nouveau, which was held at Bing's redesigned gallery in December of 1895.[81] At the same time American posters were being promoted by critics in Italy and France. A most impressive article by the insightful

Vittorio Pica appeared in the Italian journal *Emporium* and helped to establish the aesthetic value of posters on the Continent. The article was later translated into French and published in the avant-garde periodical *L'Estampe et l'Affiche* in 1897, which further escalated interest in American achievements, both artistic and public, in assimilating Japanese sources.[82] Under the watchful eye of an international audience, American poster designers responded to the Japanese art to which they had exposure both within the United States and outside the country. Consequently, the American poster renaissance flourished. Since the poster was one area in which American design kept pace with European advances — if it did not take the lead — posters were deemed central to the continued assimilation of Japanese concepts.

The Poster Renaissance

To see the emergence of the poster in America as an isolated phenomenon would mean overlooking established ties with poster design in England and on the Continent. Interest in new methods of poster design as a means of visual communication arose from simultaneous innovations in several countries. A pivotal role in this development was played by the English Arts and Crafts tradition, with its reverence for book illustration and graphic design, and the accompanying interest in Japanese art and the woodblock print.

American interest in poster making and in the ways in which Japanese motifs had influenced earlier European printmakers was sparked by the continental prints that had been seen and collected in the United States as early as the 1870s. These prints verified that a well-established brand of European Japonisme had already affected etchers and lithographers, among others. Printmakers such as Félix Bracquemond, Jules Jacquemart, and later Henri de Toulouse-Lautrec and Henri Rivière, demonstrated how stylistic elements of Japanese prints could be utilized, particularly in flattening shapes and integrating large color zones.[83]

In the 1890s, color-field images by Henri Rivière (1864–1951), who was strongly indebted to Japanese prints and artifacts, were known to other poster designers, especially to those Americans, such as Louis Rhead, who frequently traveled to France.[84] Since Rivière was also a habitué of the major Parisian dealers in Japanese art (particularly Hayashi and Bing), and he was familiar with Bing's private collection of Japanese prints, he quite likely passed on his knowledge of these objects to others in his circle. In much the same way, Toulouse-Lautrec's lithographs (fig. 34), with their silhouetted shapes and carefully orchestrated integration of image and text, led American printmakers to discover how they could employ similar techniques in their own colored posters.[85]

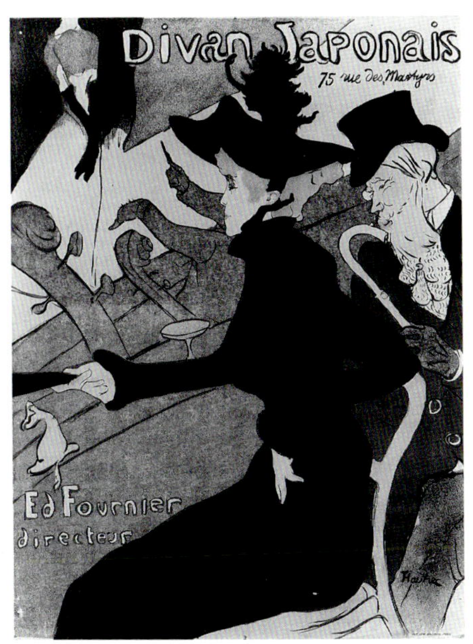

34. Henri de Toulouse-Lautrec, *Divan Japonais,* 1893. Color lithograph. The Jane Voorhees Zimmerli Art Museum, Rutgers, The State University of New Jersey. Class of 1958 Art Purchase Fund, 15th Anniversary Gift

English books and periodicals also helped to promote the American vogue for Japan. Walter Crane's children's books, which became popular in the United States, introduced flat color zones and simple border designs that had been adapted from Japanese sources.[86]

Louis Rhead and the Japanesque Tradition

Louis Rhead (1858–1926) used to good advantage his early training in England in the decorative arts and in the Arts and Crafts tradition. Not only was his work well appreciated on the European continent, he eventually became a major force in the creation of American posters as well. Through his independent commissions and precocious study at the South Kensington National Art School, the English-born Rhead came to the attention of the London representative of the New York publishing house of D. Appleton.[87] When he was offered the position of art director in New York City, in 1883, his career was launched. Rhead worked for

Appleton for six years, all the while building his private clientele. Among his earliest American works were book-cover designs that were reproduced in New York and Boston magazines. Along with one series that appeared in *Art Age* (1886), Rhead noted the relationship of his designs to "Japanese flowers."[88]

Rhead later met the editors of the American periodical *The Art Interchange, A Household Journal,* a publication that endorsed the most current aesthetic tastes in home furnishings and interior decoration. Beginning in 1885, it also reproduced a series of designs for ceramic plates (fig. 35) and decorative platters that had been inspired by Japanese sources and designers' adaptations of Japanese-style motifs. While it is not known whether these illustrations were used in the creation of specific pieces, their designs clearly emanated from a well-established tradition that dated back to the Bracquemond-Rousseau Japanese-style table service of 1866–67.[89] Even though Rhead's designs cannot be identified with certainty — much of his American work of the 1880s was unsigned and unattributed — he was recorded as working actively for *The Art Interchange* in 1886.[90] In support of the speculation that these designs were by Rhead is the fact that the term "Japanesque" was applied to some of *The Art Interchange*'s designs from 1885. With Rhead working and developing his own signed versions of Japanese motifs, he quite possibly helped to transmit a popular English term to an American audience. In any event, this usage reveals how an English-oriented term was infiltrating American designs in popular periodicals.

The 1885 Japanesque designs in *The Art Interchange* bore captions that taught American readers how to make their own versions of Japanesque designs. Although Rhead probably did not collect Japanese woodblock prints or own many books on Japanese art, he did come from a family that was intensely interested in the decoration of ceramics.[91] In the early 1870s, Rhead worked for Minton's Art Pottery Studio along with his brother Frederick Alfred Rhead, who became a pottery designer in

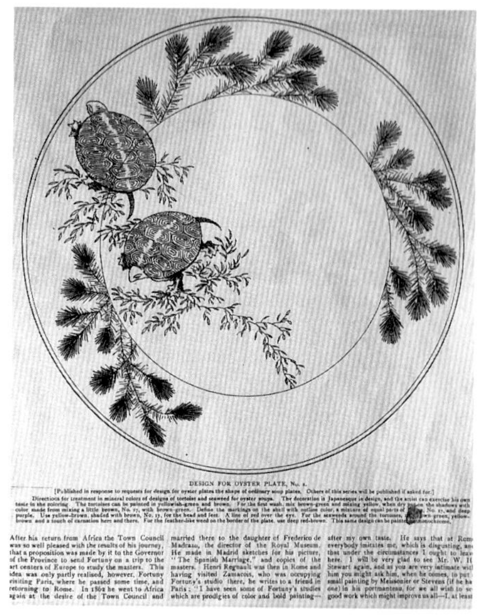

DESIGN FOR OYSTER PLATE, No. 2.

[Published in response to requests for design for oyster plates the shape of ordinary soup plates. Others of this series will be published if asked for.]

Directions for treatment in mineral colors of designs of tortoise and seaweed for oyster soups. The decoration is Japanesque in design, and the artist can exercise his own taste in the coloring. The tortoises can be painted in yellowish-green and brown. For the first wash, mix brown-green and mixing yellow, when dry put on the shadows with color made from mixing a little brown, No. 17, with brown-green. Define the markings on the shell with outline color, a mixture of equal parts of [illegible], No. 17, and deep purple. Use yellow-brown, shaded with brown, No. 13, for the head and feet. A line of red over the eye. For the seaweeds around the tortoises, [illegible]own-green, yellow-brown and a touch of carnation here and there. For the feather-like weed on the border of the plate, use deep red-brown. This same design can be painte[illegible] monochrome.

After his return from Africa the Town Council was so well pleased with the results of his journey, that a proposition was made by it to the Governor of the Province to send Fortuny on a trip to the art centers of Europe to study the masters. This idea was only partly realised, however, Fortuny visiting Paris, where he passed some time, and returning to Rome. In 1862 he went to Africa again at the desire of the Town Council and married there to the daughter of Frederico de Madrazo, the director of the Royal Museum. He made in Madrid sketches for his picture, "The Spanish Marriage," and copies of the masters. Henri Regnault was then in Rome and having visited Zamacois, who was occupying Fortuny's studio there, he writes to a friend in Paris: "I have seen some of Fortuny's studies which are prodigies of color and bold painting— after my own taste. He says that at Rom everybody imitates me, which is disgusting, an that under the circumstances I ought to lea here. I will be very glad to see Mr. W. H Stewart again, and as you are very intimate wit him you might ask him, when he comes, to put small painting by Meissonier or Stevens (if he ha one) in his portmanteau, for we all wish to se good work which might improve us all—I, at leas

35. Louis Rhead, attr., *Design for Oyster Plate.* Page from *The Art Interchange,* May 12, 1885

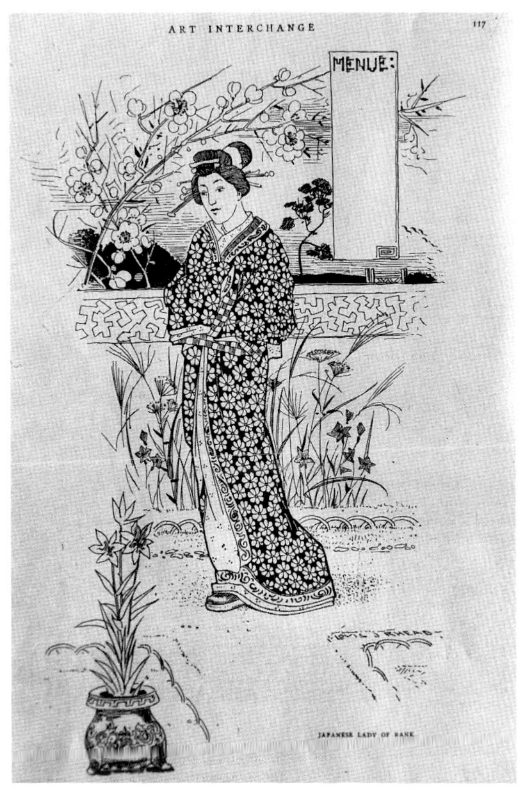

36. Louis Rhead. *Japanese Lady of Rank.* Engraving. From *The Art Interchange,* April 13, 1889

Staffordshire. Quite likely through these ties and his own involvement with ceramic decoration, Rhead gained familiarity with Japanese motifs and their application on ceramics.[92] Rhead would also have been fortuitously aware of many facets of the international Japonisme movement through his travels, especially after 1890, and his awareness of artistic developments in London, Paris, and New York. Due to his background as well as to the burgeoning American taste for a Japanesque style, Rhead was called upon by *The Art Interchange* in 1889 to decorate their "special issue" dedicated to Japanese taste.

For this edition Rhead (whose name appears in a Japanese style in some designs) created images of ethereal women dressed in Japanese-style garments (fig. 36). As forerunners of the seemingly Pre-Raphaelite women that filled his popular posters of the 1890s, these early images show how he grafted a Japanesque approach (here largely a matter of costume) onto an essentially Western way of depicting women in a garden setting. Other of his designs were Japanesque drawings for saucers, cups, and plates with color notations at the end of the issue to serve as a guide for the reader to follow when decorating ceramic blanks. A two-page spread of an abstracted chrysanthemum motif also demonstrated how Rhead was bringing his English Arts and Crafts talents to bear on an interior frieze that was decorated with Japanese design elements. An accompanying text in the magazine examined the differences between a Japanese and a Japanesque room, emphasizing how Americans could adapt Japanese motifs and colors to make their home interiors appear more timely.

The publication of this special issue of *The Art Interchange* and Rhead's active involvement in the creation of a Japanesque style in America could not have been more opportune. France experienced renewed interest in Japan through the Exposition Universelle of 1889 just as American fascination with the Far East was cresting—particularly for the interior designs of homes.

Louis Rhead and Poster Design

During the second half of the nineteenth century, Japanese art was an essential element in the evolution of avant-garde European art from academic realism toward a greater emphasis on simplification, two-dimensional design, and nonnaturalistic use of color. The decorative aspects of ukiyo-e prints, in particular, served as a precedent for and reinforcement of the tendency for abstraction on the part of European artists. In addition Japanese prints offered Western artists examples of artistically successful combinations of text and image; in so doing, Japanese prints gave credibility to the role of artists as poster designers.

Rhead was an important artistic link between Europe and the United States. His posters for American journals were a highly visible and influential affirmation in America of the developing international style of poster art in which Japanese motifs and aesthetics were assimilated. In some cases as in Penfield's design for *Collier's* (fig. 37), the Japanese ingredients of subject and style are relatively obvious within the context of an international style (fig. 38). However, in other posters — some, for example, by Rhead and Bradley — the influence of Japanese art, per se, is less discernible. In these instances Japonisme is marked by the strong integration of Japanese traits within an international style and jargon that are epitomized, for instance, by Beardsley's and Grasset's curvilinear designs of women in landscapes and that one may refer to as, for lack of a better term, Art Nouveau. It is fair to say that the art of Beardsley and Grasset could not have achieved its extreme design effects without each artist's awareness at some point in his career of Japanese art. The same may be said about American poster art. While avant-garde European poster art and graphic design were a major influence on that in America, the intervention of Japanese art was an equally important influence on American poster artists. In fact, European Art Nouveau and Japanese art reinforced, in a positive manner, each other's stylistic and thematic impact on American graphic arts.

Rhead's ability to think both as a designer and as a decorator, common in the period, as well as his skill in integrating his understanding of design with image and text, led him to create posters. In them, he displayed some of his Japanese-inspired attitudes, which became a seminal force in the poster renaissance that burst upon two continents.

Although Rhead received commissions for posters in 1889 (about the same time he joined the Grolier Club — important for its style-setting exhibitions), he did not fully anticipate the popularity of the poster in the United States.[93] The next year he moved his family to Paris, only to find that by 1894 he was forced to return to America to obtain commissions as a poster designer. In the first six months of 1894, he produced over ninety poster designs, which he easily sold to such

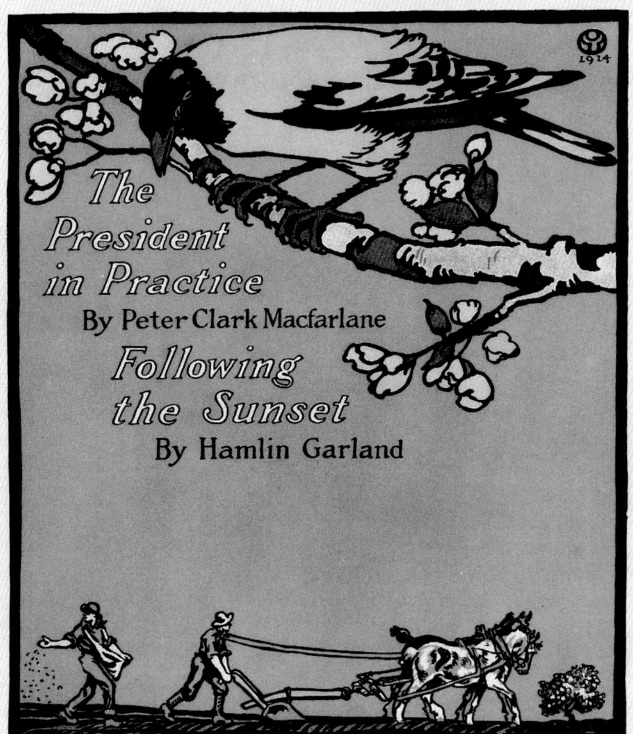

37. Edward Penfield, cover for *Collier's* magazine, April 18, 1914. Zincograph in color. Sterling and Francine Clark Art Institute, Williamstown, MA. Gift of Walker Penfield, Swarthmore, PA, Williams Class of 1919

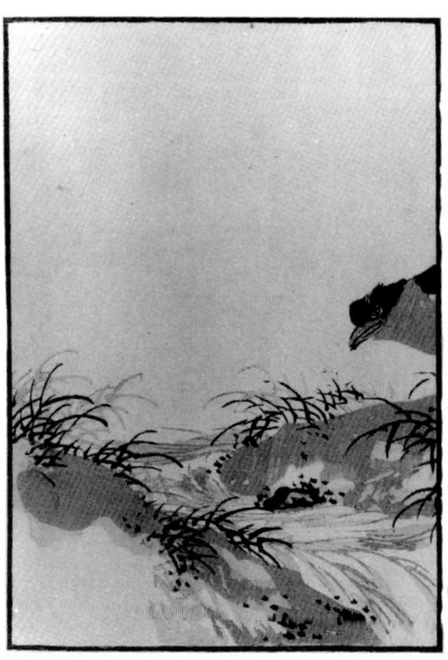
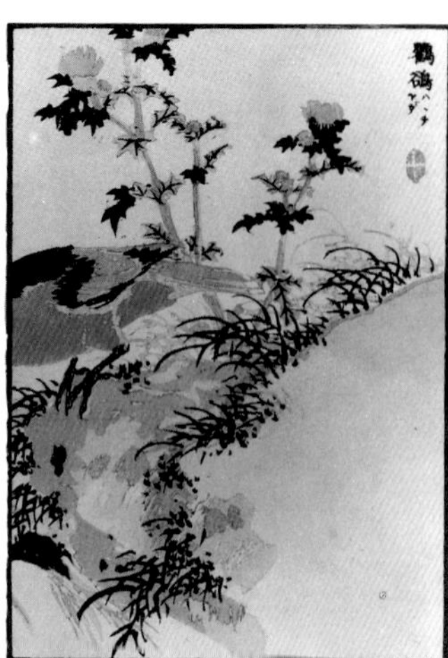

38. Kōno Bairei (1844–95), *Magpie.* From *Bairei hyakuchō gafu* (Bairei's Book of One Hundred Birds), 1881. Page from a color woodblock printed book. Private collection

magazines as *Harper's Bazar, The Century Magazine,* and *Scribner's.* By January of the next year he had an exhibition of his posters at the Wunderlich Galleries in New York, an event that elicited a review in *The American Bookmaker* in March 1895. This first one-person poster exhibition catapulted Rhead to the forefront of poster designers in the United States.

During this period Rhead received a number of awards, including a gold medal and recognition at an international poster exhibition that was held in Boston in 1895. He won considerable foreign popularity and showed at exhibitions in London and Paris.

Just as the poster craze reached its zenith in 1896, Rhead designed a poster for the London-based *Cassell's Magazine* (fig. 39) in which the women's dresses remind the viewer of his earlier Japanesque models. Rhead, however, added other layers of influence, such as the stylistic influence of the posters of his model Eugène Grasset, to create a decidedly Western adaptation of Japanese women wearing kimonos. The print's curvilinear rhythms and partially flattened space also intimate that he was joining other poster makers in turning to inspiration from Japan.

By 1897, Rhead's fame as a poster designer led the publishers of the periodical *Le Journal de la Beauté,* in Paris, to utilize for their own purposes an image that the artist had produced for the magazine *La Plume* (figs. 40 and 41). As with many of his other designs, Rhead here drew on the English Arts and Crafts tradition, the emerging curvilinear rhythms of the Art Nouveau aesthetic, and Japanese sources for inspiration.[94] He united the graceful curves of the peacock's plumage (a reiteration of elements that Whistler had employed in his Peacock Room of 1876–77) with a swirling pattern that moved from the lower left and behind the bird upward toward a flowing fountain.[95] These arabesques, suggestive of a garden path, can be traced to patterns in water that appear in Japanese paintings and decorative arts.[96] At the same time, however, the use of peacocks, which had become icons of the aesthetic movement in England,

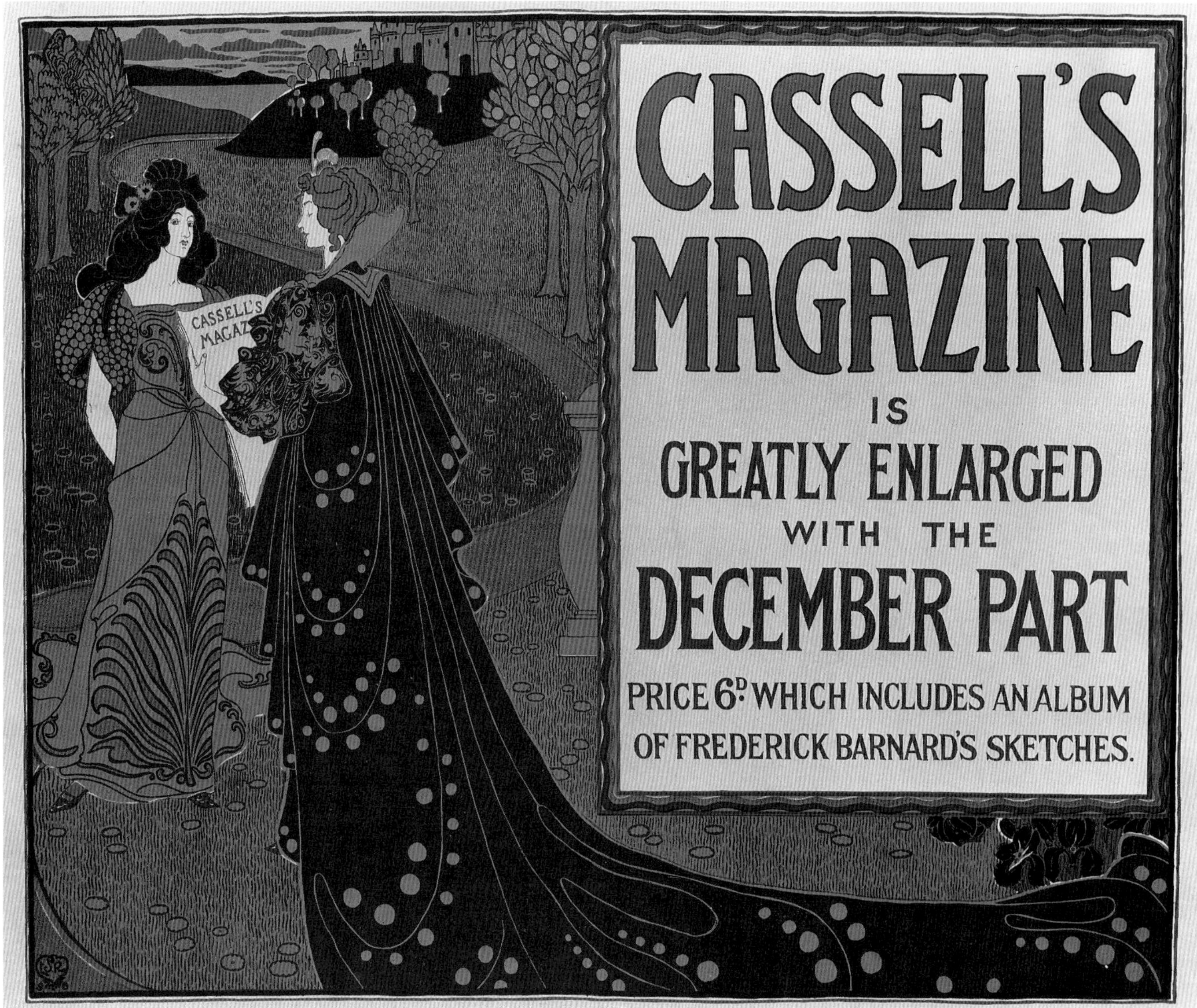

39. Louis Rhead, poster for *Cassell's Magazine,* 1896. Color lithograph. The Metropolitan Museum of Art, New York. Purchase, the Lauder Foundation, Leonard and Evelyn Lauder Fund Gift, 1985

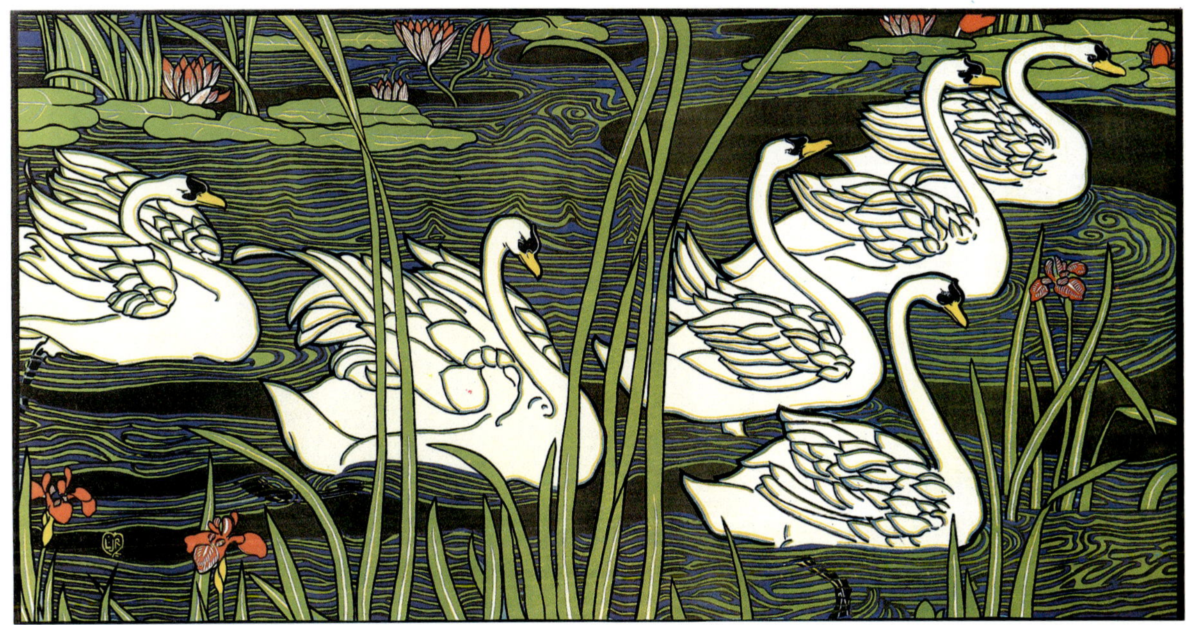

40. Louis Rhead, *Swans,* 1897. Color lithograph. The Jane Voorhees Zimmerli Art Museum, Rutgers, The State University of New Jersey, Ralph and Barbara Voorhees American Art Fund

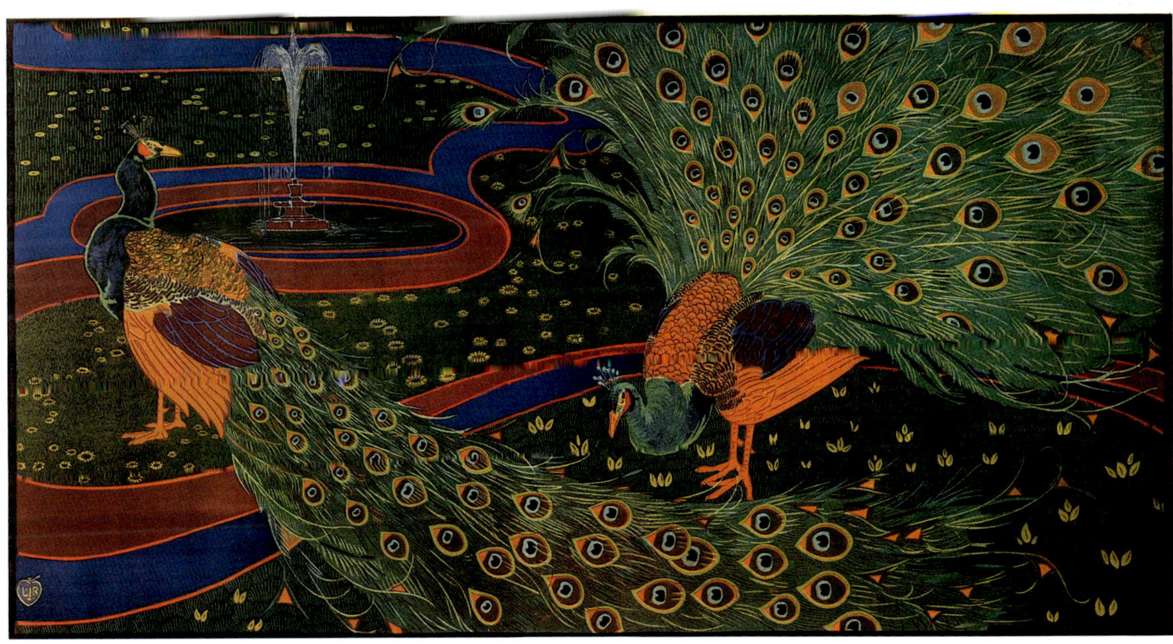

41. Louis Rhead, *Peacocks,* 1897. Color lithograph. The Jane Voorhees Zimmerli Art Museum, Rutgers, The State University of New Jersey, Ralph and Barbara Voorhees American Art Fund

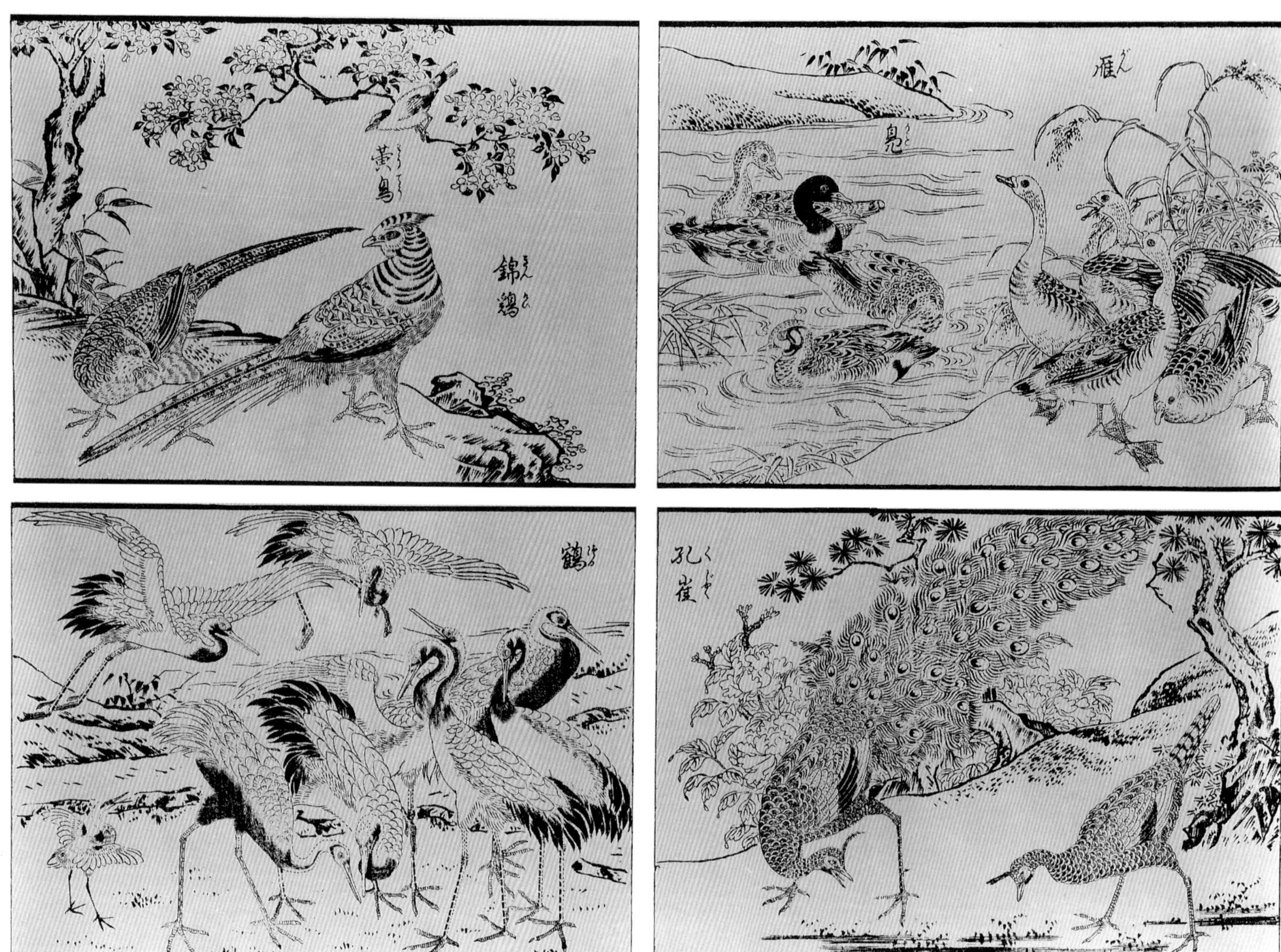

42. Page from *The Keramic Art of Japan,*
by G. A. Audsley and J. L. Bowes, 1875

could have been reinforced by images that Rhead might have seen in books such as *The Keramic Art of Japan* by Audsley and Bowes (fig. 42).

Given Rhead's penchant for ceramic decoration, his knowledge of ceramic traditions, and his awareness of Whistler's work, he would have had an ample range of sources to which to turn when developing posters. Japanese sources merely reinforced his predilections. Since he further abstracted shapes and filled largely two-dimensional surfaces with motifs, he can also be seen to satisfy the tenets of Art Nouveau design. These posters, which were frequently reproduced in art journals during the 1890s, advanced Rhead's position in the poster movement but did not certify him as dean of American poster makers. This honor was awarded to Will Bradley for his most original designs.

Will Bradley

Of all the American poster makers, Will Bradley (1868–1962) garnered the lion's share of attention in the 1890s. Much of his early work was in book illustration — another area heavily influenced by Japanese art — and the style, if not the content, of his designs was often compared to that of his English contemporary Aubrey Beardsley (1872–98), an artist with whom Bradley was frequently compared.[97] In addition to what he learned from Beardsley, especially in the use of black shapes and curvilinear rhythms, Bradley also encountered Japanese art at the Chicago Columbian Exposition of 1893.[98] For Bradley, the opportunity to examine Japanese fabrics and prints must have proved extremely useful at that moment in his career when he was becoming more drawn to abstract poster designs.

Enterprising businessmen took advantage of the strong interest in posters as a way to advertise their products. In 1894, the publishing company of Stone and Kimbell of Chicago commissioned Bradley to design posters for a new periodical called *The Chap-Book* (fig. 43). The

The Chap-Book

WILL H BRADLEY '94

43. Will Bradley, poster for *The Chap-Book,* 1894. Color lithograph. The Jane Voorhees Zimmerli Art Museum, Rutgers, The State University of New Jersey, Ralph and Barbara Voorhees American Art Fund

first of these posters was dubbed "The Twins" since the format Bradley developed was based on the repetition of remarkably similar shapes that seemed to move in unison. A critic writing in the December 1894 issue of *The American Printer* complained that he had considerable difficulty in explaining the image.[99] Admittedly, it was complicated to decipher exactly what Bradley had in mind. Nevertheless it is clear in this first poster for *The Chap-Book* that he had been studying Japanese prints of women dressed in kimonos (figs. 25, 26, and 44) as inspiration to create a "new" format for his Art Nouveau designs. The curvilinear rhythms and the dark and light patterning of the kimono were translated into an abstraction of flattened shapes. In addition, the decidedly stylized, almost lozenge-shaped face and hair could have been derived from Japanese images of courtesans with highly schematized appearances.

One of Bradley's most effective designs was completed in 1895 for *The Chap-Book* (fig. 45). In this image the woman carrying a tray of food was most likely based on Japanese textiles as well as prints. The swirling design of her skirt forms a decorative pattern that is both abstract and reminiscent of Japanese kimonos.

Although is is not known whether Bradley had his own personal collection of Japanese prints as other artists in Chicago (such as Frank Lloyd Wright)[100] did, the fact that illustrators, including Robert Blum, possessed collections attests to the wide diffusion of prints in America. In an attempt to satisfy the growing demand for a "modern" look, American designers seized on the readily available Japanese prints to provide the concepts and principles that would enable them to attract and hold an audience.

44. Kawabe Mitate (1837–1905), after Iwasa Matabei, *Courtesan Writing a Letter,* 1890–1900. Woodblock print. Cincinnati Art Museum, Gift of William J. Baer

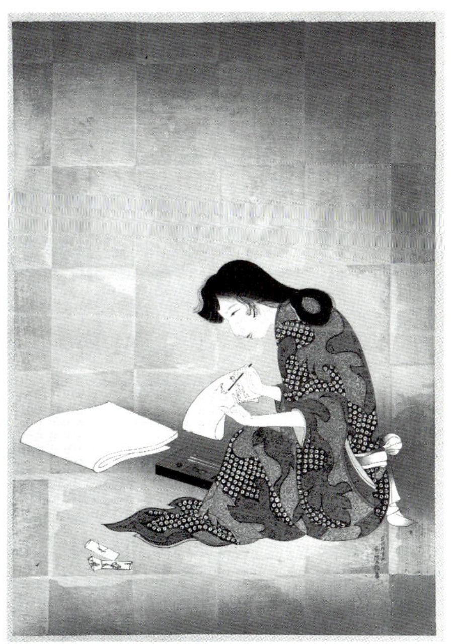

By 1894, Bradley had moved from Geneva, Illinois, to Springfield, Massachusetts, ostensibly to find more commissions. (He also would have had greater access to collections of Japanese art in the East.) Nevertheless, his designs for both large placards and small book illustrations were helping to establish an American variant of the

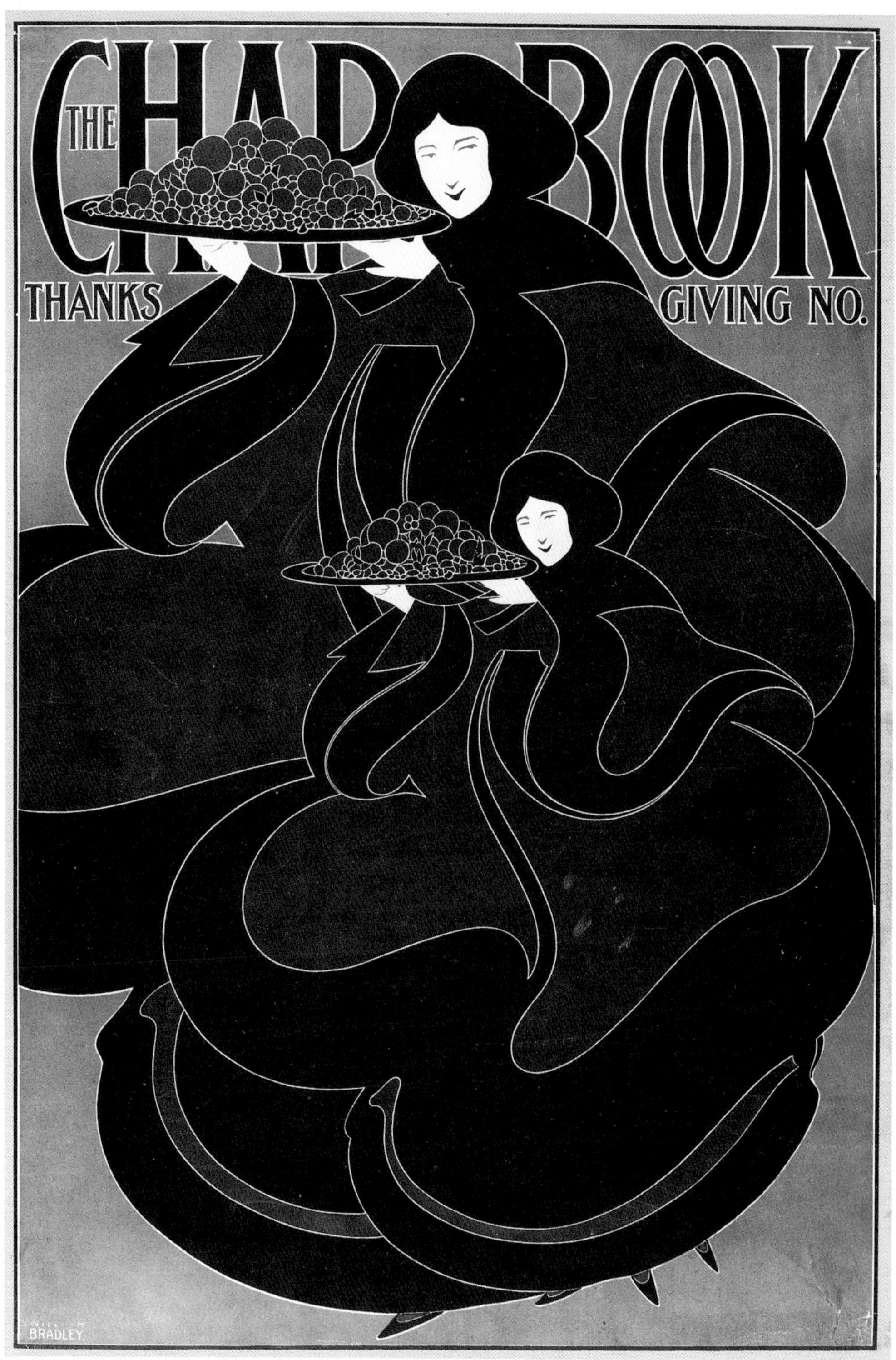

45. Will Bradley. Poster for *The Chap-Book, Thanksgiving No.*, 1895

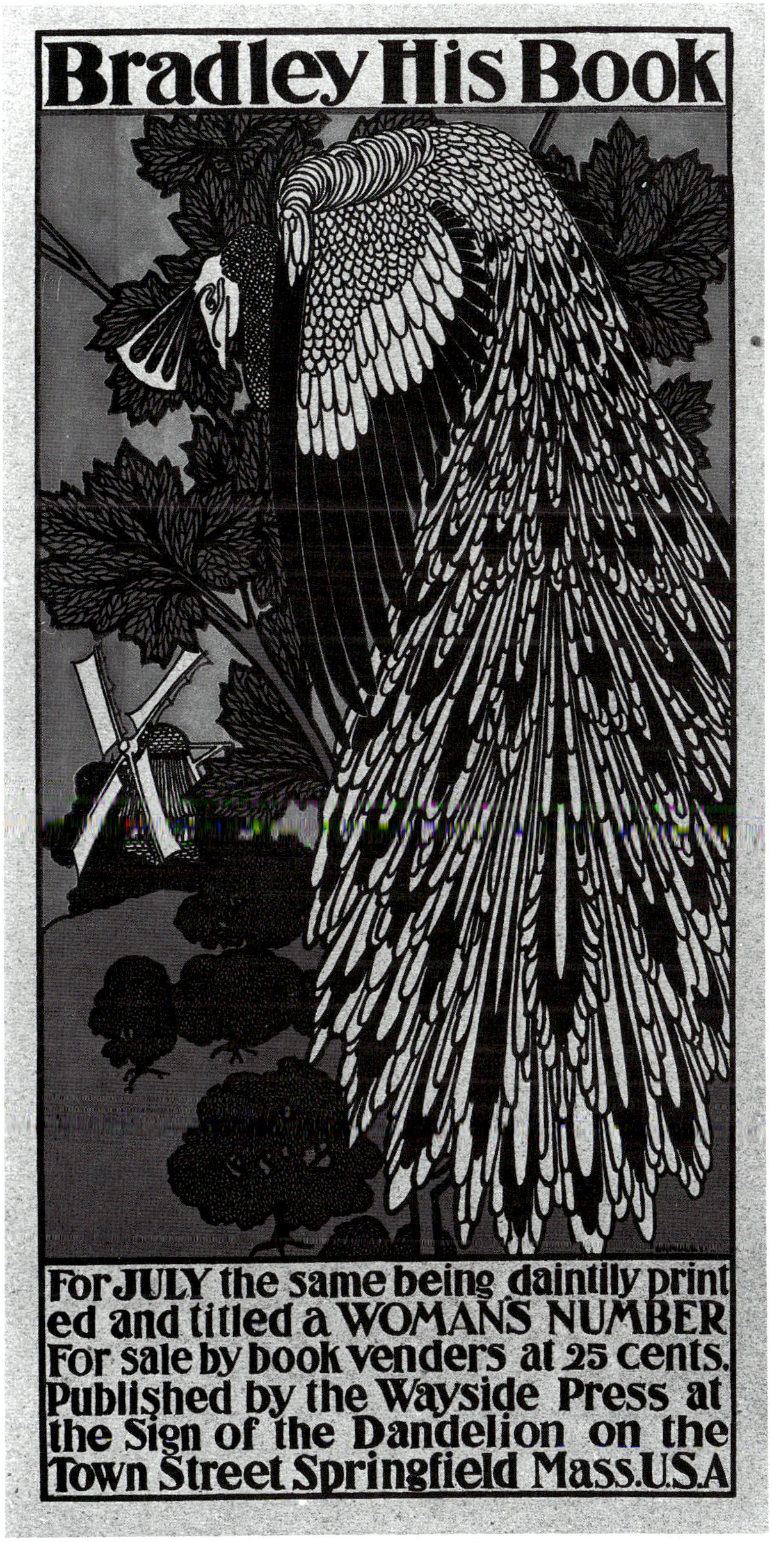

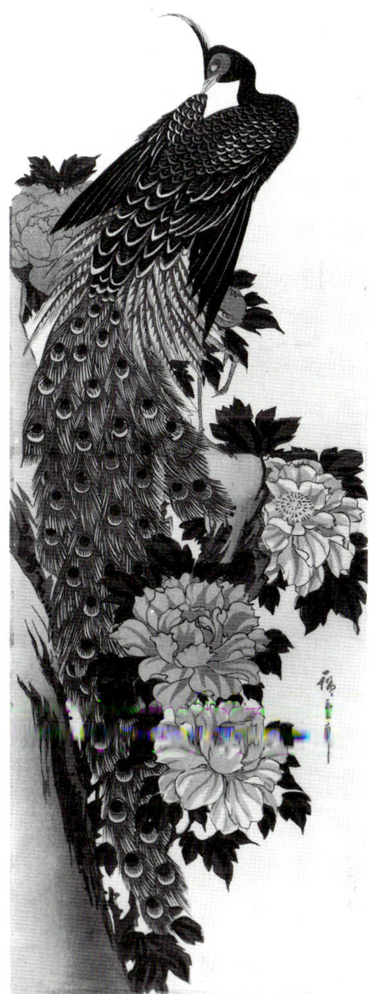

47. Utagawa Hiroshige, *Peacock and Peonies,* c. 1832. Woodblock print. Museum of Art, Rhode Island School of Design, Providence. Gift of Mrs. John D. Rockefeller, Jr.

46. Will Bradley, poster for *Bradley His Book,* 1896. Lithograph, commercial relief process, and letterpress. The Metropolitan Museum of Art, New York. Leonard A. Lauder Collection of American Posters, Gift of Leonard A. Lauder

international Art Nouveau movement. He subsumed references to specific Japanese sources in order to create the freely rhythmic designs of the Art Nouveau patterns that were then dominating the art world. To produce these designs, however, American as well as European artists had to assimilate several interlocking sources.

The curvilinear and Art Nouveau qualities of Bradley's work set the tone for posters and ornamental illustration throughout 1895 and 1896.[101] Other designers who began to work in a Bradley-inspired mode helped to initiate a large-scale poster renaissance in the United States.[102] By mid-1896, Bradley started production of his own magazine — a short-lived publication that nonetheless contributed significantly to the interrelationship between the written and the visual arts (fig. 46). This poster had a peacock motif that suggests a Japanese source, such as Hiroshige's *Peacock and Peonies* (fig. 47). The narrow vertical format of the print might have compelled Bradley to compose his own cover design this way. With the inclusion of text at the top, the cover's final effect was to convince the reader that Japanese sources, even nonspecific ones, had been influential. Far Eastern design principles also appeared on the book jackets he designed during the same period. In one, for *Lyrics of Earth* (fig. 48), the elegant arabesques of the "new" design permitted Bradley to create a subtle, asymmetrical pattern that elevated American book design to a level competitive with that of Europe.

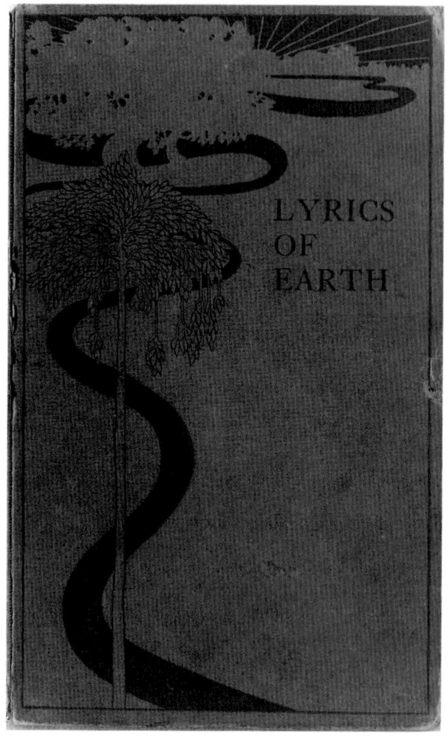

48. Will Bradley, cover for *Lyrics of Earth*, 1895. Ink and cardboard on paper. Wolfsonian Foundation Collection, Miami, FL

Despite the accolades he received for his numerous posters, Bradley, like other popular artists, realized that the poster movement could only go so far in the United States. Questions of cost and market saturation affected the poster's utility in advertising. By the mid-1890s, Bradley had redirected his energies to the design of books and their covers, which called upon other aspects of his artistic training. Since this work was not as public an enterprise as poster making, Bradley basically became a retiring businessman who wanted to work alone. He relinquished his position at the center of the public consciousness that revolved around posters and the promotion of new products. As general enthusiasm for posters waned, the number of artists who worked in this area naturally decreased. The creation of eye-catching posters had declined by 1900, just when Japonisme found additional support through exhibitions at the Exposition Universelle of 1900 in Paris. Even though Japonisme still thrived in America at the turn of the century, the great period of innovative poster design had given way to other artistic areas in which artists could renew their interest in Japanese art.

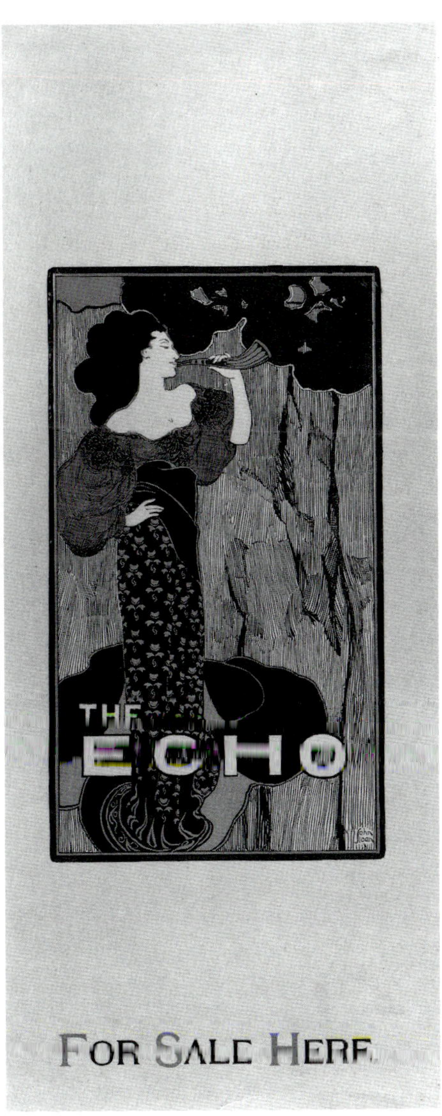

49. John Sloan, poster for *The Echo*, 1896. Hood Museum of Art, Dartmouth College, Hanover, NH

John Sloan's "Brush" with Japonisme

One other American artist stands out in the creation of Japanese-inspired posters. John Sloan (1871–1951), an artist most frequently associated with American realism and social concerns after the turn of the century, produced some drawings and posters that suggest Japanese influence.[103] Sloan's involvement with Japanese sources began in 1893, when he met Kubota Beisen, an artist for the Tokyo daily newspaper *Kokumin Shimbun*, at the Chicago World's Columbian Exposition.[104] Kubota recorded this meeting in a drawing he did of Sloan's colleague Robert Henri. (It was also inscribed in Sloan's hand.)[105] While it is unknown how deeply Kubota himself influenced Sloan, the fact that the American artist saw his Japanese counterpart produce brush drawings with stick ink must have remained ingrained in his mind. As Sloan later reported, shortly thereafter "Henri and I got the idea of carrying a bottle of Higgins ink around in our pockets, and made a lot of sketches on the spot."[106] Kubota's interest in spontaneity may have influenced Sloan in the drawings he produced for newspapers, particularly in studies for *The Philadelphia Inquirer*, beginning in the mid-1890s.

By 1895, Sloan had turned his attention to creating designs in "simplified patterns of black and white." His posters, such as the one he completed for Percival Pollard, the editor of *The Echo,* in 1896 (fig. 49), display two-dimensional decorative patterning in red and black that owes its effect to Japanese prints as well as to the work of Aubrey Beardsley.[107] Even though Sloan denied the latter influence, Beardsley's images were well known in the United States, and they had already played a seminal role in the work of Will Bradley. Sloan's narrow poster also suggests links with Japanese prints, although the overall effect is that the artist filtered his approach to design through a sensibility that was informed both by other poster makers and by Japanese art.

Whatever the direct inspiration for his flirtation with Japanese art, Sloan's interest in this area faded the more he became enmeshed in the graphic realities of the world. His infatuation with Japan disappeared just as the poster renaissance began to die out, which suggests that for some of the younger artists, Japonisme no longer beckoned as the wave of the future.

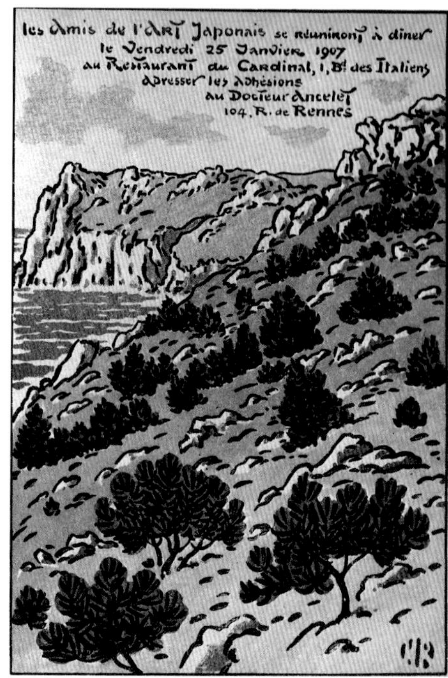

50. Henri Rivière, Invitation to a Japanese dinner, 1907. Woodcut. Courtesy Victoria Dailey, Los Angeles

1900 as a Watershed Year

Just as American involvement with Japonisme took on new ramifications around 1900, so did French commitment to Japan. This was due in part to exhibitions of Japanese art at the Exposition Universelle in Paris in 1900.[108] Led by scholars and connoisseurs, the appreciation of Japanese art in France became deeper and more thorough. Collections were perfected, and Japanese objects entered official museums such as the Musée du Louvre or Musée Guimet through gift or purchase.[109] Serious groups of collectors and connoisseurs met on a regular basis to discuss the merits of specific objects or to appreciate the works that had been acquired by the jeweler Henri Vever (1854–1942) and others. These shared experiences, which were often preceded by convivial dinner parties, led to the formation of the Friends of Japanese Art, a loosely structured group that originally included Bing and sometimes involved Americans.[110]

A side effect of these gatherings, which were held until World War One, was the production of numerous woodcut or lithograph invitations that were sent to active members of the group. Designed by some of the day's leading printmakers, including Henri Rivière (fig. 50), these small works document another way in which Japanese art was being assimilated on the Continent. These dinners and meetings also imply that after the Exposition Universelle of 1900, a network existed of individuals who were interested in discussing Japan and its culture. This fascination with Japan continued among the younger generation in France and in the United States, many of whom were not content to remain armchair travelers. As trips to Tokyo increased, American artists continued to assume formalistic devices in their work that certainly could not have been anticipated by earlier artists who had initially been enticed by Japan.

By starting more slowly and by maintaining close ties with fellow enthusiasts in England and France, American artists had a wider range of sources from which to choose when creating their images. Also aware of the accomplishments of English and French designers, Americans could freely compete on the international market. They continually tried to push for aesthetic change, especially in light of the opportunities afforded them through contact with the Far East and their ability to commercialize in part their interest in Japanese culture and art.

After 1900, the American public was greatly assisted in its perception of Japan by two factors: Japan's new dominance as a major world power; and Japan's increasingly important representation at world's fairs, such as the Louisiana Purchase Exposition in St. Louis in 1904.

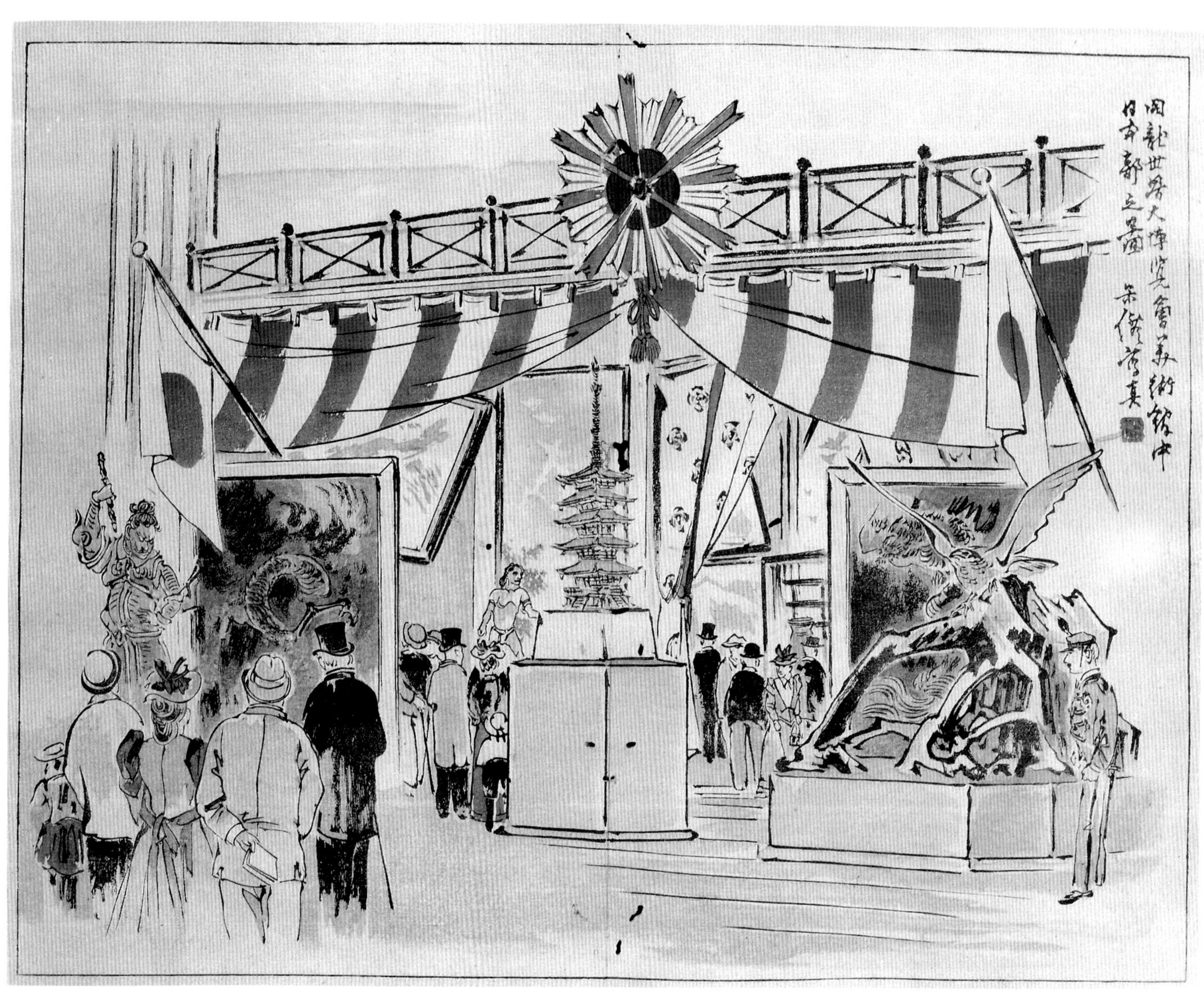

51. Kubota Beisen, *Japanese Exhibit at the World's Columbian Exposition.* From *Kakuryū sekai hakurankai bijutsuhin gafu* (Picture Book of Art Works in the World's Columbian Exposition), 1893. Color woodblock printed book. The Metropolitan Museum of Art, New York. Gift of Lincoln Kirstein, 1959

Julia Meech

REINVENTING THE EXOTIC ORIENT

Henry P. Bowie

Henry P. Bowie (1848–1920) was an American artist who came to Japan through the French connection, but whose total capitulation to Oriental art and culture sets him far apart from others. Born in France, he served as a judge in the International Court of Law at the Hague. While studying music composition at the Conservatoire in Paris as a young man, he had come to know the Goncourt brothers, who introduced him to ukiyo-e prints and awakened his interest in Japanese art. In 1893 he went on a short visit to Japan. The following year he returned to settle in Kyoto where he embarked upon a course of intensive language study and was eventually able to read and write like a native.

His first painting teacher was Nishikawa Tōrei. "It was as though the skies had opened to disclose a new kingdom of art," wrote Bowie.[111] For two years or more he worked assiduously daily from noon till nightfall, sitting on his knees in Japanese style to paint on silk or paper spread flat on the tatami mat in front of him. His next teacher was the maverick Kyoto painter and illustrator Kubota Beisen (1852–1906), who had documented the Sino-Japanese War and traveled in the West, recording, among other things, the Chicago World's Columbian Exposition of 1893 (fig. 51). In America he met artist John Sloan (see pages 91–92) and

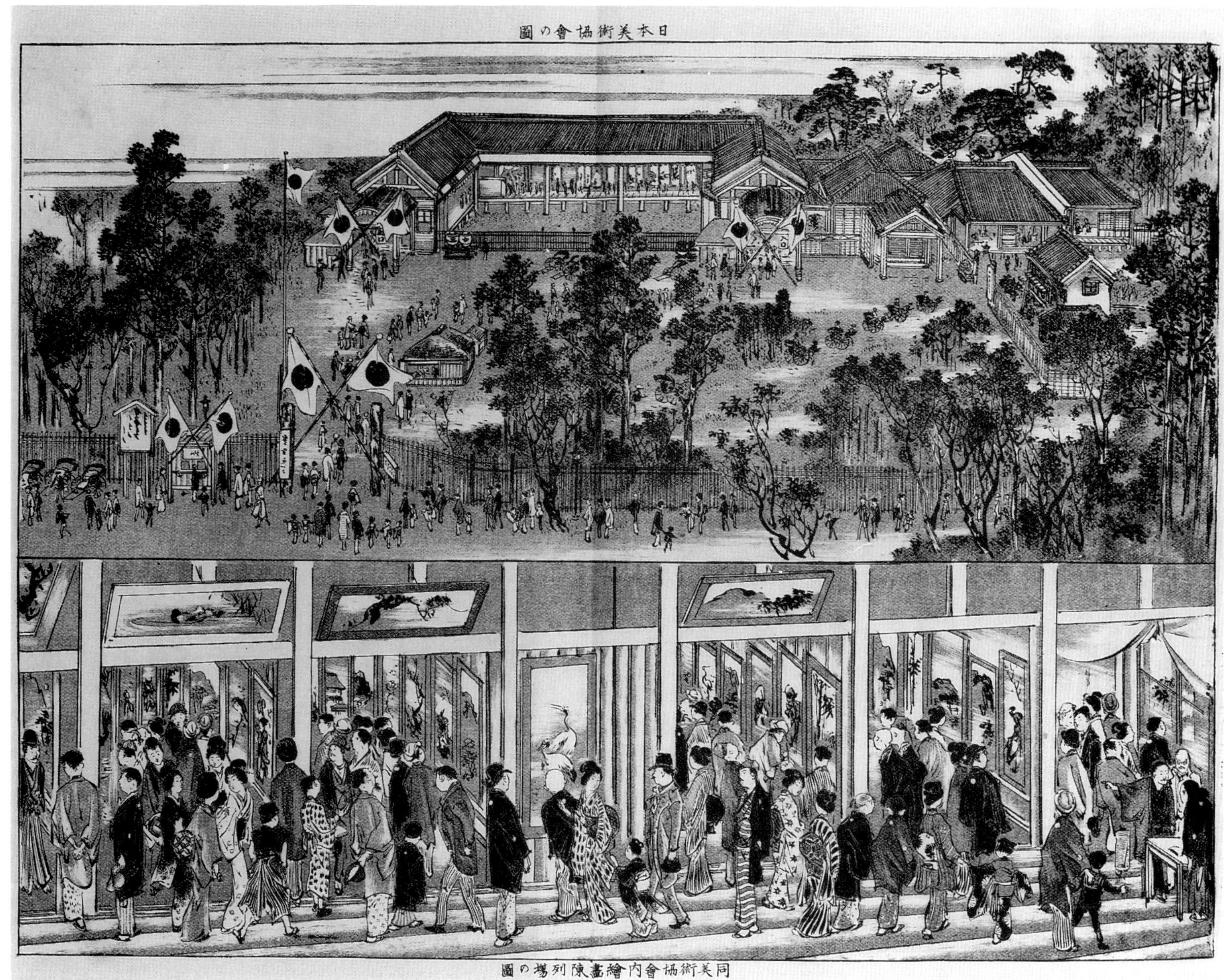

52. Exhibition Hall of the Japan Painting Society in Ueno Park, Tokyo, c. 1900

inspired him to do some poster work and newspaper illustrations in a spontaneous black and white manner.[112] Beisen's international outlook may have predisposed him to be sympathetic to foreign students such as Bowie, who claimed to have worked tirelessly under his guidance every day, including Sundays, for five years.

Bowie and an American named Francis Gardner Curtis (1868–1915), who became associate curator of Asian art at Boston's Museum of Fine Arts in 1907, were among twenty-seven second-place prizewinners (and the only foreigners) who participated in the seventh biennial joint exhibition of the prestigious Japan Painting Society (Nihon kaiga kyōkai) and Japan Fine Arts Academy (Nihon bijutsuin) at Ueno Park in Tokyo in 1899 (fig. 52). The latter was a private school for *Nihonga* artists founded in 1898 by Okakura Kakuzō—art critic, philosopher, and interpreter of the East to the Western world (most notably as the author of *The Book of Tea* and *Ideals of the East*). These two groups, which initiated juried exhibitions in 1896 and 1898 respectively, were spawned along the lines of the Paris salon system, just as the art school mirrored the conservative Ecole des Beaux-Arts. Exhibitions were generally enormous, with up to 800 entries by over 400 artists; there were nearly 13,000 visitors to the exhibition in 1900.

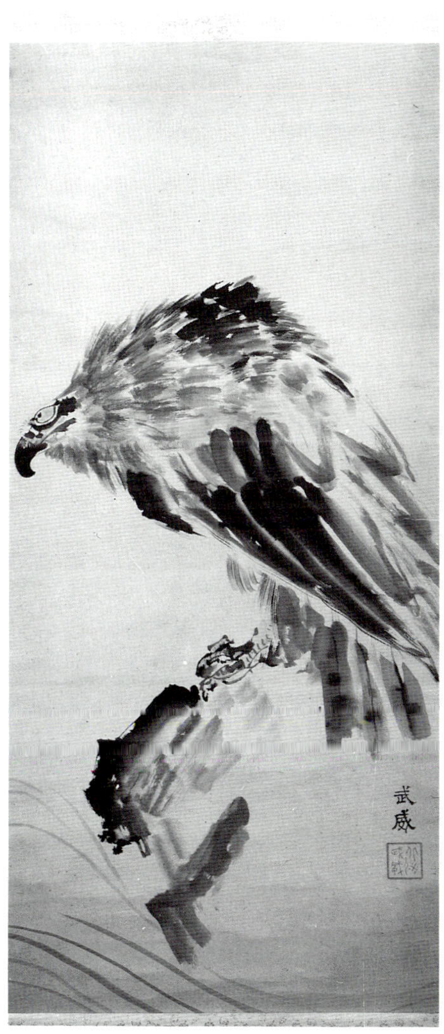

53 Henry P. Bowie, *Hawk*, c. 1900. Hanging scroll, ink on paper. Remi Hirano Collection, Tokyo

After moving to Tokyo, Bowie continued his painting studies with Shimada Sekko and Shimada Bokusen, hosted a salon of poets and painters, and took a Japanese wife. When he left Japan after nine years, he settled in San Mateo; he died in New York City.

Bowie was apparently lionized by the Japanese, who must have considered him a real curiosity. At one public exposition he submitted a painting of pigeons flying across a bamboo grove and "no one could believe that this was the work of a foreigner" (He signed himself with two Chinese characters that are read "Bu-i"; fig. 53). According to one Japanese admirer, "his reputation soon spread far and wide and requests for his paintings came in such numerous quantities that to comply his time was occupied continuously." His *Maiko,* showing a young courtesan and her attendant distracted by a butterfly, is stiff and rather flat, a competent if not particularly original work imitating the figure style of Beisen and Sekko (figs. 54 and 55).

To his credit, however, Bowie did more than simply master the foreign technique; in 1911 he published *On the Laws of Japanese Painting,* the first serious Western-language study of this subject. (Fenollosa's *Epochs of Chinese and Japanese Art* was published posthumously the next year.) Bowie's approach was that of an insider's detailed "how-to" manual for students and would-be artists, complete with explanatory drawings by Sekko (fig. 56). Although Bowie did feel compelled to devote a few pages to the history of woodblock prints, he speaks of them with not a little condescension. "The great painters of Japan have never held this school in any favor," he wrote.

At one time or another I have visited nearly every distinguished artist's studio in Japan, and . . . I have never seen a Japanese print in the possession of any of them, and I know their sentiments about all such work. A print is a lifeless production, and it would be quite impossible for a Japanese artist to take prints into any serious consideration. They rank no higher than cut velvet scenery or embroidered screens.

He is forced to concede, however, that prints did first attract the world's attention to Japanese art, even though they were no more than a "cheap substitute for art with the lower classes, just as Raspail says garlic has always been the camphor of the poor in France." (Faint praise, indeed.) As for Fenollosa,

had he possessed the training necessary to paint in the Japanese style I do not think he would have devoted so much time to Japanese woodcuts.

Visiting me in Kyoto, where I was busily engaged in painting, "Ah!" he cried, "that is what I have always longed to do. Sooner or later I shall follow your example." But he never did. Instead he issued a large work on Japanese prints.

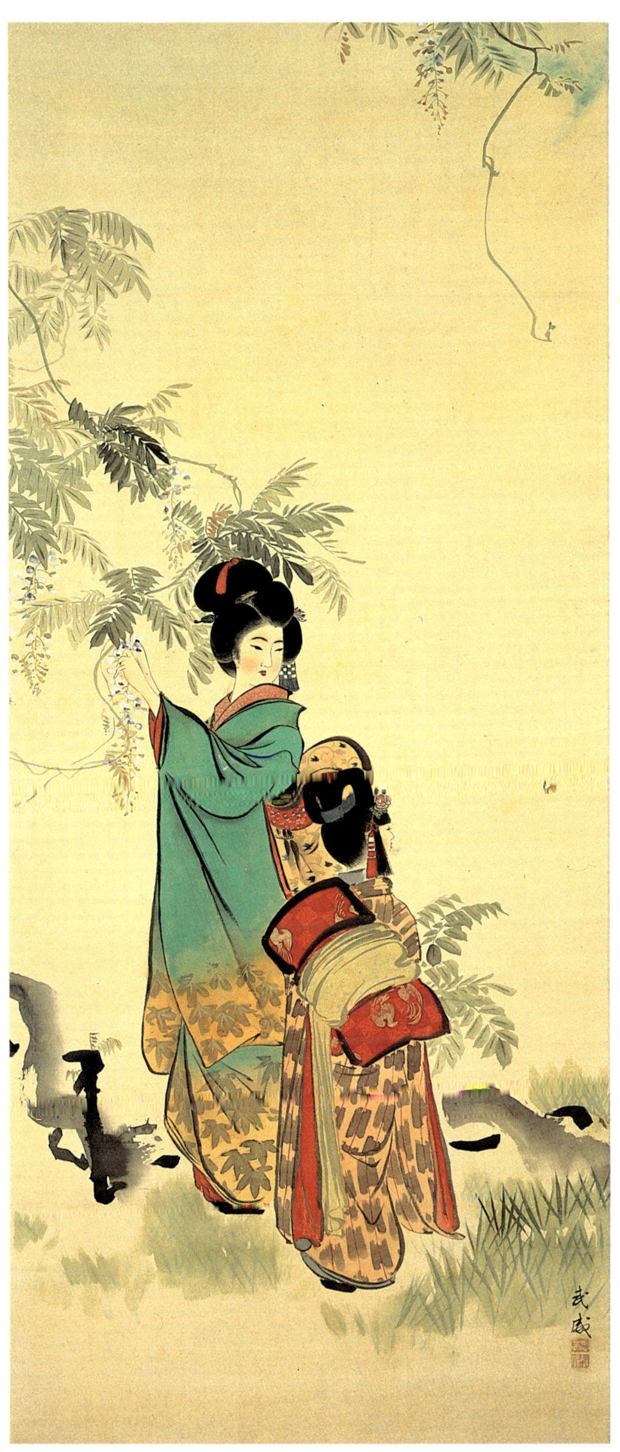

54. Henry P. Bowie, *Maiko,* c. 1900. Hanging scroll, ink and color on paper. Remi Hirano Collection, Tokyo

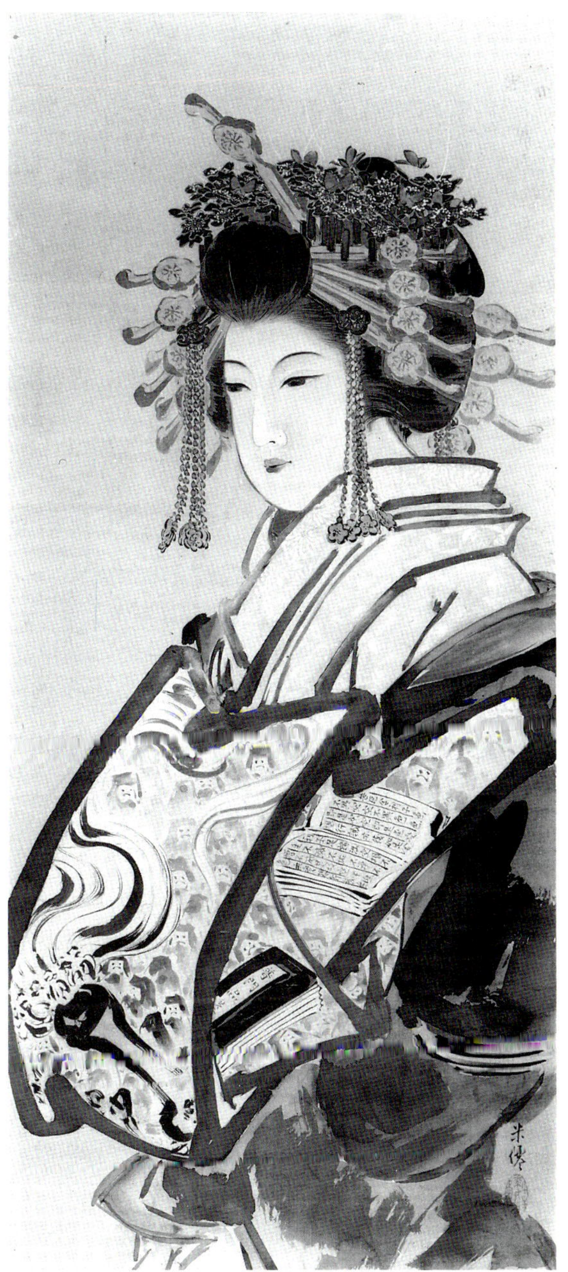

55. Kubota Beisen, *Hell Courtesan,* c. 1890. Hanging scroll, ink and color on paper. Fukutomi Tarō Collection, Tokyo

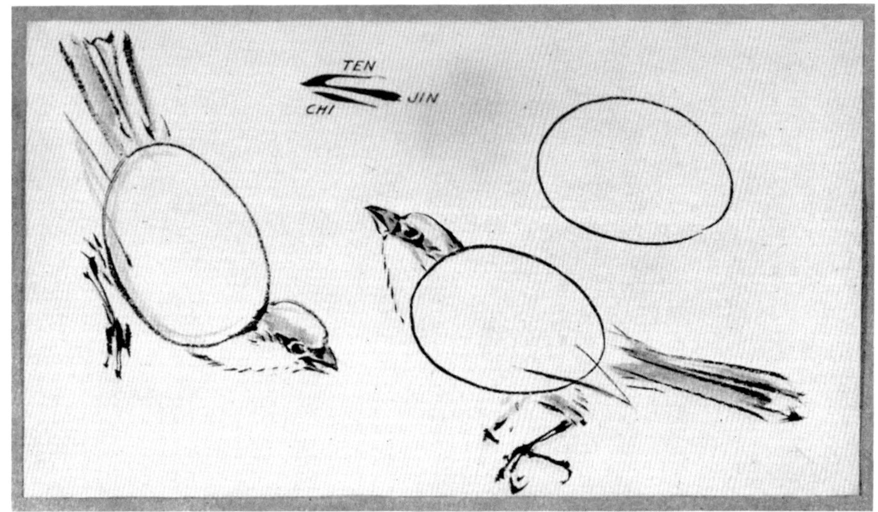

56. Shimada Sekko, illustration for Henry P. Bowie, *On the Laws of Japanese Painting,* 1911

Bowie writes with the humorless zeal of a convert to a new religion, but his book has had lasting value as an exposition of the principles of Japanese paintings. He would never admit, however, that the ideas or methods of Japanese art could be successfully transplanted into or influence Western painting. It was his opinion that the two countries have nothing in common, and the introduction of Japanese elements into Western art would actually have undesirable and unfortunate results. His only concession was in the case of Japanese composition — "their way of presenting a subject"; here, there might be a common meeting ground. But the essence of the art of Japan was a mystery understood only by the chosen few (including, of course, himself). "It is said that Whistler as a painter was influenced by Japanese art," he wrote.

In some of his landscapes the composition may have been suggested by Hiroshige prints which he imitated, but that hardly justifies the statement that Whistler as a painter was influenced by the essential principles of the art of Japan.[113]

Overly proud of his own hard-won skills, Bowie missed the larger picture, the gradual diffusion and intermingling of Eastern and Western styles that was beginning to break down national boundaries (between not only East and West but also Europe and America) at the turn of the century.

Helen Hyde

Two American graphic artists, Helen Hyde and Bertha Lum, set high standards of craftsmanship in the woodcut medium in America by exploiting the skills of native Japanese artisans. Both women spent long periods of time in Japan, favored rather sweet, anecdotal figure subjects, and were hugely successful during their lifetimes: their work was exhibited in America, Europe, and Japan. By the time of their deaths, however, they looked old-fashioned, and their public reputations quickly faded. Not only did they stand apart from the mainstream of modernism, but they also seem to have been perceived primarily as illustrators, like Robert Blum before them. It is time now to reconsider their contribution as popularizers of Japonisme in America.

Helen Hyde (1868–1919) — "Nellie" to her family — grew up in San Francisco, where her father was an inventor and civil engineer and her mother a teacher. Her father died when she was thirteen and Hyde was taken under the wing of her wealthy aunt, Augusta Hyde Bixler, who furnished her with a studio in the family's unused barn and financed a solid if conventional art education, first in San Francisco with Ferdinand Richardt (1819–95) and Emil Carlsen (1853–1932), then in New York at the Art Students League, and finally in Europe. In Berlin she studied portraiture with Franz Skarbina (1849–1910), and for several years in Paris she worked under Raphaël Collin (1850–1916) and Albert Sterner (1863–1946).[114]

She credited her association with Félix Régamey (1844–1907), painter, illustrator, teacher, and traveler, with sparking her enthusiasm for fine Japanese art:

To him there was no art except Japanese art, no women except Japanese women, and no life except Japanese life. He thrilled me with his descriptions of the loveliness of things Japanese, and as he had been to Japan many times and had lived there for long

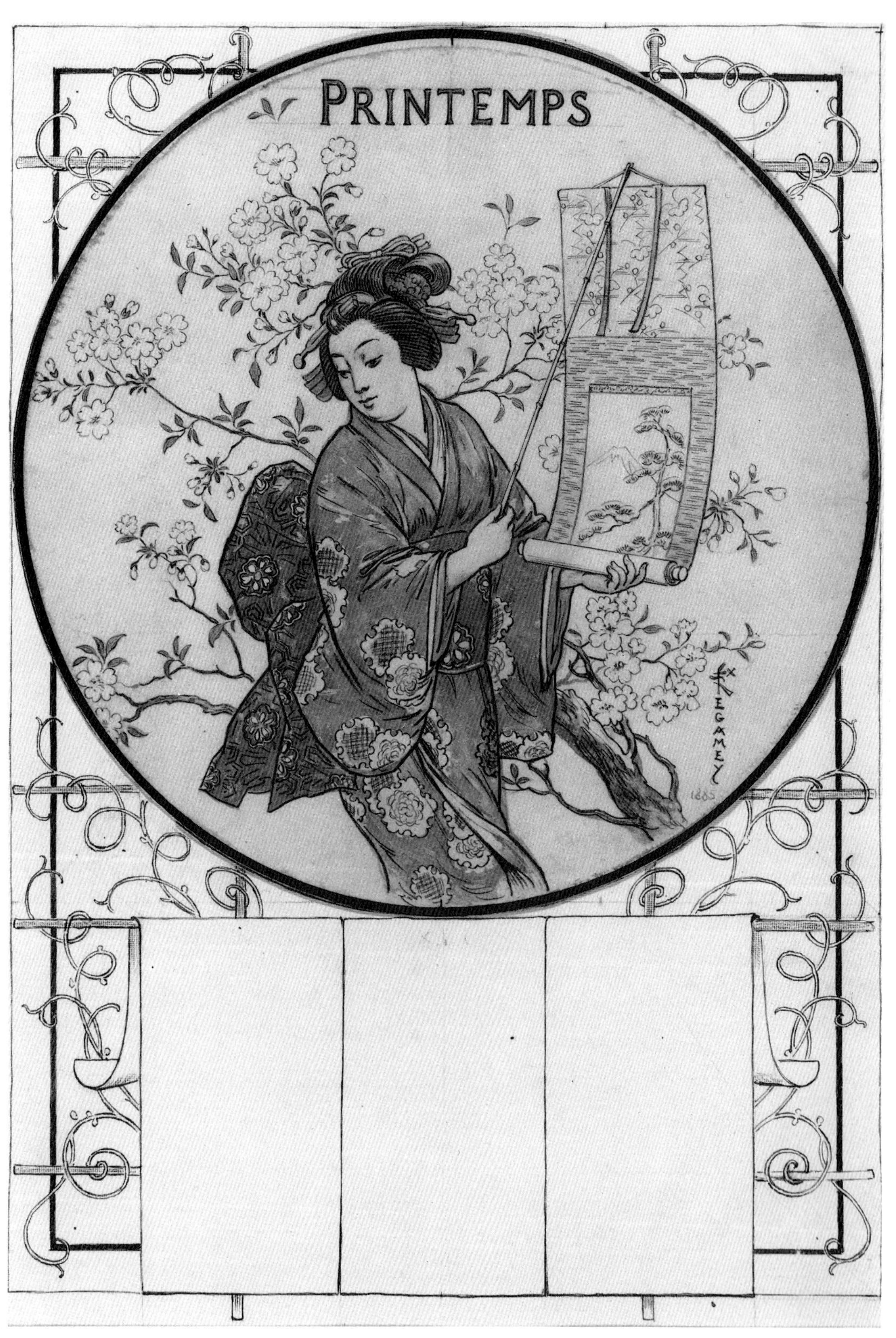
PRINTEMPS
F. RÉGAMEY
1885

57. Félix Régamey, *Study for Calendar: Spring,* 1885. Watercolor and crayon. The Jane Voorhees Zimmerli Art Museum, Rutgers, The State University of New Jersey. Acquired in the name of The Dai-Ichi Bank, Ltd.

periods, he knew his topic thoroughly. He . . . was not recognized so much as a clever artist as he was for his ability to enthuse others and provoke ideas in them. Working under Régamey's instructions, I fully made up my mind to become a professional illustrator.[115]

Régamey, who worked in a descriptive, sentimental style not unlike that adopted by Hyde, made the first of many visits to Japan in 1876 in the company of French industrialist Emile Guimet (1836–1918; fig. 57). In 1878 the two collaborated on *Promenades japonaises,* an account of their trip to Japan, with text by Guimet and illustrations by Régamey; and in 1889 Guimet opened a museum in Paris housing his Asian collection.[116]

When Hyde returned to San Francisco in the mid-1890s after a ten-year absence, she, like her contemporary the photographer Arnold Genthe, explored the artistic possibilities of the only Asian subject near at hand, the densely crowded eight-block area of Chinatown. The children, with their "exotic" colored silk costumes and long braids were especially intriguing to her (fig. 58). (The "child cult" runs through much of late nineteenth century art.) Between 1897 and early 1899 she produced about twenty colored copperplate etchings devoted to this theme ("like hunting for tropical birds," as she described it) with the encouragement of her friend, the etcher Josephine M. Hyde (b. 1862, no relation), who printed some of her plates.[117] Helen Hyde used a curious portable press that was made for her in San Francisco. It was not very sturdy and would not have withstood much pressure, but her etchings tended to be miniatures (fig. 59).[118]

58. Helen Hyde, *Standing Boy in Purple,* c. 1898. Color etching. The Jane Voorhees Zimmerli Art Museum, Rutgers, The State University of New Jersey, Ralph and Barbara Voorhees American Art Fund

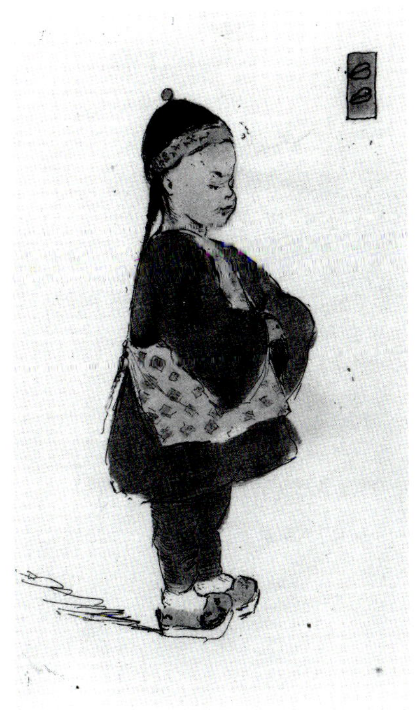

The etchings were an immediate financial success, but Hyde realized she would have to expand her horizons. In the summer of 1899, at the age of thirty-one, she sailed for Japan with Josephine Hyde, intending to spend six months. Although she often returned for extended visits (the years 1910–12 were spent in the States, with a productive interlude in Mexico; fig. 60), it was not until fourteen years later, in October of 1914,

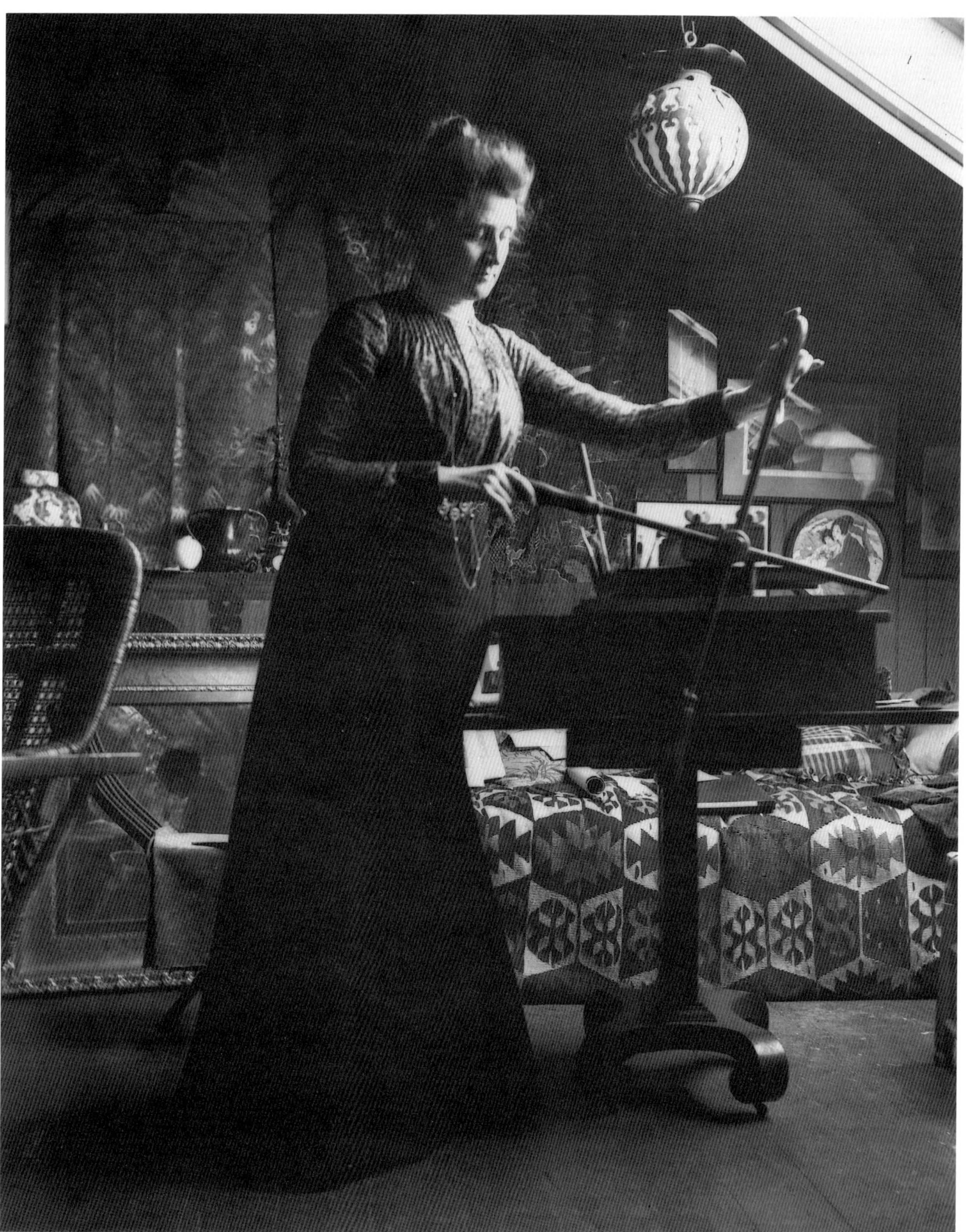

that she finally left Japan for good and settled in Chicago, where her sister Mabel Hyde Gillette lived.[119] Her summers were spent at Nikkō, where she rented the house of a Buddhist priest. Nikkō, site of the ornate mausoleum of Tokugawa Ieyasu, the founder of the Tokugawa shogunate, was a great tourist attraction and favorite scenic retreat several hours north of the capital (see figs. 21 and 22).

In Tokyo she started off in the foreign enclave in Tsukiji but quickly relocated to Akasaka, a purely Japanese neighborhood. (In 1899, following the revision of the original commercial treaties of 1858, restrictions on foreigners' residence, travel, and trade activities within Japan were lifted. Hyde was able to move about freely.) Her luxurious two-story wooden house was built to her design as were the chairs and many of the other furnishings (fig. 61).[120] She installed tatami and shoji, but did not give up her creature comforts to live entirely in Japanese style; rugs covered her tatami. Smitten by the Japanese use of family crests, she used her decorative "HH" monogram throughout her home; it was cast in the metal saucers of her Kutani-ware teacups, dyed on the window curtains and the garments of her servants, and even painted in gold on her rickshaw (figs. 62 and 63). Pretentious, perhaps, but this was a lady with style who knew her own mind—a strong personality. There was nothing modest or self-effacing about Helen Hyde; she was her own best publicist and had to be—she was a commercial artist. As one critic wrote in 1904, "Everybody who knows anything about art or artists knows who Helen Hyde is."[121] A tall, fuzzy-haired blonde, she was considered a great beauty whose appearance compelled "ecstatic worship from her male contemporaries."[122] Friends described her as ambitious and clever, always gracious and cheerful, and she was very sociable; while she devoted her mornings to uninterrupted work in her studio, her afternoons were filled with tea parties and theatrical events.

59. Helen Hyde with her portable etching press, c. 1901. Photograph. The Jane Voorhees Zimmerli Art Museum, Rutgers, The State University of New Jersey, Ralph and Barbara Voorhees American Art Fund

Among her close acquaintances in Tokyo was the English potter and etcher Bernard Leach (1887–1979). Leach, who was born in Hong Kong

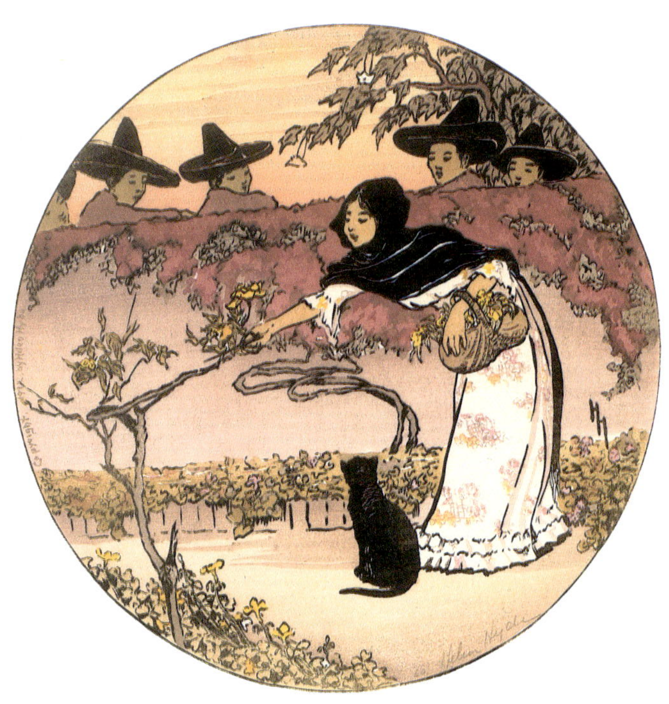

60. Helen Hyde, *A Mexican Coquette,* 1912. No. 60. Color woodcut. The Fine Arts Museums of San Francisco, Achenbach Foundation for Graphic Arts, DeYoung Museum transfer

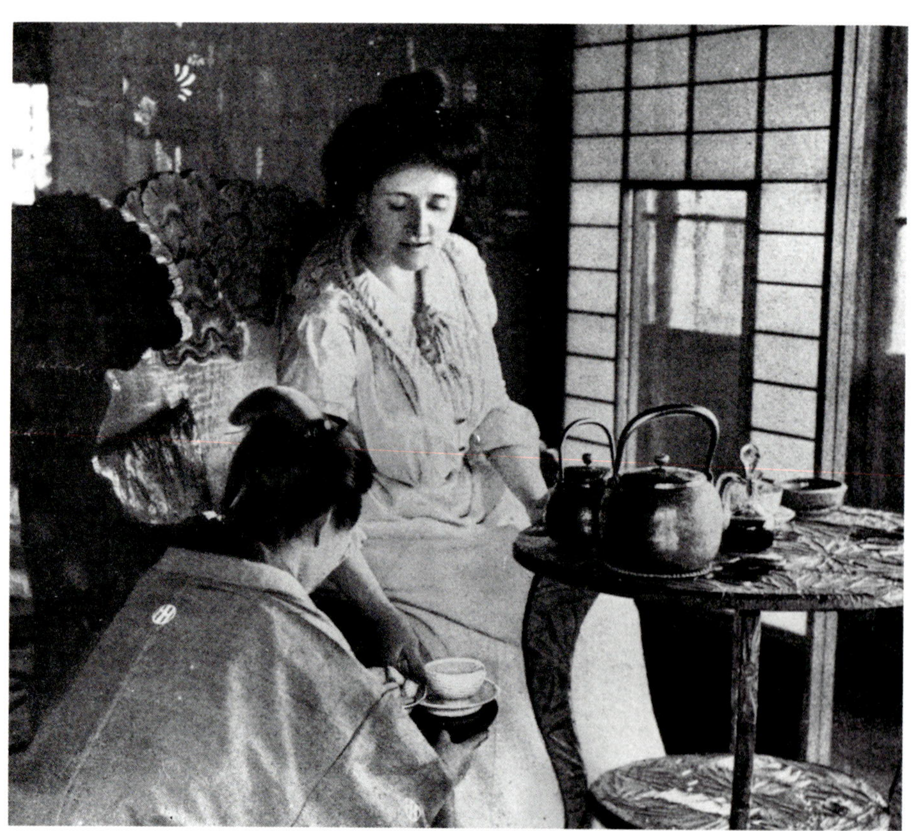

61. Helen Hyde in Tokyo. Photograph. From *Harper's Bazar,* January 1906

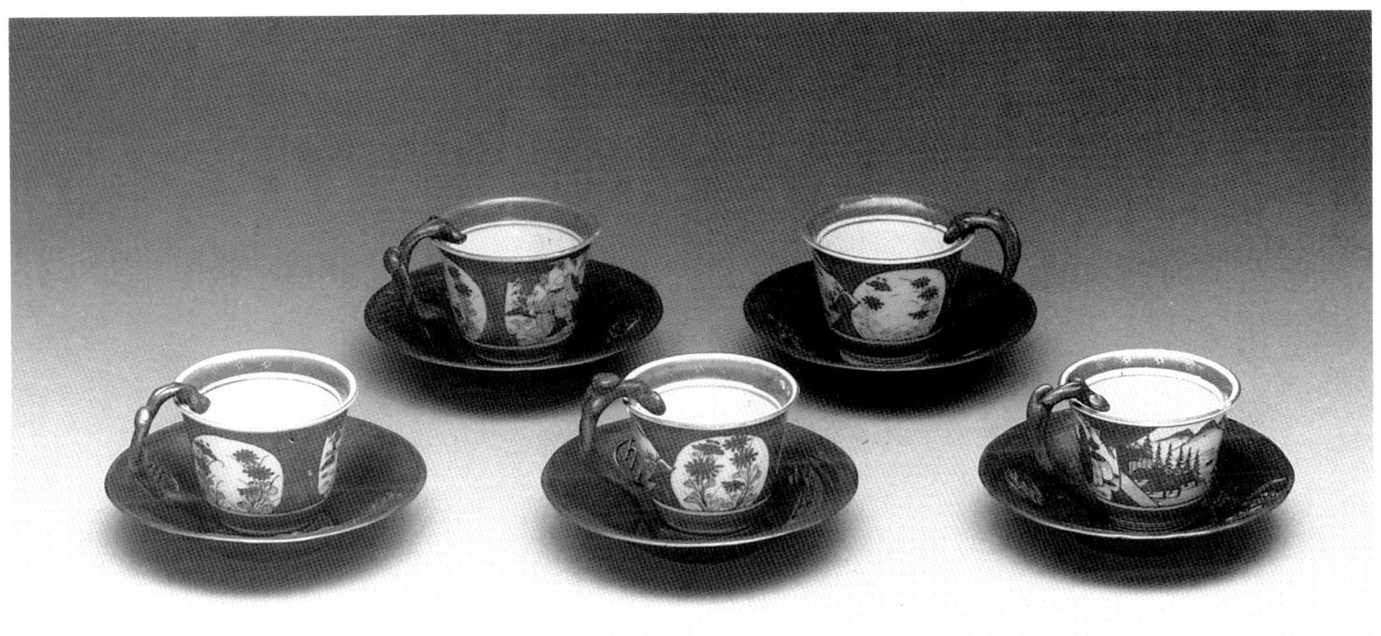

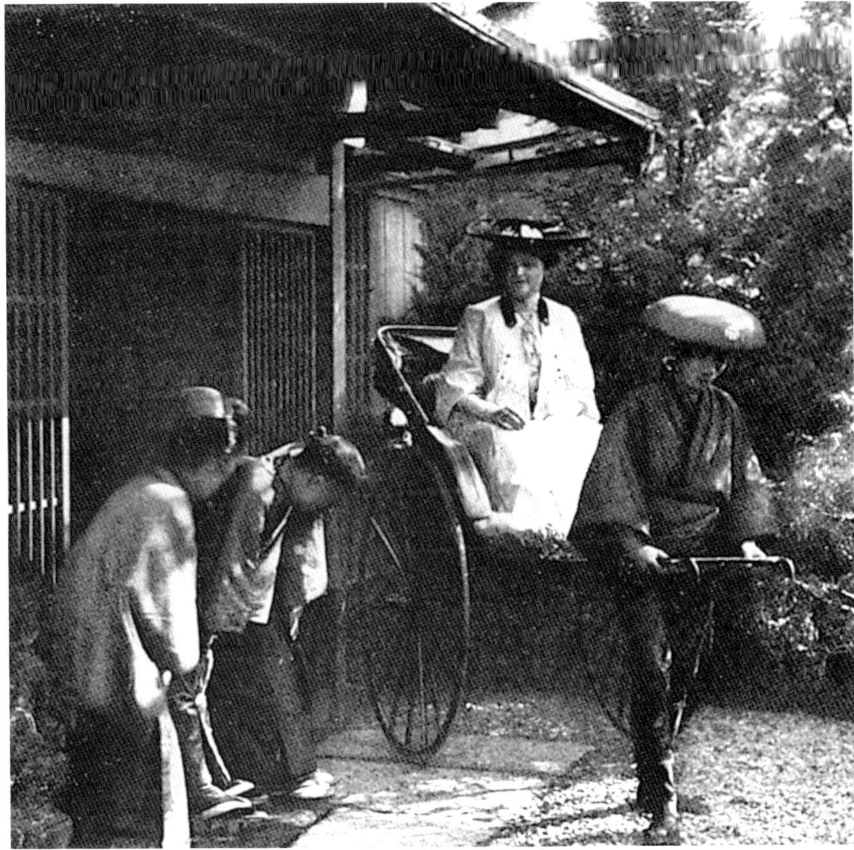

62. Helen Hyde's tea service. Kutani porcelain cups with metal fittings and "HH" monogram designed by Hyde. Richard Miles Collection

63. Helen Hyde in her rickshaw. Photograph. From *Harper's Bazar,* January 1906

and educated in London, arrived in Japan at age twenty-one in 1909 with his wife and spent eleven years, the first of many visits in his ongoing search for a meeting of East and West. Trained as an artist, he brought with him a large etching press and gave the first lecture on this subject in Japan at his home in 1910.[123] Hyde, who continued to make etchings throughout her years in Japan, consulted with Leach when she had technical problems.

It was a disappointment to Hyde that she did not succeed as an illustrator of children's books; only two or three are known to have been published during those first years in Japan, others were left unfinished.[124] A 1901 watercolor maquette illustrated by Hyde exists for an unpublished album of Japanese children's songs harmonized and loosely translated by her sister Mabel during a one-year visit to Japan in 1900 (fig. 65). The songs, most of which were composed during the Meiji era, range from the national anthem (*Kimigayo*) to simple ball-bouncing verses. It was a period when Western music and education exerted a strong influence in Japan, and many of these tunes are taken from Spanish and German folk songs.[125] The verses of the *Diamond* song were composed by the empress herself in 1887 under the inspiration of one of Benjamin Franklin's twelve virtues of industry, a truly cross-cultural mix.

Hyde's maquette contains many illustrations which she later reworked into single-sheet prints. The source for some of these images (all populated with her own characteristic tiny tots) was contemporary photography—the images of quaint "Old Japan" that were bound into albums for the tourist trade or the Western armchair traveler. Like Robert Blum, she included a camera in her working equipment, and she too owned at least one album of hand-tinted photos of Japan.[126] The Drum Bridge at Tokyo's Kameido Shrine in wisteria season, for example, was a popular scenic spot and was captured on film by many Japanese photographers in the 1880s and 1890s (fig. 66).

Jingles from Japan, published in 1902, is another charming integration of

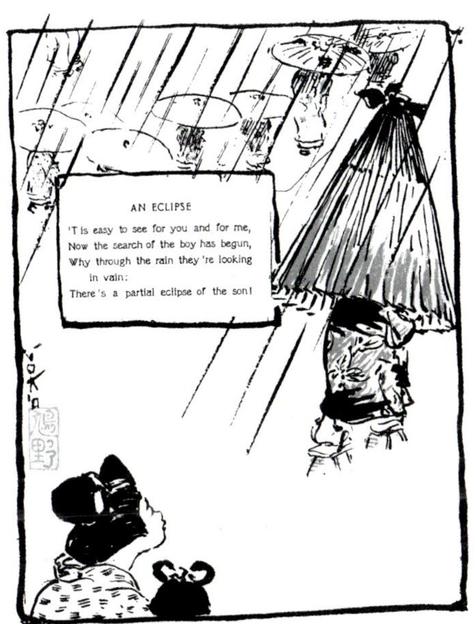

64. Helen Hyde, page from *Jingles from Japan,* 1902. Photorelief. Ravicz Collection

image and verse, the latter composed by her sister Mabel (fig. 64). One detects a healthy note of skepticism in some of the verses in this book: for the antique dealer catering to foreigners, for example, "any old junk will do," including reproductions of woodcuts aged in brown tea. The calligraphic style of the drawings is a tribute to Hyde's two years of training in the Japanese ink-painting technique with the grand old master Kano Tomonobu (1843–1912; figs. 67 and 68). As described in her hometown newspaper in 1901:

every day, with the regularity of clockwork, click, click on the porch fell the wooden shoes of the closely shaven and bald-headed old Master Kano, come to give a lesson to his foreign pupil, of whom he was more than proud. Down on his knees in the studio he would mark out the lesson. Then withdraw to a soft mat and with his cup of tea proceed to enjoy himself while he watched with admiring eyes the struggle of the American girl to acquire the deft turn of the wrist, wherein lies the secret of success in Japanese art. He is not accustomed to the sticktoitiveness of our American people, and he shook his wise old head and marveled at the great progress made in so short a time by his apt pupil.[127]

Tomonobu was the ninth-generation master of the Hamachō Kano family (one of several Kano school lineages). In his youth he was an official painter-in-attendance to the shogun, but with the advent of modernization he also studied Western oil and watercolor techniques (British correspondent and illustrator Charles Wirgman (1832–91), a resident of Yokohama, was one of his teachers). Around 1881 he became a supporter and collaborator with Ernest Fenollosa in the latter's drive to modernize traditional Japanese painting. Tomonobu was one of the original seven members of the Painting Appreciation Society (Kangakai) founded by Fenollosa in 1884. It was an art study and appraisal group established on the basis of the close friendship between Fenollosa and fellow Bostonian William Sturgis Bigelow, who had an unlimited budget; their joint goal was to save old Japanese art by exhibiting and thus

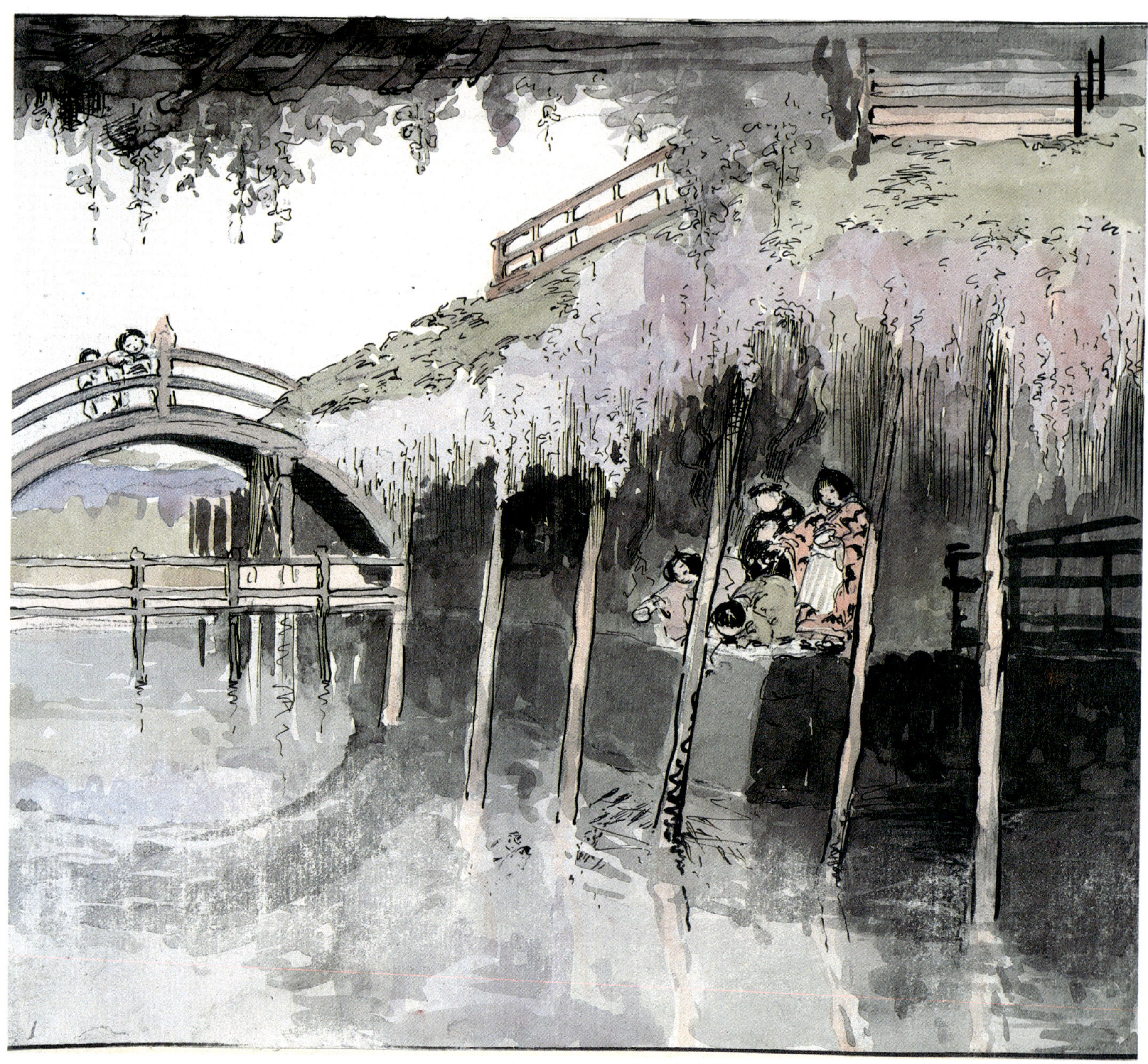

65. Helen Hyde, *Kameido,* page from a maquette for the album *Songs of the Japanese Children,* c. 1901. Watercolor on paper. The Jane Voorhees Zimmerli Art Museum, Rutgers, The State University of New Jersey, Ralph and Barbara Voorhees American Art Fund

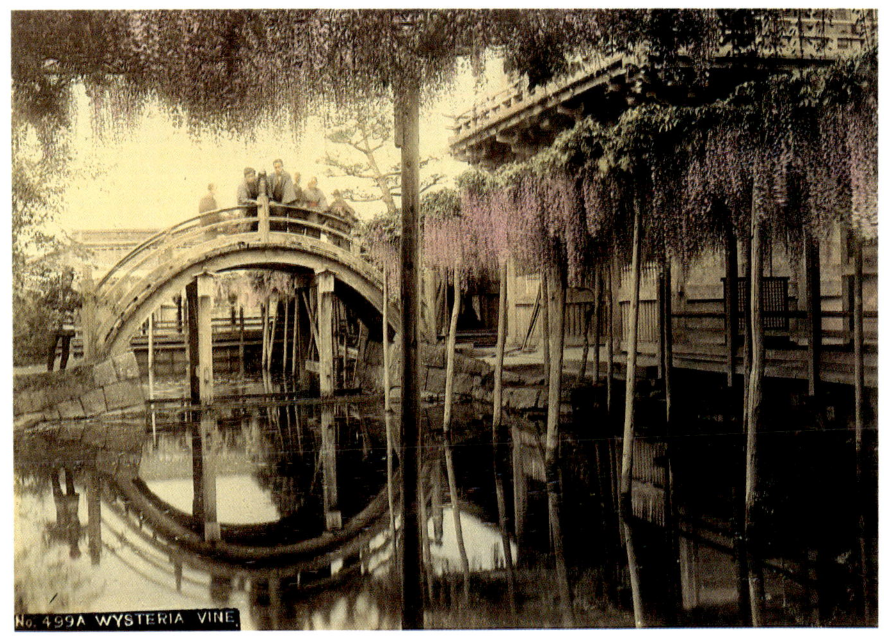

66. Anonymous, Japanese, *Wysteria Vine* (Drum Bridge at Kameido Shrine), c. 1880. Hand-colored albumen print. Courtesy E. and J. Frankel Gallery, New York

publicizing the works of member artists (most of which were purchased by the two Americans and today reside in the Museum of Fine Arts in Boston).

In 1889, three years after Fenollosa and Okakura returned from their investigation of art education in the West, the Tokyo School of Fine Arts opened. Okakura was de facto director of the school from 1890 to 1898. Tomonobu and other artists favored by Fenollosa were appointed to the faculty. Although Fenollosa returned to Boston in 1890 to take up his position at the Museum of Fine Arts, during the year 1889–90 he himself was on the staff lecturing on aesthetics, a theoretical approach quite new, if not alien, to the Japanese. He spoke in broken Japanese, or used Okakura as interpreter (students made a point of avoiding his class), but his salary was one-half the meager annual school budget.[128]

Tomonobu, strictly an academician, taught beginners at the art school; his own work is rather mundane, but he was a much-beloved, patient teacher, and it was he who took on the foreign students. In the spring of 1901 he urged Helen Hyde to submit three of her ink paintings, *Ebisu, In the Rain* (Chinese children under a large umbrella), and *Beloved Child* — also

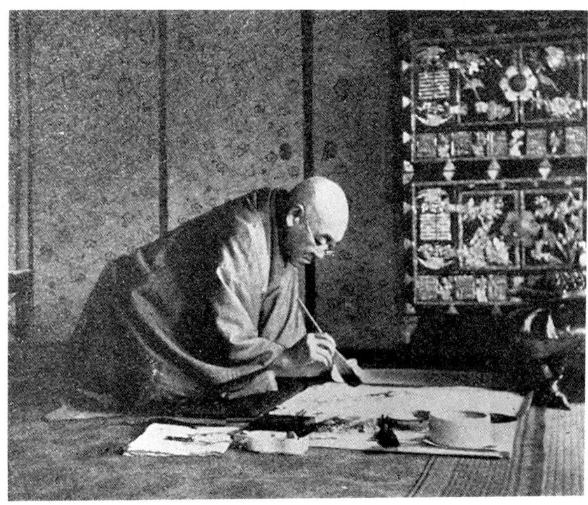

67. Kano Tomonobu in Helen Hyde's studio. Photograph. From *Harper's Bazar,* January 1906

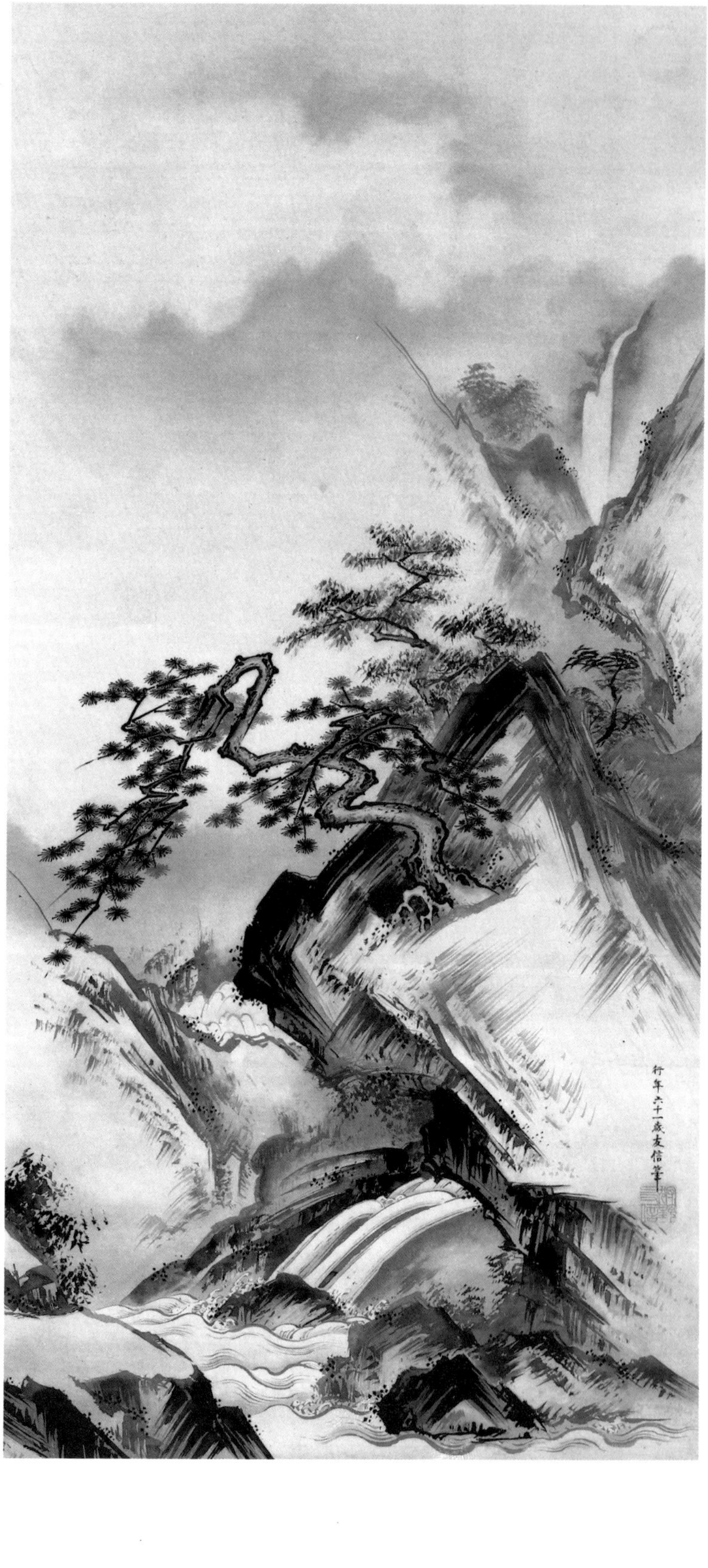

68. Kano Tomonobu, *Landscape,* 1903. Hanging scroll, ink on paper. Tokyo National Museum

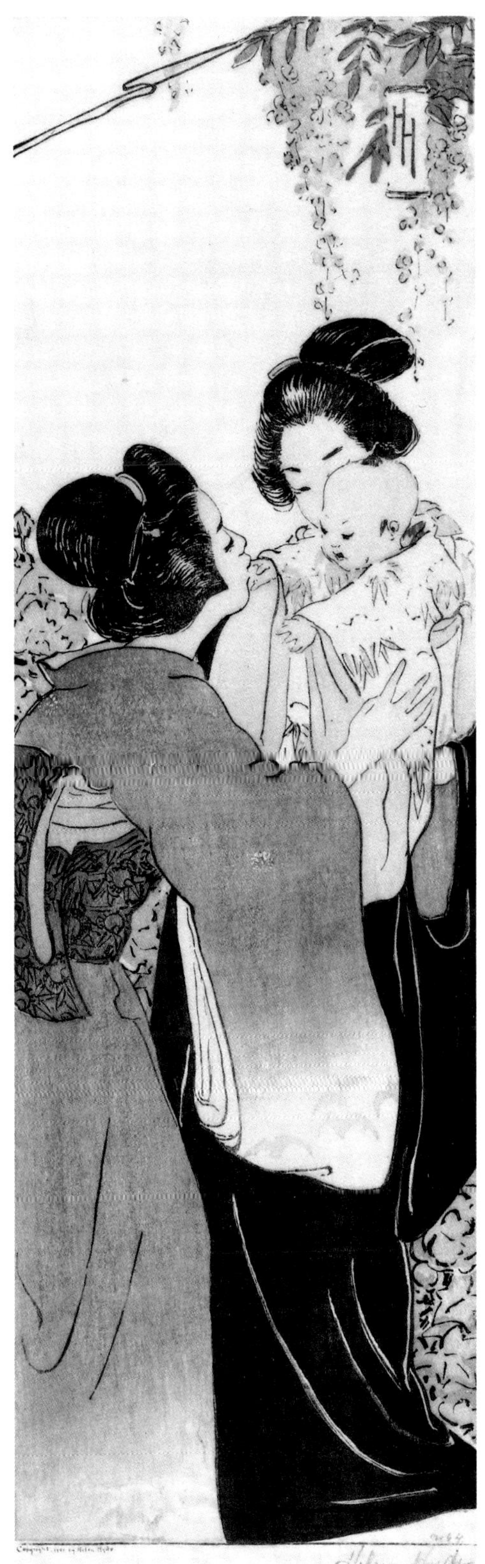

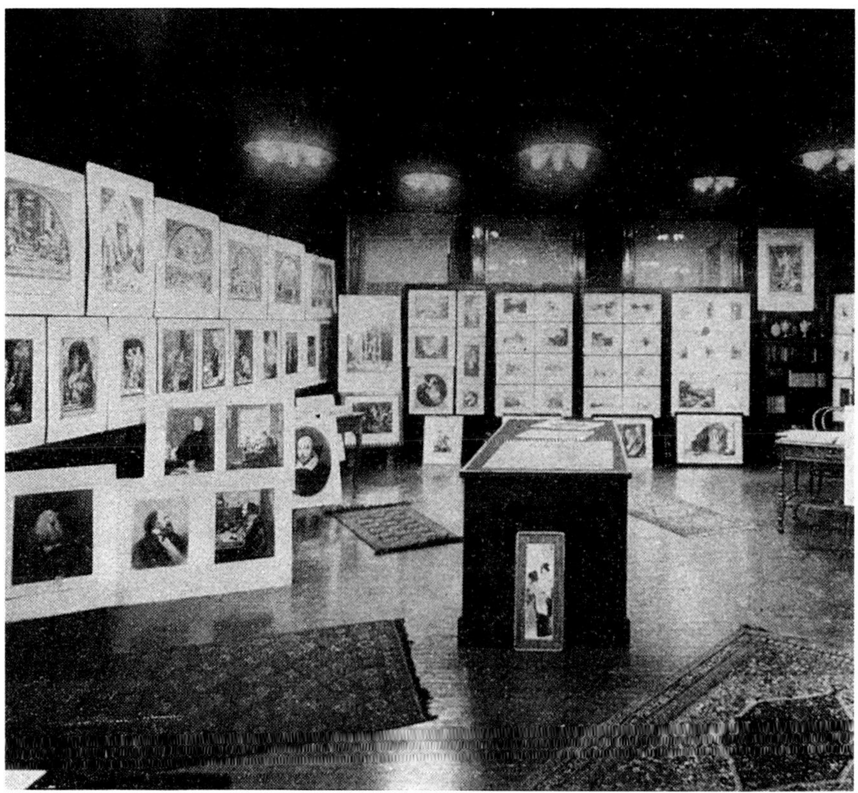

70. Hyde's *Monarch of Japan* on display at Albert Roullier's Art Rooms, Chicago, 1902. Photograph. © 1989 The Art Institute of Chicago, All Rights Reserved

69. Helen Hyde, *Monarch of Japan,* 1901. No. 64. Color woodcut. © 1989 The Art Institute of Chicago, All Rights Reserved. Gift of Mrs. Gillette and Mrs. Irwin, 1920

known as *Monarch of Japan* — to the spring exhibition of the Japan Fine Arts Academy and the Japan Painting Society.[129] Hyde was reportedly awarded a first prize for *Monarch of Japan.* Although the original painting is not known to have survived, she did reproduce the prizewinner that same year in the form of a color woodcut (figs. 69 and 70).

Her earliest work in the color woodcut technique dates from 1900, and she acknowledged as her teacher the Prague-born artist Emil Orlik (1870–1932). He taught her to carve her first blocks and even gave her some of his tools.[130] Orlik had come to Japan in 1900 for two years expressly to learn the art of Japanese printmaking. Deploring evidence of Western influence, which he considered to have set back Japanese taste, he produced a group of woodcuts and etchings that documents his close involvement with Japonisme (fig. 71). Kano Tomonobu modeled for the image of the artist in Orlik's well-known triptych *The Artist, the Carver, the Printer* (fig. 72).

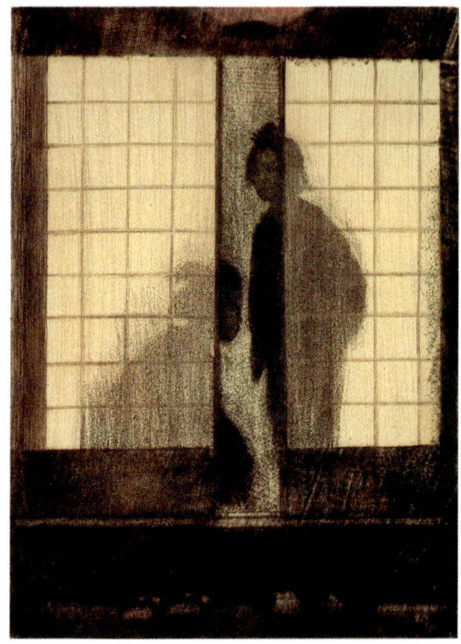

71. Emil Orlik, *Two Japanese Women Seen Through a Window,* c. 1902. Soft-ground etching, roulette, drypoint, printed in color. Print Collection, Miriam and Ira D. Wallach Division of Art, Prints and Photographs, The New York Public Library, Astor, Lenox and Tilden Foundations

In the late nineteenth century, when Western artists were just beginning to experiment with the color woodblock medium, the Japanese, with a heritage of nearly two centuries of multicolor printing, could depend upon a highly specialized division of skilled labor that guaranteed a final product of high technical quality. The artist, carver, printer, and the publisher who commissioned and distributed the product, worked together as a team to create harmonious artistic effects.

The artist's design, copied in outline onto thin tracing paper, is pasted face down on a block of hard wood, usually cherry. The engraver cuts away parts of the block, leaving lines in relief to be printed. This is known as the "key" block, from which the line image is printed with black ink. Additional blocks are carved for each color. Absolute accuracy of register is secured by carving an angle at the lower corner and a straight line along one side of the block. Next, the printer brushes a combination of rice paste and pigment mixed with water onto the raised surface of the color blocks. The pigments are vegetable extracts, minerals,

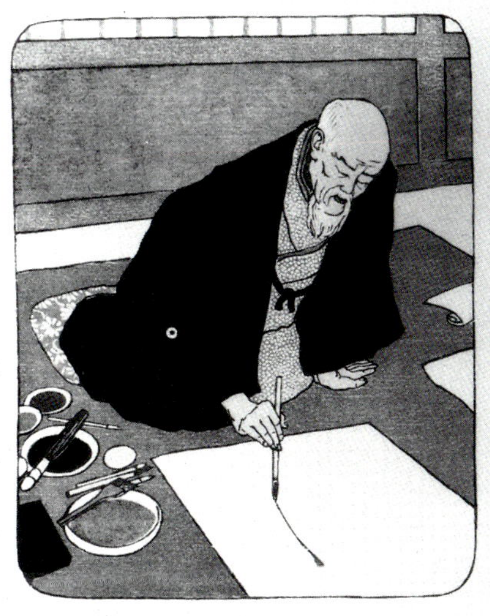

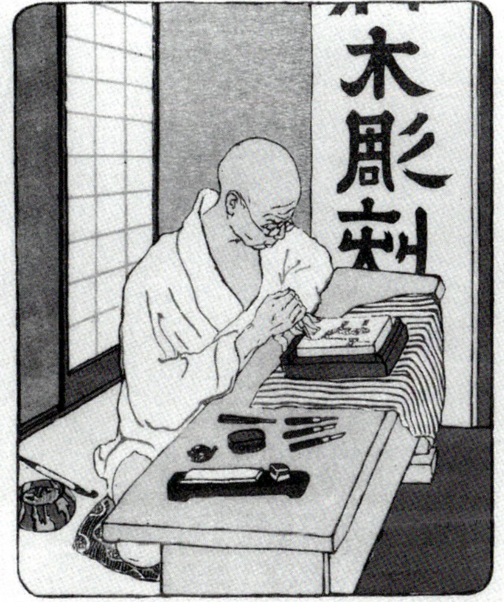

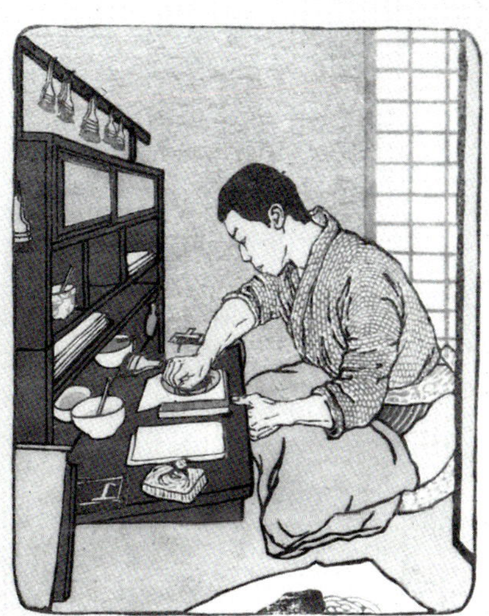

72. Emil Orlik, *The Artist, the Carver, the Printer,* 1902. Color lithograph reproduction of a color woodcut triptych of 1901. Sterling and Francine Clark Art Institute, Williamstown, MA

73. Helen Hyde, *Bamboo Fence,* 1904. No. 62. Color woodcut. The Jane Voorhees Zimmerli Art Museum, Rutgers, The State University of New Jersey, Ralph and Barbara Voorhees American Art Fund

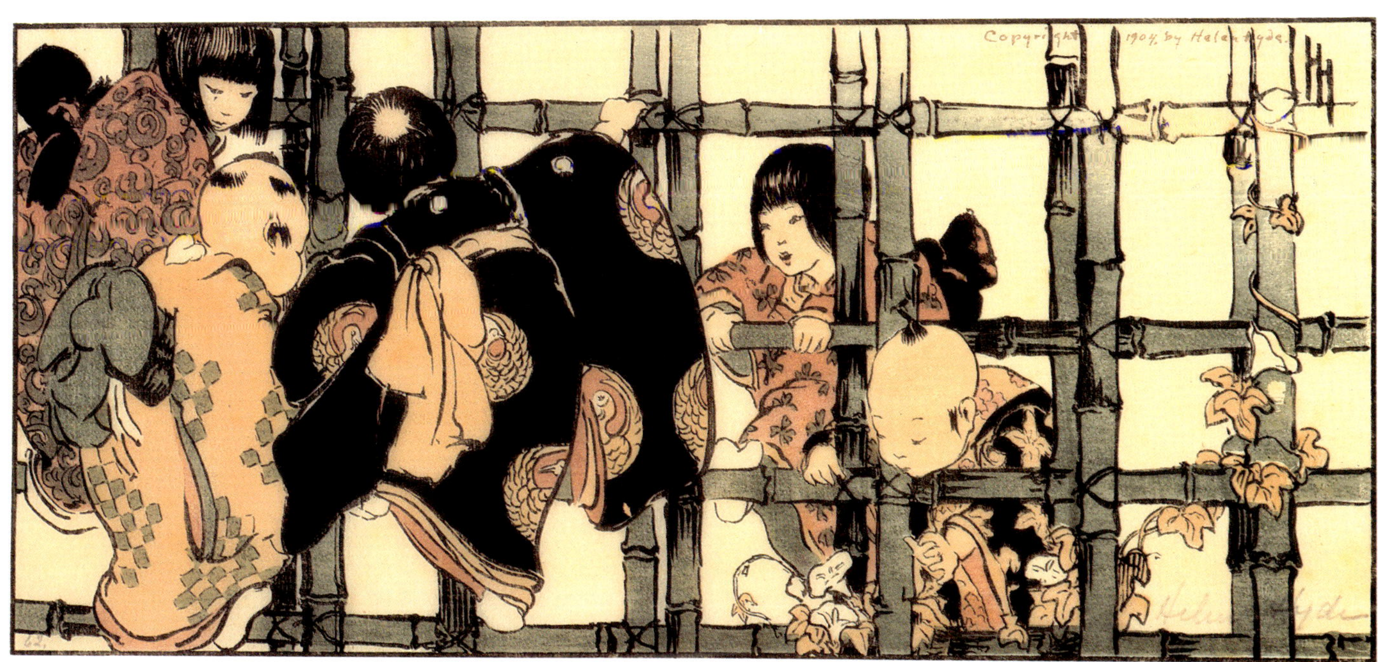

and since the 1860s, chemical dyes. The printer places the key-block-printed sheet of handmade mulberry-bark paper face down on a color block and rubs the moistened, sized paper with a hard circular pad until the color is transferred. The process is repeated with each color block until all the colors are printed.

Another of Orlik's Western "students" of the woodcut in Tokyo in 1900 was the Dutch painter S. C. Bosch Reitz (1860–1938), whose growing involvement with Asian art led him to New York in 1915 as the first curator of Far Eastern Art at the Metropolitan Museum of Art (fig. 74).[131] The museum acquired the bulk of its Japanese prints under his tenure — including those sold by Frank Lloyd Wright in 1918 and 1920.

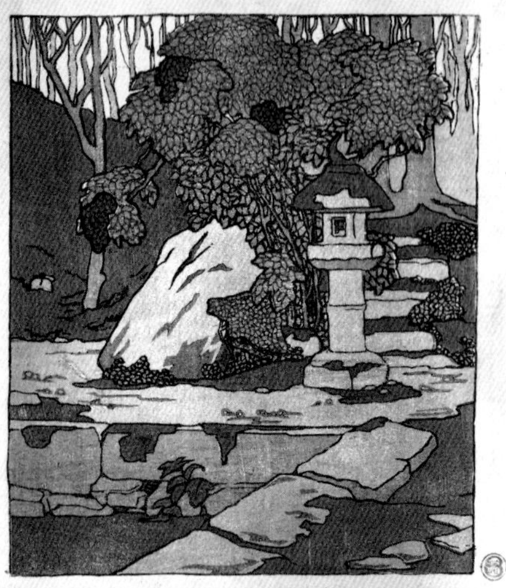

74. S. C. Bosch Reitz, *Japanese Garden*, 1900. Color woodcut. H. S. Six Collection, Laren, Holland

The format and theme of Hyde's woodcut *Monarch of Japan* is taken from an eighteenth-century pillar print such as that by Torii Kiyonaga (1752–1815) depicting a maid handing a baby over to a young mother to be nursed, with a tree branch (wisteria in the case of Hyde) filling the space in the upper corner (fig. 75). The Japanese use the term *hashira-e* (literally, "pillar picture") for a tall narrow print format varying in size from about 26 by 4 inches to 26 by 6 inches. Because she specialized in mother and child themes, one charitable critic called Hyde the "Mary Cassatt of the West."[132] Like Cassatt, she was unmarried and extremely proper, even prudish. Hyde's women are never shown suckling their babies, bare breast exposed and toes twitching in ecstasy. She is also much less dynamic than Kiyonaga in her linear rhythms. She consistently favors the pale colors of faded or toned eighteenth-century prints — the kind that appealed especially to the French connoisseurs and that are found in some Cassatt images.

There is no question that sweetness and "quaint" subjects were what her audience wanted (fig. 73). She had a keen commercial instinct and pandered to the popular taste. Many of her themes — *Winter* and *Summer Shower,* for example — call to mind the hand-tinted photographs of pretty Japanese women self-consciously posed with umbrellas against a backdrop

75. Torii Kiyonaga, *A Mother Taking Her Child from a Young Woman,* 1781. Color woodcut. Museum of Fine Arts, Boston, Spaulding Collection

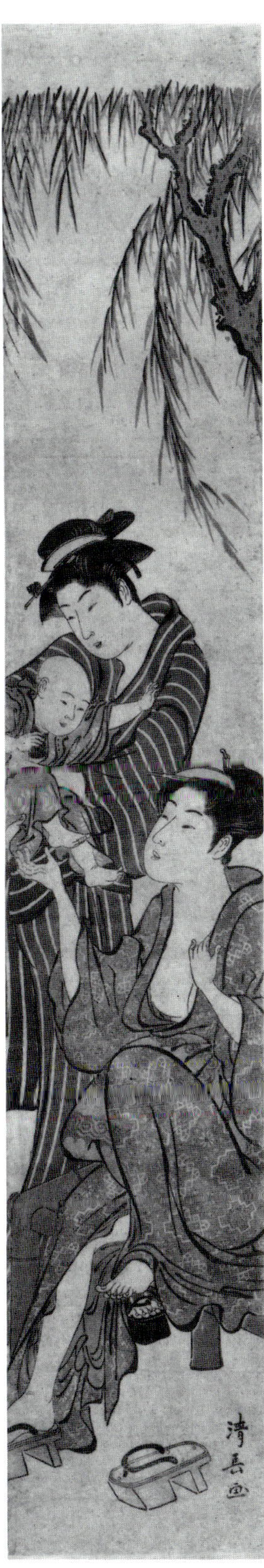

of rain or snow, images favored by the Western tourist (figs. 76–78). The contemporary Japanese audience craved very much the same thing. By the late 1890s the single sheet ukiyo-e print went into decline in Japan, its documentary role usurped by newspapers, photographs, and chromolithography. Simultaneously, however, there emerged a new source of life for color woodcuts as frontispiece illustrations for books and magazines featuring modern romantic fiction and boasting circulation in the tens of thousands.

Small fold-out color woodcuts such as *Cherry Blossom Shower* by Takeuchi Keishū (1861–1943) were bound into these popular monthly journals as luxury supplements illustrating the bizarre melodramatic stories that were then in vogue (fig. 79).[133] The prints, which must have been familiar to Hyde and which mirror the taste of her American audience, emphasize the age-old subject of idealized feminine beauty. Japanese artists were of course inevitably touched to some extent by widespread knowledge of Western art dispersed through magazines like *Jugend* or the work of those who studied abroad.

Although Hyde did learn the Japanese printing techniques, she soon realized that in the interest of saving time (not to mention achieving a superior level of quality) she would do well to hire native craftsmen; thanks to this joint venture, she ultimately produced seventy-one color woodcut designs. Some of her early work was distributed and probably printed for her by Fenollosa's partner, Kobayashi Bunshichi. *A Japanese Madonna* of 1900 has Kobayashi's seal reading "Hōsūkaku" (the name of his publishing house) stamped in the lower left margin (fig. 80). Beginning around 1903, her printer was Murata Shōjirō, who had worked on designs by Hiroshige III (fig. 81). The carving was done off premises, but when the blocks arrived, she would carefully supervise the printing, done over a period of two to three months each winter in her upstairs studio (figs. 82 and 83). The names of her carver (Matsumoto) and printer (Murata) are engraved in the key block of only one of her prints,

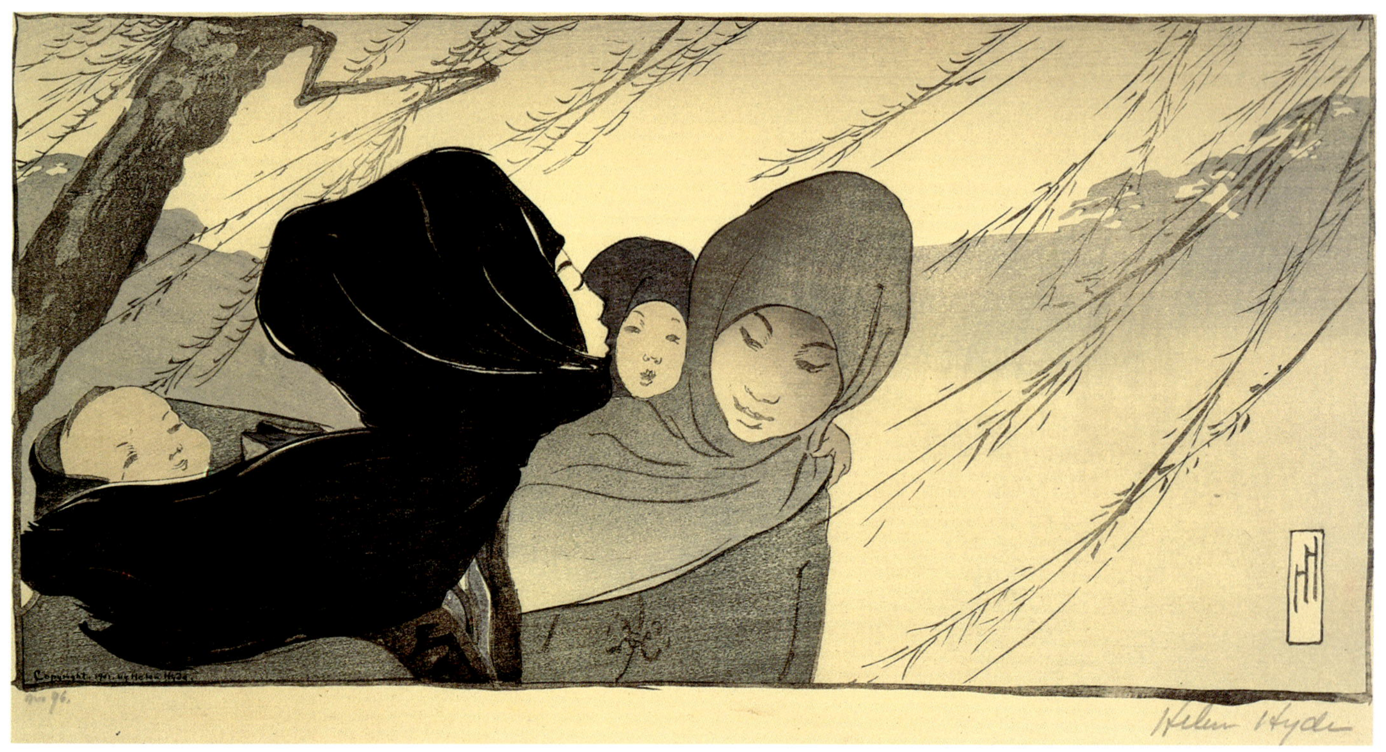

76. Helen Hyde, *Winter,* 1901. No. 96. Color woodcut. Print Collection, Miriam and Ira D. Wallach Division of Art, Prints and Photographs, The New York Public Library, Astor, Lenox and Tilden Foundations

77. Helen Hyde, *Summer Shower,* 1909. No. 204. Color woodcut. The Fine Arts Museums of San Francisco, Achenbach Foundation for Graphic Arts, DeYoung Museum transfer

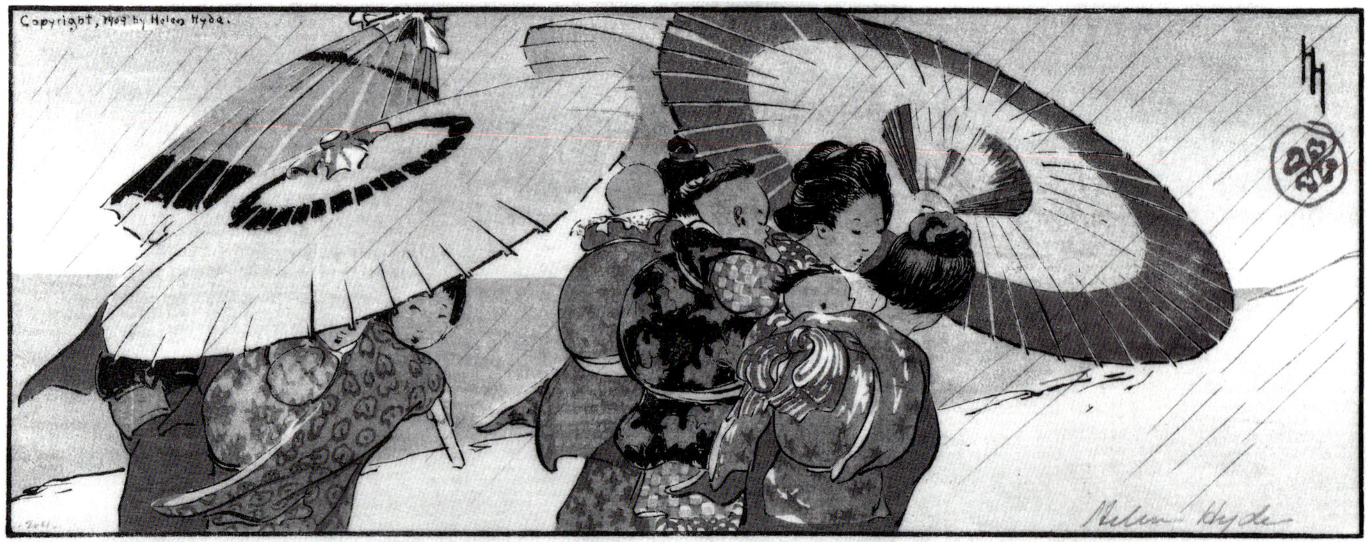

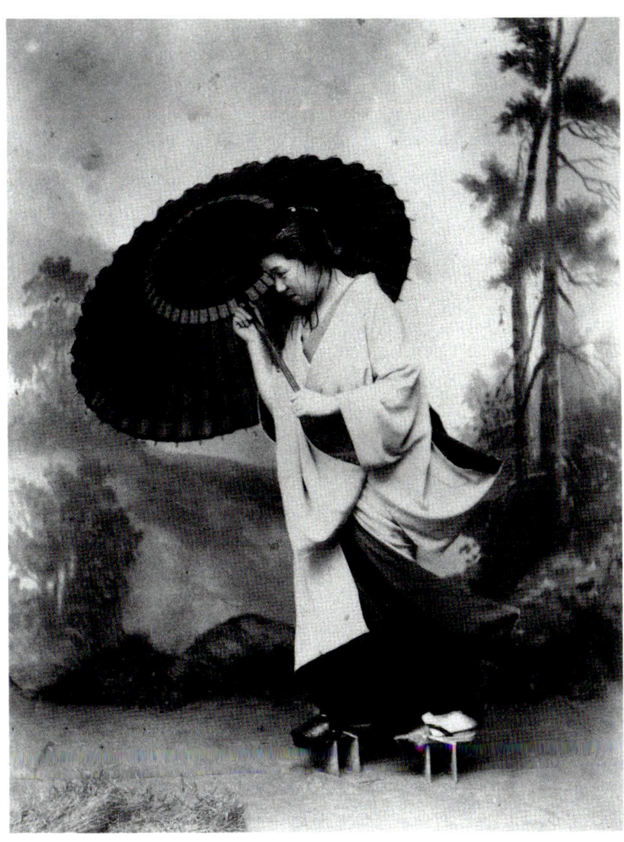

78. Anonymous, Japanese, *Woman with Umbrella,* c. 1890. Hand-colored albumen print. The Jane Voorhees Zimmerli Art Museum, Rutgers, The State University of New Jersey

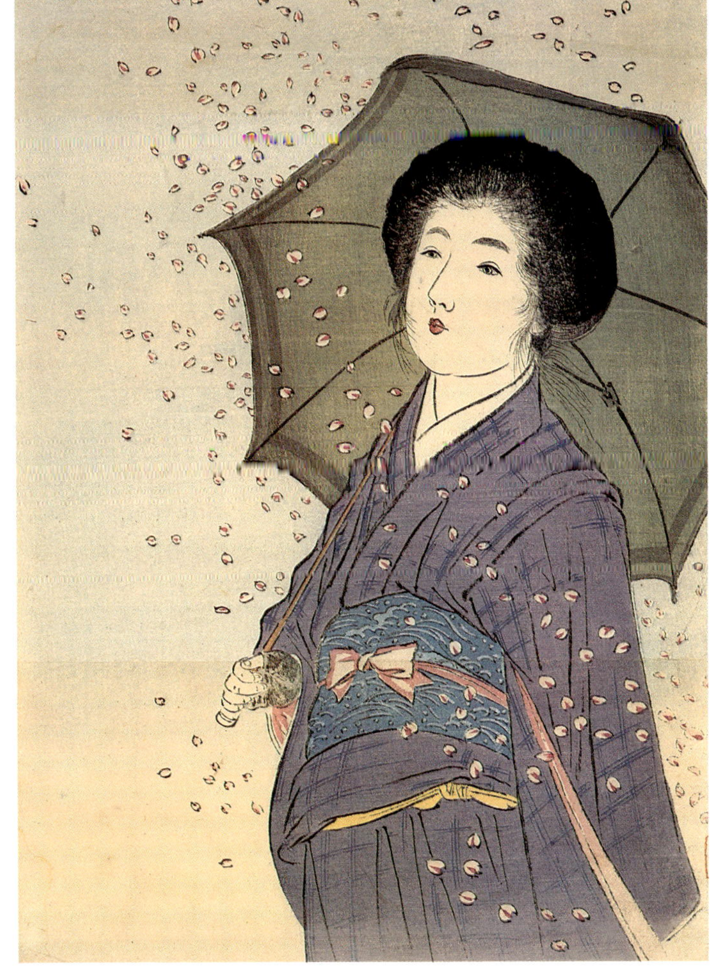

79. Takeuchi Keishū, *Cherry Blossom Shower.* From *Bungei kurabu,* April 15, 1907. Color woodcut. Robert O. Muller Collection

Baby Talk of 1908 (fig. 85).[134] Her "HH" monogram and red four-leaf clover seal appear on the sliding door at the far right of the oval — and the names of her Japanese craftsmen are at the outer edge (fig. 86). *Baby Talk* is a stylized reworking of a watercolor painted a year earlier (fig. 84).

Although Hyde remains unmistakably Western in form and content, the exquisite gradation of pigments, precision of carving, and masterly use of line typical of her prints were of course welcomed by her public as genuinely Japanese. However, the technical virtuosity precipitated a kind of backlash among her British colleagues, including Frank Morley Fletcher, Alan Seaby, William Giles, and others who dedicated themselves to carrying the torch for the Arts and Crafts movement. For them, an "original" color print was created, carved, and printed by the artist — the interpolation of an artisan-interpreter could only cause art to deteriorate to the level of mere craft. To publicize their cause they founded a journal called *The Original Colour Print Magazine* in 1924. Giles, the editor, pointed out that when Americans came into the print movement it was not unusual

> *for her woodblock cutters to go to Japan, especially those living on the Pacific coast. They are not content with learning the craft, but exploit the services of the skilled Japanese Block-Cutter, and Printer, to translate their work, though they do not hesitate to sign their own names. Is it sheer lack of humour, when they state they destroy the blocks "with their own hands" when the edition is complete!*[135]

Hyde was quite an accomplished watercolor artist; her works in this medium, which sometimes served as preliminary studies for her prints, are surprisingly close in style and even theme (Japanese women) to her contemporary, Kuroda Seiki (1866–1924; fig. 87). Kuroda had been a student of Raphaël Collin in Paris at the same time as Hyde — hence a certain similarity of style — and was hired as the first teacher of Western painting at the Tokyo School of Fine Arts in 1896. That same year he founded the White Horse Society for Japanese artists working in what

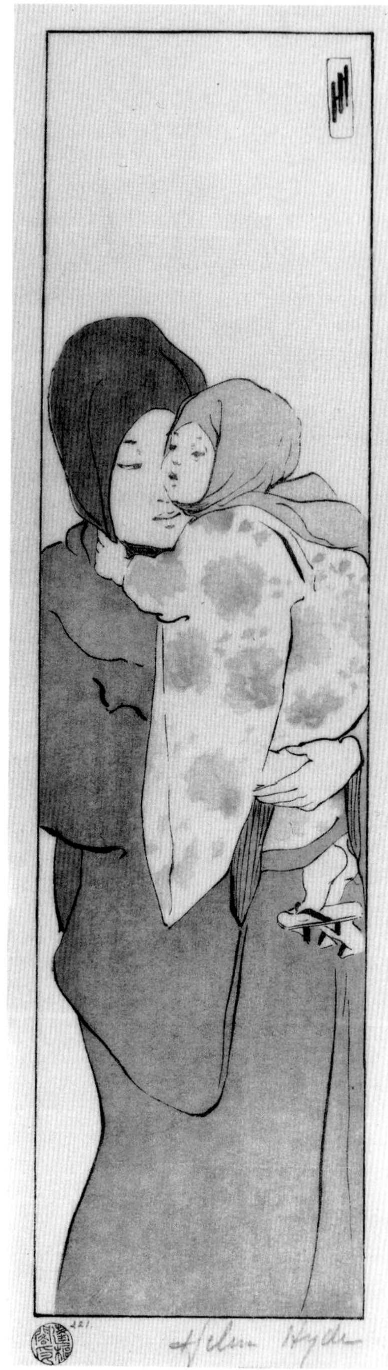

80. Helen Hyde, *A Japanese Madonna*, 1900. No. 221. Color woodcut. The Fine Arts Museums of San Francisco, Achenbach Foundation for Graphic Arts, DeYoung Museum transfer

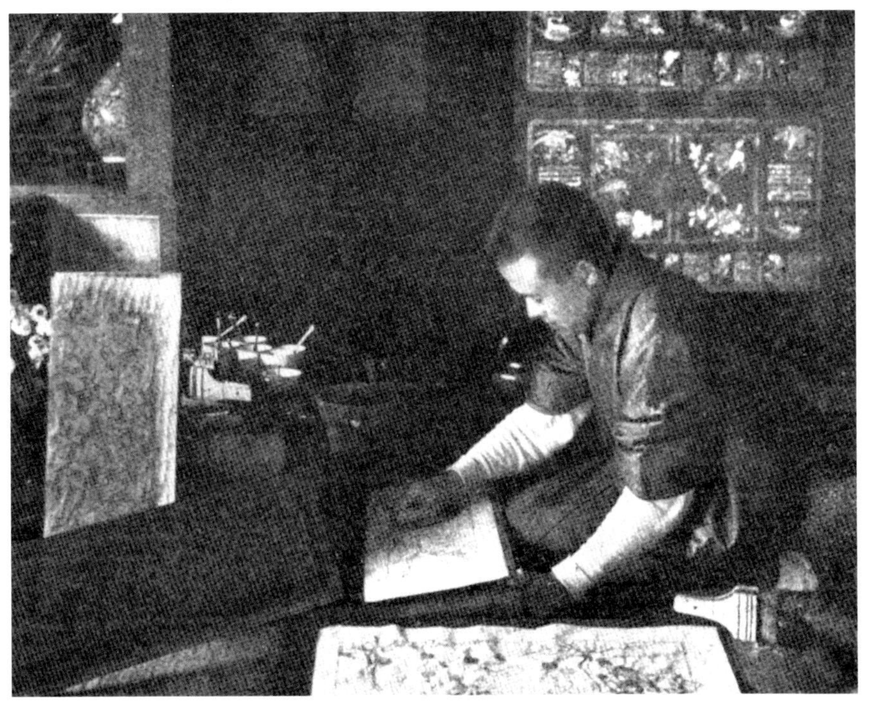

81. Murata Shōjirō in Hyde's studio. Photograph. From *Harper's Bazar,* January 1906

82. Helen Hyde, Wood key block and color block for *The Daruma Branch,* 1910. (Key block canceled by the artist.) Print Collection, Miriam and Ira D. Wallach Division of Art, Prints and Photographs, The New York Public Library, Astor, Lenox and Tilden Foundations. Gift of Helen Hyde, 1914

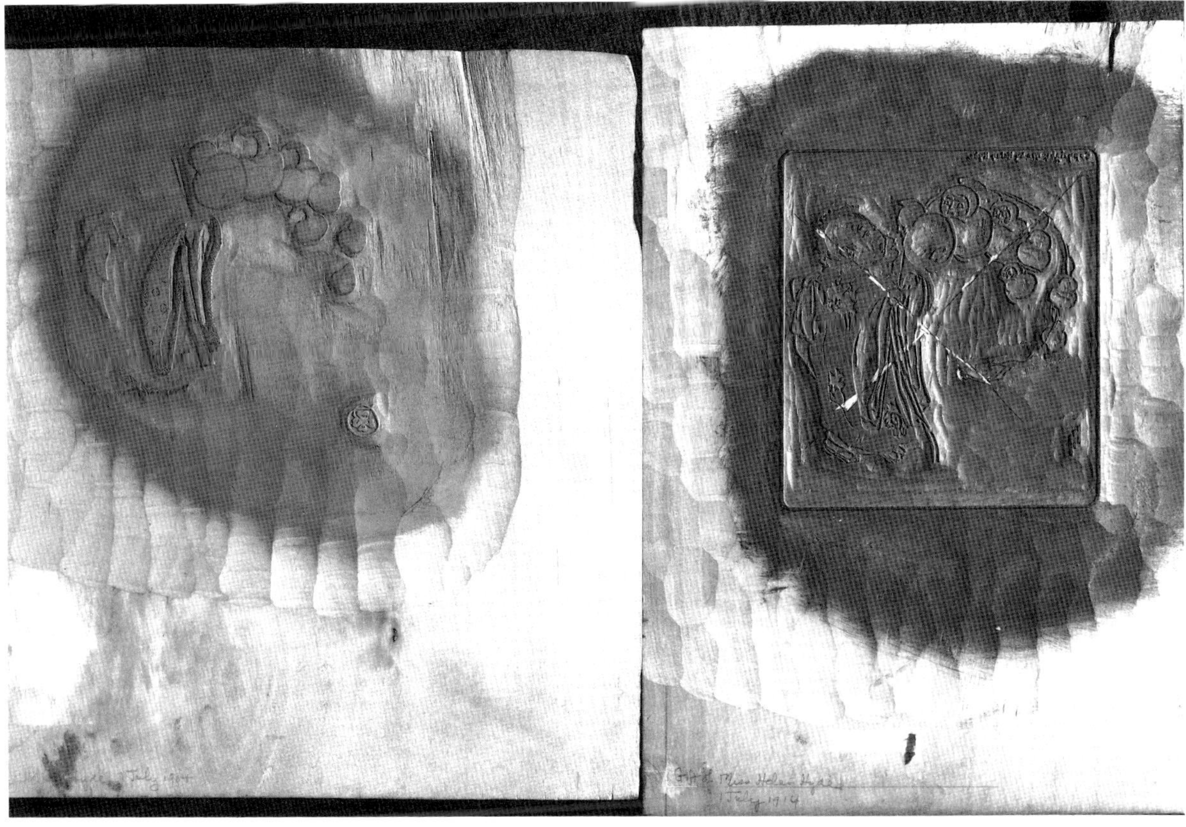

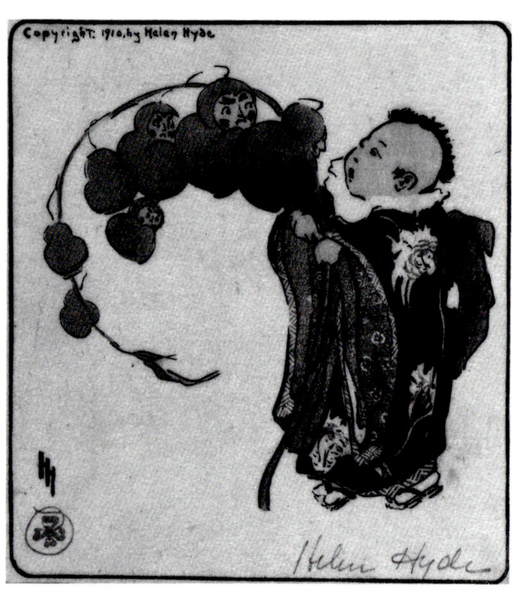

83. Helen Hyde, *The Daruma Branch,* 1910. Color woodcut. Print Collection, Miriam and Ira Wallach Division of Art, Prints and Photographs, The New York Public Library, Astor, Lenox and Tilden Foundations. Gift of Helen Hyde, 1914

84. Helen Hyde, *Baby Talk,* 1907. Watercolor on paper. Museum of Art, University of Oregon, Eugene

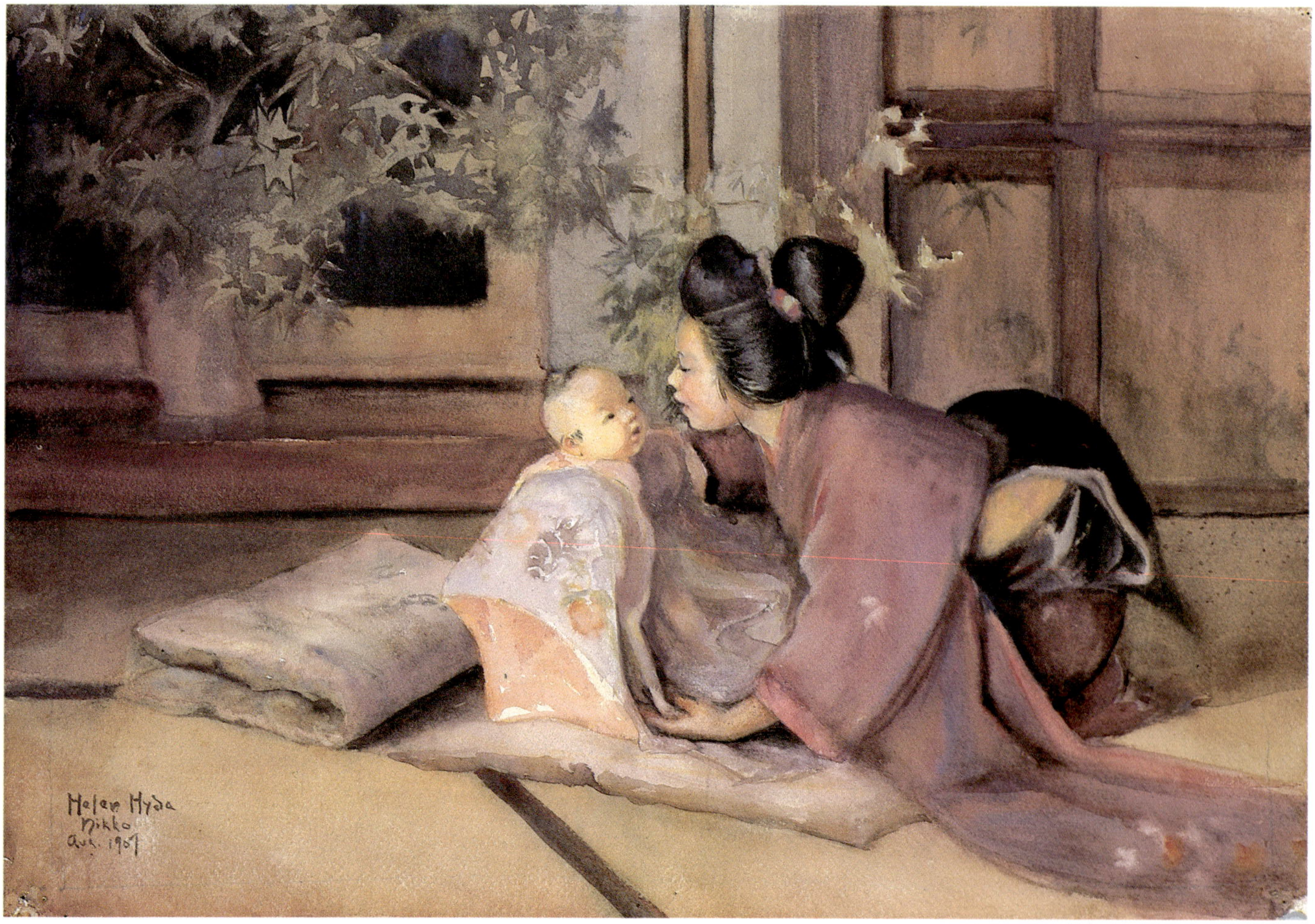

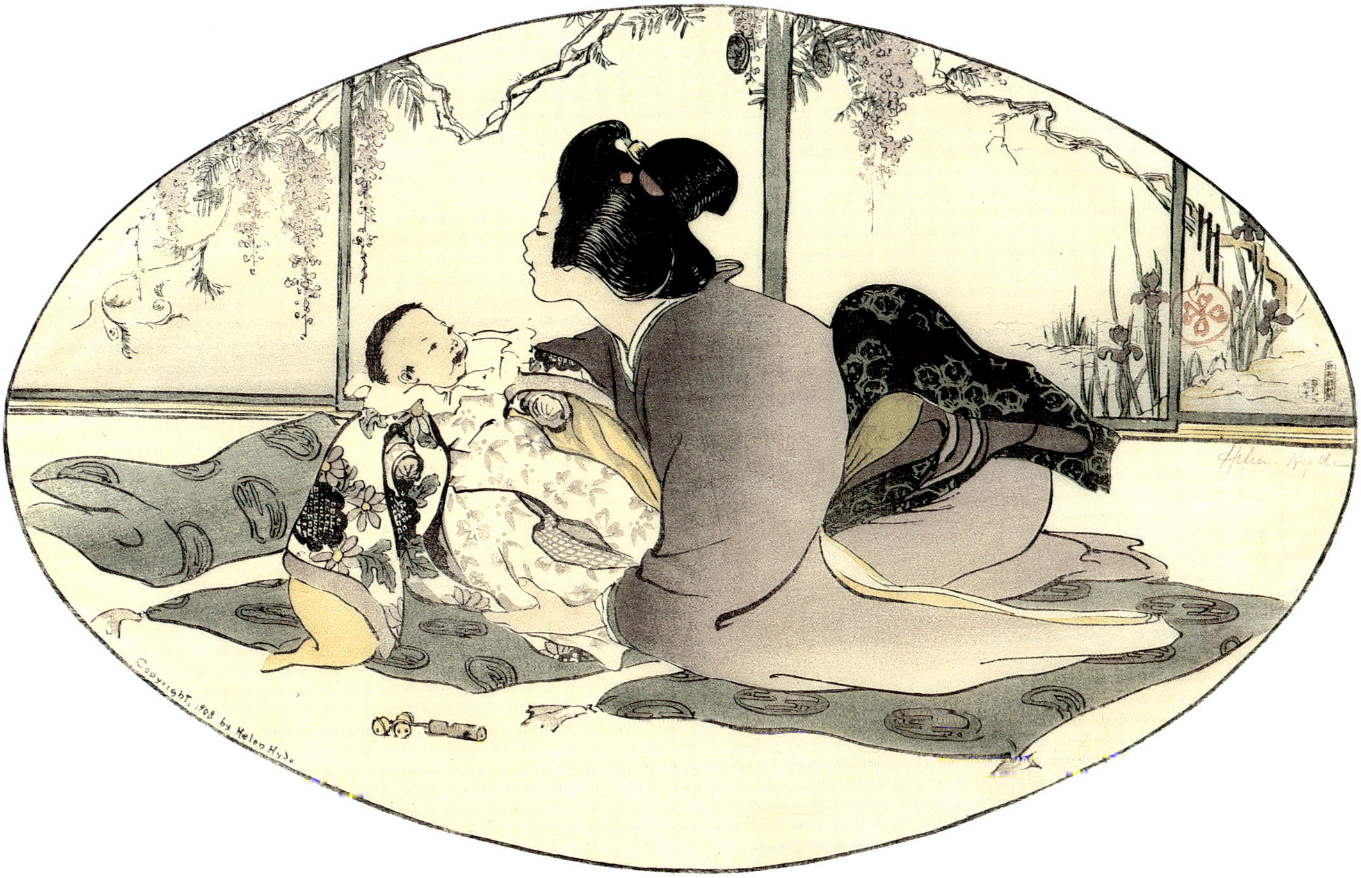

85. Helen Hyde, *Baby Talk,* 1908. No. 4. Color woodcut. The Jane Voorhees Zimmerli Art Museum, Rutgers, The State University of New Jersey, Ralph and Barbara Voorhees American Art Fund

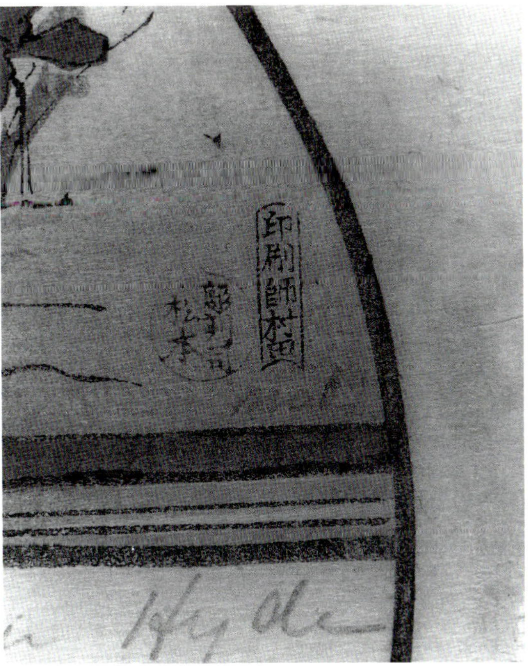

86. *Baby Talk,* detail of seal at right (above signature)

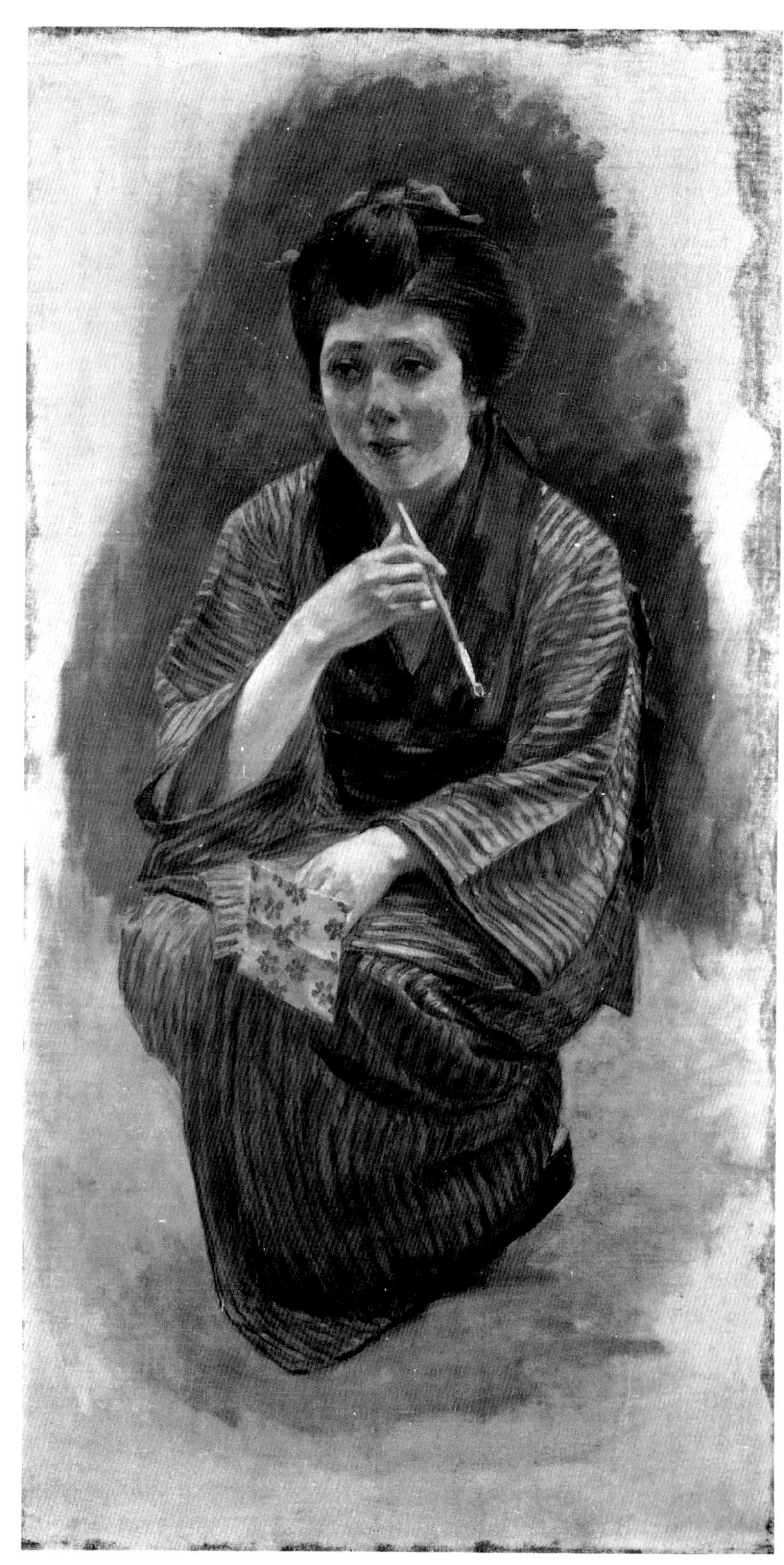

87. Kuroda Seiki, *Study for Telling an Ancient Romance: A Serving Maid,* 1896. Oil on canvas. Tokyo National Research Institute of Cultural Properties

was taken to be a modern style of brightly colored "Impressionism" associated with Collin.

Hyde was never drawn into the vortex of modernist experimentation. A critic for *The New York Times* in 1906 wondered whether, in devoting her life to paintings of Japanese, she might run the risk of losing track of Western ideas, people, and methods "without becoming thoroughly anything else than an exiled Occidental."[136] Like others of her time, Hyde was lured to Japan by what she called the "charming quaintness of the environment."[137] There is a touch of condescension in the way she and those who praised her work describe the "little brown men" of Japan. To a group in San Francisco she explained the Japanese worship of natural beauty as follows: "The Japanese are a people so lacking in physical beauty themselves," she said, "that . . . they must compensate for their deficiencies, and one becomes so fascinated with this acquired, quaint beauty that it amply compensates for the niggardliness of fate."[138] The mixture of admiration and superiority toward the Japanese was shared by many Westerners at the time. Art historian Elisa Evett studied the critical reception of Japanese art in late nineteenth-century Europe and concluded that

> *as long as Japan remained remote, Europeans could safely perpetuate their myths about it and cultivate an idealistic reverence for it. By preserving their distance from Japan, they could worship their romantic, fanciful images of it in tranquility. When it threatened to come too close, to encroach on the sacred domain of Western values, a new kind of distancing was adopted to replace the old—a vertical detachment, so to speak, of aloof superiority.*[139]

In her favorite theme of Chinese and Japanese children, Hyde found little noble savages of her own. Playing to an imagined stereotype, she draped her hired models in special costumes stored in an old Korean chest, and portrayed them in such a manner that "the foreigner sees in them the Japan of his dreams. . . ."[140]

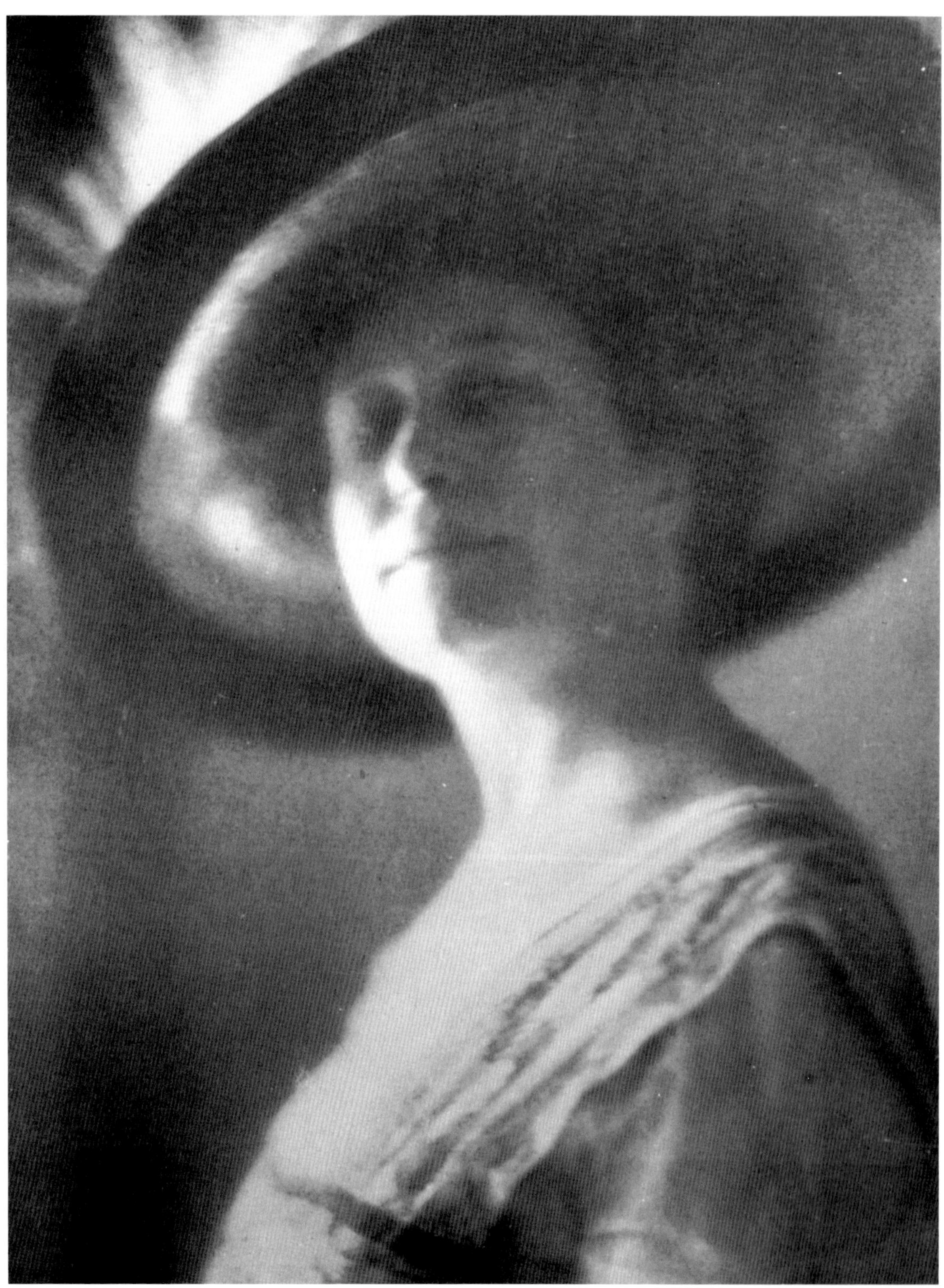

88. Bertha Lum. Photograph, 1912

Bertha Lum

Bertha Lum (1879–1954) was a remarkable woman, large-boned and statuesque with green eyes and titian hair (fig. 88). It is said that "conversation stopped when she entered a room!"[141] She is also described as imperious, strong-willed, and condescending toward the Japanese, but this does not seem to have hindered her cause in the least.

She would never tell anyone the date of her birth (it may have been a few years earlier than 1879), and certainly in later years the date on her passport was far from correct. She was born Bertha Boynton Bull, daughter of the lawyer Joseph W. Bull, in Tipton, Iowa; both parents are said to have been amateur painters. She went on to study in Chicago at the Art Institute art school, and she was not the first to become fascinated there by Japanese woodblock prints. She took additional instruction in Chicago from Frank Holme, at that time conducting the Holme School of Illustration, and then spent several years as a student of Anne Weston, the designer of stained glass.

Lum was unusually reticent about her life — deliberately so, it would seem — and her biography is pieced together with difficulty.

In 1903 she married Burt Francis Lum, a prominent attorney in Minneapolis. The craze for Japonisme was already in full swing in Minneapolis when Lum arrived there. A leading exponent was the city's foremost interior designer, John Scott Bradstreet (1845–1914), who combined the Oriental influences (both Moorish and Japanese) that were popular among American decorators in the late nineteenth century (thanks to the Centennial Exposition in Philadelphia) with the formal design principles of the Arts and Crafts movement. In 1904 Bradstreet opened a workshop and salesroom known as the Craftshouse, staffed by about thirty Scandinavian and Japanese artisans. Here he sold Asian antiques acquired during biennial visits to Japan that had begun in 1886, designed furniture inspired by Japanese motifs (fig. 89), and even hoped to remodel an island in downtown Lake of the Isles as a recreation of a temple island (probably Miyajima) that he had admired in Japan (fig. 90).[142]

When Lum went to Japan on her honeymoon, a friend who had studied with her at the Art Institute of Chicago asked her to find some woodblock tools. "I dragged my husband all over Japan looking for the things," she recalled later with some amusement.[143] It seems that after nearly giving up in despair, on the day of sailing she finally found a shop where they reproduced old prints. During the one hour available to her she learned a few things about the process and bought thirteen tools for twenty dollars (they were replaced when she later found them to be inferior as well as overpriced).[144] "I did no work in the shops then," she wrote of that first trip. "Buying tools, brushes and everything necessary for printing, I worked out the process after my return home."[145]

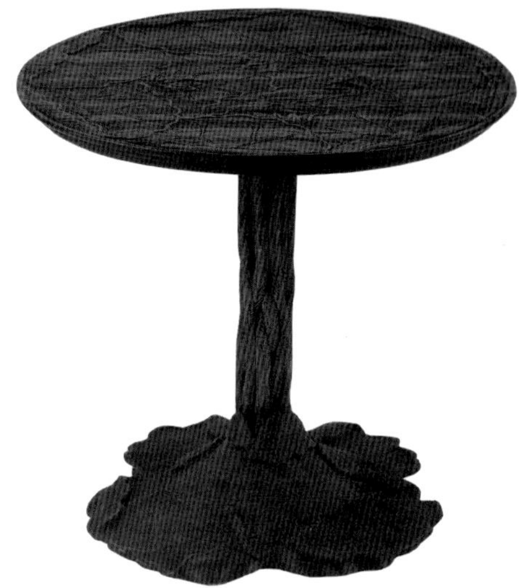

89. John Scott Bradstreet, center table from the William Prindle House, Duluth, MN, c. 1905. Cypress. The Minneapolis Institute of Arts. Gift of Wheaton Wood

Homecoming, printed in 1905 in Minneapolis from a black key block and two color blocks (a gray-blue block and a yellow-orange block), was an early success (fig. 91). Her inspiration was probably a simple black and white drawing in the style of Hiroshige showing fishermen under an arched bridge illustrated in Bing's *Artistic Japan* in June 1888 (fig. 92). The flock of descending geese is obviously a decorative addition of her own. Like Whistler before her, whose lyrical interpretations of Old Battersea Bridge were modeled on Hiroshige, she is more interested in the structure of the bridge than in the narrative element that animates the Japanese print; she also delights in the reflection of the bridge on the water, a realistic touch quite foreign to Hiroshige. Tentative and experimental in its technical execution, the image is nonetheless effective in its simple curvilinear rhythms. The format is that of the small Japanese *hosoban,* a narrow print measuring roughly 12½ by 5 inches. Furthermore, she used an unusual thin Japanese paper with a beautifully shimmering mica surface. The edition numbered over four hundred, roughly double the number she generally produced in later years.

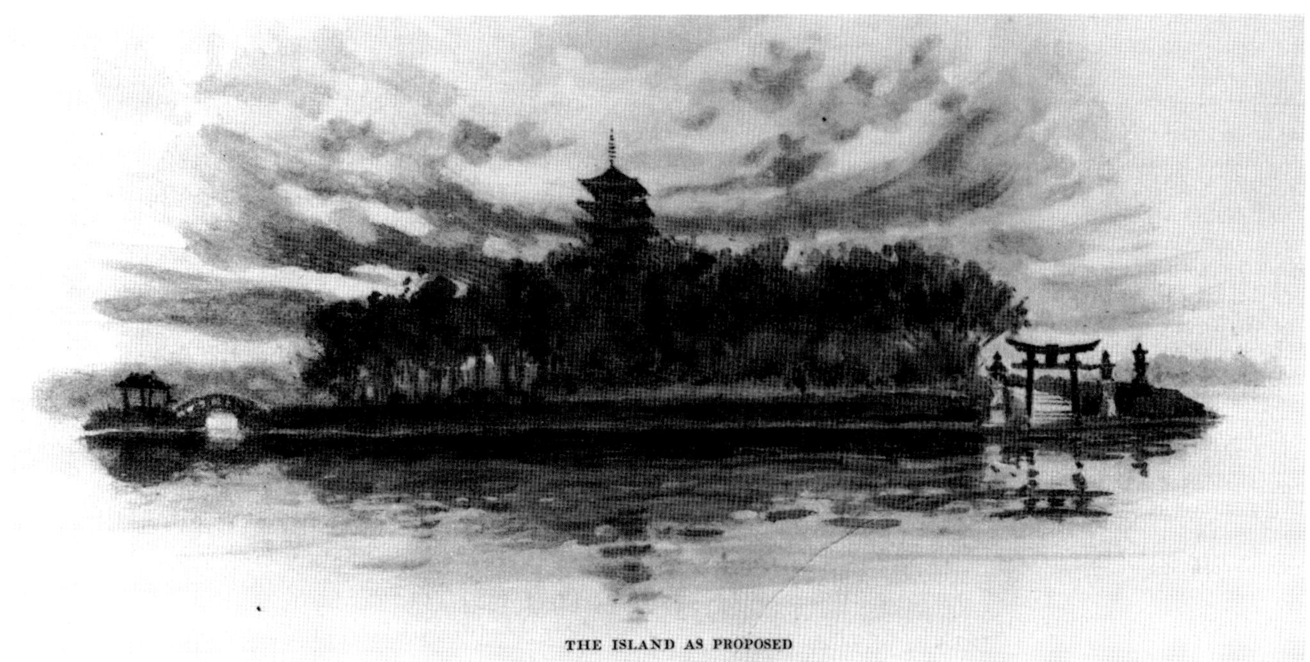

90. John Scott Bradstreet, design for "Bradstreet Island" in Lake of the Isles, Minneapolis. Engraving of sketch. From *The Bellman,* January 20, 1912

A word about Japanese print formats is in order here. Single-sheet prints were made in a number of standard, closely regulated sizes. In addition to the *hosoban,* there is the small *koban* (roughly 9 by 6¾ inches), the medium-size print called *chūban* (roughly 11 by 8 inches), the *chū-tanzaku* (15 by 5 inches), the larger *tanzaku* (15 by 6¾ inches), the *hashira-e,* or pillar picture (see page 116), and the *ōban,* or standard large print format (roughly 15 by 10 inches). The individual sheets were often composed as diptychs (both vertical and horizontal), as well as triptychs, pentaptychs, and even larger combinations.

LUM AND BONKOTSU

In the spring of 1907 Lum set off on her second visit to Japan, this time for serious study. She was armed with a letter of introduction to Iwamura Tōru (1870–1917), an art critic and professor of Western art history at the Tokyo School of Fine Arts. As a young man, Iwamura had spent five years in America and France studying painting, and he had

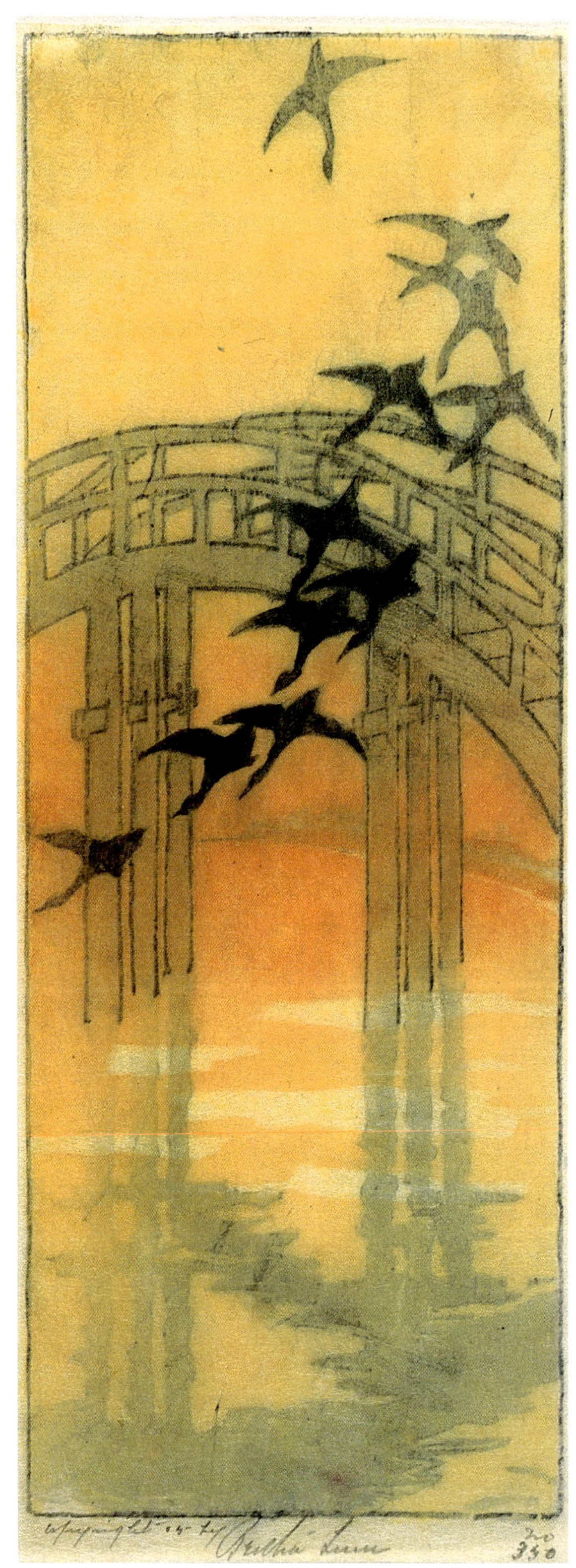

91. Bertha Lum, *Homecoming,* 1905. No. 350. Color woodcut. The Minneapolis Institute of Arts. Gift of Ethel Morrison Van Derlip, 1916

mistake arose from an immoderate as well as an indiscreet application of them. Time has now toned down this eagerness, and the opportune moment for beginning again, with matured experience, on another plan, seems to have arrived. Within the last few years extensive and successful research has brought the finest models of Japanese industry to western countries, and henceforth choice may be made from amongst them of specimens not only racy of the soil, but possessed of that eclectic beauty which is of no country. Especial care therefore ought now to be given to the selection of subjects which lend themselves readily to the requirements and customs of our western culture, with scrupulous avoidance of all those which would encourage mere trick, or degrading imitation. Such are the tendencies which will prevail in the choice of the specimens which will compose the collection of which a first instalment is now offered to the public, and which will gradually accumulate in the series that we shall continuously offer in this periodical. By them we hope that we shall be enabled to estimate the marvellous fertility of that Japanese imagination which has formed an endless variety of brilliant designs, all bearing the stamp of the purest and most ingenious taste.

Our producers will not we trust allow such valuable resources to remain unutilised, for there is not one among technical designers, book illustrators, architects, decorators, manufacturers of papers, printers, weavers, potters, bronze-workers, or goldsmiths, and even the workers in the numberless small industries, who may not derive benefit from consulting a collection which will form a repertory of centuries of Japanese fine art.

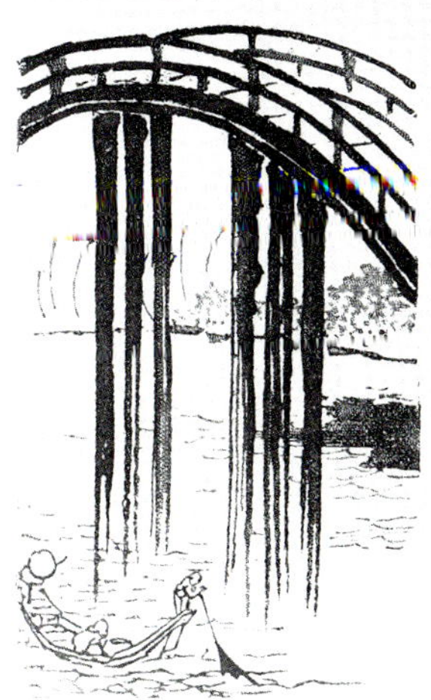

It will not suffice, however, merely to borrow the designs of these models; they must be thoroughly analysed and studied, with a view to arriving at their original conception. This they will be found to be well worthy of, for undoubtedly to discerning minds their aspect will suggest extremely serious reflections upon the fundamental principles of Japanese ornament as compared with the traditions of our own schools. For whilst strict limits have been placed, by the rigorous laws which we call our "styles," to the bounds within which our imagination has been permitted to wander, and whilst our industrial arts have in consequence assumed

5

92. Drawing in the style of Hiroshige. From *Artistic Japan,* 1, No. 1 (June 1888)

served as Japan's commissioner of fine arts at the 1904 Saint Louis World's Fair. Well-connected in the art world, Iwamura took Lum to the studio of Igami Bonkotsu (1875–1933), a block carver who was a friend of his, and she worked at his shop every day for three months, cutting blocks.[146] According to a rare interview with Lum, in the *Los Angeles Times*,

> *his two helpers, boys twelve years of age, acted as teachers, while the master block cutter twice daily passed on her work. She put in eight hours daily . . . working in a small house in the poorest quarter of the city. The next step was that of printing and with due ceremony she was taken by the professor and the master cutter and presented to a printer in whose shop she spent four weeks. She did no actual work, but spent her time seeing her designs transferred from her own blocks. Her rickshaw boy acted as interpreter during this time at the print shop.*
>
> *"Following this," says Mrs. Lum, "I returned to my home and for three years worked independently, absorbing what I had learned in Japan and using my own ideas and theories. Then I went back to Tokyo, took a house and went on a hunt for my old printer and block man. This hunt lasted a month."*[147]

She did find her chief aides, the cutter and printer, and worked with them for two years from 1911 (immediately following the birth of her youngest daughter) through 1912. The young apprentices who had assisted her on her first visit were both dead, which Lum attributed to "the wretched conditions that surrounded a handful of people who know the secrets of this art."

It happens that Lum's arrival in Japan in 1907 coincided with the birth of the so-called creative-print (*sōsaku hanga*) movement in Japan, and that Bonkotsu, the carver with whom she apprenticed, was deeply involved in this movement. In contrast to the classical ukiyo-e system, in which the artist merely designed the print, many of the newer print artists believed that they should be involved at all levels to ensure more direct personal expression. They valued personal creativity over craftsmanship. The status of the woodcut at the time was that of a lowly reproductive medium, quite similar to the situation that had existed in Europe before the revival of the color woodcut as an independent art form by Auguste Lepère (1849–1918) and Henri Rivière (see pages 74–75) in 1889. New Western-style photomechanical techniques were coming to usurp even the illustrational role of the woodcut. Publishers who once supported the single-sheet print industry had gone out of business or had converted to newspapers. It was necessary for the modern Japanese artist to look at his own, indigenous woodcut tradition through the eyes of Europeans in order to take up this medium once more as an original art form. In 1904 a Japanese oil painter, Yamamoto Kanae (1882–1946), was the first of his generation to try his hand at using the woodcut medium to create an original work of art in a modern (international) style, designing directly on the block with the carving knife. Four years later he and other Western style painters including Ishii Hakutei (1882–1958) formed a boisterous artists' drinking group called Pan, who, like French counterparts, gathered at a favorite café, where they thrashed out issues of ukiyo-e and modernism. One of the loudest and most unruly drunks in the crowd was their block carver, Bonkotsu. What was a traditional ukiyo-e artisan doing in the midst of a group of up-and-coming young Western style painters? Bonkotsu was unusual not only because he was accepted as one of them — in fact, he was the life of the party — but because he had the gift of being able to translate their designs successfully into printed form as illustrations for the avant-garde art journals, notably *Myōjō* and *Kōfū*, that these young painters sponsored. In his carving he imitated perfectly the light, sketchy quality of a Western-style pencil drawing. It is just this quality of a fine, wavering pencil-like key-block outline that characterizes the best work of Bertha Lum during her mature "Japan" period, when she was apprenticed to Bonkotsu (fig. 93).

Bonkotsu, for his part, was so impressed by the serious, hard-working Western artist who had set out to create her own prints as independent

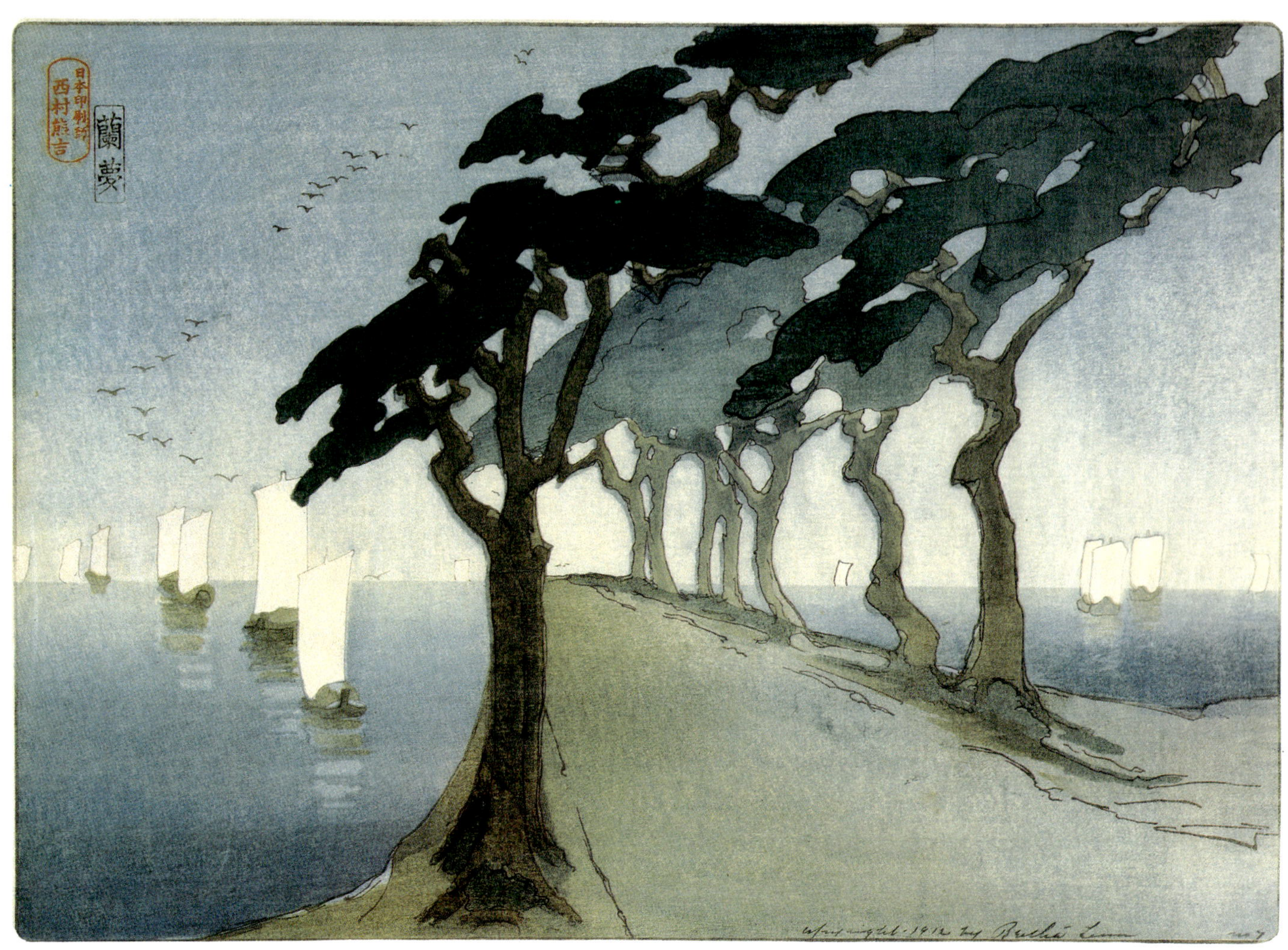

93. Bertha Lum, *Pines by the Sea,* 1912. No. 7. Color woodcut. © 1989 The Art Institute of Chicago, All Rights Reserved. Brian Lathrop Collection

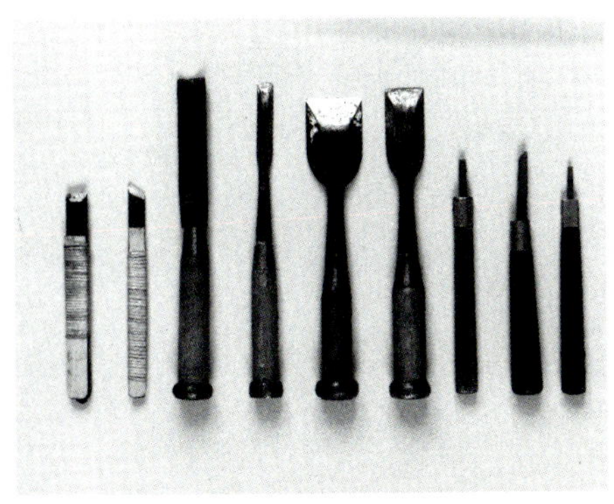

94. A selection of Bertha Lum's Japanese block carving tools: engraving knives, chisels, and gouges. (Lum's name is incised in Japanese phonetic script ["Ramu," literally "Orchid Dream"] on the handles of most of her tools.) The Fine Arts Museums of San Francisco, Achenbach Foundation for Graphic Arts, Gift of Mr. and Mrs. Edouard J. Bourbuisson

works of art — a model for her Japanese colleagues, he felt — that he wrote about her in the Waseda University journal only a month after meeting her. In his opinion the color woodcut, because it was neglected by serious artists, was in danger of becoming an extravagant but useless craft. He acknowledged that although the woodcut was best suited to reproduce designs by modern Japanese-style painters, they seemed uninterested and were on the whole a rather stuck-up lot, difficult for someone like him to approach — quite the opposite of the easygoing, less elitist Western-style painters. It was Bonkotsu's theory that woodblock carving and printing should be incorporated into the curriculum of art schools in Japan. While recognizing that Bertha Lum's technical abilities were still limited, he was struck by the fact that she had come with her own tools (fig. 94) and spent every day except Sunday in his studio. "If this trend continues," he wrote with a mixture of admiration and concern, "perhaps the art of the Japanese color woodcut will be taken over by foreigners! This is truly worrisome."[148] Sets of Lum's key blocks and color blocks are preserved in both the Achenbach Foundation for Graphic Arts in San Francisco and the Museum of Art, University of Oregon (figs. 95 and 96).

Bonkotsu introduced Lum to the printer with whom he always worked, Nishimura Kumakichi (1861–?1941). His name is stamped on prints by Lum dated 1912 and 1913 (fig. 97).[149] Nishimura was trained as a printer from the age of nine and had his own workshop from 1877, at which point he printed for most of the big names in the world of ukiyo-e — Yoshitoshi, Kuniyoshi, and later Kiyokata and Shinsui.

A large number of Bertha Lum's prints dating from her 1907 study trip and first exposure to Nishimura are gray night scenes with artificial illumination (fig. 98), which immediately call to mind the work of the great Meiji print artist Kobayashi Kiyochika (1847–1915). This is probably no coincidence, for Nishimura had started working for Kiyochika around 1880. It was his most challenging assignment; Kiyochika

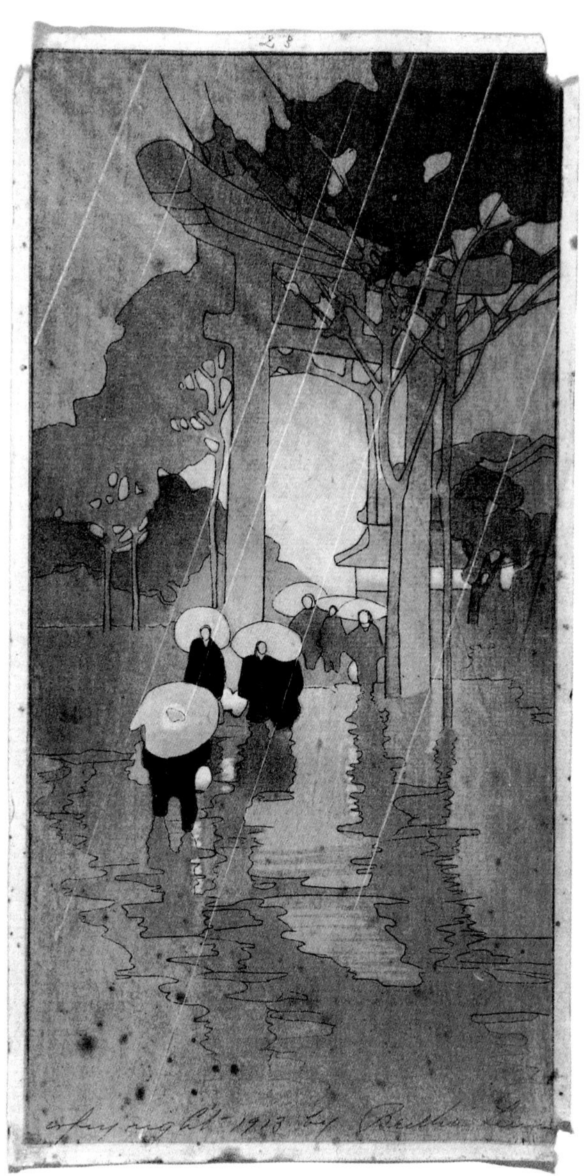

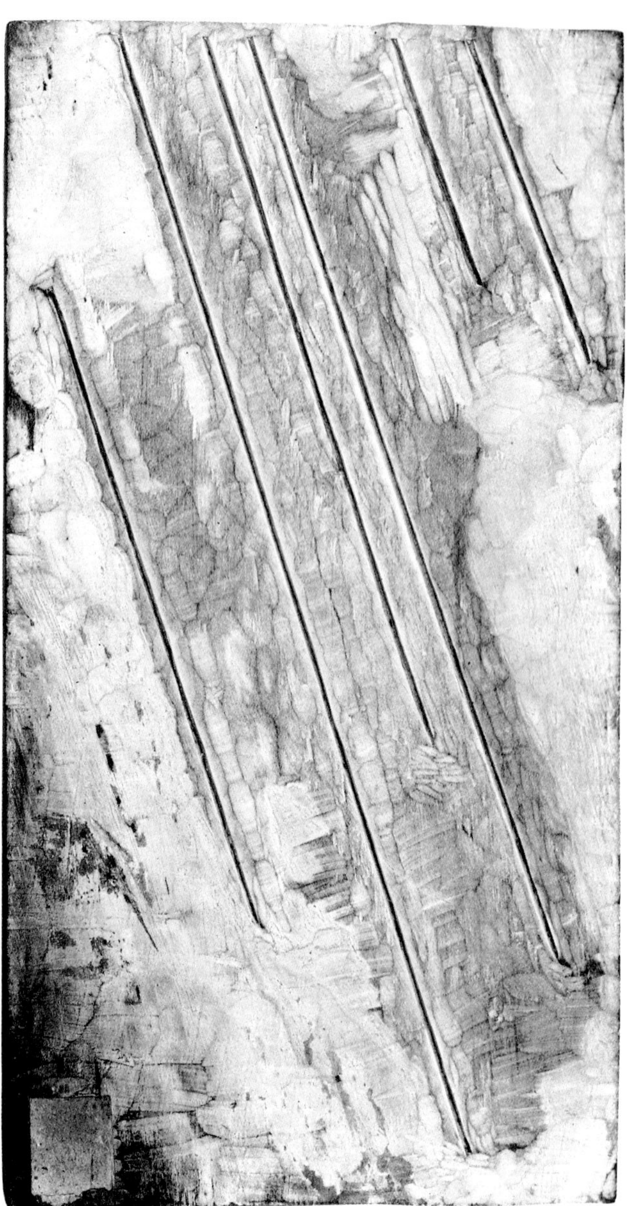

95. Bertha Lum, *Temple Gate,* 1913. (first issued in 1912). Color woodcut and color block for rain. Museum of Art, University of Oregon, Eugene

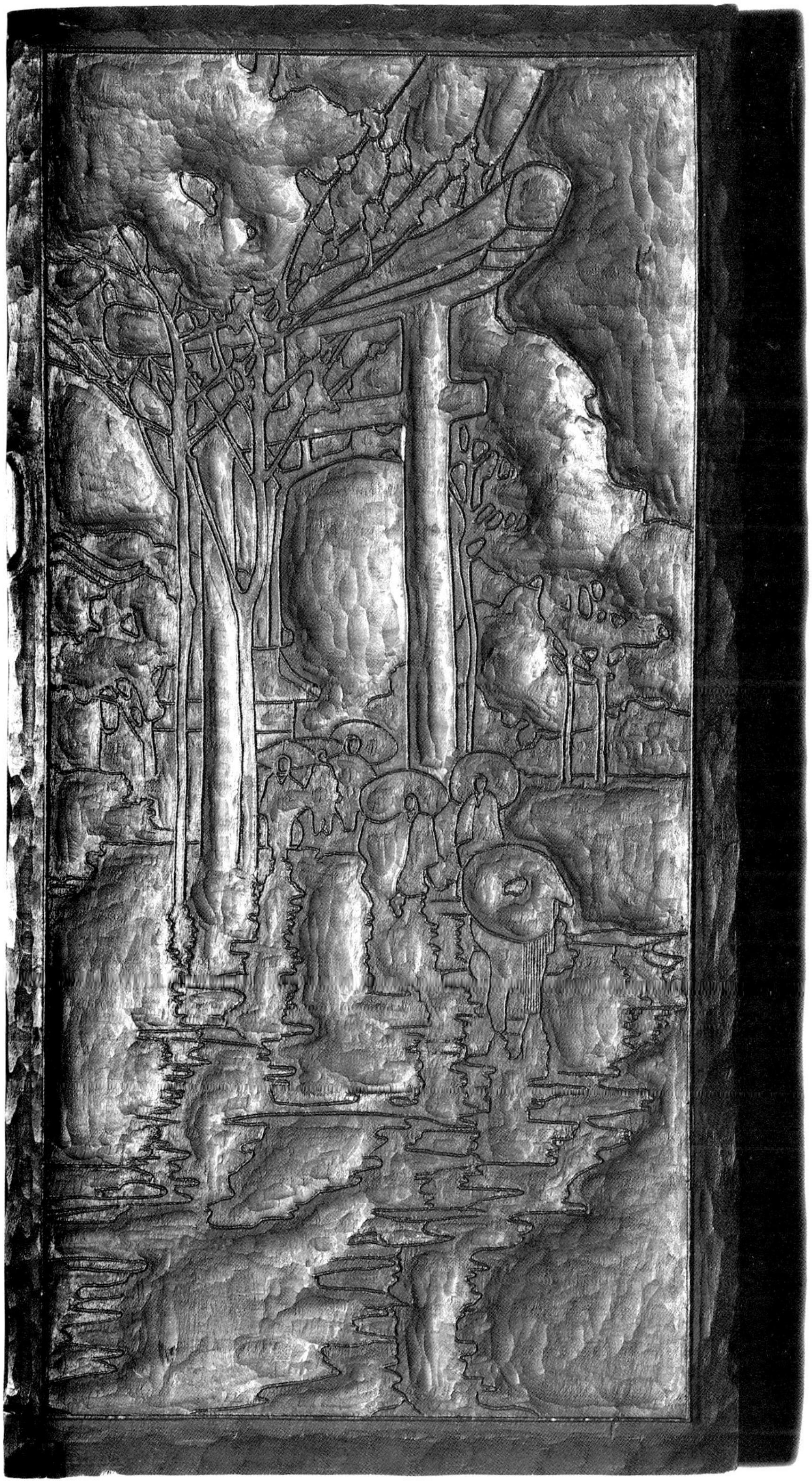

96. Key block for *Temple Gate,* 1912. Museum of Art, University of Oregon, Eugene

97. Detail of artist's seal, "Ramu," and printer's seal, "Nishimura Kumakichi." From Bertha Lum, *Pines by the Sea* (see fig. 93)

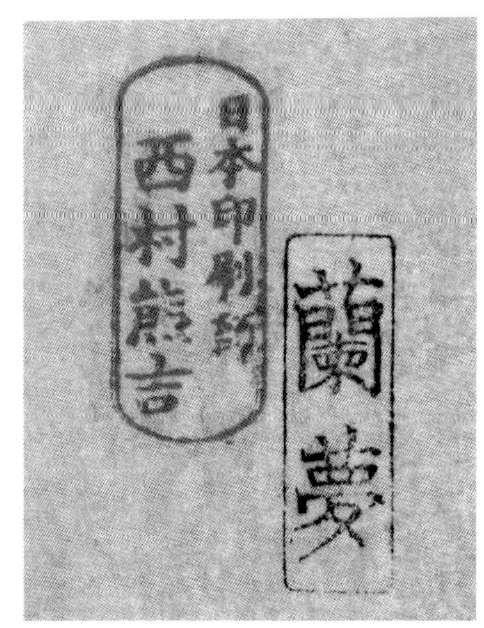

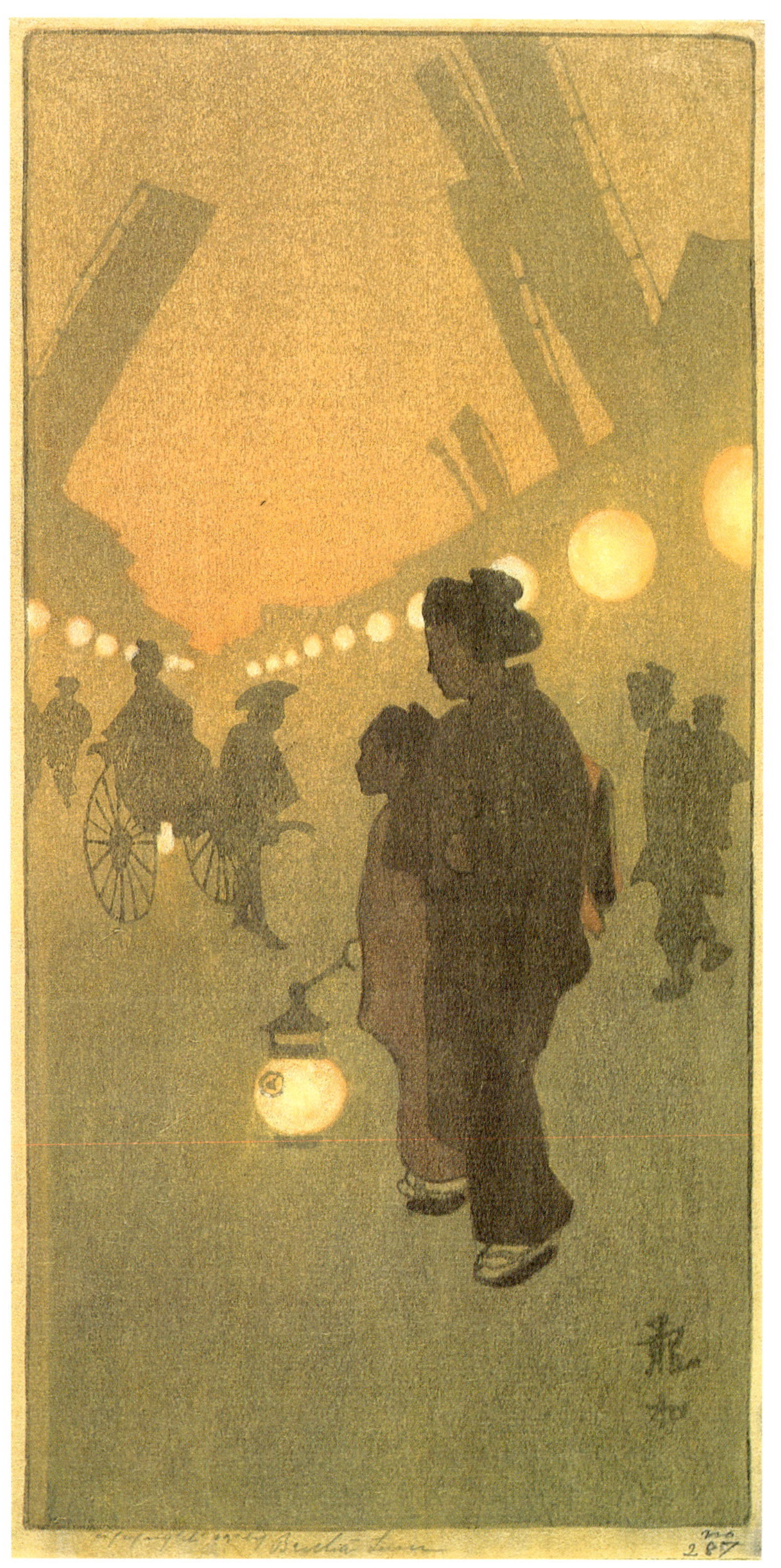

98. Bertha Lum, *Theater Street, Yokohama,* 1907. No. 287. Color woodcut. The Minneapolis Institute of Arts. Gift of Ethel Morrison Van Derlip, 1916

was familiar with Western-style painting and specialized in chiaroscuro effects, delighting especially in innovative night scenes with artificial illumination and cast shadows (fig. 99). Nishimura, a simple, illiterate craftsman, had never seen an oil painting and it took him many days to get the right effect. It was his work with Kiyochika that brought him to the attention of the Japanese Western-style painters at the turn of the century.

A footnote to Lum's role on the fringes of Japan's creative-print movement was her participation in the tenth annual public exhibition of the Pacific Painting Society (Taiheiyō gakai) at Ueno Park in Tokyo in the spring of 1912, an event that set her professional career in motion.[150] The Pacific Painting Society was founded in 1901 by a group of conservative Western-style oil painters led by Yoshida Hiroshi (1876–1950), who is best known today for the woodblock prints he started to make in the 1920s. Beginning in 1900, Yoshida and his group came to America often for commercial exhibitions in Boston, New York, Detroit, Indianapolis, Saint Louis, and elsewhere. They brought with them watercolors showing the picture postcard variety of traditional tourist beauty spots, aimed at the popular taste (fig. 100).[151] *Japanese Junks* was a recurrent subject; it is the theme also for one of the prints Lum produced under her own steam during her interval back in Minneapolis between 1908 and 1911 (fig. 101).

The Minneapolis prints are rather broadly conceived, without the delicacy of line and printing typical of her Japanese work — or, one should properly say, of the work of her teammates Bonkotsu and Nishimura. In any case, it was a "Minneapolis" print from 1909, *Fox-Women,* that was submitted to the 1912 exhibition at Ueno Park in Tokyo — the only work by a Westerner (and by a woman) and, as far as one can judge by the illustrated catalogue, the only woodcut (fig. 102). The Japanese entries were oils, watercolors, and sculptures, all in a naturalistic Western style. Her *Fox-Women* was accepted because, as the

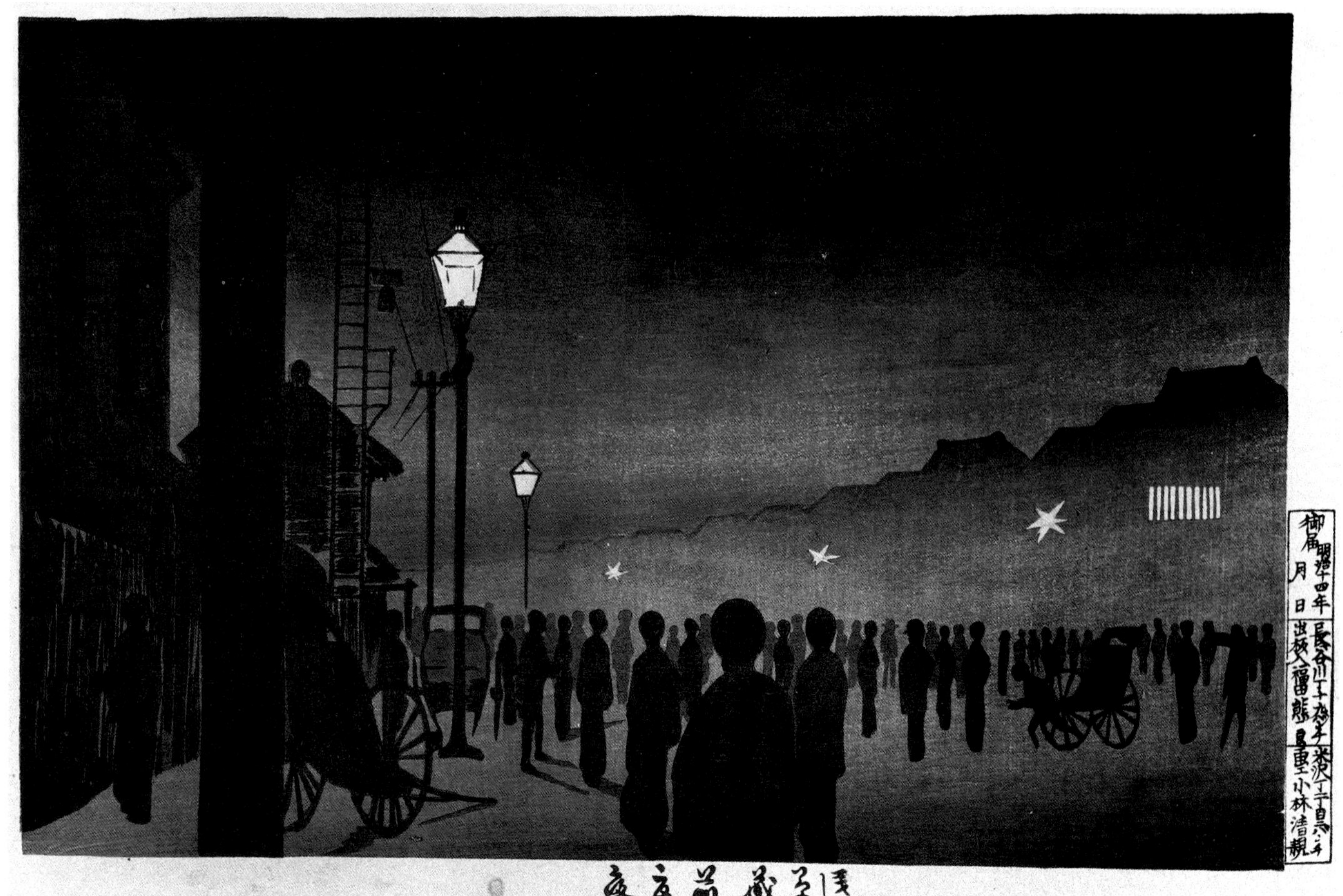

99. Kobayashi Kiyochika, *Summer Night at Asakusa Kuramae,* 1881. Color woodcut. The Santa Barbara Museum of Art, Gift of Mr. and Mrs. Roland A. Way

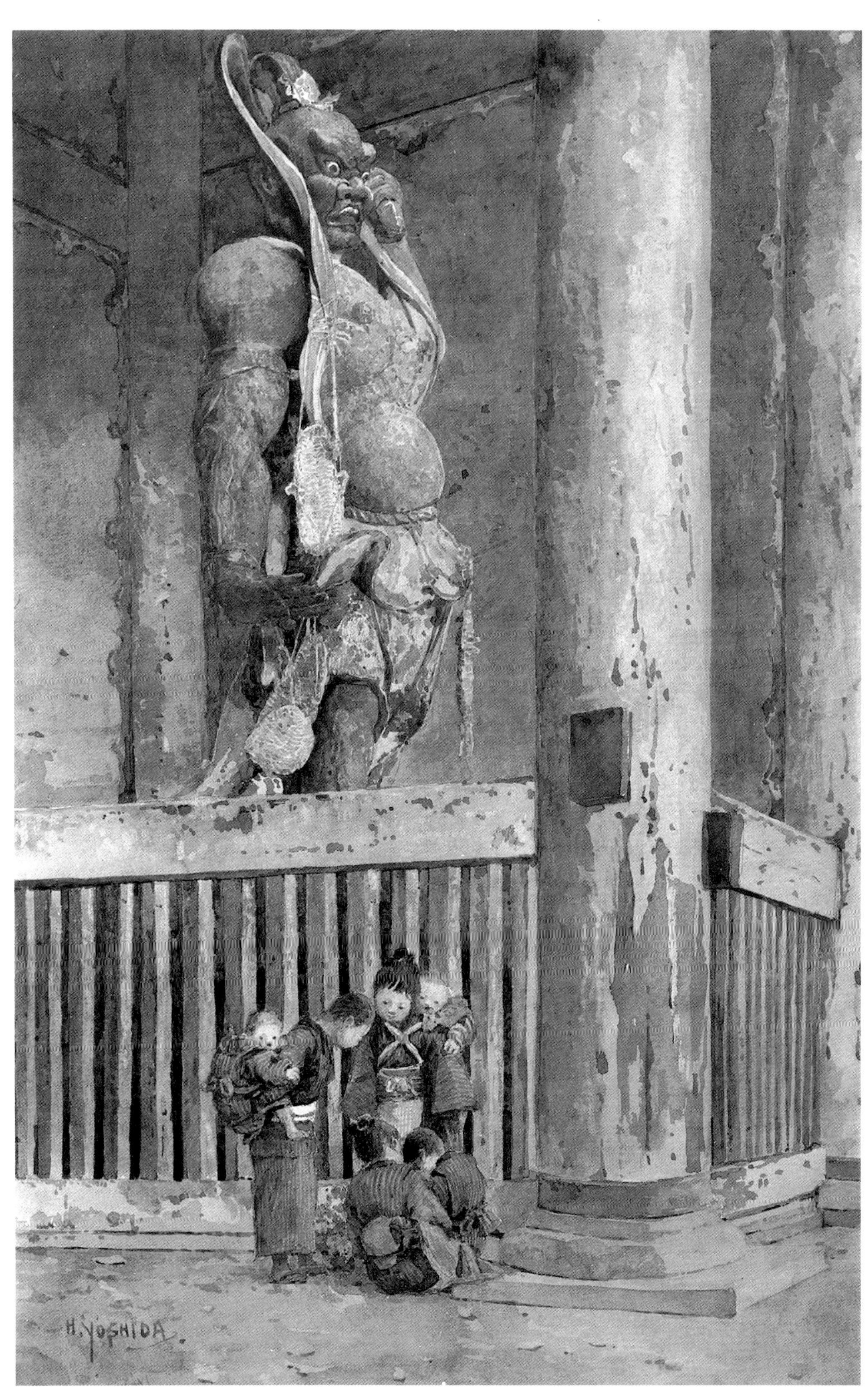

100. Yoshida Hiroshi, *Children at Gate of Myogi Shrine,* c. 1900. Watercolor on paper. Museum of Fine Arts, Boston. Abbott Lawrence Fund

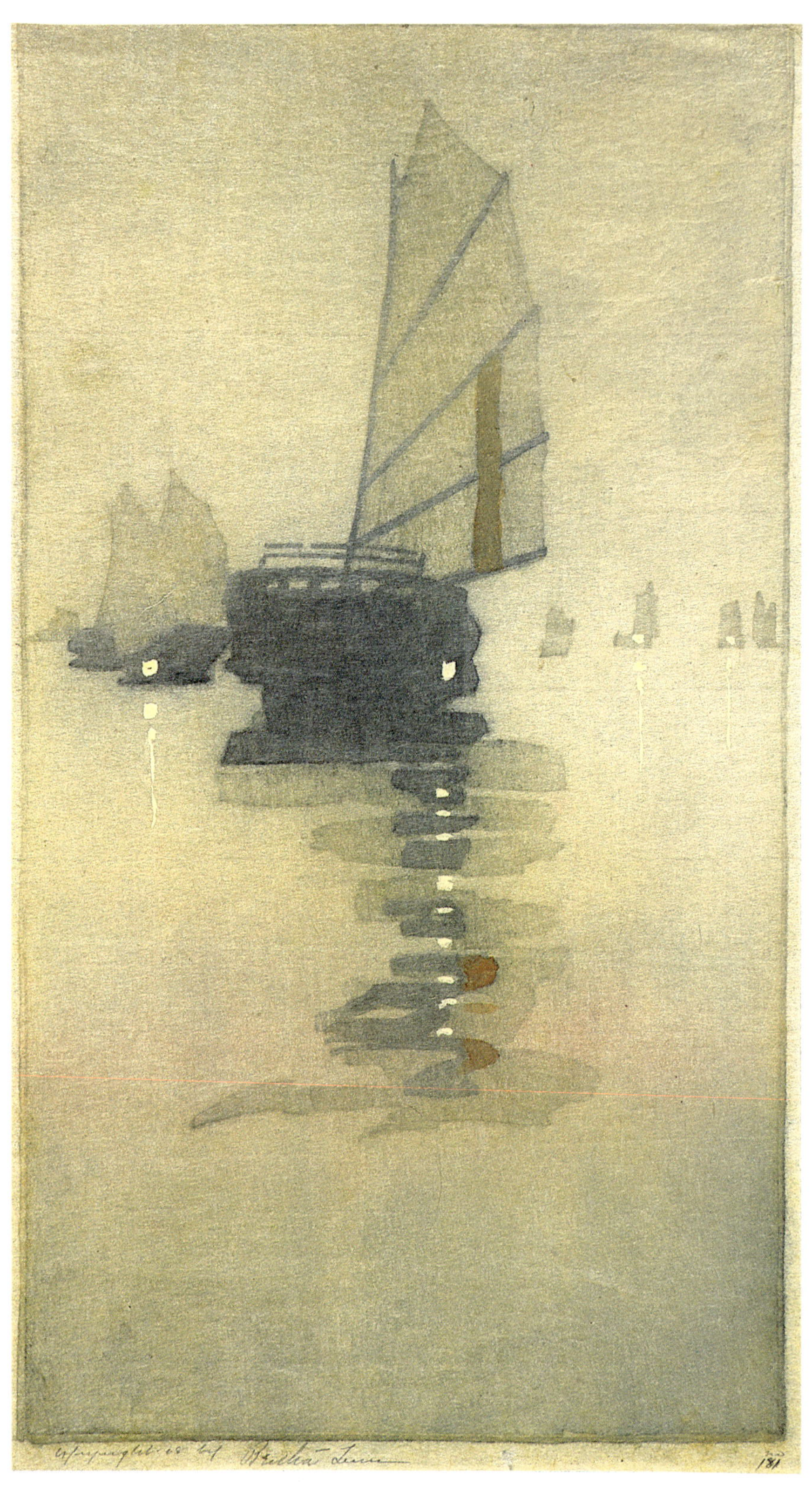

101. Bertha Lum, *Junks in the Inland Sea,* 1908. No. 181. Color woodcut and watercolor. The Minneapolis Institute of Arts. Gift of Ethel Morrison Van Derlip, 1916

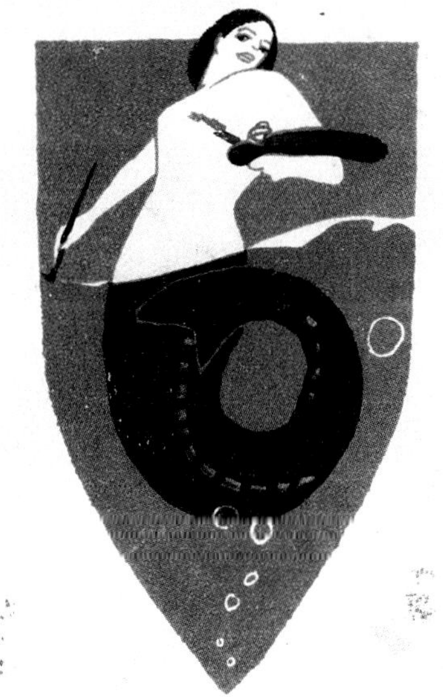

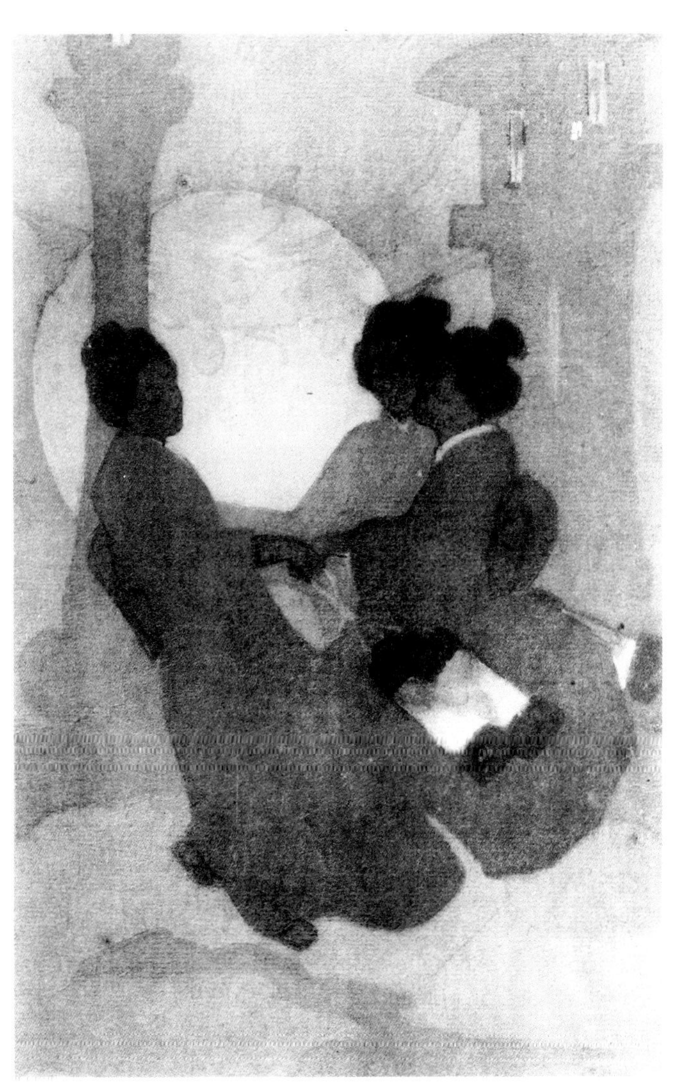

102. Cover and illustration of *Fox-Women,* 1909. From the Pacific Painting Society exhibition catalogue, Tokyo, 1912

catalogue makes clear, it was an example of *jisaku,* i.e., "self-made," a fact still remarkable at that time in the Tokyo art world.

In the long run, the self-made print was something of an exception in her career. Lum, like Hyde became dependent on her Japanese craftsmen; she would take the watercolors she painted in California to Japan for printing. She was prevented by immigration officials from bringing her assistants to California. She did succeed, however, in taking two men with her to Peking when she moved there in the 1920s.[152] As an artist carefully directing the work of artisans, she was following the practices not of the new creative-print movement but of the best traditional ukiyo-e printmakers. In terms of composition and style her work during her Japan period is often heavily derivative of Hiroshige; close comparisons can be found for *Pines by the Sea* (fig. 93), *Wind and Rain* (figs. 104 and 105), or *The Bamboo Road* (fig. 106), for example. Her publicists in later years liked to present her as a "western reviver of the glories of Hiroshige and Hokusai," and a remarkable headline in the *Chicago Evening Post* in 1932 read "Woman from Iowa Outdoes Orientals at Their Own Game."[153]

Lum, like Helen Hyde, preferred to use a thin tracing paper for her prints in order to get an especially delicate effect closely resembling a watercolor. Traditional Japanese printmakers never used this kind of paper for their finished work. *The Bamboo Road* of 1912 is typical of her best designs: it is sensuous, feminine, and rather lyrical, printed with technical finesse and delicate color gradations. Her model was probably Hiroshige's depiction of a famous scene from a thirteenth-century battle epic, in which Tokiwa Gozen, widow of the general Minamoto Yoritomo, flees the capital in a heavy snowstorm hoping to save her three young sons from certain execution at the hands of a victorious rival (fig. 107). It is a story instantly familiar to a Japanese audience, but we can assume that Lum was ignorant of the literary content of her model. Rafael Fernandez, curator at the Sterling and Francine Clark Art Institute, went

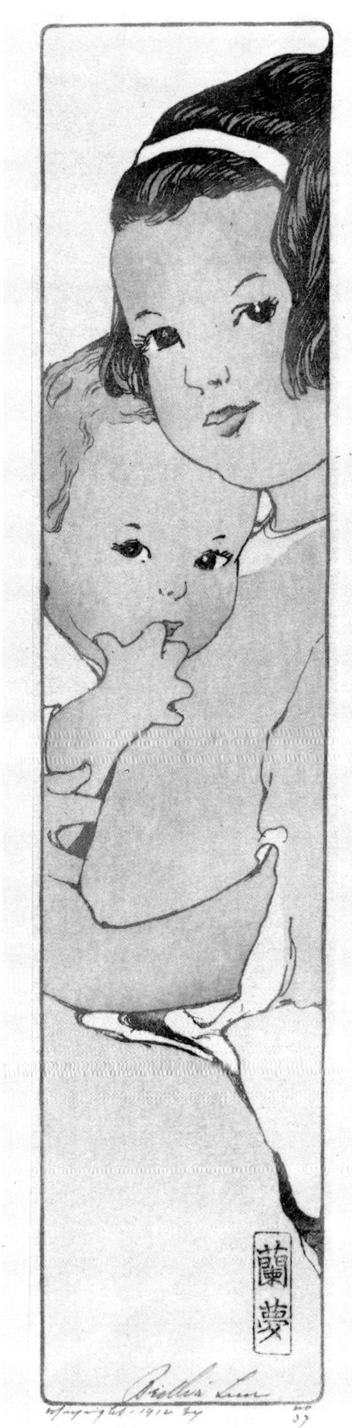

103. Bertha Lum, *My Children,* 1912. No. 37. Color woodcut. The Minneapolis Institute of Arts. Gift of Ethel Morrison Van Derlip, 1916

to the heart of the issue when he wrote that

> *much of the fascination of Japanese prints rested on the fact that few of their dedicated Western admirers could tell what they were about. . . . The numerous inscriptions and references that are such an essential part of* ukiyo-e *went unread for the most part. . . . However, lack of knowledge of what information was encoded in a print allowed and encouraged a purely visual experience.*

The topical, storytelling elements were inaccessible to most Western artists and collectors of Japanese art. They were free to

> *see the prints as pure graphic gesture, mere play of lines and color, simply as "significant forms" (as Roger Fry would have it). They could ignore those conventions and limitations which so encumbered the Japanese artists and structured the way the Japanese themselves perceived them.* Ukiyo-e *conventions were strictly imposed from above. Censorship prescribed use of colors, established approved sizes and shapes, and kept the stiffest control over subject matter.*[154]

Lum is especially interesting when she experiments with Japanese formats. *My Children* (1912), which shows her two little girls, uses the narrow vertical poem-paper shape (*tanzaku*) to great advantage (fig. 103). Her daughters, Catherine (also known as "Balliet," d. 1983) and Bettina ("Peter Boy," 1911–83), were born in Minneapolis. Peter Lum, who married the British diplomat Sir Colin Crowe in 1938, became a writer specializing in children's books and in East Asian myths and legends; clearly, she was deeply influenced by her mother, with whom she traveled back and forth to Asia during most of her early years. Both she and her elder sister, who married the Italian aristocrat Anthony Riva and moved to Genoa, Italy, tried their hand at color woodcuts; Peter Lum's *Tourists* (fig. 108), printed in 1920 when she was only nine, and *Oriental Roofs,* done in China in 1924, are rather simple and derivative, in a monochromatic palette, but very effective.

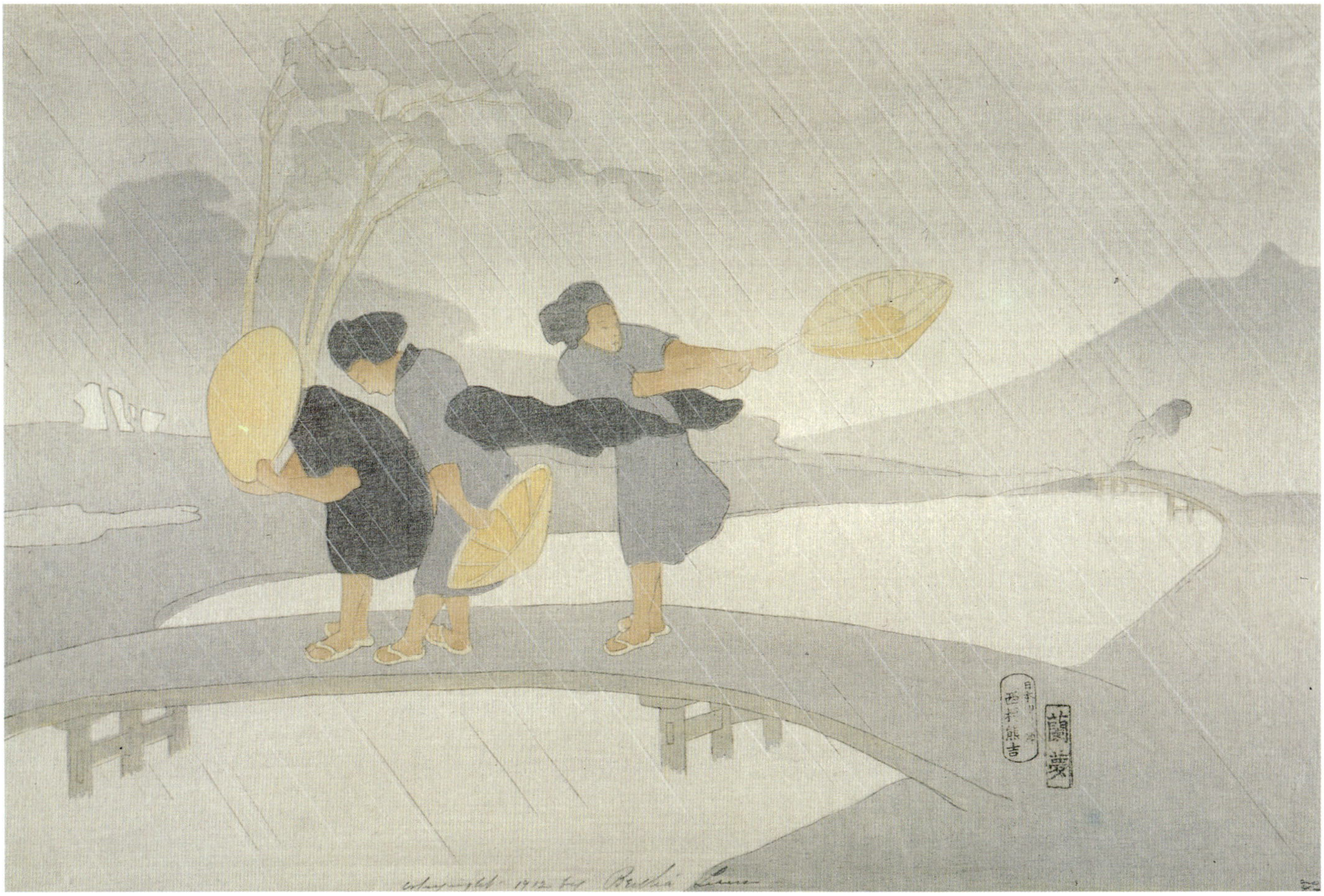

104. Bertha Lum, *Wind and Rain,* 1912. No. 42. Color woodcut. The Minneapolis Institute of Arts. Gift of Ethel Morrison Van Derlip, 1916

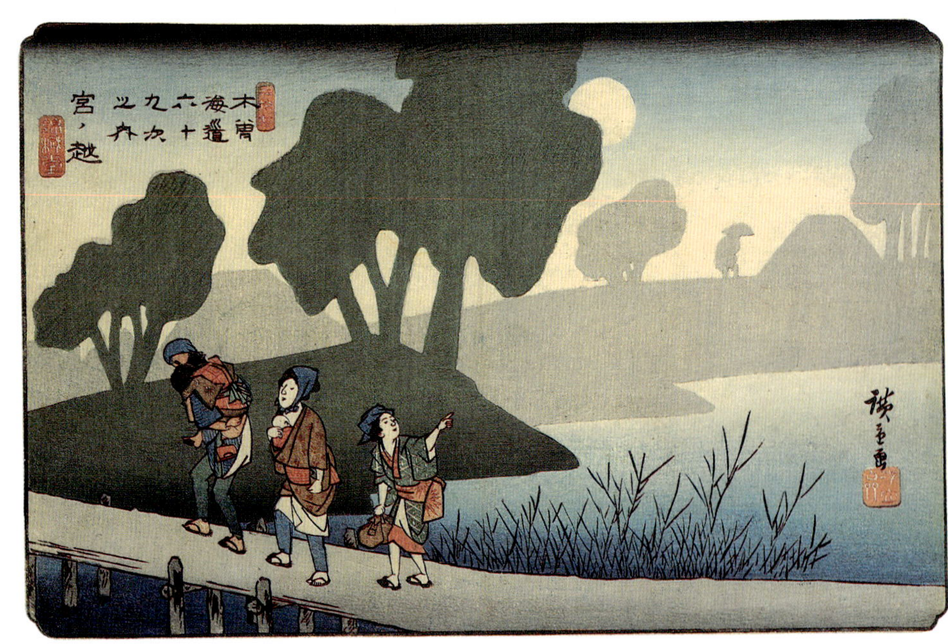

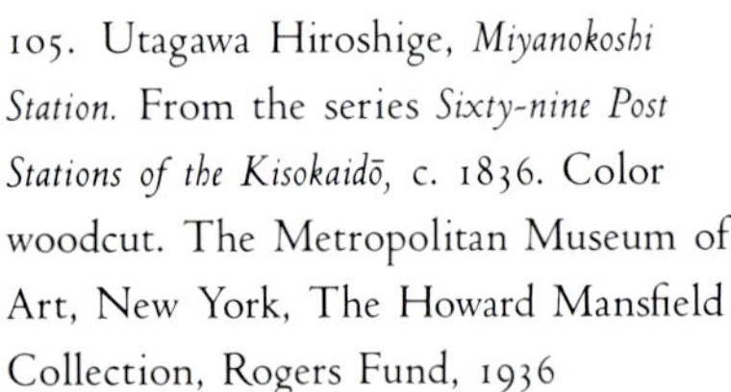

105. Utagawa Hiroshige, *Miyanokoshi Station.* From the series *Sixty-nine Post Stations of the Kisokaidō,* c. 1836. Color woodcut. The Metropolitan Museum of Art, New York, The Howard Mansfield Collection, Rogers Fund, 1936

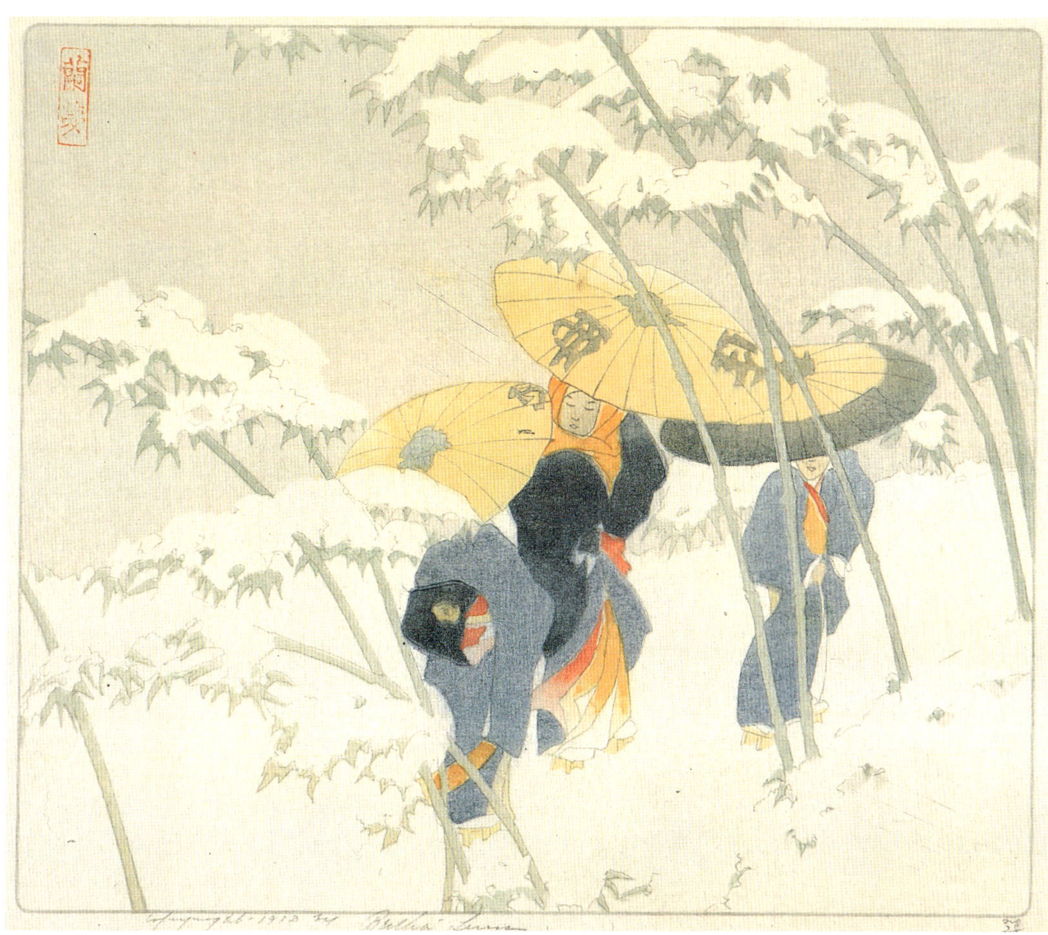

106. Bertha Lum, *Bamboo Road,* 1912. No. 28. Color woodcut. The Minneapolis Institute of Arts. Gift of Ethel Morrison Van Derlip, 1916

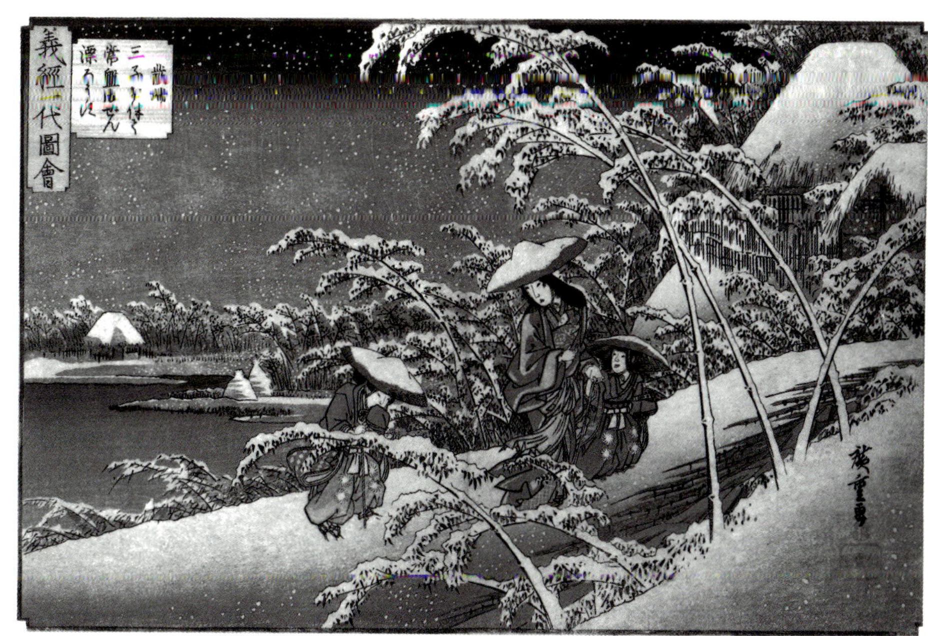

107. Utagawa Hiroshige, *The Winter Flight of Tokiwa Gozen with Her Three Children.* From the series *Yoshitsune ichidai zue* (Scenes from the Life of Yoshitsune), c. 1836. Color woodcut. © 1989 The Art Institute of Chicago, All Rights Reserved. The Clarence Buckingham Collection

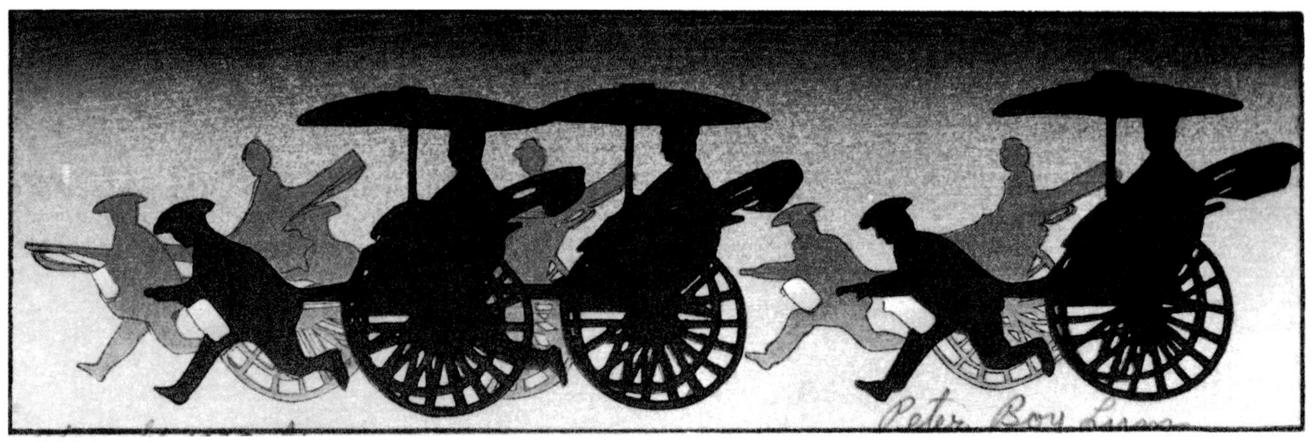

108. Peter Boy Lum, *Tourists,* 1920. Color woodcut. The Fine Arts Museums of San Francisco, Achenbach Foundation for Graphic Arts, Gift of Mr. and Mrs. Edouard J. Bourbuisson

LUM AND HEARN

Much of Lum's subject matter is taken from the stories of Lafcadio Hearn (1850–1904), whose romantic interpretations of Japanese legends and folklore were enormously popular in the United States. His best stories appeared often in the *Atlantic Monthly* toward the turn of the century. An American of Greek-Irish parentage, Hearn attended boarding schools in Europe and France, worked for a while as a reporter in America, and moved to Japan in 1890, where he spent the last fourteen years of his life teaching English literature. He died a Japanese citizen. His writings include about thirty ghost stories with Japanese themes; the old stories were read aloud to him by his Japanese wife, and he would translate and expand them for Western taste, taking into account the sensibilities of his American and Victorian readers, most of whom were women. His own macabre temperament and taste were also at work in transforming the original tales with added drama and detail (figs. 109 and 110).[155]

The ghostly heroines of two stories in Hearn's *Kwaidan* (1904)—Aoyagi, or Green Willow, and Yuki-Onna, or Snow Woman—inspired Lum prints (fig. 111). Typically Hearn's ghost appears in the guise of a

109. Bertha Lum, *Spirit of the Sea,* 1916. No. 56. Color woodcut. The Metropolitan Museum of Art, New York, Harris Brisbane Dick Fund, 1924

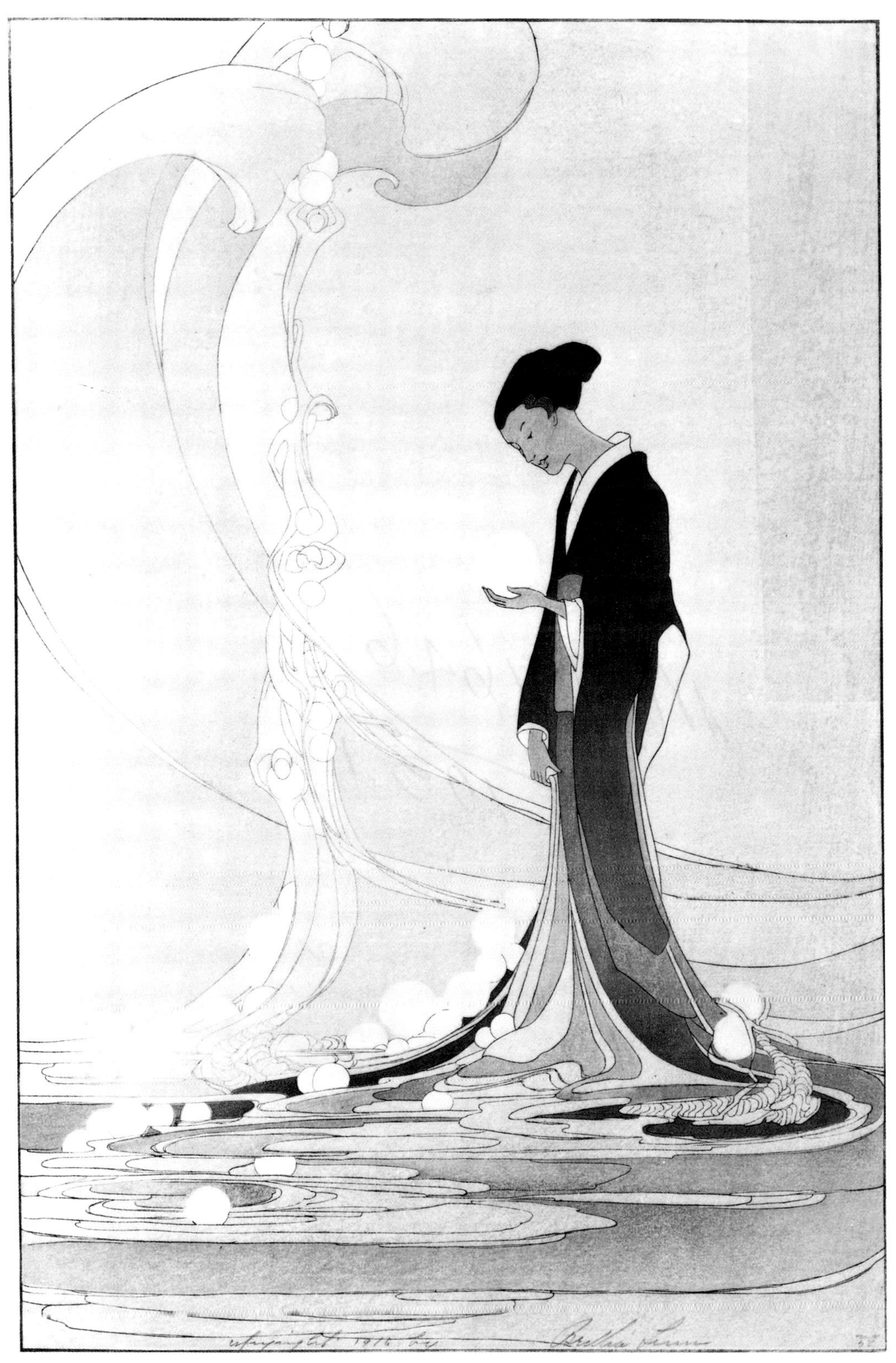

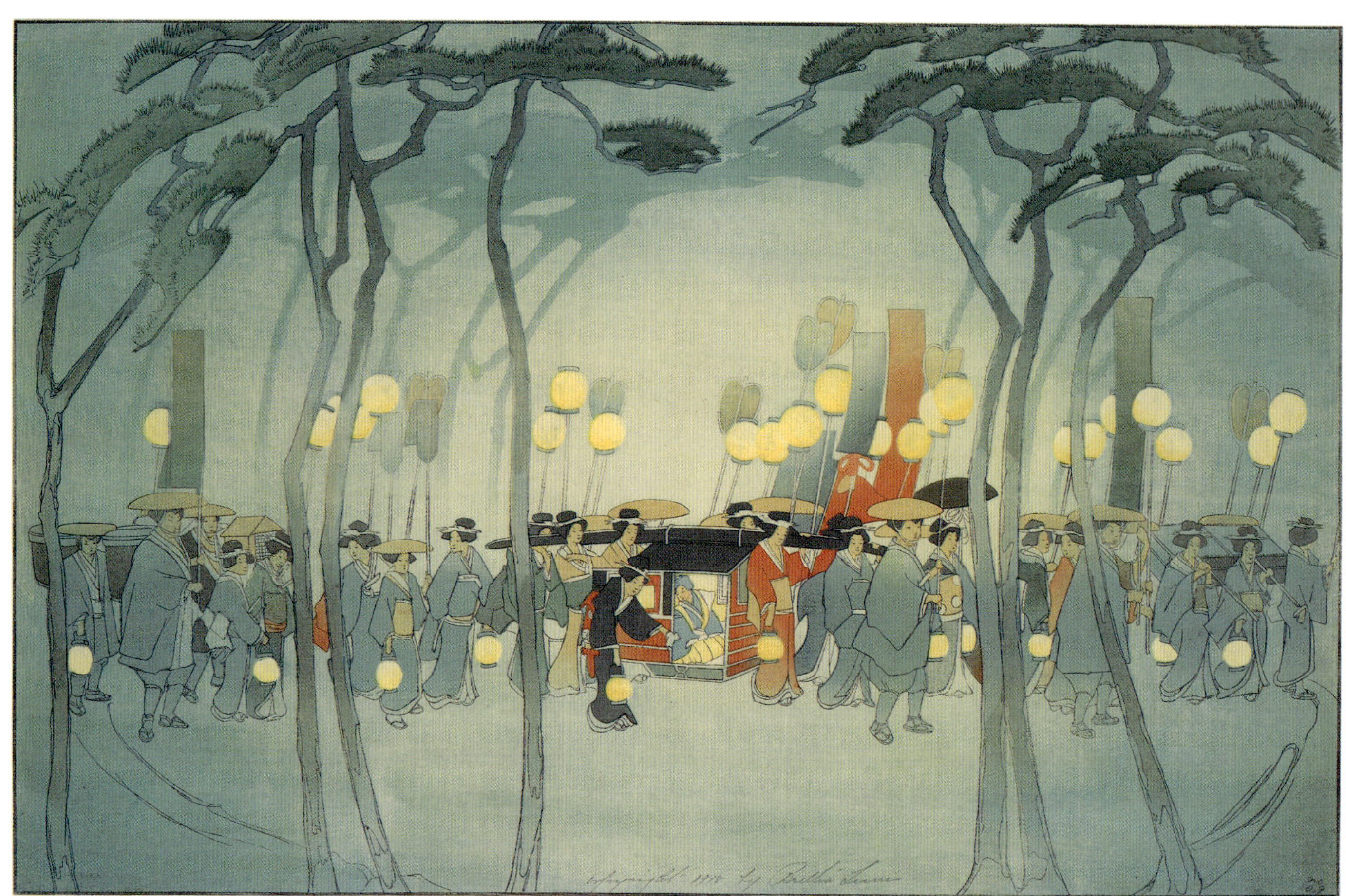

110. Bertha Lum, *The Procession,* 1918. No. 29. Color woodcut. The Metropolitan Museum of Art, New York, Harris Brisbane Dick Fund, 1924

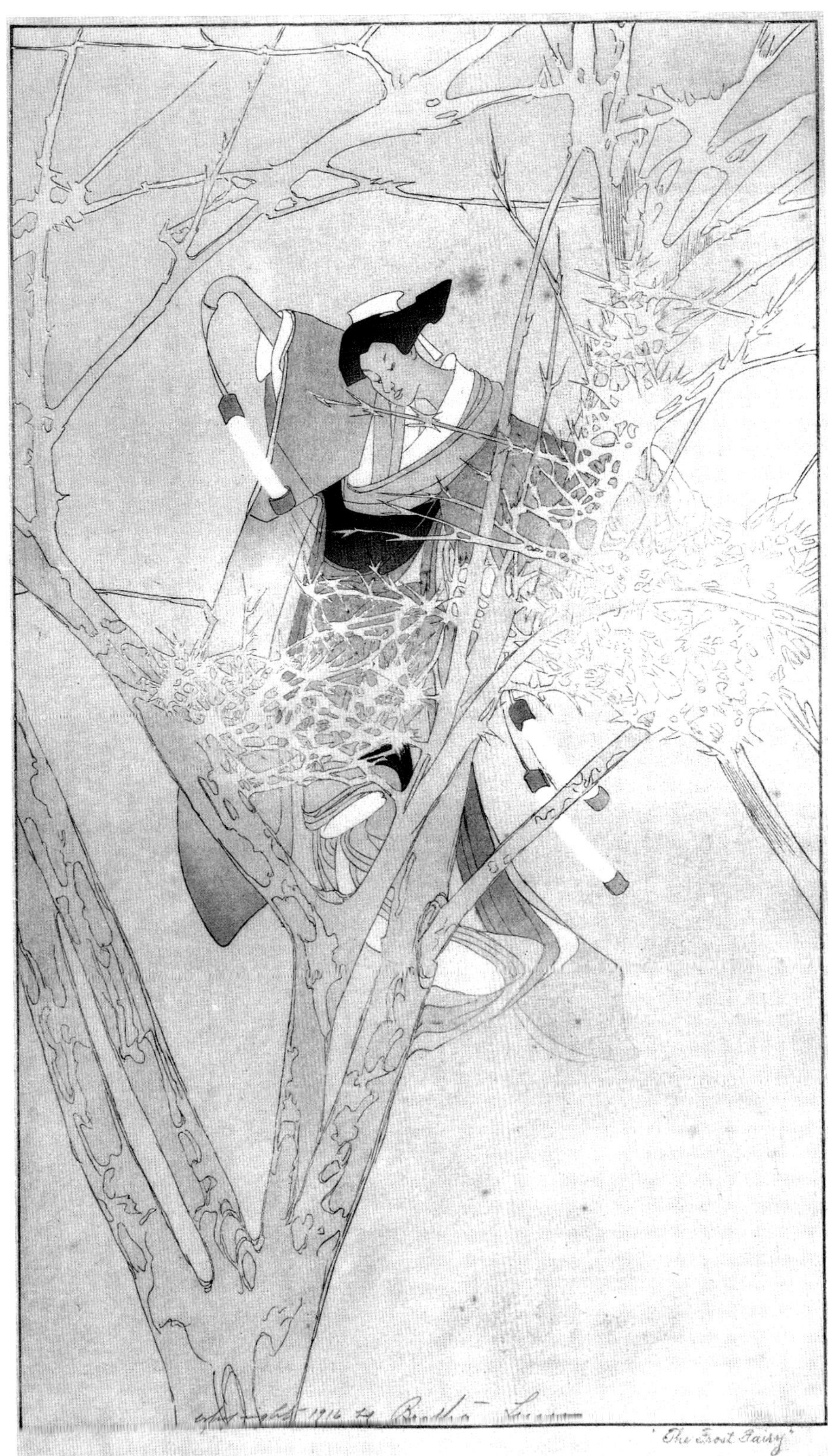

111. Bertha Lum, *Frost Fairy* (*Snow Woman*), 1916. Color woodcut. The Jane Voorhees Zimmerli Art Museum, Rutgers, The State University of New Jersey, Ralph and Barbara Voorhees American Art Fund

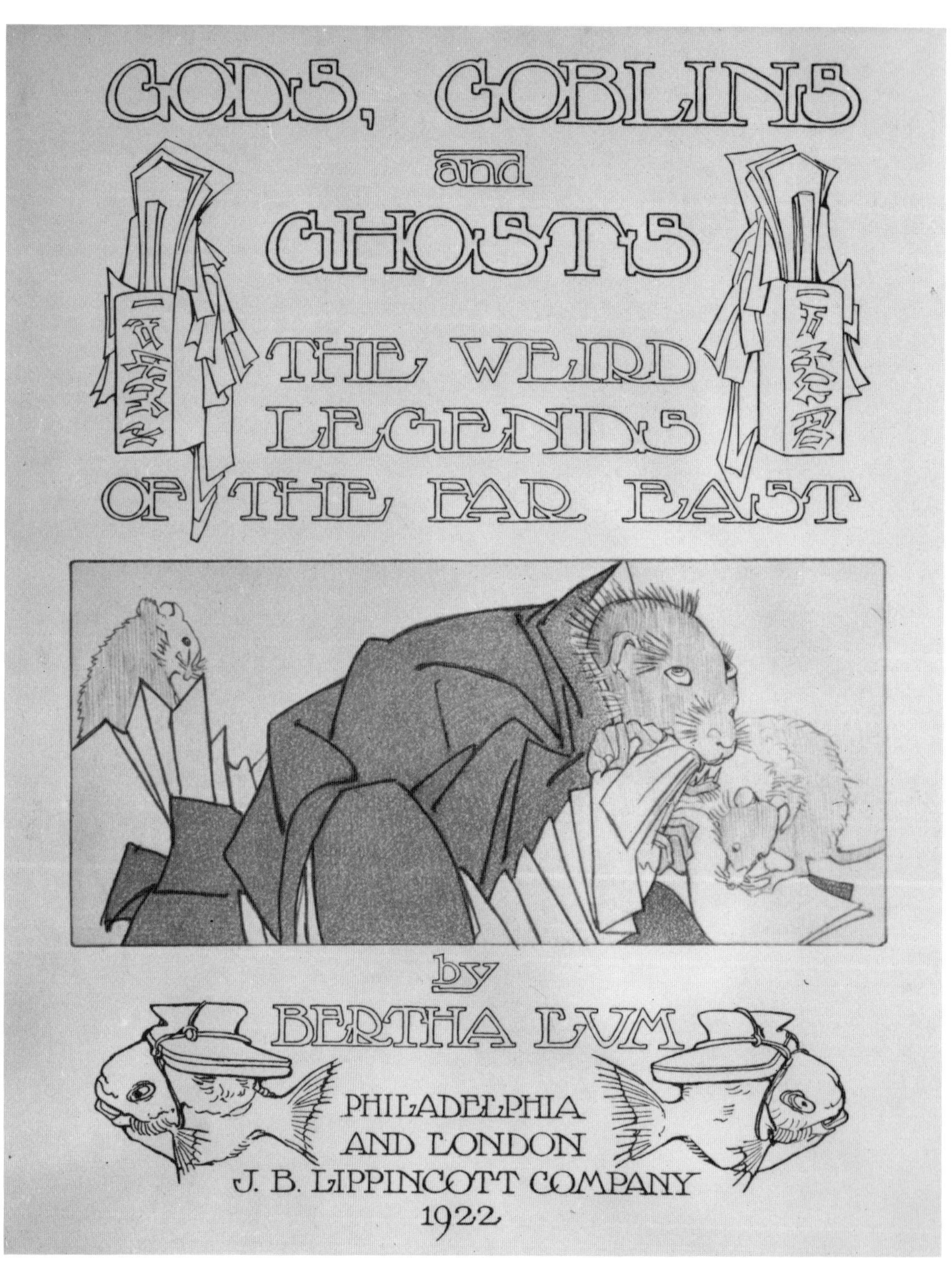
GODS, GOBLINS
and
GHOSTS
THE WEIRD
LEGENDS
OF THE FAR EAST
by
BERTHA LUM
PHILADELPHIA
AND LONDON
J. B. LIPPINCOTT COMPANY
1922

112. Bertha Lum, title page of *Gods, Goblins and Ghosts,* 1922. Ravicz Collection

beautiful woman who falls in love with and marries an unsuspecting young man; but after several years she reverts mysteriously to her true form and disappears. The Snow Woman, or Frost Fairy, appears on a bitter winter night, for example, dressed all in white, and freezes one young man to death, but spares his companion, for sentimental reasons. The youth is sworn never to divulge her moment of weakness. Later he marries a beautiful girl named O-Yuki (Snow), and they live happily together until, inevitably, he makes the mistake of telling her the strange tale of the Snow Woman. His wife, screaming with rage, reveals herself to be the woman in question, and melts into a bright white mist, never to be seen again.

Another favorite theme for Lum — she used it at least four times — was that of goblin fox-women (see fig. 102). Hearn devotes a chapter to "Kitsune" (Foxes) in *Glimpses of Unfamiliar Japan* (1894). The goblin fox assumes the form of a beautiful woman for the purpose of deluding mankind, haunts solitary places, and at night is fond of making queer ghostly lights resembling lantern fires. (This was the subject also of one of Hiroshige's best known prints, *Fox Fires at Ōji* from the series *One Hundred Famous Views of Edo.*) Several Lum prints were exhibited in the Minneapolis Institute of Arts in 1917 with the appropriate Hearn quotations appended to their mats.[156]

Lum later wrote and illustrated a book of her own along the lines of Hearn. Published by Lippincott in 1922 as a luxury volume, thread-bound in imitation of Japanese hand-sewn bindings, it is entitled *Gods, Goblins and Ghosts: The Weird Legends of the Far East* and has specially designed full-page color plates (fig. 112). The author mingled stories adapted from the Japanese by way of Hearn, such as "Aoyagi," with insights of her own about Japanese customs and culture. Like Hearn and many other Japanophiles of the time, her attitude is one of disillusionment and regret at the rapid passing from the scene of the quaint and exotic "Old Japan":

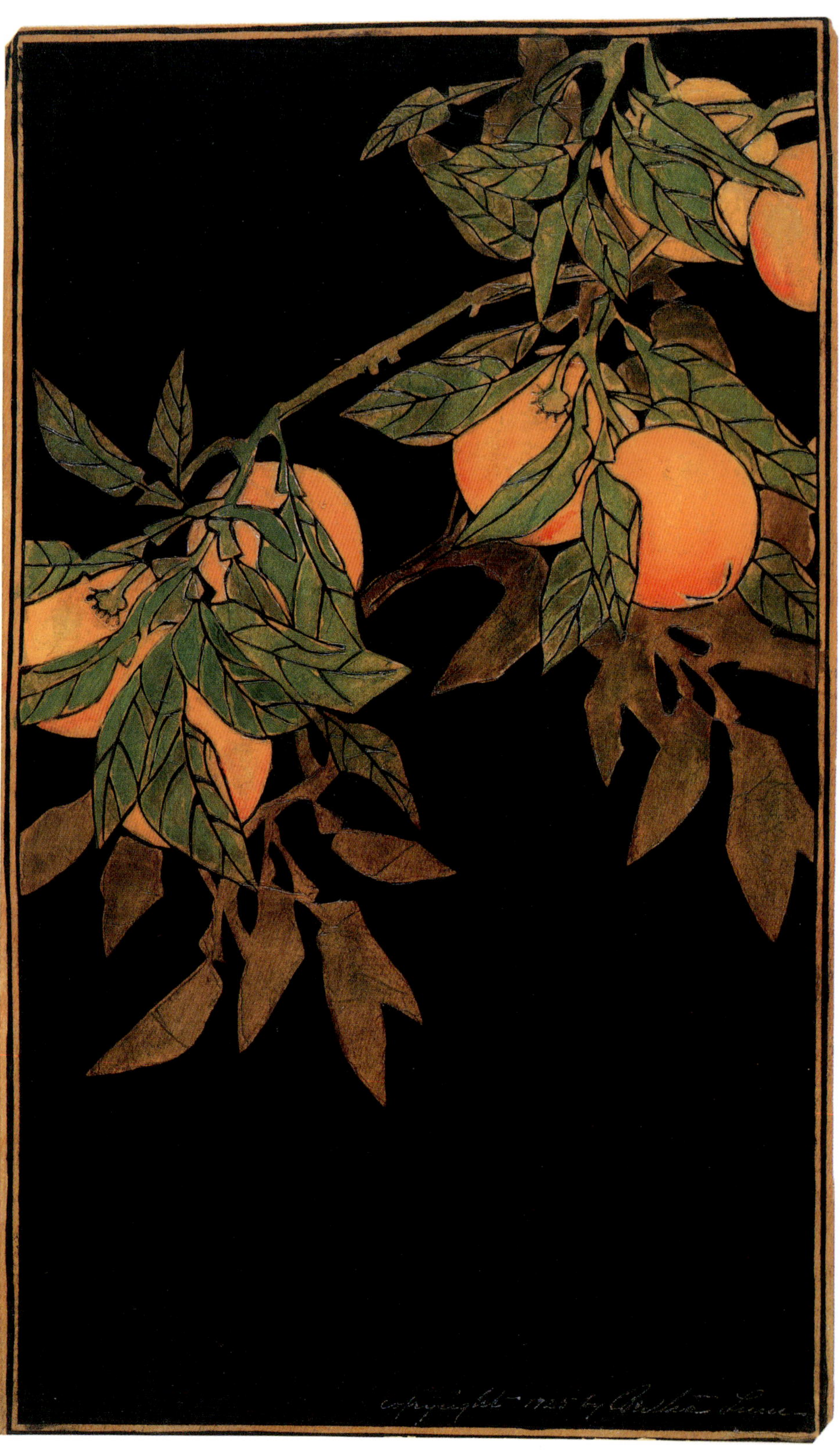
copyright 1925 by

Japan can, if she will, turn, and, gathering up that universal idealism, weld modern civilization with Oriental symbolism and lead the East if not the world. But, instead, she is flooding the world with cheap toys, exporting embroideries that have neither color, workmanship or design to recommend them. The best ivory carver in Japan runs a push-cart and the few block cutters and printers are hunting for work, and one asks why color-prints of any value are no longer produced.[157]

THE INVENTION OF "RAISED-LINE" PRINTS

The Lums moved from Minneapolis to San Francisco in 1917 or 1918.[158] By 1928, around the time Burt Lum moved his practice to Los Angeles, he and Bertha, who spent more time in Asia than in America, were divorced. Between 1923 and 1926 Bertha Lum and her daughters lived in Peking and during this time she invented the hand-colored "raised-line" print, a technique whose "secret" she jealously guarded during her lifetime (fig. 113). Learning from the Chinese method of woodblock printing, she found a new way to use the carved printing block: the paper is laid on a block that has been carved so as to leave the outlines of the image in relief, in the manner of the Japanese key block. But in this case it is not the block that is inked, but rather the paper: after the paper is pressed into the carved depressions, the ink is brushed onto the raised lines. When removed from the block, the paper retains the texture of the raised lines and depressions. The depressed areas of the print are then hand colored. There are some similarities with the textured effect of a rare style of oversized Japanese print called "stone-rubbing picture" (*ishizuri-e*), dated to the late eighteenth century. Lum's 1925 *Branch of Oranges* also resembles a famous set of decorative black-printed bird and flower prints by Itō Jakuchū (1716–1800), designed in imitation of stone rubbings, which were originally published in 1771 and reprinted around 1900.[159] Lum commuted between Peking and her home in Pasadena (her studio was in Hollywood) from 1929 until World War Two, exhibiting

113. Bertha Lum, *Branch of Oranges*, 1925. Relief print with hand color. The Fine Arts Museums of San Francisco, Achenbach Foundation for Graphic Arts, Gift of Mr. and Mrs. Edouard J. Bourbuisson

regularly in China and America. Her last dated prints, suggestively titled *Brandied Mice* and *Green Dragon Cocktail,* were made in 1937. (According to her son-in-law, she was in failing health by 1938.) From 1948 to 1953 she was in Peking again, living with her daughter Peter and her son-in-law. She was placed under house arrest when the Communists took power; her daughter Catherine's husband was killed in front of their house. In 1953 she moved to Catherine's home in Genoa, and that is where she died in 1954.

Until the mid-1930s Lum was very prolific. She published two books of her own, illustrated several others, and designed at least one hundred graphic images for woodcuts, not to mention unknown numbers of paintings and raised-line images. She had favorable press until the time of her last known exhibition, in Los Angeles in 1941, but her reputation did not endure and she was soon all but forgotten, her work found only in old-fashioned California homes and antique shops.

Charles Hovey Pepper

When Charles Hovey Pepper (1864–1950) and his family arrived in Japan in 1903, they soon met up with Helen Hyde, who was by that time an old Tokyo hand (fig. 114). She advised them to follow in her footsteps by taking a house in Nikkō. There, a local hotel manager found three young women to model for the artist, and they became the subject of a set of four handsome color woodcuts (figs. 115 and 116). He also painted thirty or more watercolors in Japan, several of which are now in the Colby College Museum.[160] Like so many of his colleagues, he worked from photographs after posing his models in various settings (fig. 117).

All but unknown today, Pepper was a well-regarded watercolorist in his day and a significant force in the Boston art world. It is of special interest that throughout his long career, critics drew attention to the

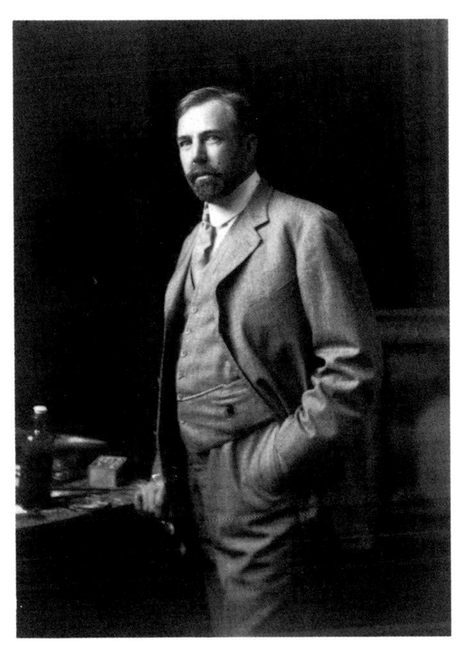

114. Charles Hovey Pepper, c. 1900–10. Photograph. Courtesy Frances Pepper Tarson

Japanese element in his work — a preference for calligraphic lines, flat planes of color, and aerial perspective (fig. 118). Born in Waterville, Maine, where his father was president of Colby College, he himself graduated from Colby in 1889 and headed for New York to spend two years at the Art Students League studying with William Merritt Chase; perhaps he even overlapped there with Helen Hyde. Between 1893 and 1899 he lived in Paris, first as a student at the Académie Julian and then working in a studio of his own in Paris, with interludes in Italy and Spain. He was evidently an independent sort, wealthy, dapper, and well traveled. It is also apparent that he came to Japanese art through France. In 1905 an admiring critic revealed that

Going one day into the Musée Guimet he saw his first Japanese prints, and the effect on him was immediate; as he says himself, they struck him pretty hard. From that time he studied them. Beginning in a small way to collect, he has since bought them with such persistence and discrimination that now he has one of the best collections in America.

"I think," he says, "I learned more about color from the prints than from any other source. More also about line and composition." It is the simple directness of the Japanese that appealed to him, as a relief from our more complex civilization.[161]

Pepper began purchasing prints of quality from Bing in Paris, and was well repaid when Bing gave him his first one-man show in 1897 at his gallery L'Art Nouveau.[162] The Peppers returned to live in Concord, Massachusetts, but in 1903 they set off for a year of travel in Asia with a long stopover in Japan. Pepper went seriously into the business of enlarging his collection of ukiyo-e prints.

From Kyoto he wrote home to his parents: "I am adding to my collection of prints and have since I came bought about 600 . . . very fine ones. I was at first discouraged when I found the price of a single good print — 30 ¥ + 50 ¥ — but [from] some men who had no shops but brought prints to one, and [from] an auction where a collection was sold,

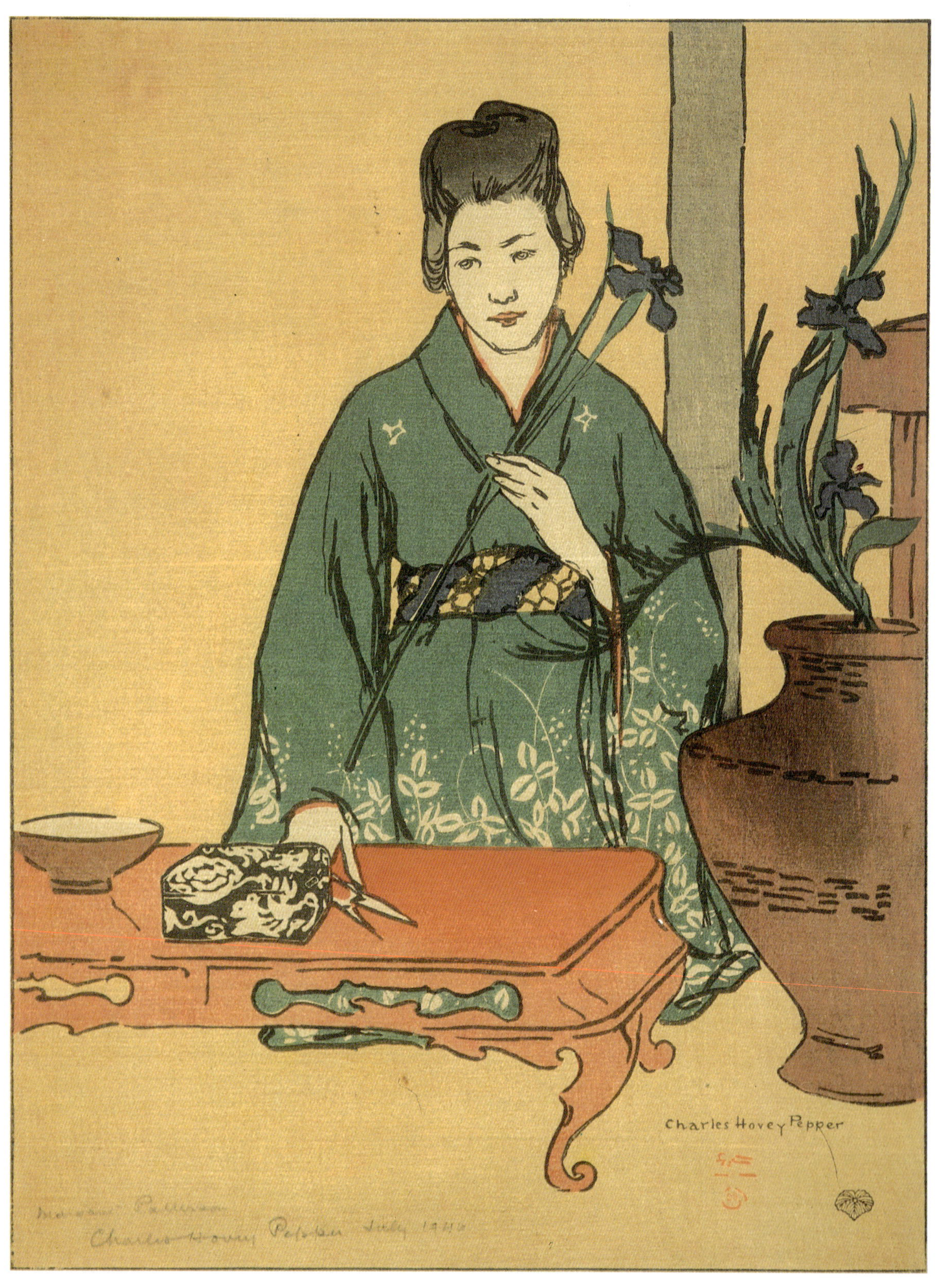
Charles Hovey Pepper

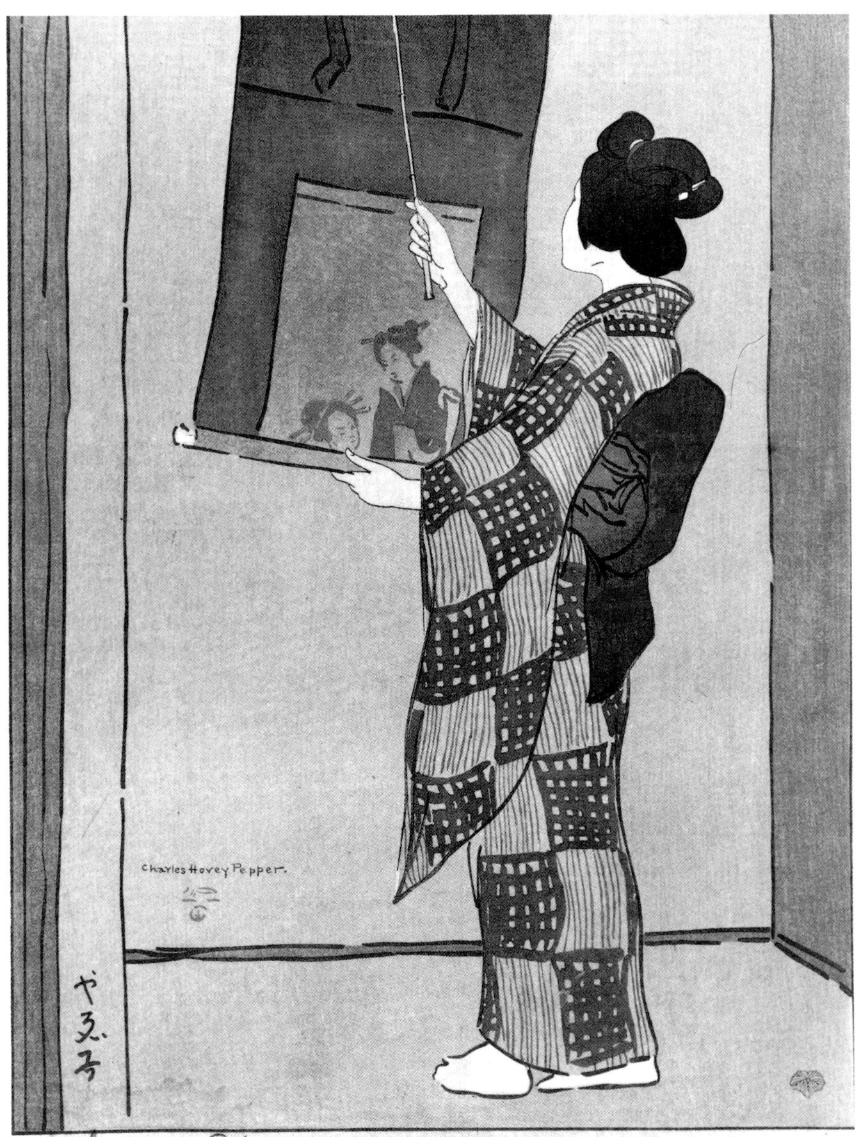

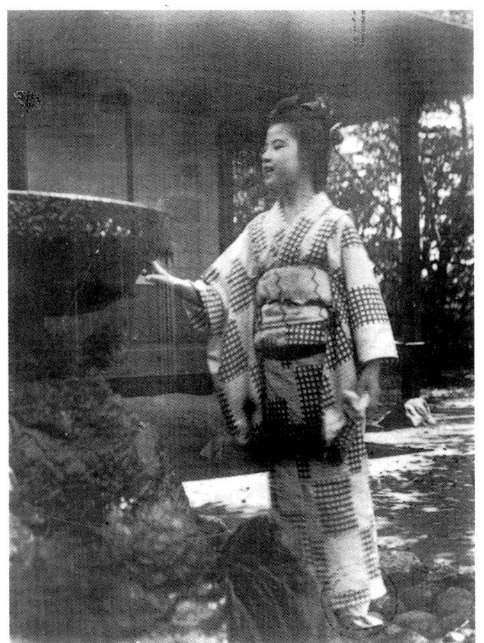

117. Charles Hovey Pepper, *Yayako in the Garden at Nikkō,* 1903. Photograph. Courtesy Frances Pepper Tarson

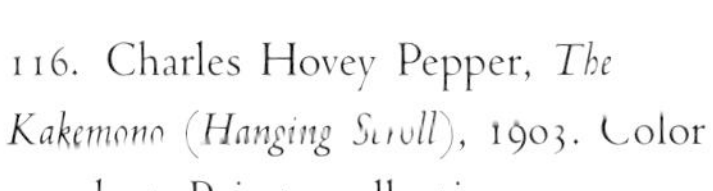

116. Charles Hovey Pepper, *The Kakemono (Hanging Scroll)*, 1903. Color woodcut. Private collection

115. Charles Hovey Pepper, *Ikebana,* 1903. Color woodcut. Rose Ann O'Connor Collection

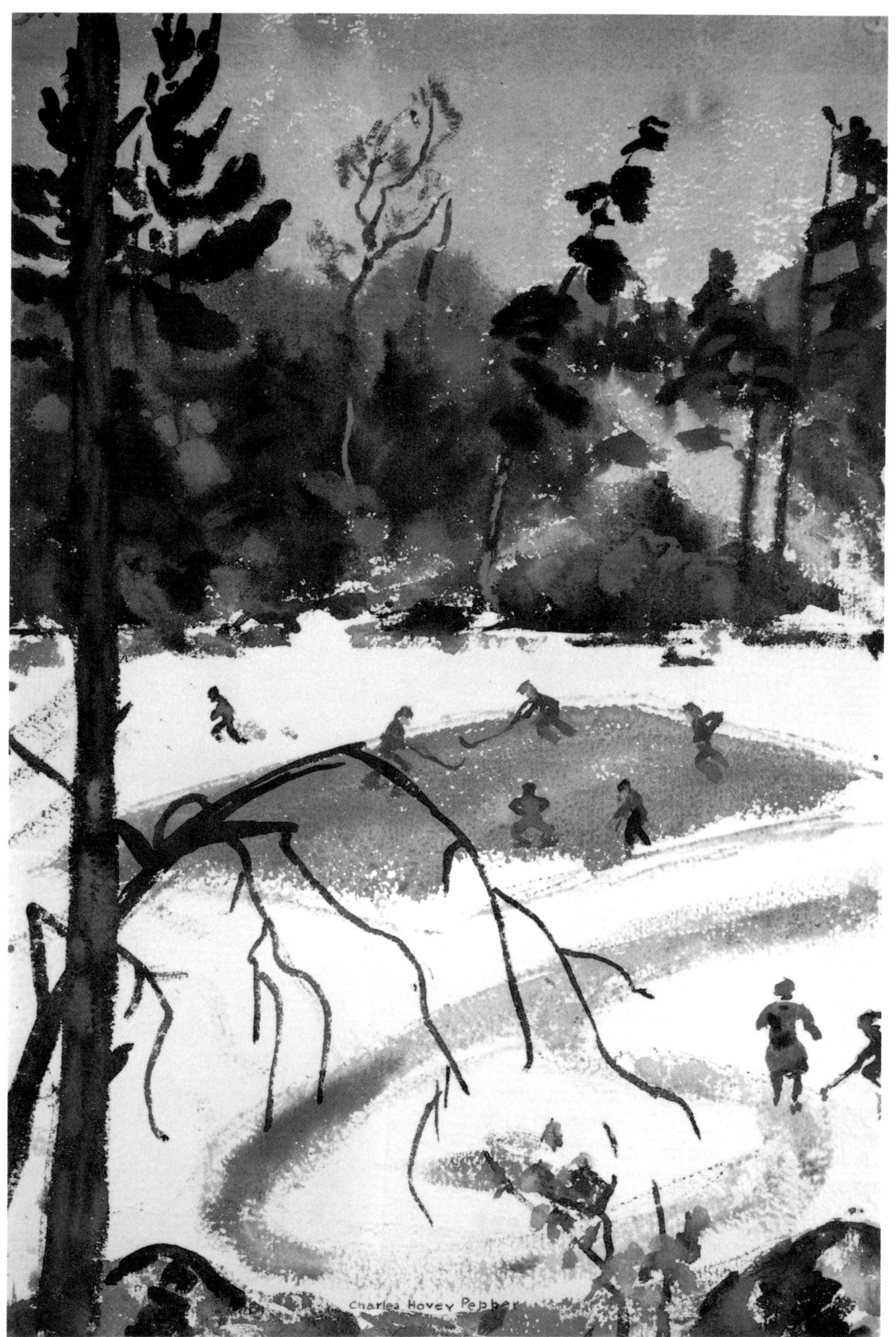
Charles Hovey Pepper

I succeeded in buying reasonably some beauties."[163] Dealers came nightly to his hotel room in Tokyo to show their wares and were surprised to discover that Pepper's son Stephen, age twelve, "displayed discriminating taste and already knew the ideographic signatures of the leading artists."[164] (Stephen, a philosopher, later became a professor of aesthetics and ethics and Chairman of the Department of Art at the University of California at Berkeley.)

Pepper's designs for woodcuts were carved, printed and published for him by none other than Kobayashi Bunshichi, whom he surely found through Hyde. His biographer also records that "he later sent this same wood-block printer a Dutch and a French water-color which, in due time, came back reproduced in a set of beautifully done prints without a trace of oriental characteristics."[165] The French example must be his best-known print, *The Conspirators* (fig. 119), presumably based on a watercolor of the same title which was shown in Tokyo in the 1906 Ueno Park exhibition of Yoshida Hiroshi's group, the Pacific Painting Society. The painting, in turn, was based on a photograph taken in Paris. His paintings were surely valued by Japanese who, not having Western art collections of their own, were still starved for the "real thing." An October 1903 issue of the new art periodical *Bijutsu shinpō* (Art News) records Pepper's comments (probably made in the course of a public lecture) on contemporary Japanese Western-style painters working in oil and watercolor.[166]

Arthur Wesley Dow's Japan diary sheds further light on Pepper's brief career as a print designer. When Dow landed in Yokohama in October 1903, his first stop, the morning after arrival, was the local branch of Kobayashi's print shop: "We were shown a print designed by Mr. Pepper—two figures in color. K. is printing them for him."[167]

Dow, who had been making woodcuts on his own for over a decade, followed up quickly, his curiosity obviously piqued. He met Pepper in Tokyo the following week at the Hotel Metropole ("a very shabby

118. Charles Hovey Pepper, *Skating, Concord,* undated. Watercolor on paper. Museum of Fine Arts, Boston, Anonymous gift

building in Western style"): "He has been making a set of figure prints, the work being done by Kobayashi. K. charged him 30 yen for the first 100 and 20 yen for each 100 after that, K. to keep the blocks." A few days later the process itself was demonstrated for Dow—his first exposure to the authentic technique: "Spent the morning at Mr. Pepper's seeing a printer work. He sat upon the floor with the blocks in front of him. . . . He was printing a set of Harunobu blocks that Mr. Pepper had bought."[168]

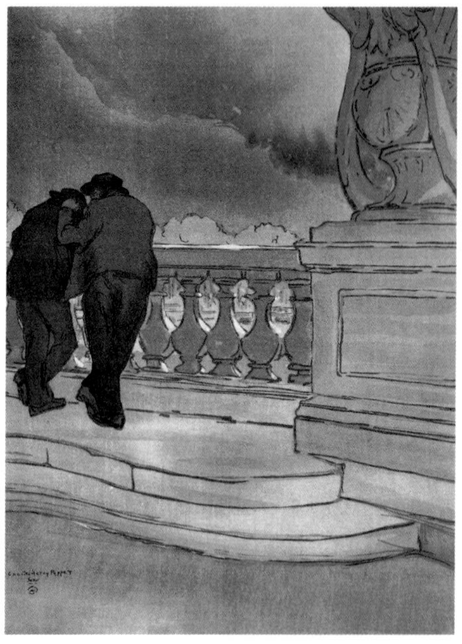

119. Charles Hovey Pepper, *The Conspirators*, c. 1906. Color woodcut. Museum of Fine Arts, Boston, Bequest of John T. Spaulding

In 1905, following his return to Concord, Pepper wrote *Japanese Color Prints,* a book on the technique and history of ukiyo-e.[169] It was published by Walter Kimball, whose Boston gallery showed Pepper's Japan watercolors. Although modest in scope, the book is likely to have been widely read at the time. Pepper begins with an apology for treating such a humble art form, and then gives an exceptionally clear and thorough description of the technique of printmaking, singling out the block cutter for special praise. The appeal of the prints to Westerners is fourfold, he says: (1) simplicity: "They eliminate all unessentials" (this phrase appealed to Frank Lloyd Wright, who used it in his own writings on Japanese prints); (2) because the artist works with a brush, the composition conveys a fluid linear rhythm; (3) prints teach good balance of color masses; and (4) their color harmonies and contrasts are both subtle and daring. Here he sounds a theme familiar from Arthur Wesley Dow's 1899 *Composition.*

Pepper continued to buy prints at auction in New York, and this interest may have accounted in part for his deepening friendship with John T. Spaulding (1870–1948).[170] Both John and his brother William (1865–1937) emerged as serious ukiyo-e print collectors around 1910. (It was the Spaulding fortune that supported Frank Lloyd Wright's print purchases in Japan in 1913; Wright designed—but never executed—a print viewing room for the Spauldings in 1919.) Pepper and the younger Spaulding were active on the exhibition committee of the Boston Art

Club, helping to champion modernism in an arch-conservative town. In January 1920 they presented an exhibition of woodblock prints by Americans; works by the newly formed society known as Provincetown Printers (including Edna Boies Hopkins) dominated the show.

Aesthetic Reform and Japanese Art

Around the turn of the century, at the peak of the Arts and Crafts movement in America, Japanese art was enlisted in the service of social responsibility and the search for an indigenous, organic American culture. Reacting against industrialization and Victorian eclecticism, reformers with a social message who chose art as their medium gave birth to societies and schools of design. Designs for better living were sought by architects like Frank Lloyd Wright, designing for the future, and by art teachers in classrooms across the country. Art schools began teaching a broad curriculum of arts and crafts; Arthur Wesley Dow, who taught at the School of the Boston Museum of Fine Arts, the newly founded Pratt Institute in Brooklyn, and the Department of Fine Arts at Columbia University Teachers College, exemplifies the ideal teacher for these modern times.

Arthur Wesley Dow

At age twenty-seven Arthur Wesley Dow (1857–1922) left his hometown of Ipswich, Massachusetts, for five years of art study abroad at the Académie Julian and at Pont-Aven, in Brittany. However, it was not until his return to Boston, where he met Ernest Fenollosa at the Museum of Fine Arts, that his interest in Japanese painting and prints was awakened. The two became fast friends and collaborated on theories of aesthetics

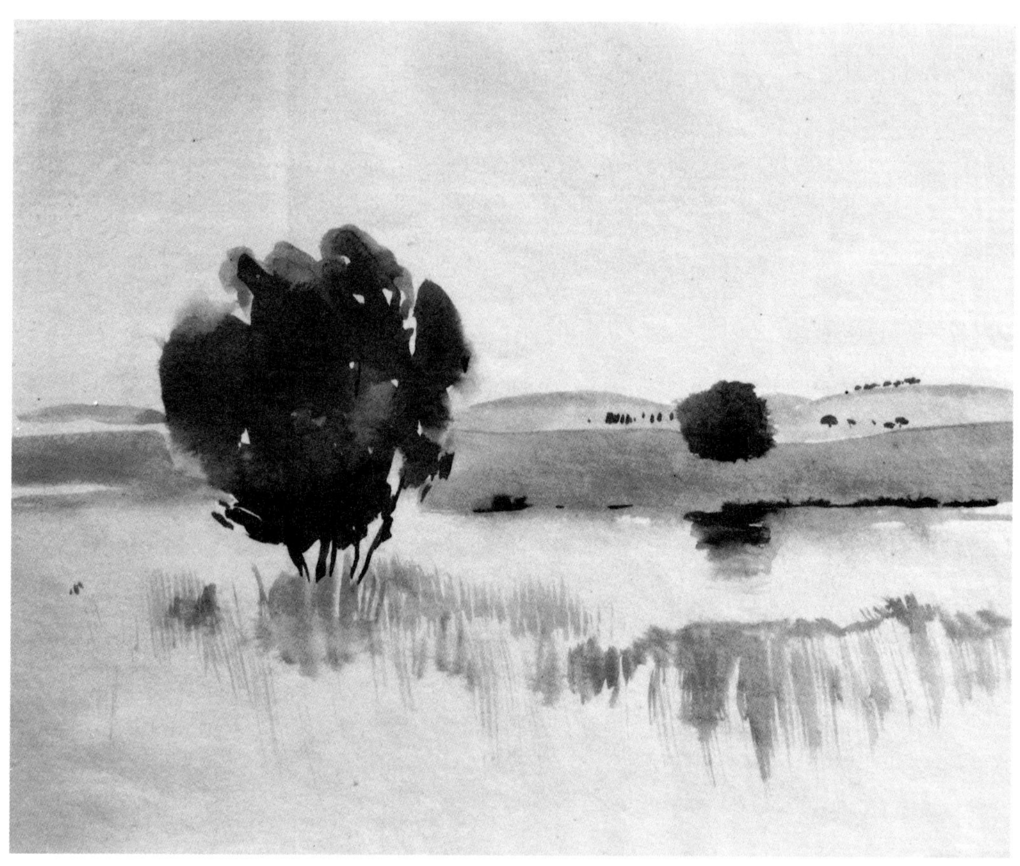

120. Arthur Wesley Dow, *Pond,* c. 1893. Ink-wash from sketchbook. Ipswich Historical Society, MA

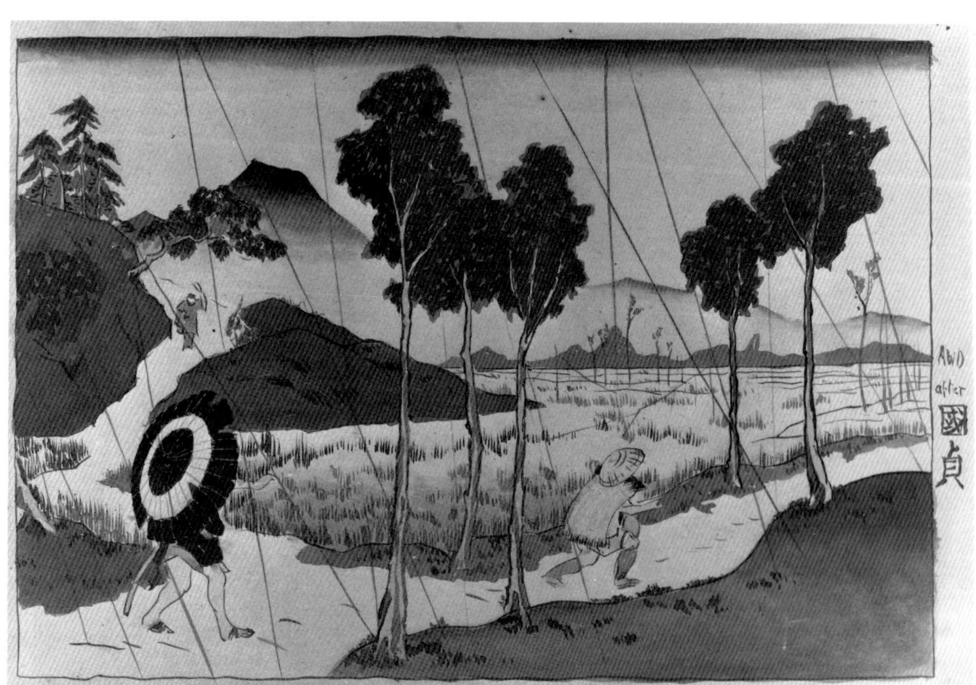

121. Arthur Wesley Dow, Copy of Utagawa Kunisada (1786–1864), *Act V.* From the series *Kanadehon Chūshingura,* early 1830s. Watercolor on paper. Frank J. Dowd, Jr., Collection

and art education for many years to come. Both men were drawn to the abstraction inherent in Japanese art and rejected the imitation of nature typical of the West.

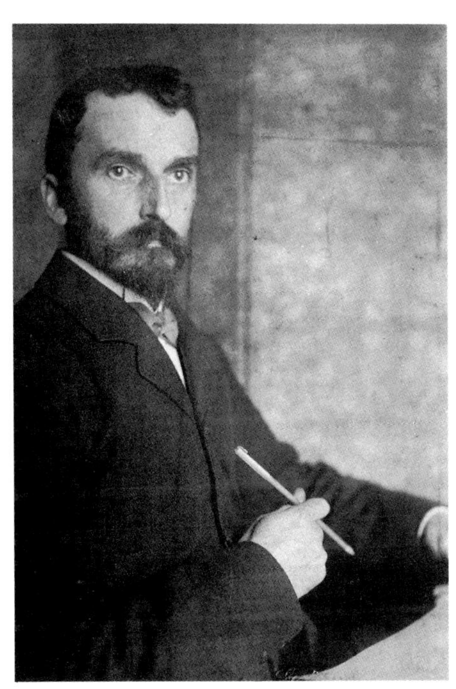

122. Gertrude Käsebier, *Arthur Wesley Dow,* c. 1900. Platinum print. Mr. and Mrs. George N. Wright Collection

In the early 1890s Dow was initiating the Japanese splashed-ink (*haboku*) technique of painting and was copying Japanese woodblock-printed designs (figs. 120 and 121). Japanese art became a major source of inspiration to him — a key to his liberation from Western naturalism and to a new mode of self-expression. The thrill of discovery is palpable in a letter he wrote in 1893: "At dusk I go down to the museum and look over [Japanese illustrated] books. We have classified a large file now, separated into *straight line* and *composition.* The mere looking them over is a great stimulus — I feel an actual power coming from them, and shall begin now to put this power into my landscapes and into designs of some kind in color and line."[171]

Dow soon began to build his own collection of Japanese prints, which eventually numbered into the thousands. About five hundred of the best of these were sold at auction in 1923, after his death. The carefully annotated and illustrated catalogue of the sale gives a vivid picture of his patterns of collecting, ranging from a rare early eighteenth-century standing beauty by Kaigetsudō Doshin, to landscapes by Hiroshige. Included were many printed books and manuscripts useful for his classroom exercises: books of kimono patterns, designs for lacquerware and sword ornaments, even architectural drawings. The catalogue was prepared by his friend of thirty years and near neighbor in Salem, Matsuki Bunkio (see page 53). A measure of the collection's quality can be judged by the discriminating New York buyers who were present: the Metropolitan Museum's Bosch Reitz, Howard Mansfield, photographer Arnold Genthe, and Harold G. Henderson (1889–1974), who was to become a professor of Japanese language and art history at Columbia University. Also in the bidding were Harvard graduate Arthur Davison Ficke (1883–1945), an attorney, poet, and print connoisseur from

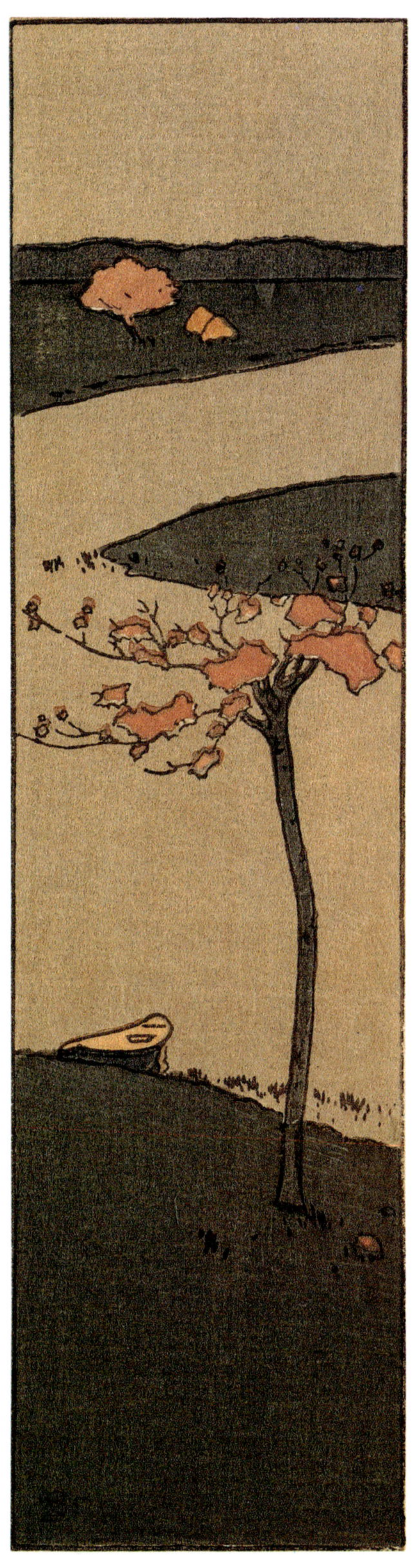

123. Arthur Wesley Dow, *Bend of a River*, c. 1895. Color woodcut. Museum of Fine Arts, Boston, Gift of Mrs. Ethelyn H. Putnam

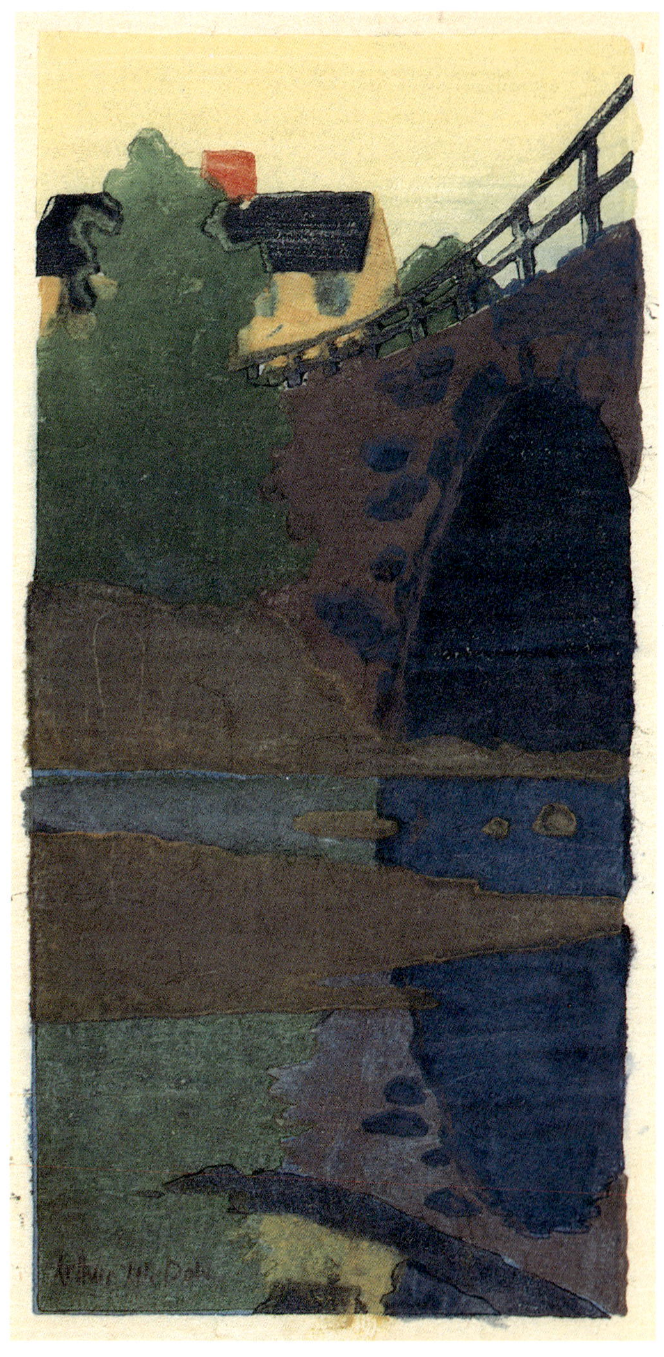

124. Arthur Wesley Dow, *Ipswich Bridge*, c. 1893–95. Color woodcut. The Jane Voorhees Zimmerli Art Museum, Rutgers, The State University of New Jersey, Ralph and Barbara Voorhees American Art Fund

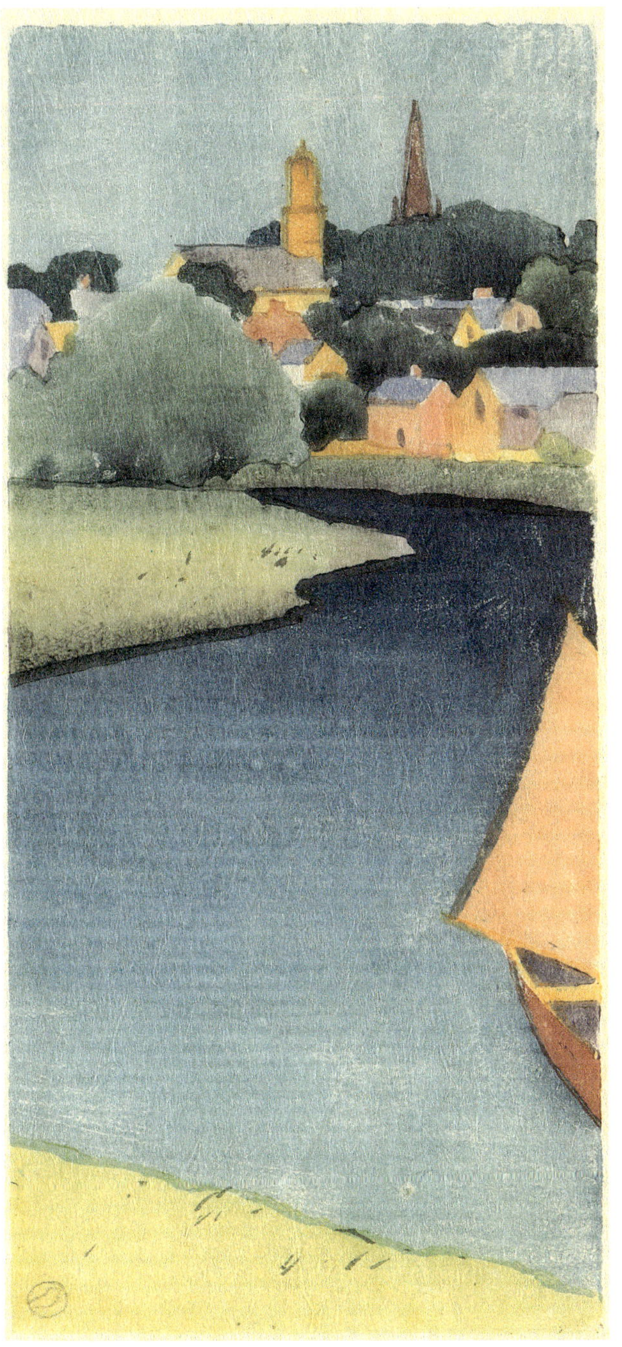

125. Arthur Wesley Dow, *View in Ipswich (Sailboat)*, c. 1893–95. Color woodcut. Museum of Fine Arts, Boston, Gift of Mrs. Ethelyn H. Putnam

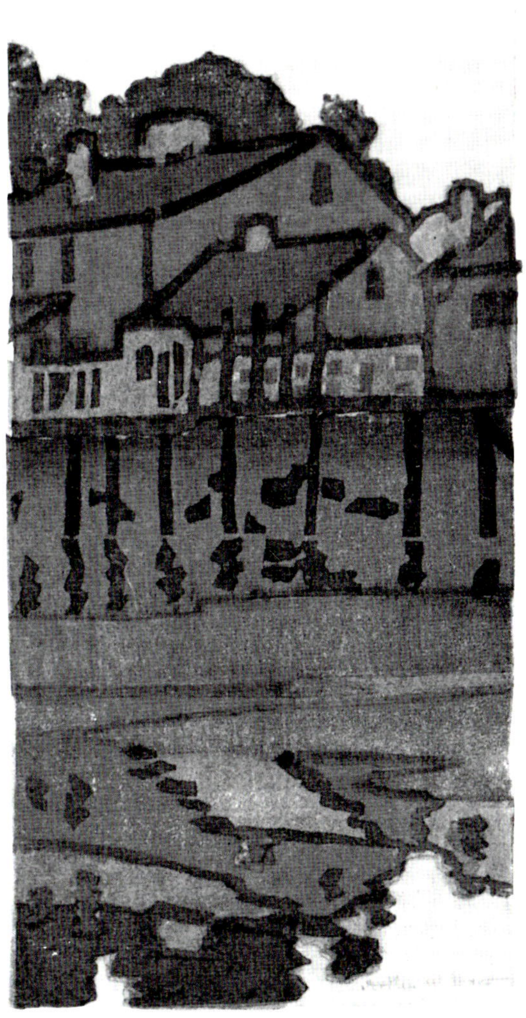

126. Arthur Wesley Dow, *Above the Old Bridge, Ipswich*, c. 1893–95. Color woodcut. The Metropolitan Museum of Art, New York, Gift of Mrs. W. L. Putnam, 1942

Davenport, Iowa, who wrote *Chats on Japanese Prints* (1915) and whose collection was later dispersed through public auction, and Harvard-trained Arthur B. Duel (1870–1936), a New York ear, nose, and throat surgeon whose 4,000 prints entered the Fogg Art Museum in 1933 — in short, almost all of the serious collectors.[172] In addition, the Dow estate deposited at Columbia University Teachers College and now in the C. V. Starr East Asian Library numbers some 200 titles of Japanese woodblock printed books in approximately 600 volumes.

The calligraphic line of Japanese art was a stimulus to Dow and he insisted that his students practice line drawing with Japanese materials — namely, Japanese paper, brush, and ink (fig. 122). Dow had a good teacher in Fenollosa, and he had the Bigelow and Fenollosa-Weld collections to guide him, but judging by ukiyo-e still extant from his estate, he freely purchased reprints and gaudy late designs if they could be useful to him in his work.

Fenollosa made clear his admiration for Dow when he hired him as a part-time assistant in the fall of 1893. Two years later Dow moved to New York to teach at Pratt, but in September 1897 he was appointed keeper of Japanese Paintings and Prints at the Museum of Fine Arts for two years.[173] In 1895 Fenollosa staged an exhibition of woodcuts by Dow in the corridor of the museum's Japanese gallery. Dow had been experimenting with woodcuts since 1891; his small vertical *Bend of a River* is overtly Japanese not only in its shape but in its flat planes and decorative curving rhythms (fig. 123). Dow also created what he called a "picture book" of woodcuts, a portfolio of single-sheet prints showing views along the Ipswich River, and claimed as his immediate stimulus Hiroshige's series the *Fifty-three Stations of the Tōkaidō* (see fig. 134; figs. 124–26). These prints are tiny, about 5 inches high by 2¼ inches wide. Why so small? Because unlike Helen Hyde or Japanese printmakers, Dow had to work through every step of the printing process himself — he was the designer, carver, and printer. Timid about handling a large block of wood, he chose a small piece of soft pine (fig. 127). Although a Japanese carver and printer could work with lightning speed, producing dozens of prints in a single day, the process was very slow and time-consuming for Dow. On the other hand, he was riding the crest of the Arts and Crafts movement and admired the personal craftsmanship involved in making woodcuts; it was a way of proclaiming his self-sufficiency in the face of modern standardization and mechanization. Handcraftsmanship was the Arts and Crafts ideal, buoyed by the belief that working with one's hands produced spiritual benefits. Describing Dow's work, Fenollosa boasted: "It is the work of the individual artist from start to finish. . . . Here there is no unsympathetic machinery, no division of labor between hand and hand, no apprentice's botching; neither is there any publisher to interpose his superior conception of the public taste."[174] In this respect, of course, Dow's prints are very un-Japanese; the impersonal division of labor is what ensured high quality and mass production of Japanese prints.

One obvious model for the miniature vertical compositions and even the use of monochrome color schemes (all blue, for example) that Dow used are the little "pictures within pictures" in prints by Kuniyoshi (1797–1861), Toyokuni, and others, of which he owned many versions (fig. 128). Hiroshige's Tokyo river scenes in the medium *tanzaku* size from his series *Famous Places in the Eastern Capital,* while larger in scale, provide another point of reference in terms of subject and composition (fig. 129). By the late nineteenth century miniature replicas of Hiroshige's popular series were in production for the tourist trade; Dow may have collected these, as well.

Dow was attracted to the woodcut medium as a good way to develop a mastery of composition, which he defined as the art of putting together line, color, and *notan* (contrasting masses of dark and light), in an expressive and harmonious manner. These were the elements he admired in Japanese art. Trained as a painter, he called his woodcuts "wood-painting" and they presented to him the challenge of creating a new

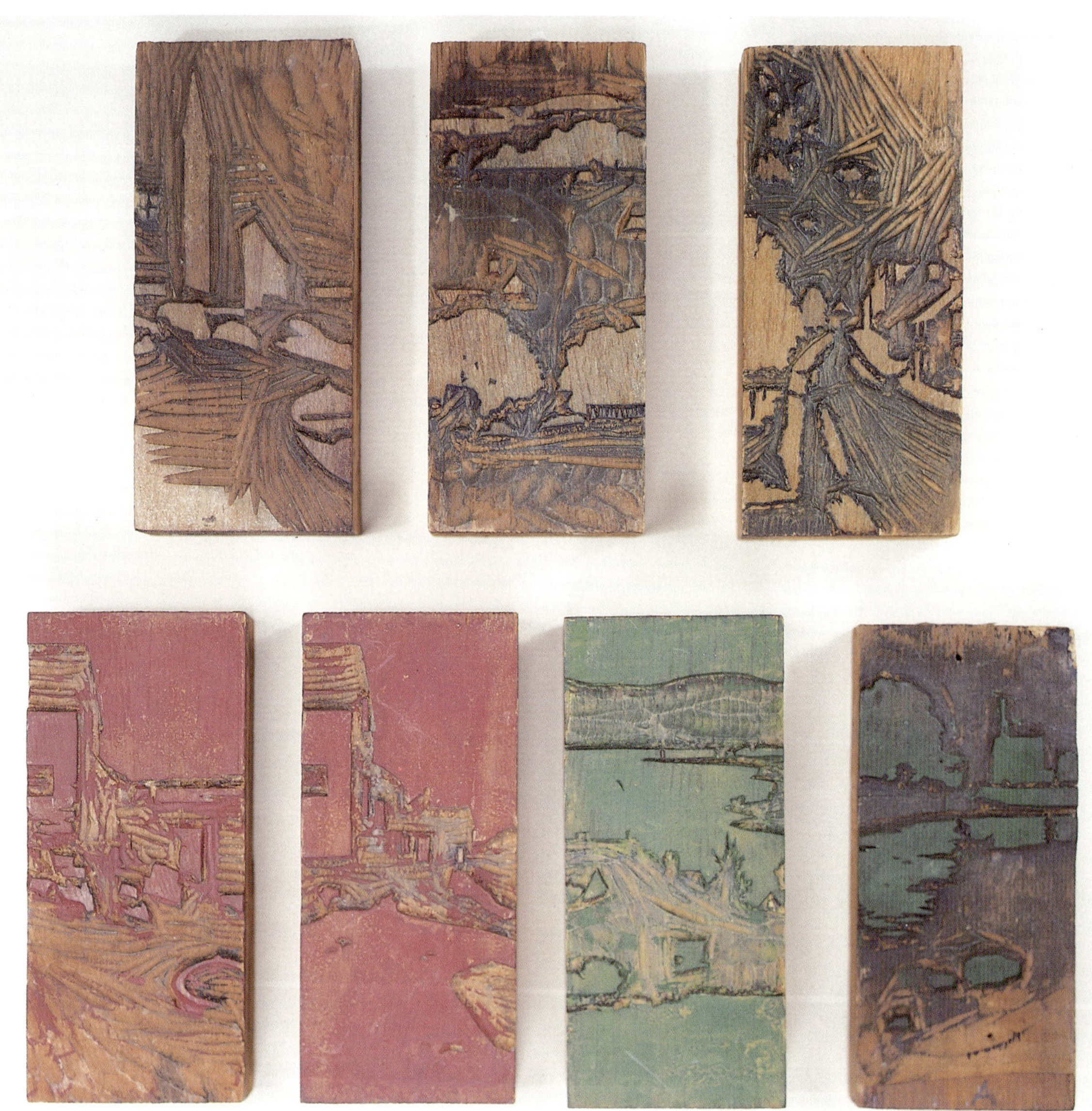

127. Arthur Wesley Dow, Color blocks for Ipswich prints, c. 1893–95. Frank J. Dowd, Jr., Collection

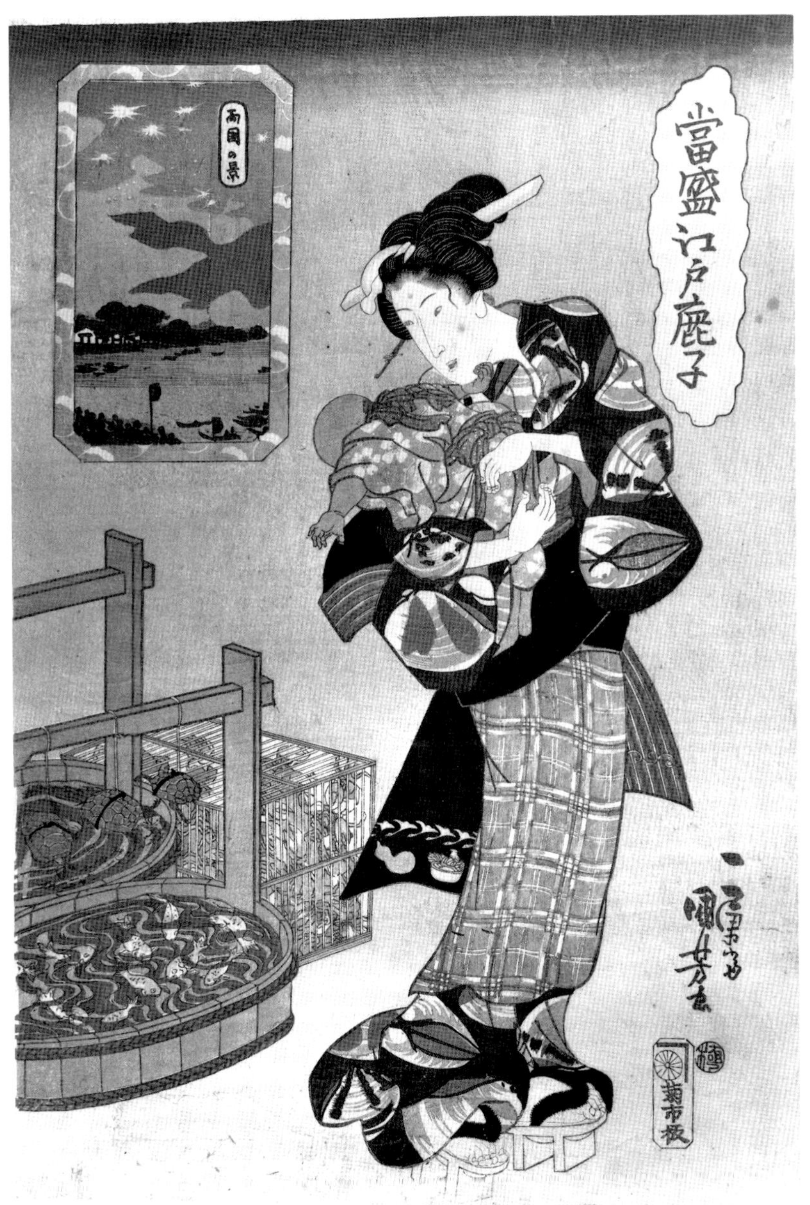

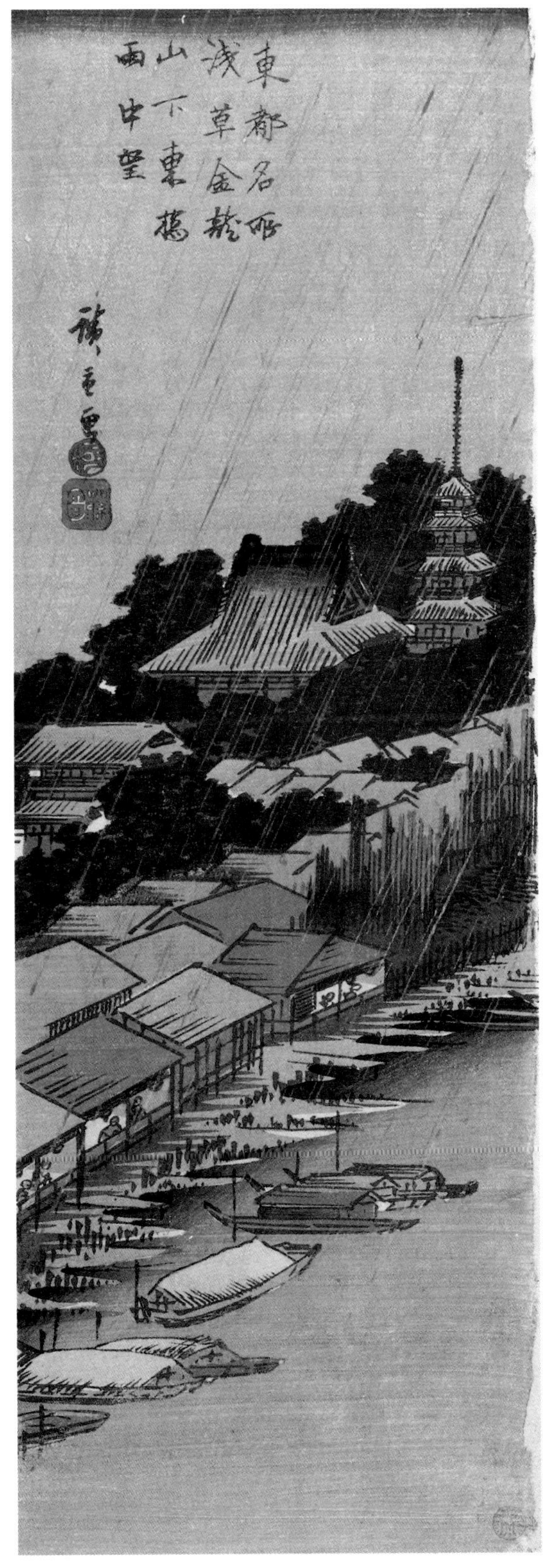

128. Utagawa Kuniyoshi, *View of Ryōgoku: Tōmori Edo Kanoko,* 1830s. Color woodcut. Frank J. Dowd, Jr., Collection

129. Utagawa Hiroshige, *Asakusa Temple Seen Through the Rain.* From the series *Famous Places in the Eastern Capital (Tōto meisho),* c. 1838–39. Color woodcut. The Metropolitan Museum of Art, New York, Rogers Fund, 1914. Formerly Spaulding Collection

color scheme on every print, from light gray monochromes to deep rich colors: no two are alike. As for the use of color, he wrote that the

method of expression would lose all its charm if obliged to serve the ends of literal representation. Its strength lies in free interpretation, in a playing with colors, so to speak, rather than in a forced realism. It lends itself readily to a suggestive rendering of effects of nature; a twilight, moonlight, sun and shadow, rain, gray days and morning mists, but it as easily permits a departure into a purely imaginative treatment as brilliant and unreal as stained glass. If you tire of painting a river blue you can, in the next proof, change it to purple or yellow. . . . But this of course entails a new color-composition, a new scheme in the arrangements of dark and light masses and hues. The constant exercise of the inventive faculty, and the study of line involved in cutting everything in the design to a definite shape upon the block, give to the process an educational value of importance to the artist.[175]

In approaching the printmaking process as a willful educational experiment, he is again very un-Japanese. Within a given edition of two hundred or so prints, the Japanese craftsman would brush the colors onto the woodblocks with monotonous regularity. The goal was to have each and every print look alike. If one does find significant variation in colors, it is most likely a decision made by the publisher. It does not mean that the Japanese printer, a technician, was experimenting with different effects. Self-expression of that sort was not encouraged; the printer was low man on the totem pole, in any case.

Dow was a typical American pragmatist; he was concerned with the practical and technical value of Japanese art. Turning to art education and lecturing as a means of spreading his synthesis of Eastern and Western aesthetics, he published *Composition* in 1899. It is a how-to design manual for art students and teachers to train judgment in art through a series of exercises in line, mass, and color, complete with demonstrations of opposition, transition, subordination, and symmetry (fig. 130). The

130. Arthur Wesley Dow, page from *Composition: A Series of Exercises Selected from a New System of Art Education,* 1899. The Fogg Art Library, Harvard University, Cambridge, MA. Gift of Denman W. Ross. Copy inscribed by Dow to Ross

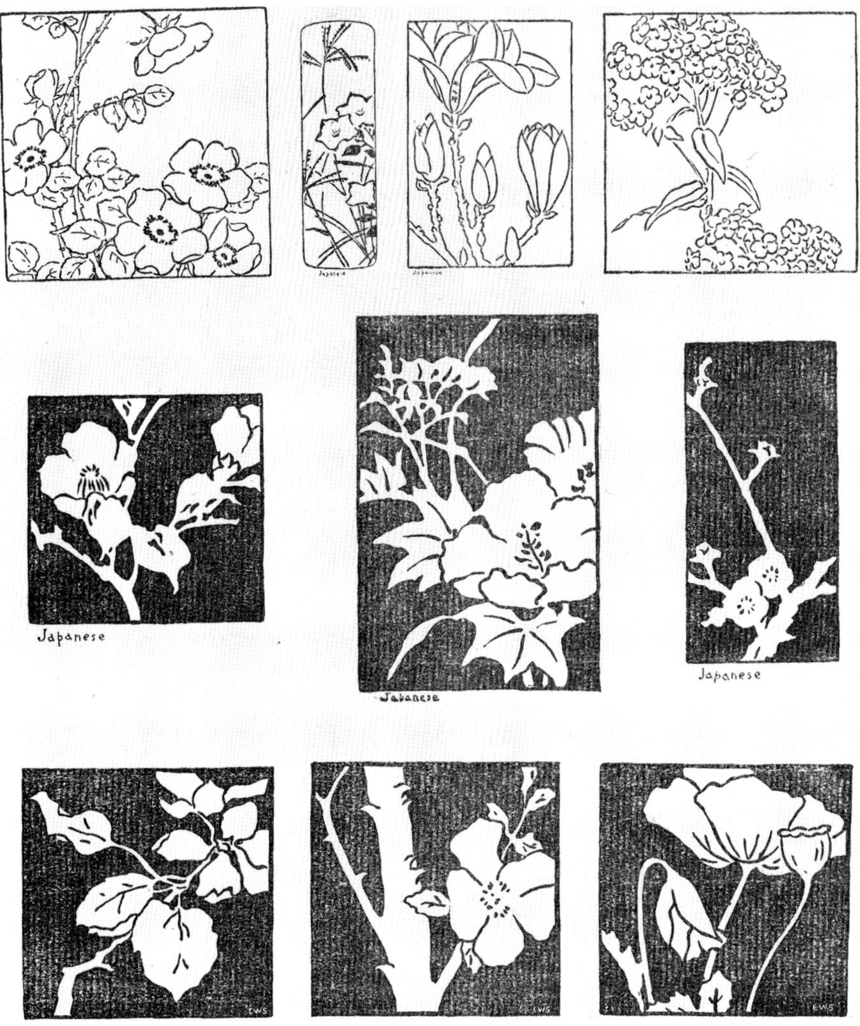

book was a huge success and went into twenty editions by 1938. Though most of his examples were taken from Oriental art, the fundamental principle that art is essentially the harmonious arrangement of lines and colors was one that was circulating among young radicals in France during his period of study in Pont-Aven, where he knew Gauguin.[176]

In 1893 he initiated a two-month summer course at Ipswich that was attended by students and future artists from all over the country. To help implement his theories he published three packets of "Ipswich Prints," intended for public schools, in editions of eight hundred using a foot-powered press.[177] Issued in 1902 and 1903, many of these engraved facsimiles were based on Japanese art in his own collection. The packet with black and white designs, for example, draws on various woodblock-printed *ehon,* or "picture books" (figs. 131 and 132). *Ehon* were themselves intended as copybooks for Japanese artists, illustrating earlier Chinese and Japanese painted models. In another Ipswich packet, the detail of trees and rocks from a design by Hiroshige (fig. 133) is probably taken from Dow's badly damaged impression (fig. 134). Dow's darkened Hiroshige may even be a late nineteenth-century replica. By that time there was already a large market in forgeries. Greedy Japanese dealers, catering to the huge foreign demand, bought up old original printing blocks and ran off new impressions, which they then aged artificially by soaking them in soot water.

Reproductions of woodblock prints by all the great masters of ukiyo-e were on the market by 1885; often dealers would cleverly mix them in with genuine examples, so they were difficult to detect.[178] Serious ukiyo-e scholarship in the West was very slow in coming because of language barriers, and early collectors had little to guide them. This having been said, it should be noted that a good reproduction might be just as useful to a Western artist (who was likely to be an easy target for an unscrupulous dealer) as an original; it was the subject, design and color that mattered, more than the age or authenticity.

When Dow finally went to Japan for three months in the fall of 1903, he was more than ready to see the country through the eyes of Hokusai and Hiroshige, but he was no romantic (fig. 135). He did, of course, buy Japanese prints — over a thousand by the end of his visit; here was just the sort of foreigner who kept ukiyo-e dealers in business. In the end, even he had to confess, "There is a great abundance of Hiroshiges — mostly bad. I am almost tired of the sight of them." But he was also a man with a mission; his goal was to visit every art school in Tokyo and Kyoto and observe the classes in design and drawing. On the whole he was not impressed; to his disgust he found they had for the most part

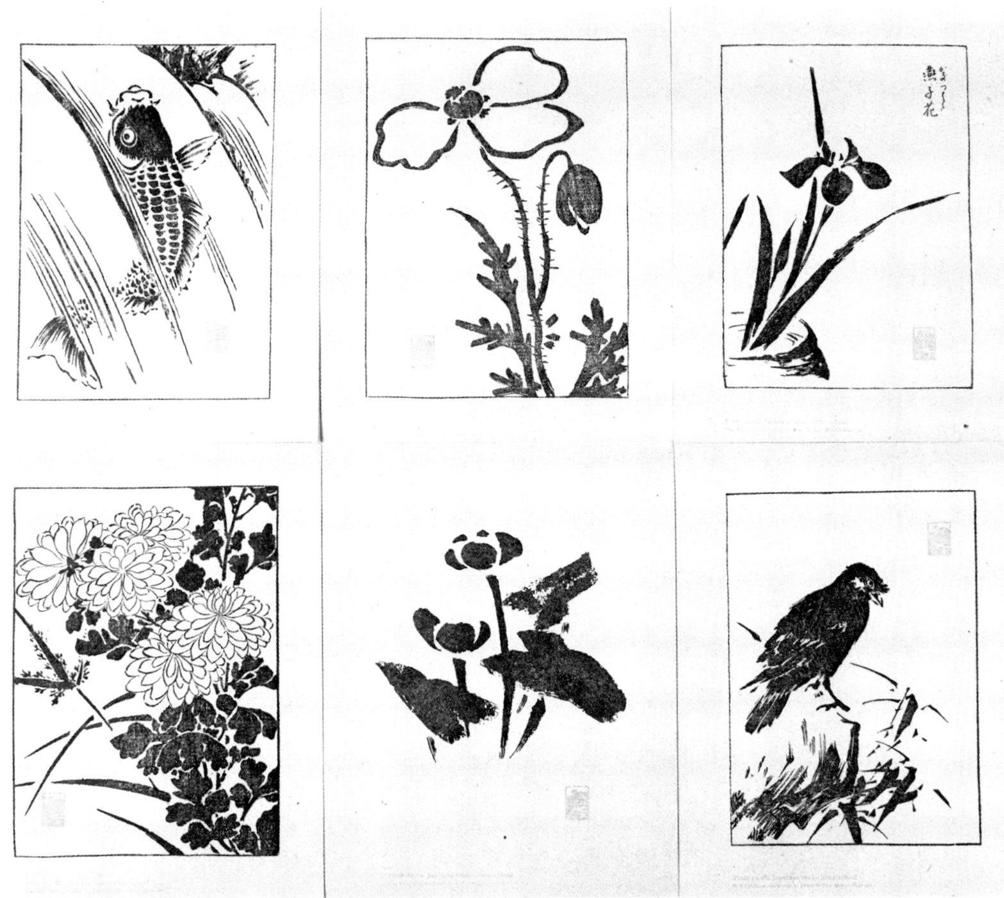

131. Arthur Wesley Dow, top, left to right: *Fish Leaping a Waterfall; Poppy; Iris;* bottom, left to right: *Chrysanthemum; Lily; Raven, Old Chinese.* From *Ipswich Prints,* 1902. Ink and engraving on paper. Mr. and Mrs. George N. Wright Collection

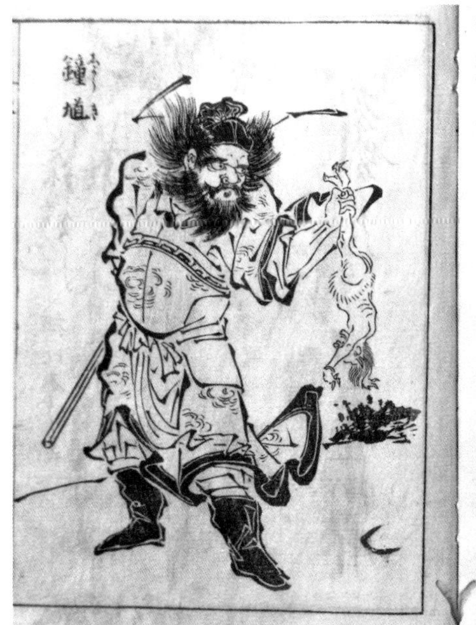

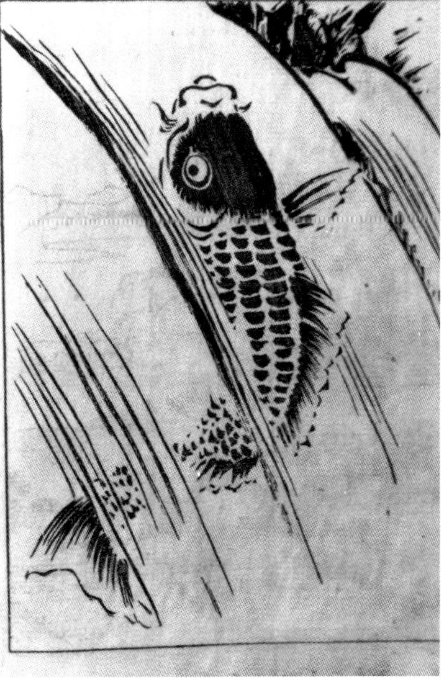

132. Terai Shigefusa (active 1744–64), *Shoki the Demon Queller; Fish Leaping a Waterfall.* From *Ehon jūyo* (Picture Book of Gathered Leaves), 1751, 1. Woodblock printed book. Ipswich Historical Society, MA

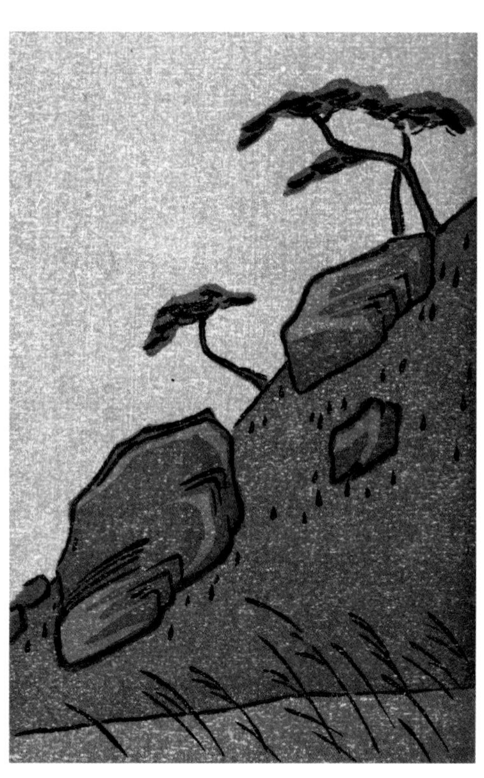

133. Arthur Wesley Dow, *Color Scheme from a Print by Hiroshige.* From *Ipswich Prints,* second set, 1902. Ink and engraving on paper. Print Collection, Miriam and Ira Wallach Division of Art, Prints and Photographs, The New York Public Library, Astor, Lenox and Tilden Foundations

134. Utagawa Hiroshige, *Hakone.* From the series *Fifty-three Stations of the Tōkaidō (Gyōsho),* c. 1840. Color woodcut. Frank J. Dowd, Jr., Collection

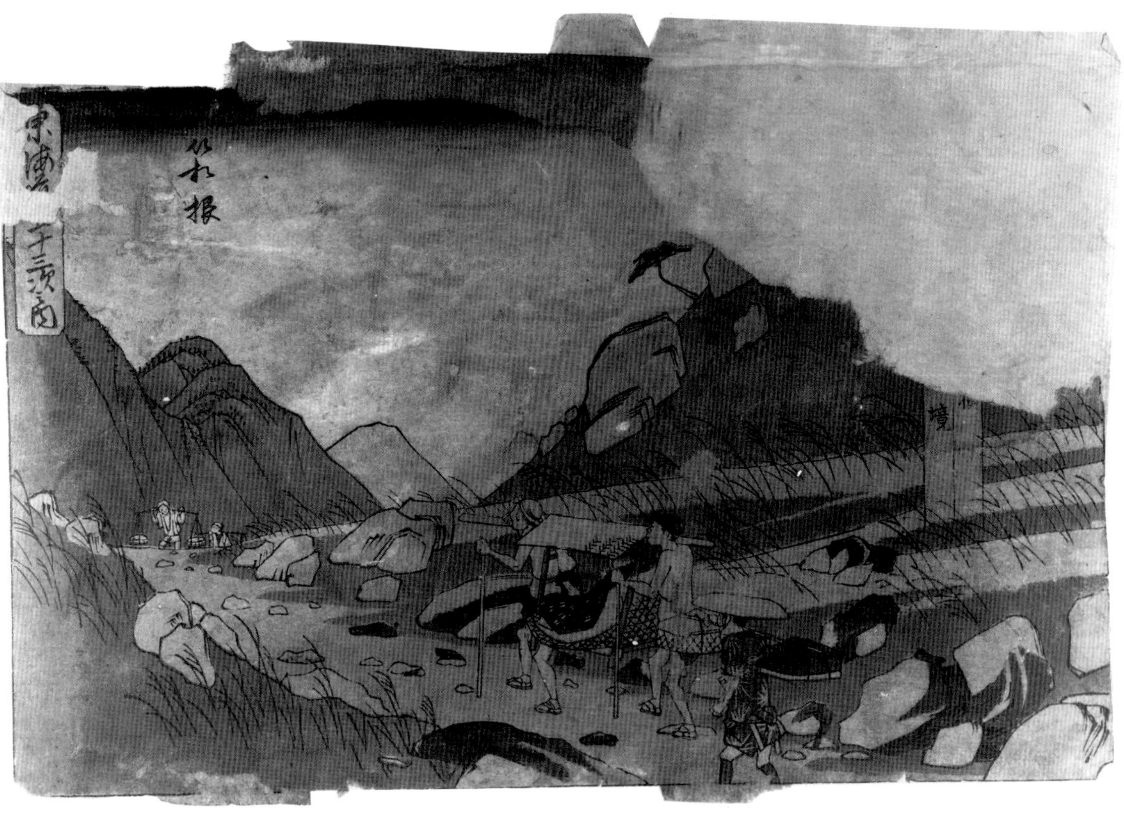

135. Arthur and Minnie Dow at Kasuga Shrine, Nara, 1903. Blue-tinted photograph. Ipswich Historical Society, MA

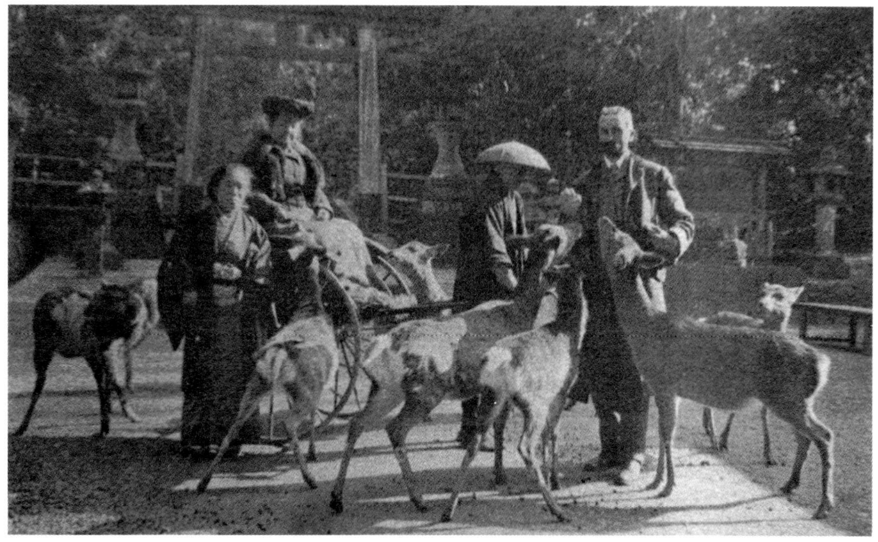

given up the old Japanese techniques for new Western ones, and he took it upon himself to deliver his views in a public lecture. As reported by the Japanese press, he claimed to have been influenced most by the early ink painters Sesshū and Nōami. American art education, he said, had suffered from the habit of learning by rote copying rather than learning art as a craft, or skill; Americans could learn from Japanese art, especially as regards the integration of painting and architecture in the interiors of the temples of Kyoto. He hoped that his own aesthetic theories might improve the general level of American society. "If I could give you a word of advice," he concluded, "then it is that you should maintain and study your own remarkable indigenous art forms. It is of no benefit to the Japanese to be intoxicated with Western art and to forget what is good about Japanese art."[179]

Dow was a diligent student, taking advantage of every opportunity to learn. He had access, through Fenollosa, to the great private collections. And he took evening painting lessons with Kano Tomonobu, which he recorded with fascination in his diary, even though the old man tended to ramble on about Fenollosa, Bigelow, and Helen Hyde. Through Charles Pepper he was introduced to his first demonstration of proper woodblock printing. He then hired Hyde's printer, Murata Shōjirō, to give him two all-day lessons, starting with how to make a *baren* (the hard, round pad used to rub the back of the paper). Dow actually went to visit Hyde at her home, but remained discreetly silent on the subject of her work. The only thing he could bring himself to compliment was her collection of Japanese hand towels![180]

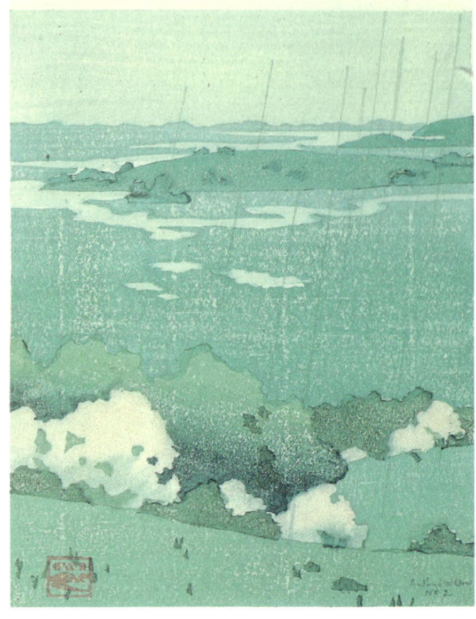

136. Arthur Wesley Dow, *Rain in May*, 1908. Color woodcut. Andrew Terry Keats Collection

During Dow's later years his own work became increasingly simplified, pared down to the essentials. The contrast between Dow's dramatic poster for the 1896 exhibition organized by Fenollosa and Ketcham in New York, and the more old-fashioned illustrational style poster commissioned by the Grolier Club for its exhibition that same year (see figs. 14 and 16) is very instructive. Dow is working here in the simplified mode of Hiroshige with an overlay of curvilinear American Art Nouveau and Arts and Crafts seen in contemporary posters by Bradley. His 1908 *Rain in May* is less decorative, moving closer to abstraction (fig. 136). The poetic *Moonrise* series of 1910–15 may represent the climax of his move toward modernism (fig. 137). But even here one may speculate about the influence on Dow of contemporary Japanese print artists. The Dow estate includes landscapes by Uehara Konen (1868–1940), who worked for Kobayashi Bunshichi at the turn of the century producing small color prints intended for the American tourist market (fig. 138), and nearly abstract landscape and floral patterns by Kamisaka Sekka (1866–1942).[181]

Dow's theories of abstract design were popular because they could be applied to painting, printing, photography, textile design, metalwork, and even woodwork. His color woodcuts were small in scale and never widely known, but with *Composition* he reached out to a wide audience. His message as an educator was a utilitarian one, typical of the didactic, even moralizing, goals of the Arts and Crafts movement. Dow was probably the most influential teacher in America at the turn of the century, numbering among his students Edna Boies Hopkins, Max Weber, Alvin Langdon Coburn, and Georgia O'Keeffe.

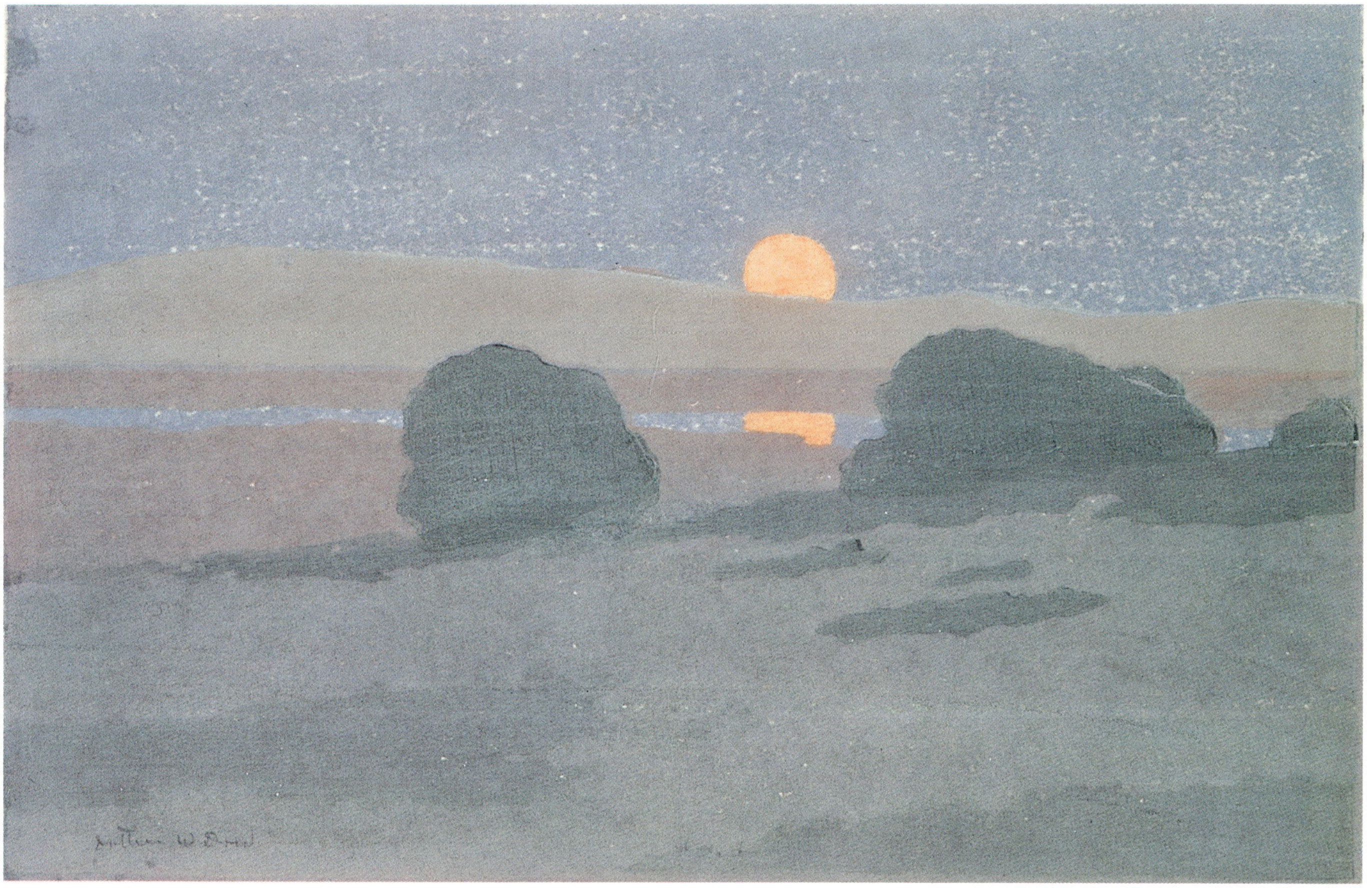

137. Arthur Wesley Dow, *Moonrise*, c. 1910. Color woodcut. Private collection

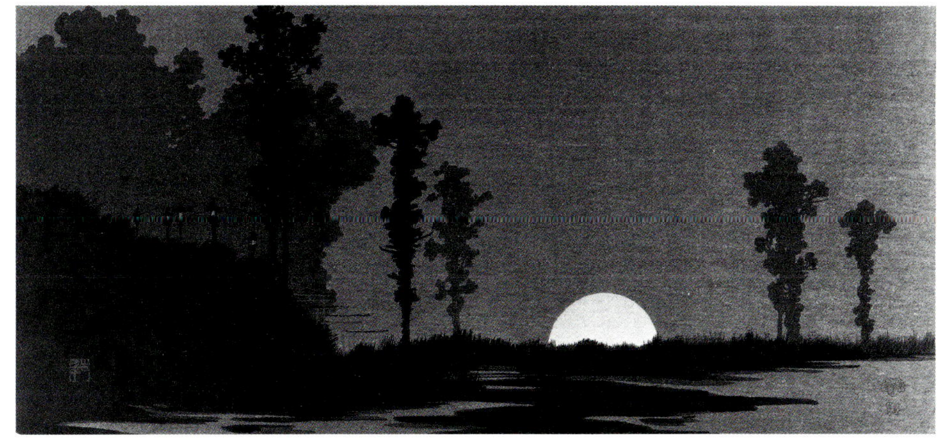

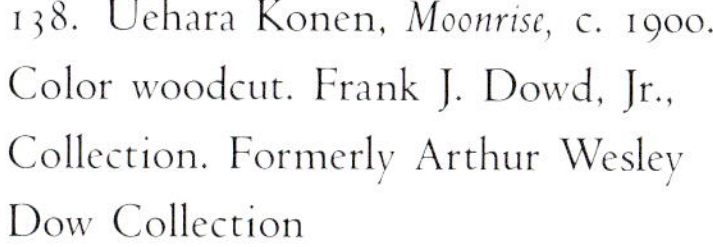

138. Uehara Konen, *Moonrise*, c. 1900. Color woodcut. Frank J. Dowd, Jr., Collection. Formerly Arthur Wesley Dow Collection

Edna Boies Hopkins

When the young widow Edna Bel Boies (1872–1937) enrolled as a new student in Dow's class in composition and design at the Pratt Institute in the spring of 1899, he described her as "very serious" and "deeply in earnest."[182] Originally from Hudson, Michigan, she had attended the Art Academy of Cincinnati from 1895 to 1899 immediately following the unexpected death of her husband, John Boies, a local banker. (He is believed to have contracted tuberculosis.) At Pratt her classmates included the Russian émigré Max Weber, who later described Dow as the greatest teacher he ever had. A photograph of one of Dow's classes taken around 1899 shows that most of his pupils were women; it also reveals two of his own Japanese prints displayed on the wall behind him for purposes of instruction (fig. 139). In March of 1899 he lent some prints to Pratt for an exhibition. He would have been teaching the techniques of color

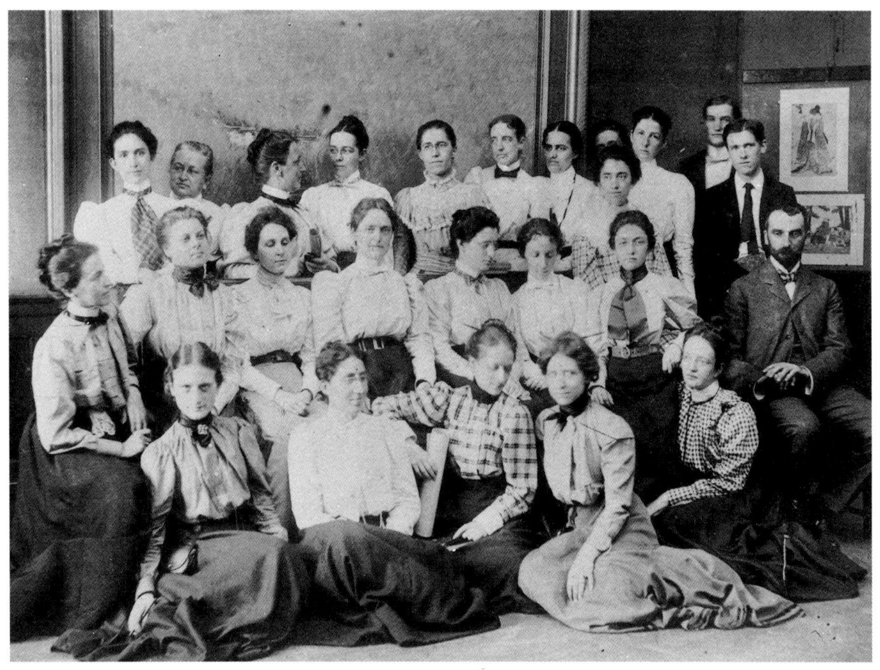

139. Dow with class, Pratt Institute, Brooklyn, New York, c. 1899. Photograph. Archives of American Art, Smithsonian Institution, Washington, DC

printing, and a careful analysis of Japanese prints as well as decorative objects and European paintings was his method of inculcating Pratt students with the universal principles of good design. Of course, 1899 was the year Dow published *Composition.*

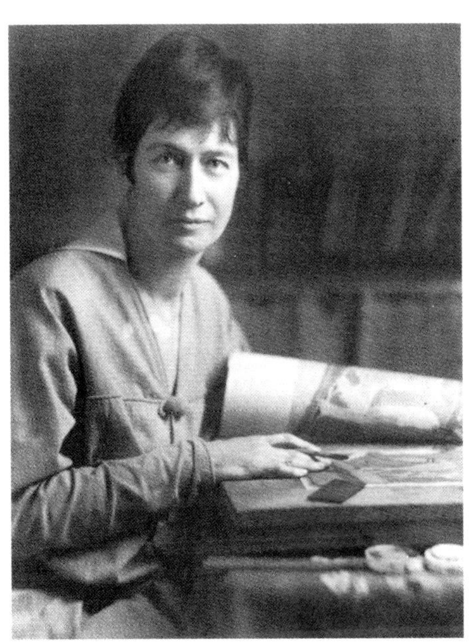

140. Edna Boies Hopkins, c. 1917. Photograph

By the spring of 1900 Boies was using her new skills to teach at the Veltin School for Girls in New York City. The scrapbook with her teaching notes for the fall of 1903 is filled with Arts and Crafts designs for pottery, lamps, and belt buckles, all showing influence of Japanese motifs. That fall she went to an exhibition of Howard Mansfield's collection of Japanese prints, and she wrote a description of Japanese printmaking based on the writings of "Mr. Fen," i.e., Fenollosa.[183]

In 1904 she married a former Cincinnati classmate, the painter James R. Hopkins (1877–1969), and for their honeymoon, her parents sent them off on a one-year trip around the world, which included — needless to say — a period of study in Japan, perhaps inspired in part by Dow's trip the preceding year. They settled in Paris in 1905, and remained there until the outbreak of the war, in 1914, when James Hopkins joined the staff of the Cincinnati Art Academy.[184] They were back in Paris from 1920 until 1923, when they finally repatriated for good. James was invited to be artist in residence at Ohio State University, where he became head of the Department of Fine Arts. A man of parts, he was also president of his hometown bank, the Mechanicsburg Farmers' Bank, and manager of a large, prosperous farm.

As was typical of many of her fellow artists, Edna Boies Hopkins ("Eddie" to her friends) appears to have been an independent, liberated woman, closely focused on her profession as a color woodblock print artist (fig. 140). Although her husband settled into the academic community in Columbus, she was a rather flamboyant, cosmopolitan type who wore pants (unusual in her day), tinted her hair red, and rented an apartment in Manhattan, where she spent most of her winters and carried on her separate career. She summered in Provincetown, in Maine, and in

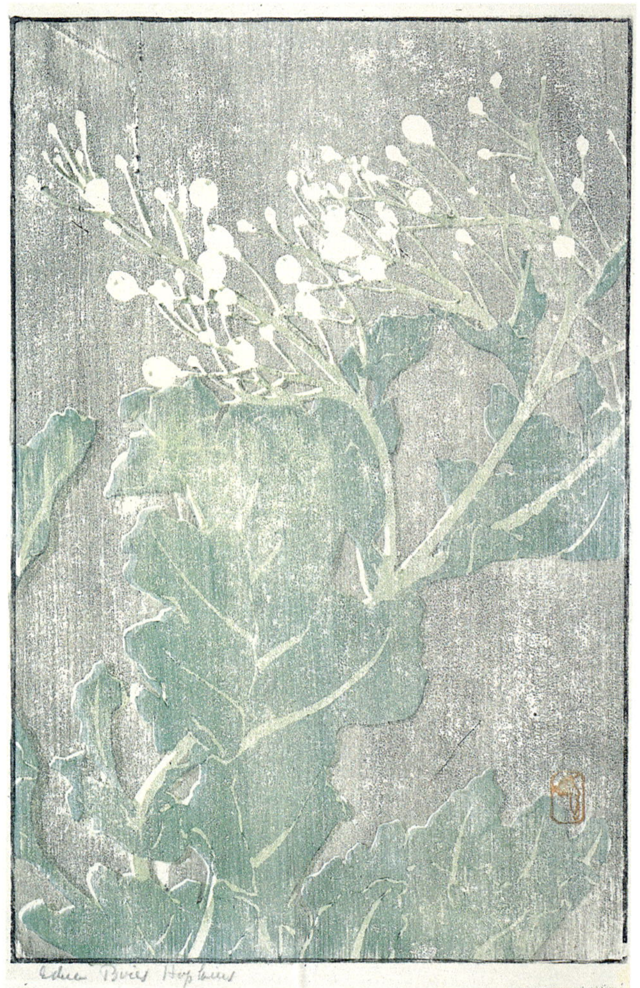

141. Edna Boies Hopkins, *Sea Cabbage,* c. 1906. Color woodcut. The Jane Voorhees Zimmerli Art Museum, Rutgers, The State University of New Jersey, Gift of University College New Brunswick Alumni Association

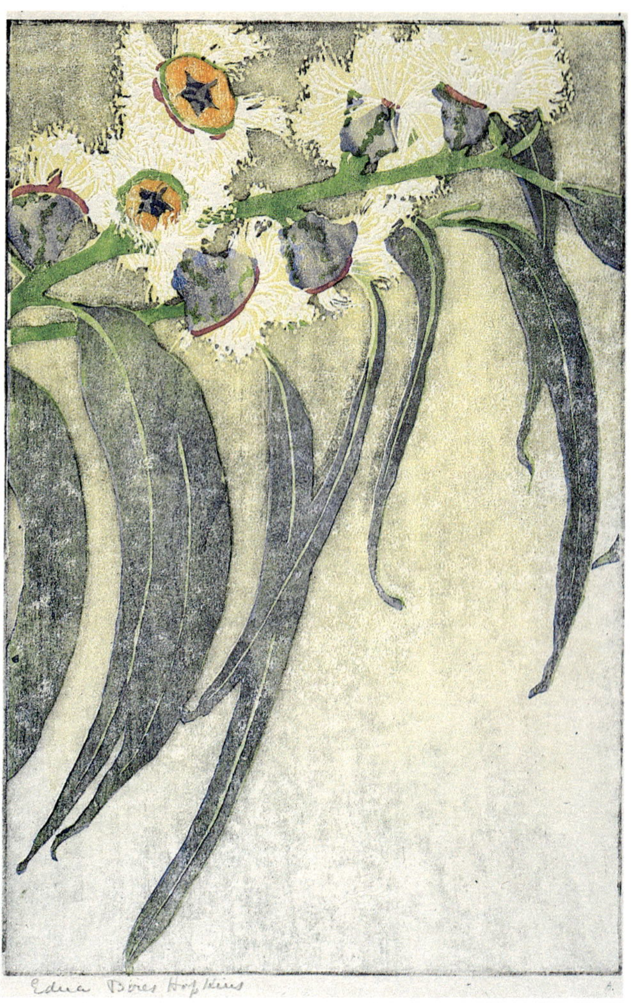

142. Edna Boies Hopkins, *Eucalyptus,* c. 1910. Color woodcut. Print Collection, Miriam and Ira D. Wallach Division of Art, Prints and Photographs, The New York Public Library, Astor, Lenox and Tilden Foundations

the Cumberland Mountains of Kentucky.

Hopkins exhibited her first prints in Paris in 1906, and her last works are believed to date from 1923; arthritis of the hands may have ended her career prematurely. She specialized in closely cropped floral studies (with an occasional bumblebee or spider) which, before her Provincetown period, generally measure 11 inches high by 7 inches wide. (A few of the earliest, perhaps from her New York years, are in miniature scale.)

She did not date her prints, but one can trace a stylistic evolution. The early designs are the most Japanese; they are delicate, often quite intricate, and feature a red peapod seal in one of the lower corners (fig. 141). The artist made careful preliminary drawings during her Paris years: studies are preserved in graphite, black ink, and watercolor (figs. 142 and 143). (Later she sometimes drew her designs directly onto the block.) Many of these studies were made at Giverny in Monet's garden.

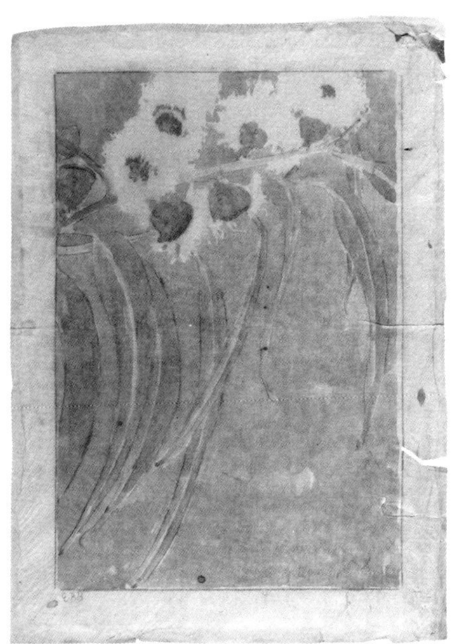

143. Edna Boies Hopkins, *Eucalyptus*, c. 1910. Watercolor. Print Collection, Miriam and Ira D. Wallach Division of Art, Prints and Photographs, The New York Public Library, Astor, Lenox and Tilden Foundations

The Japanese inspiration for her early Paris works is evident: the *Sōka ryakugashiki* (Methods of Cursive Drawing of Flowering Plants), an illustrated woodblock-printed book of floral studies by Kuwagata Keisai (Keisai Masayoshi [1764–1824]) dated 1813, is a model for her elegant compositions, weighted in one corner in the Japanese manner and often set against a soft gray ground (fig. 144). Did she have access to this book? Almost certainly: it was very popular among Western collectors. Hayashi Tadamasa reproduced it in *Paris Illustré* in 1886, and several copies are listed in Bing's 1890 catalogue for his grand ukiyo-e exhibition at the Ecole des Beaux-Arts. The example illustrated here once belonged to the Paris collector Javal. Dow is likely to have owned a copy, as well.[185] Recently an anonymous Japanese manuscript volume of botanical studies from Dow's collection has come to light; in color and often composition many of the images are clearly related to Hopkins's work, although the American is inevitably more naturalistic in her modeling, less sinuous and fluid than her Japanese model (figs. 145 and 146).

In Paris, Hopkins exhibited in the Louvre as a charter member of the

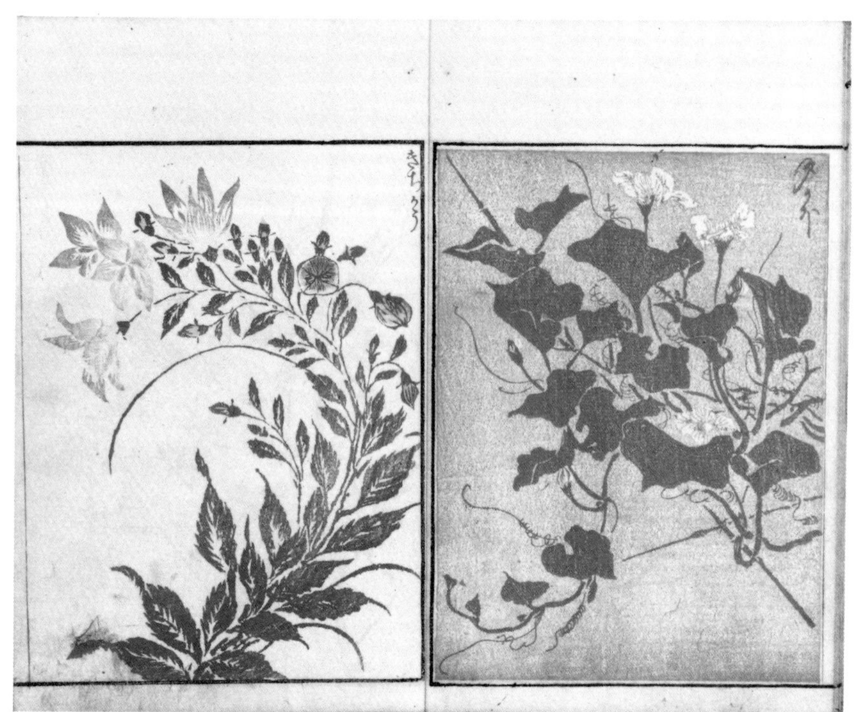

144. Kuwagata Keisai, *Calabash* and *Chinese Bellflower.* From *Soka ryakugashiki* (Methods of Cursive Drawing of Flowering Plants), 1813. Woodblock printed book. Dr. G. Pulverer Collection, Cologne

Society of Original Wood Engravers in Color, organized by the ambitious Auguste Lepère. She also exhibited regularly elsewhere in Paris, building up a significant market for her prints, which entered many European museum collections. Her lush images evolved into increasingly flattened and simplified flowers, enlarged to fill the entire block. They glow like jewels against dark blue, red, or black grounds (fig. 147). The bold design and bright color of Hokusai's *Canary and Peony* (fig. 148) compares well with a decorative print such as *Fuchsia* (fig. 149).

Hopkins's prints are satisfying not only for their strong compositions, but for their subtle gradations of velvety color washes. *Datura,* for example, has a luminosity obtained by printing purple and yellow color blocks over one another (fig. 150). In addition to layering colors to achieve an effect of overlapping veils, she avoided the hard black outlines of a key block. The softly mottled, textured effects she achieves are quite

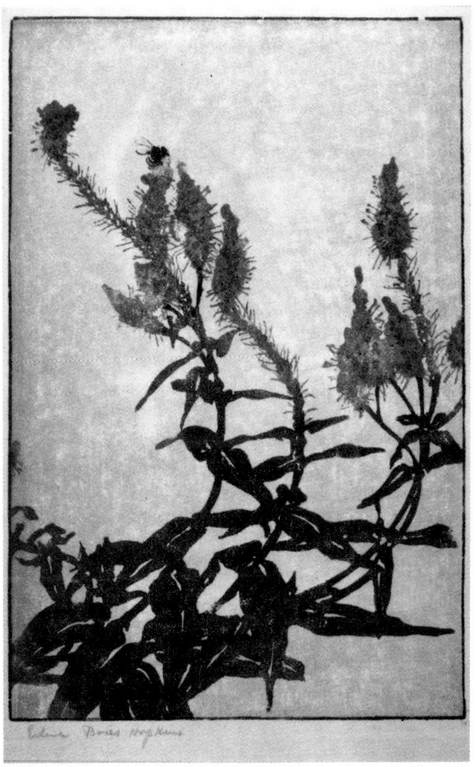

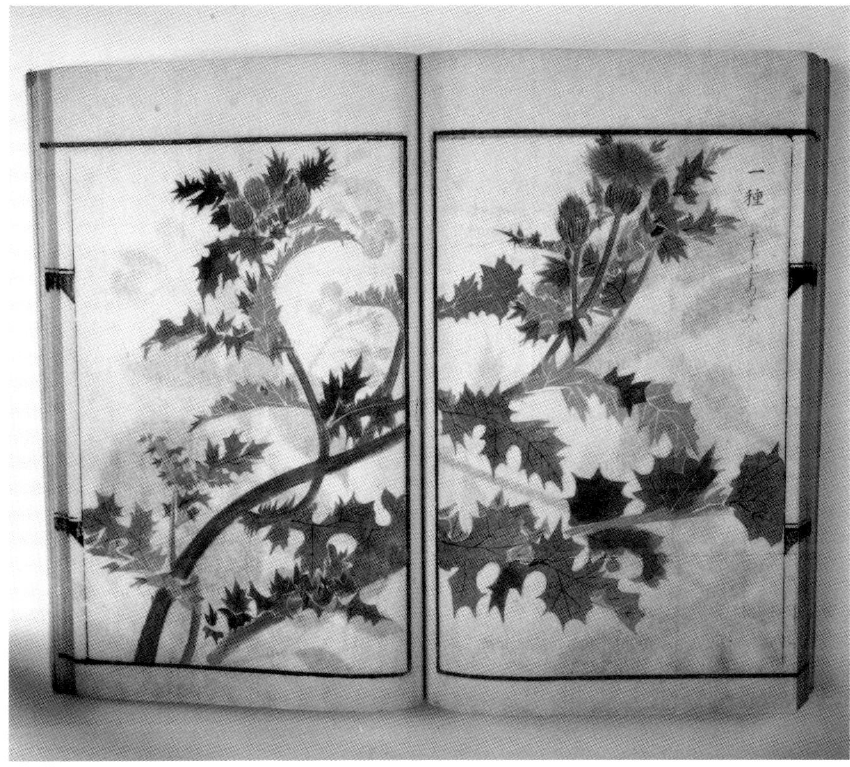

145. Edna Boies Hopkins, *Veronica,* c. 1908. No. 18. Color woodcut. The Jane Voorhees Zimmerli Art Museum, Rutgers, The State University of New Jersey, Gift of University College New Brunswick Alumni Association

146. Anonymous, *Globe Thistle.* From an album of botanical studies, c. 1800. Ink and color on paper. Roy Pedersen Collection. From the estate of Arthur Wesley Dow

unique, distinctly her own. The Japanese printmaking process described in her 1903 notebook seems prophetic:

By varying the depth of the color, the degree of moisture with which it was applied to the block, the degree of pressure, and the use of paper of greater or less absorbent quality, it was possible to obtain tones so subtle, varying, and transparent that no wash of water-color laid on with a brush can approach them. Instead of soaking into the paper, the color was often caught up, as it were, on the outer fibres only, the very whiteness of those below shining through and diluting it with light.

Hopkins often printed on a medium-weight Japanese mulberry paper (*kōzo*), not overly absorbent. She was an experimental printer who produced very small editions in which every impression varies slightly. A brochure for her 1914 exhibition at the Cincinnati Art Museum mentions

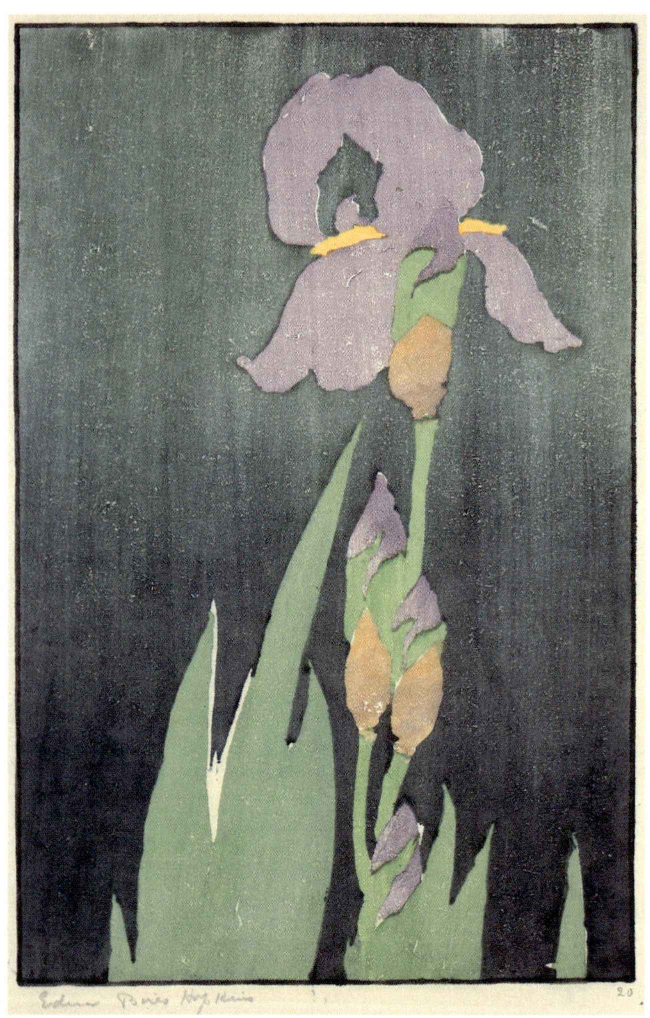

147. Edna Boies Hopkins, *Iris,* c. 1910. No. 20. Color woodcut. Museum of Fine Arts, Boston, Bequest of John T. Spaulding

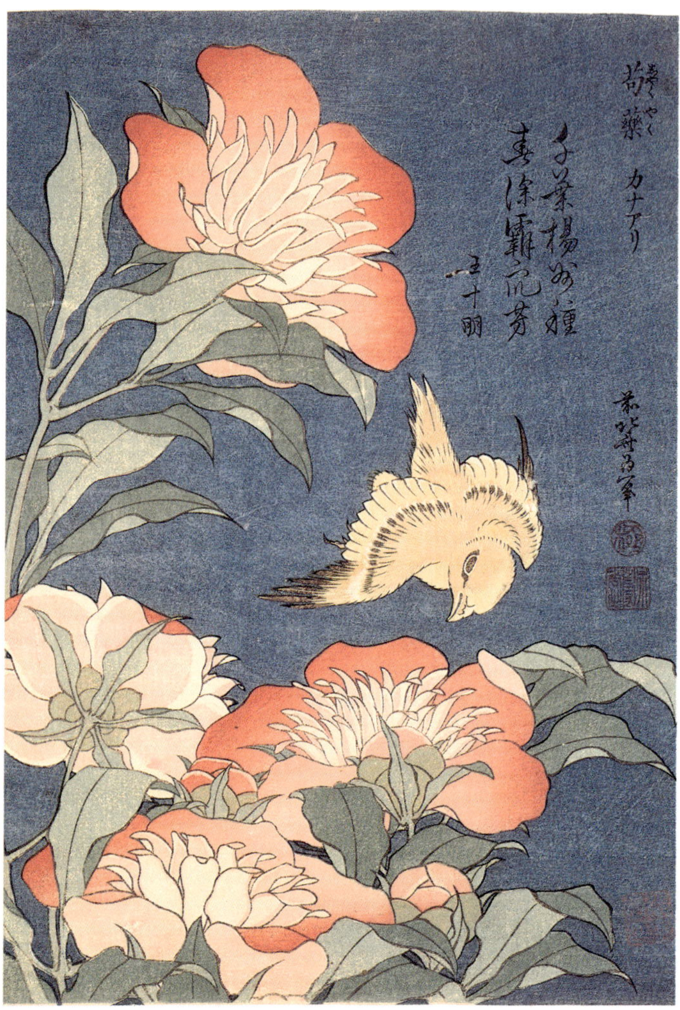

148. Katsushika Hokusai, *Canary and Peony,* late 1820s. Color woodcut. The Minneapolis Institute of Arts. Bequest of Richard P. Gale

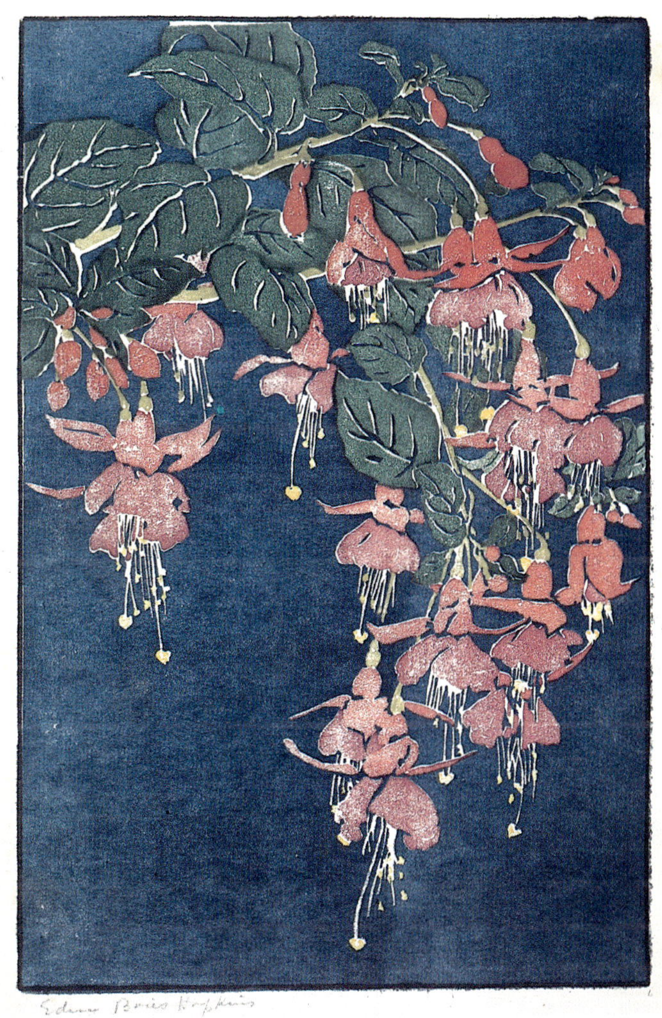

149. Edna Boies Hopkins, *Fuchsia,* c. 1910. No. 6. Color woodcut. The Jane Voorhees Zimmerli Art Museum, Rutgers, The State University of New Jersey, Ralph and Barbara Voorhees American Art Fund

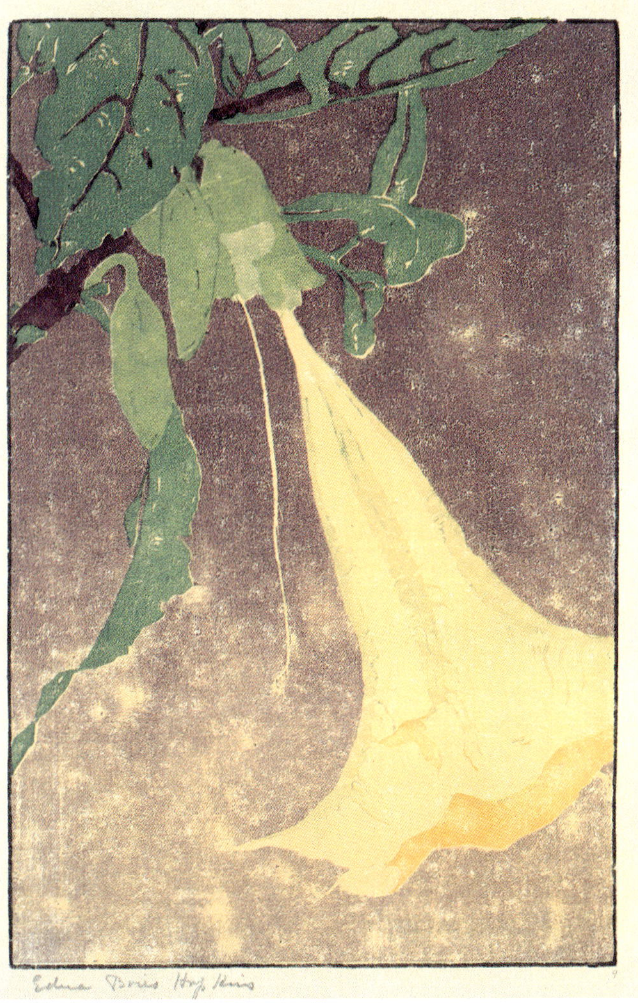

150. Edna Boies Hopkins, *Datura,* c. 1910. No. 9. Color woodcut. Museum of Fine Arts, Boston, Bequest of John T. Spaulding

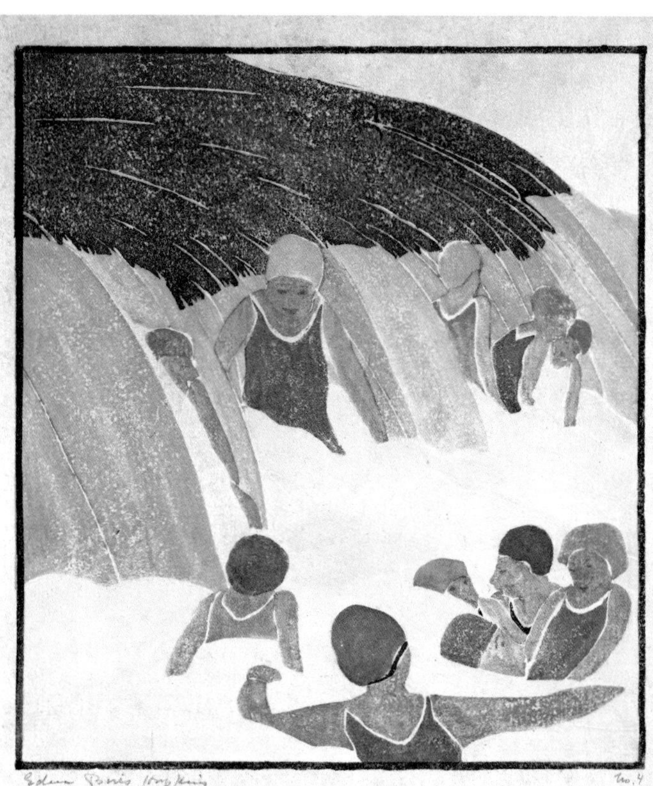

151. Edna Boies Hopkins, *Cascades,* c. 1916. No. 4. Color woodcut. Museum of Fine Arts, Boston, Bequest of John T. Spaulding

152. Tod Lindenmuth, *Low Tide,* 1915. Color linoleum cut. Print Collection, Miriam and Ira D. Wallach Division of Art, Prints and Photographs, The New York Public Library, Astor, Lenox and Tilden Foundations

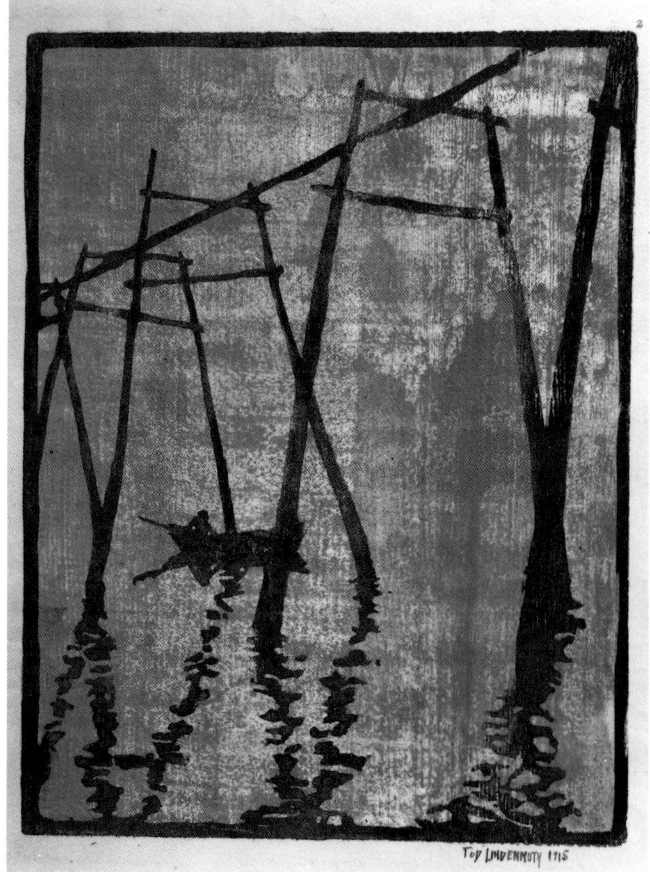

fifty numbered prints of each subject, but she may have printed and numbered them only as required; there are few examples with numbers higher than the twenties among works presently known. Perhaps she even used a hand press on occasion.[186]

Hopkins remained an active teacher. She passed on the woodblock printing technique to her friends (and former classmates from Cincinnati) Ethel Mars (1876–after March 1956) and Maud Squire (1873–c. 1955), and she conducted a class in printmaking during her summers in Provincetown. In Provincetown, under the influence of B. J. O. Nordfeldt (see page 213) and others, her palette brightened, and she achieved a less formal, more abstract style with a dazzling array of high intensity colors — a style that is no longer indebted to Japan (fig. 151).

Although the color woodcut was regularly described by early twentieth-century American critics as "still in its infancy," Provincetown during World War One was a catalyst for large numbers of block printers such as Tod Lindenmuth (1885–1976), who first exhibited there in 1915. Lindenmuth was an original member of the Provincetown Printers, a society of artists devoted to woodblock prints that was founded in 1918.[187] Born in Allentown, Pennsylvania, he studied at the Chase School of Art in New York City. The mood, composition, and striking simplicity of *Low Tide,* his earliest print, calls to mind Whistler and Hiroshige (the two names that cast a large shadow over Japonistes), as well as the pictorialist imagery of Alvin Langdon Coburn (figs. 152 and 189). Lindenmuth was, in fact, trained in photography as a child by his father, a professional. The heavily textured, rough look of the surface has to do with his choice of the linocut medium. The near abstraction of this image of the skeletal understructure of the long wharf that jutted out from Provincetown's Crown and Anchor is checked by the implied realism of its broken reflection on the water. Lindenmuth stopped making prints in 1940 and thereafter devoted himself entirely to painting.

Japanese Art and Japonisme in Chicago

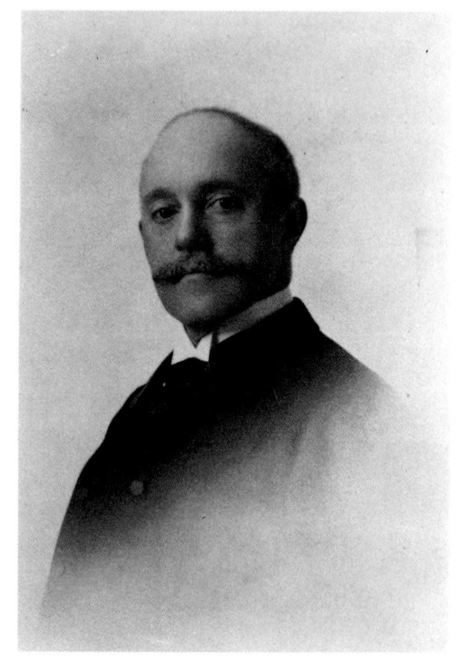

153. Clarence Buckingham, undated. Photograph.

In Chicago, as in Boston and New York, great private collections of ukiyo-e were being formed in the 1890s. Foremost among them were those of Charles J. Morse (1852–1911), a Yale graduate and civil engineer from Evanston, Frederick W. Gookin (1853–1936), and Clarence Buckingham (1854–1913), all participants in the historic Japanese woodblock print exhibition at the Grolier Club in New York in 1896 (see pages 44 and 73). Buckingham was a gregarious and cheerful real estate tycoon who accumulated an outstanding group of about 1,400 prints by the time of his death in 1913, and his collection remains the centerpiece of the Department of Asian Art at the Art Institute, of which he was a trustee (fig. 153). Always ready to share his collection with friends and fellow connoisseurs, he enjoyed hosting print study meetings at his home, with Gookin presiding as commentator. Among his guests at such events were Helen Hyde, as well as collectors Howard Mansfield of New York, Judson D. Metzgar (1869–1956), an attorney from Moline, Illinois, Arthur D. Ficke, and Helen C. Gunsaulus (1886–1954), a graduate of the University of Chicago who was later to become Assistant Curator of Japanese Ethnology at the Field Museum, and then Keeper of the Buckingham Collection of Japanese Prints at the Art Institute from 1926 until 1943.[188]

Gookin was a self-educated New Englander who began his career as a cashier at Northwestern Bank in Chicago (owned by Buckingham's father). His own collection of ukiyo-e, dating from the 1880s, was one of the earliest of its kind in the country (fig. 154). In 1902 he left the bank to become a full-time consultant and dealer in prints. A meticulous, gentle, and scholarly man, he soon gained recognition as an authority in his new field and was responsible for the serious and well-informed cataloguing of numerous public and private collections; he had a considerable influence on American collecting of ukiyo-e. In 1913, when the Buckingham collection was bequeathed to the Art Institute, Gookin's past association with the donor led to his appointment as curator of that collection, a post he held for the rest of his life.

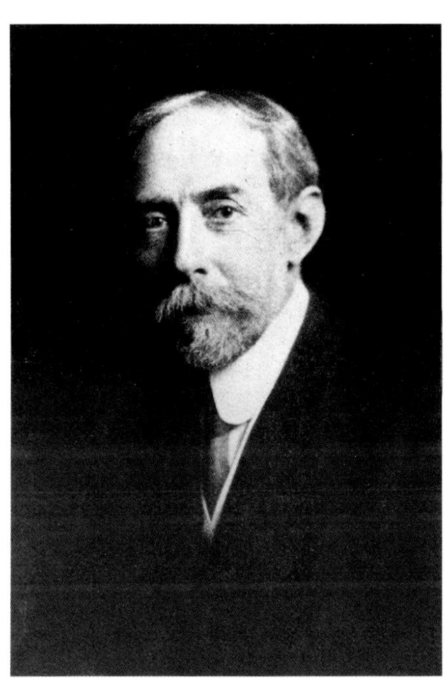

154. Frederick William Gookin, c. 1915. Photograph

Frank Lloyd Wright

The most aggressive publicist of Japanese art in Chicago was Frank Lloyd Wright (1867–1959). As an architect, he was obviously aware of the Japanese buildings at the World's Columbian Exposition in 1893, the year he set up an office of his own in Oak Park. He surrounded himself with Oriental art throughout his life, but Japanese prints, in particular, became a serious obsession and preoccupied him on many levels — as artist, vendor (he became a full-fledged dealer), writer (*The Japanese Print, An Interpretation* was published in 1912), and collector (he owned thousands of prints at the time of his death).[189] In keeping with his own search for a democratic art, he perceived Japanese prints as the art of the common people. In his Prairie School houses he espoused the principles of simplicity, geometric abstraction, and utility that point the way to the modernism of the 1920s. Simplicity ("the elimination of the inessential") is what he praised above all in ukiyo-e prints.

It was in keeping with the spirit of the Chicago Society of Arts and Crafts founded in 1897, that Wright and his good friend (and client) William H. Winslow (1857–1934) collaborated on publishing a lavish book, *The House Beautiful,* early that same year. Printed in a limited edition, the book is pervaded with youthful idealism. Winslow was the publisher, the text was written by William Gannett, a Unitarian minister, and Wright designed the graphics. Gannett stressed the Arts and Crafts philosophy of simplicity, truthfulness, and the influence of nature in ornament, and Wright found one source for his stylized ornaments in the seed pods of weeds. He photographed the wildflowers and weeds — icons of the prairie — in carefully arranged still lifes, which were reproduced in collotype and added to the flyleaf of the book in a little brochure (fig. 155). Each tiny image is outlined with a thin red line in a vertical format that obviously imitates a Japanese hanging scroll. The weed compositions, complete with square red seal in the lower right corner, have their parallel in Hiroshige's small *tanzaku* woodcut of *Snails on Nadeshiko Pinks,* a print that Wright owned until he was forced by bankruptcy to sell it at auction in 1927 (fig. 156).[190]

Wright made his first trip to Japan in the spring of 1905 and later claimed that it was made in pursuit of prints. He did return with several hundred Hiroshige woodcuts, which he catalogued and displayed the following year at the Art Institute of Chicago. It is easy to understand his lifelong preference for Hiroshige, whose work is so picturesque and accessible.

Throughout his life Wright used museum exhibitions both of his own work and of Japanese art to further his career. The prints in the 1906 exhibition, for example, were ultimately sold to Buckingham. Only two years later, in 1908, Wright contributed 218 woodcuts to a second ukiyo-e exhibition at the Art Institute (fig. 157).[191] Thought to be the largest such display ever mounted in America, it showed a total of 655 prints drawn from a handful of local collections, including those of Buckingham and Gookin. The works were mounted in six galleries whose design and display were the joint effort of Gookin and Wright. Wright even devised a small mahogany stand for narrow vertical prints, complete with a projecting ledge to accommodate Japanese-style flower arrangements, clearly visible in the photograph.

Among Wright's collaborators during his Oak Park years was George Mann Niedecken (1878–1945), who called himself an "interior architect." Niedecken, who taught at the Wisconsin School of Art in Milwaukee,

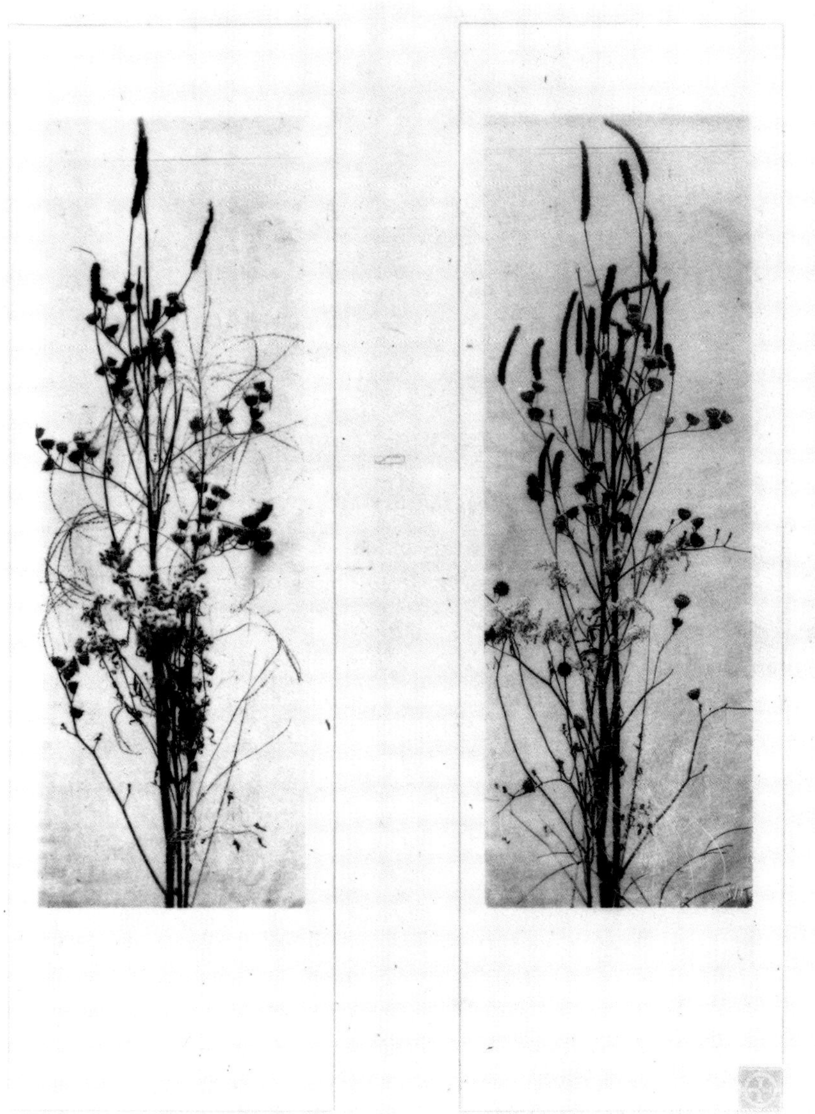

155. Frank Lloyd Wright, *Weeds and Wildflowers.* From *The House Beautiful,* by William C. Gannett, 1897. Collotype proof sheet. Kelmscott Gallery, Chicago

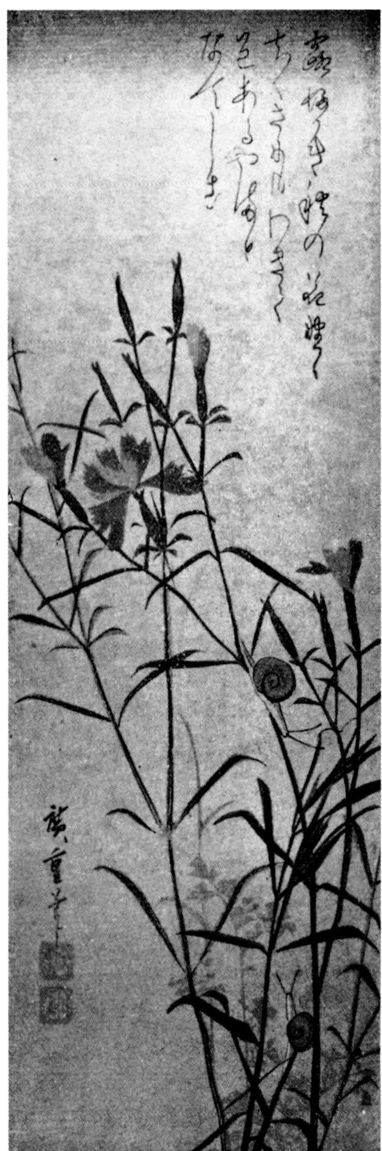

156. Utagawa Hiroshige, *Snails on Nadeshiko Pinks,* 1830s. Color woodcut. Illustrated as No. 244 in 1927 Anderson Gallery catalogue of the Frank Lloyd Wright Collection

had attended the School of the Art Institute of Chicago in 1897–98, followed, predictably, by a year at the Académie Julian, and exposure to Continental Art Nouveau. He also collected Japanese prints and Chinese ceramics, available from a local dealer in Milwaukee. The graphic arts played a key role in his profession; he became a noted muralist in the custom designing of interiors, and relied upon drawings to communicate with his draftsmen and clients.[192] Illustrated here (fig. 158) is his 1904 colored drawing for the dining room frieze he painted in Wright's new house for Susan L. Dana (Springfield, Illinois). The stylized design of sumac, purple aster, and goldenrod (prairie flowers) complemented Wright's abstract decorations and has the flattened, decorative character of late Japanese screen painting, as do many of his finished murals. Among the most dramatic is the birch tree and fern motif he created for the Coonley House (fig. 159).

One of Wright's staff architects at the time was Marion Lucy Mahony (1871–1962). Born in Chicago and the first woman to graduate with a degree in architecture from the Massachusetts Institute of Technology, she worked on and off in Wright's studio for nearly fourteen years, from 1895 to 1909, when he left for Europe, closing the Oak Park studio for good. Mahony was often responsible for designing the furniture and decorative details of his interiors (leaded glass, lighting fixtures, and glass mosaics), but she is renowned for the perspective drawings she made for clients or created expressly for exhibition and publication.

Wright liked to see his clients build on a spacious site with ample room for landscape gardening; his concept of organic architecture meant integration with nature, as in Japan. Likewise he was concerned with creating an attractive foliate setting for his perspectives and always encouraged his draftsmen to enhance the buildings with trees, flowers, and shrubs. It is surely no coincidence that Mahony's finest renderings, filled with the spirit of Japonisme, date from between 1905 and 1907, in the wake of Wright's Japan trip and his Hiroshige exhibition. Wright

157. Exhibition of Japanese prints at The Art Institute of Chicago, 1908. Installation designed by Frank Lloyd Wright. Photograph. © 1989 The Art Institute of Chicago, All Rights Reserved

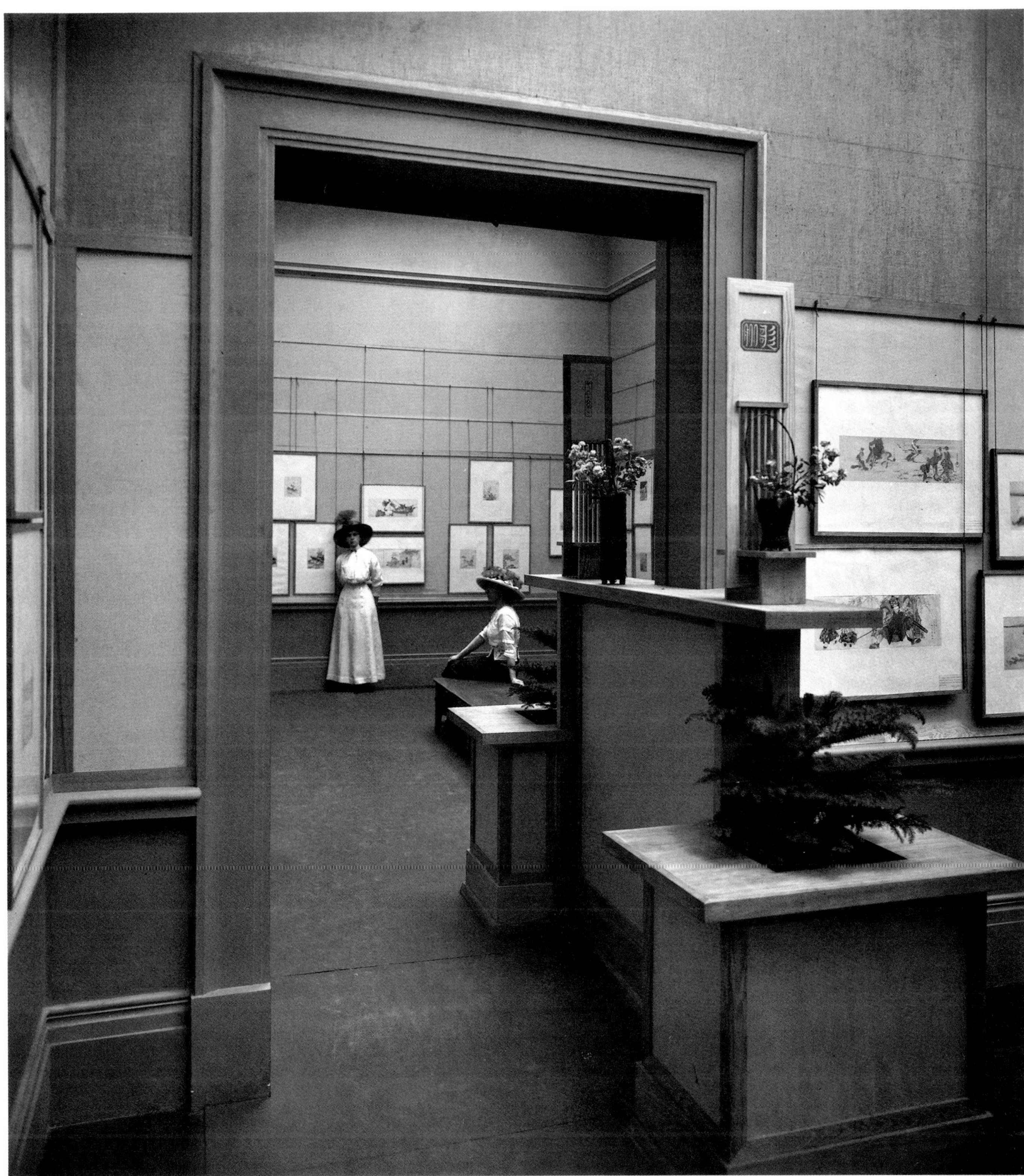

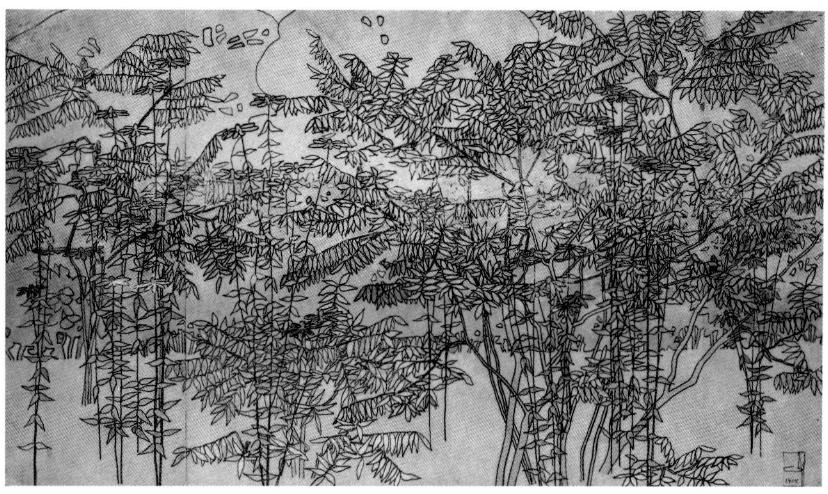

158. George Mann Niedecken, *Sumac*, 1904. Ink and watercolor on paper. Kelmscott Gallery, Chicago

159. George Mann Niedecken, *Birch Tree and Fern Mural in the Interior of Frank Lloyd Wright's Avery Coonley House, Riverside, Illinois*, c. 1908–09. Photograph. Kelmscott Gallery, Chicago

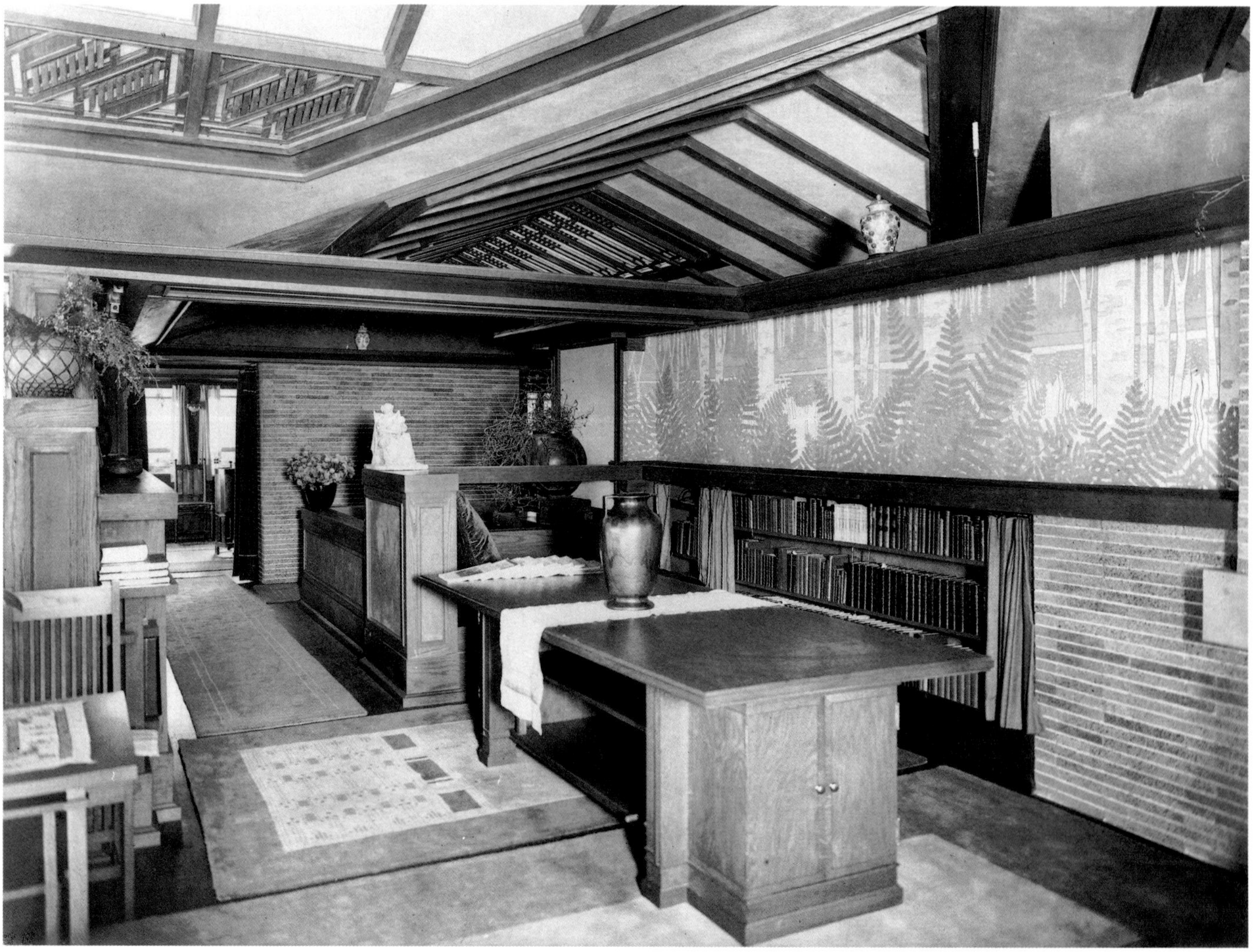

later penciled a notation on the drawing for the 1906 K. C. De Rhodes house in South Bend, Indiana: "Drawn by Mahony after FLLW and Hiroshige" (fig. 160). The remark was obviously occasioned by the arbitrary insertion of an enlarged detail of a bird on a flowering branch in the lower left corner, but Wright must also have been conscious of her use of the framing device of flattened tree trunks cropped at the sides and rising out of the composition in the immediate foreground with a canopy of foliage overhead, leaving a sort of window opening through which the viewer looks into deep space. The technique was adopted by Hiroshige in *Maples at Mamma* from his last and one of his most commercially and artistically successful series, the *One Hundred Famous Views of Edo,* dating from 1857–58. Mahony's dense foliage of trees, flowers, plants, and vines all but obscures the house itself, being rather more ornate and detailed than the tightly structured designs of the Japanese master.

Likewise, an unusual rendering of the 1904 Hardy house in Racine, Wisconsin, imitates the distinctive shape of a Japanese pillar print (fig. 161). The house itself is perched dramatically high on a hill, seen from below, with most of the area given over to empty space, very similar to Hiroshige's 1834 composition of a daimyo cortege climbing toward a castle on Kameyama (fig. 162). It was an unusual choice of angle, because most people saw the house from its street approach, rather than from the Lake Michigan shoreline. The striated sky is a technique often used by Hiroshige to indicate rain and the branch protruding arbitrarily into the empty center cannot but remind us of his well-known narrow vertical print *Swallows and Aronia* (fig. 163).

Wright's involvement with Japan gained momentum in 1916 with the commission for the Imperial Hotel in Tokyo, a project he completed in 1922. Wright never returned to Japan, but it remained a source of solace and inspiration.

William Sturgis Bigelow, a sensitive, troubled man who escaped to

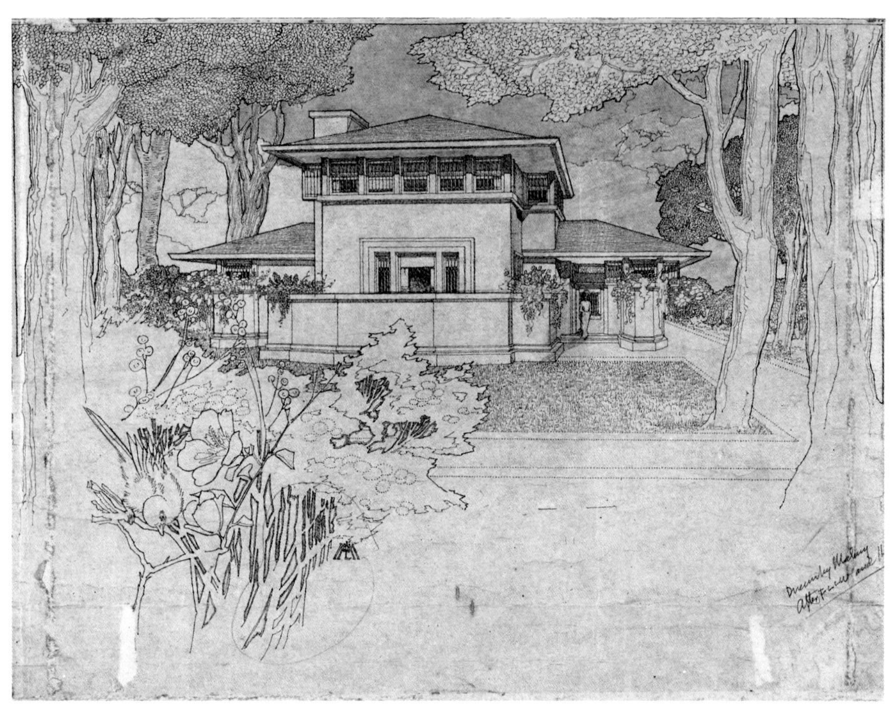

160. Marion Mahony, *Rendering of K. C. De Rhodes House, South Bend, Indiana,* 1906. Ink and watercolor on paper. © 1962 The Frank Lloyd Wright Foundation. Courtesy The Frank Lloyd Wright Archives

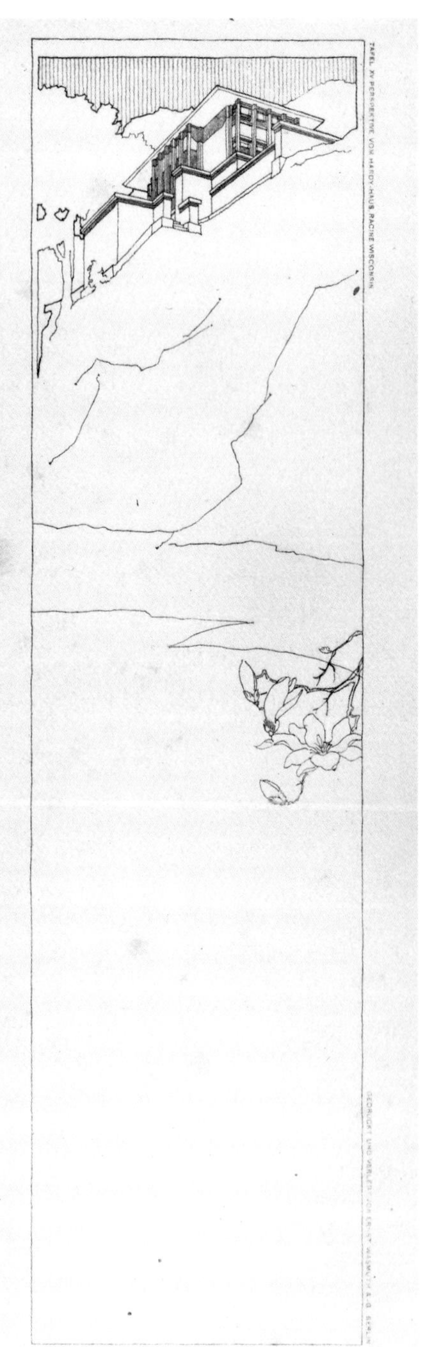

161. Frank Lloyd Wright, *Perspective of Hardy House.* From Wasmuth portfolio, 1910. Kelmscott Gallery, Chicago

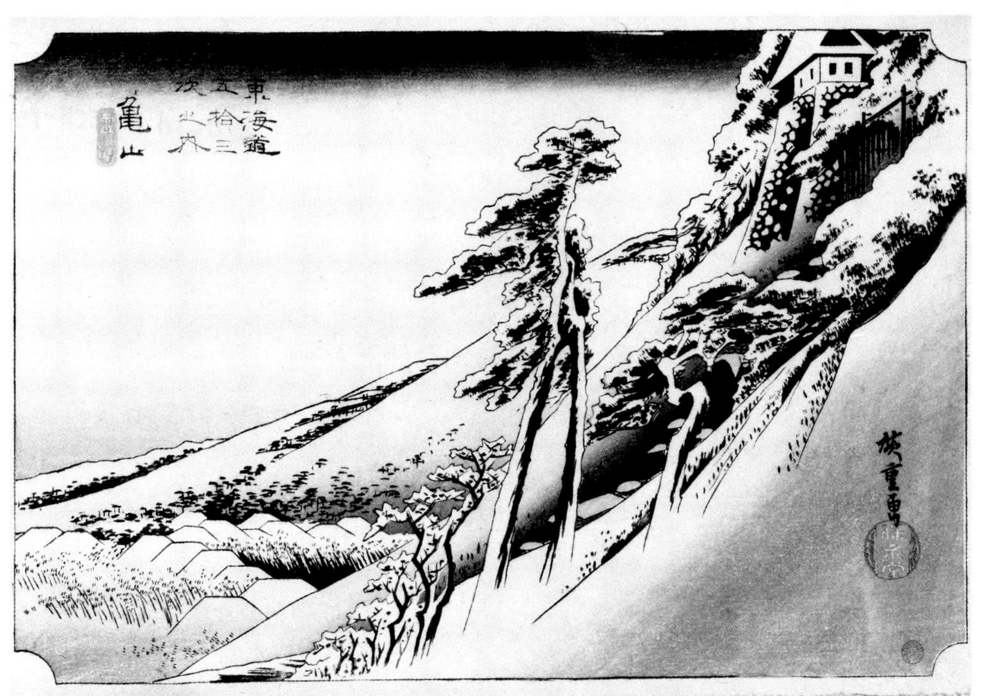

162. Utagawa Hiroshige, *Kameyama, Clearing Weather after the Snow.* From the series *Fifty-three Stations of the Tōkaidō,* 1833–34. Color woodcut. The Metropolitan Museum of Art, New York, Rogers Fund, 1918

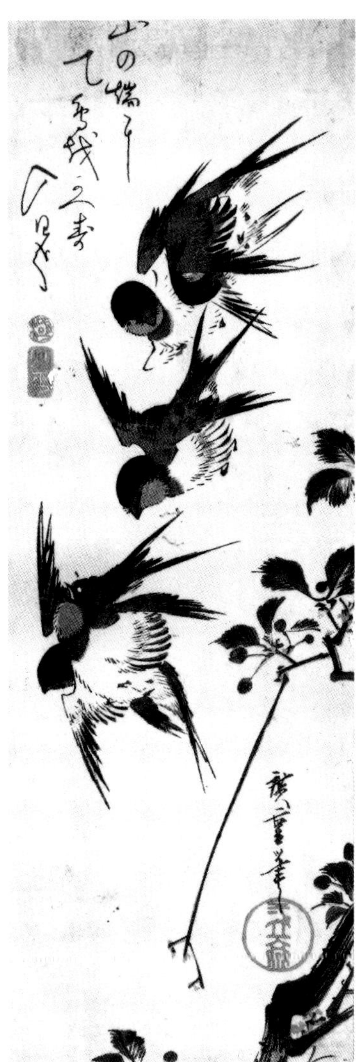

163. Utagawa Hiroshige, *Swallows and Aronia,* c. 1835. Color woodcut. The Grunwald Center for the Graphic Arts, University of California, Los Angeles. Purchased from the Frank Lloyd Wright Collection

Japan to embark on a serious Buddhist pilgrimage and amass a comprehensive collection of Japanese art, is a classic example of a thoughtful Westerner dissatisfied with modern culture (see pages 51–52). Wright, too, acknowledged an element of escapism in the lure of the Orient, and his interpretation of prints betrays a typically romantic nineteenth-century view of Japan as a primitive country, whose people were naïve and childlike. It was an imaginary vision of "uncivilized" Japan that led him to praise the spiritual appeal of Hiroshige woodcuts. Then, too, he touted his prints as rare and unique, confirming his own self-image as a genius, a man of superior insight and refinement.

B. J. O. Nordfeldt

The School of the Art Institute of Chicago, one of the largest and best in the United States, produced some outstanding graphic artists around the turn of the century. Among them were George Niedecken, Elizabeth Colwell, Bertha Lum, and B. J. O. Nordfeldt (1878–1955), all of whom were drawn to Japanese art (fig. 164). In 1906, the year of Wright's Hiroshige exhibition at the Art Institute, Nordfeldt made a set of color woodcuts that were clearly intended as his own "Hiroshige" suite. Trained in England, birthplace of the Arts and Crafts movement, Nordfeldt adopted the "do-it-yourself" philosophy of handcraftsmanship. At the same time his Japanese models helped modernize and simplify his imagery.

Nordfeldt's artistic career spanned sixty years, reaching maturity in the period between the wars in Santa Fe and Minneapolis, before he settled in Lambertville, New Jersey. He is well known as an American expressionist painter and as an etcher; his brief encounter with color printmaking during his early years in Chicago has been largely forgotten.

Nordfeldt was born in Sweden and moved to Chicago with his family in 1891, at age thirteen, joining a cohesive but ethnically isolated Swedish

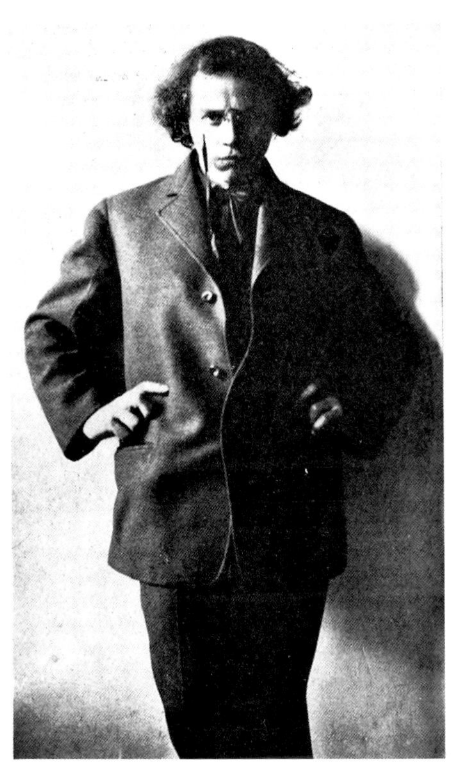

164. B. J. O. Nordfeldt, c. 1905. Photograph

community. He worked as a printer's devil and compositor for the local Swedish newspaper, and when he enrolled at the School of the Art Institute in 1899, a year after Niedecken, he was dependent at first on the museum's Swedish janitor for translations. He was an indrawn young man, whose "sense of cultural distinction stayed with him all his life."[193] Instructor Albert Herter chose him as his assistant on a major mural project for the Paris Exposition Universelle and Nordfeldt traveled to Paris in 1900 to see the works in place. There, at age twenty-two, he attended the Académie Julian for a few weeks before finding his own studio. This was followed by a year in England and a year in Sweden in a cottage near the sea.

It was in England that he learned block carving and printing techniques under the guidance of Frank Morley Fletcher (1866–1949), a portrait painter who was director of the art department at Reading University College from 1896 to 1906. Fletcher's first print was *Meadowsweet,* published in a limited edition of seventy-five by his friend and supporter John Dixon Batten in 1897 (fig. 165).[194] Batten had been experimenting with color printing from wood and metal blocks for several years, although at that time he did not have access to Japanese tools and paper. His insights into the future of block printing in the West were published in an interview in the art periodical *The Studio* in 1884:

"There is no need, and it would show, I think, but little wisdom on our part, to imitate the art of the Japanese. *They are supreme in their own realm, and a large realm it is, but it is not the universe. Japan need not block the way. Many generations of men might work at this very method of colourprinting without coming in touch with the deadening influence felt by those who attempt to imitate, too closely, what men of another nation or age have perfected."* . . .

"You believe that [color woodcut printing] *opens a new field of art?"*

"Yes: I regard it as an art in itself, and alone; not merely one more method of

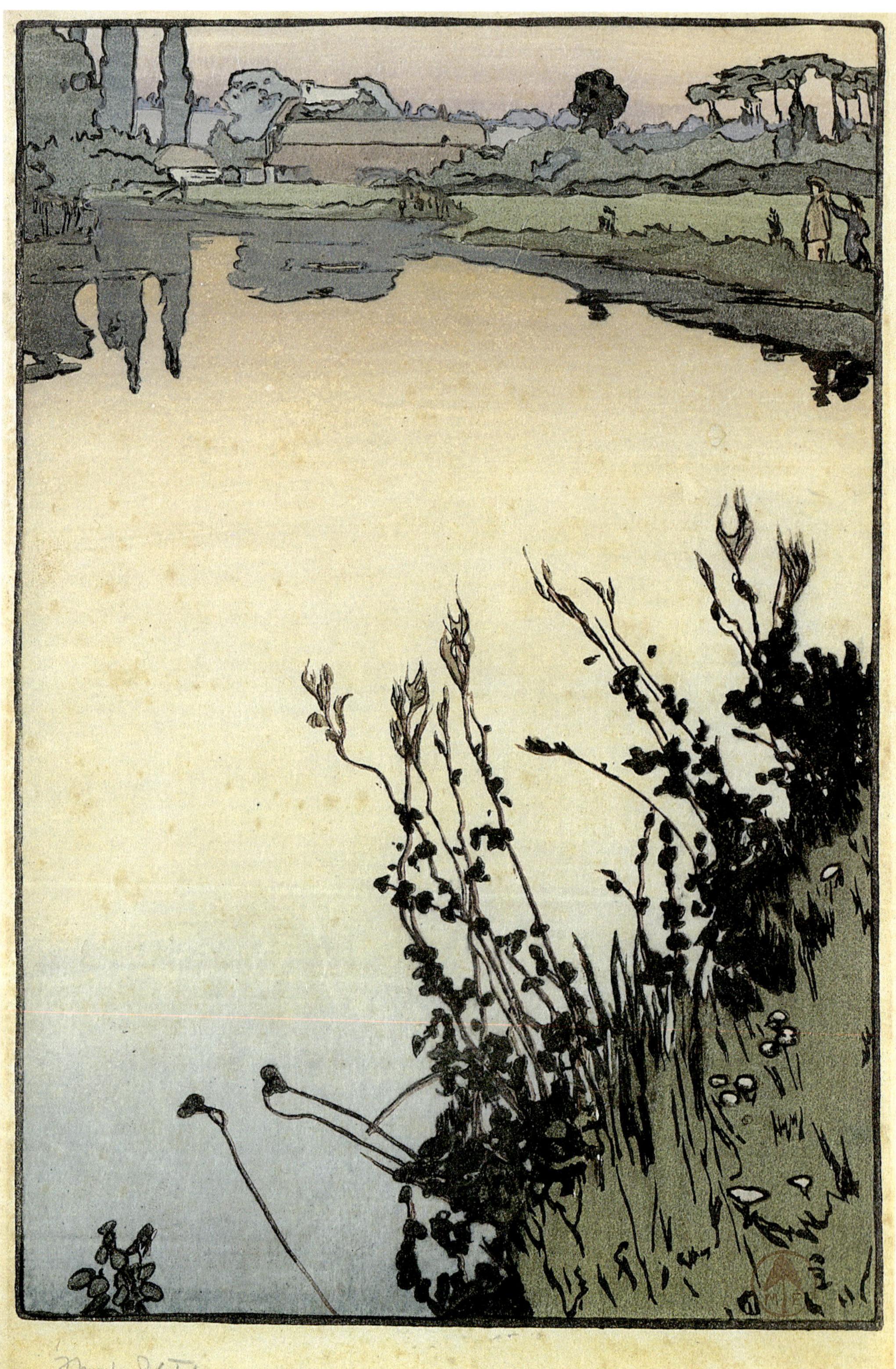
Morley Fletcher

165. Frank Morley Fletcher, *Meadowsweet,* 1897. Color woodcut. The Santa Barbara Museum of Art. Gift of Mr. and Mrs. T. Frame-Thomson

multiplying copies of originals produced by another artist. In this, the designer must design, from the first, a print, *not a painting. Nor will he find the spirit of his first intention crushed by a weight of mechanical technicalities; but, on the contrary, discover that he has a medium to express himself which will be from first to last within the control of his mind and hand."*[195]

Although a Japanese printseller in London gave them valuable hints and demonstrations, Fletcher and Batten had to learn by the slow and unsatisfactory method of studying the photographs and instructions for printing given by T. Tokuno, chief of the Bureau of Engraving and Printing of the Japanese Ministry of Finance, in a detailed account first published by the Smithsonian Institution in 1893. The text accompanied a collection of woodcutting and printing equipment given to the Smithsonian by the Japanese government and still on display today in the Hall of Graphics of the National Museum of American History.[196]

In 1916, while art director for the Edinburgh College of Art, Fletcher wrote *Wood-Block Printing,* a practical textbook of workshop practice aimed at the artist-craftsman and illustrated with an original example of his own work printed on Japanese paper (fig. 166). In 1923 he was invited to Santa Barbara, California, to found an art school, through which he inspired a generation of California artists. Fletcher became a naturalized American citizen in 1926.[197]

166. Frank Morley Fletcher, *Position of the Hands in Using the Knife and Baren.* From *Wood-Block Printing,* 1916

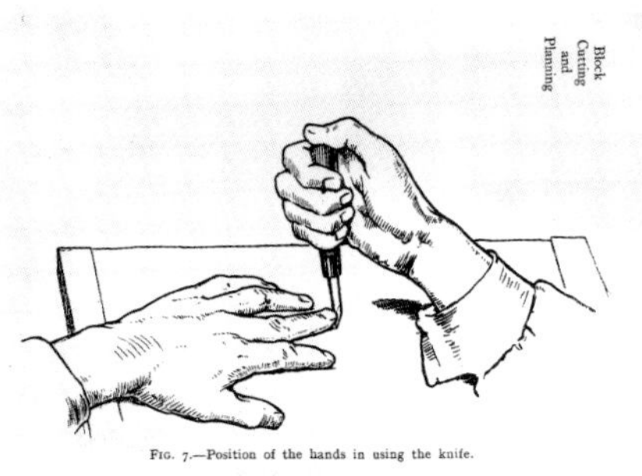

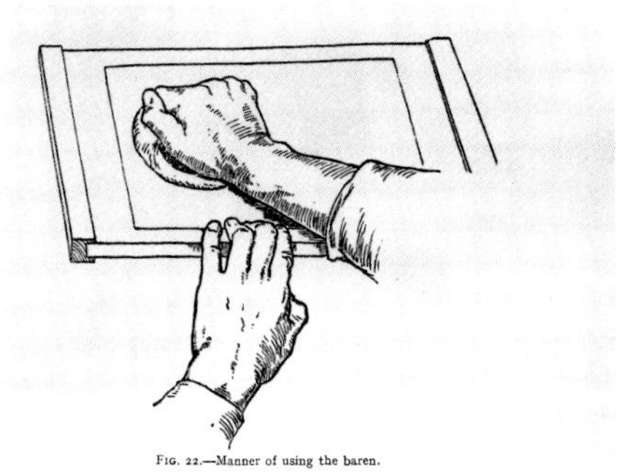

Nordfeldt, his student, made his first original woodcut as soon as he returned from Europe and set up his studio in Chicago in 1903. In his own evolution toward abstraction and modernism he created a brand of Japonisme taking as its starting point the examples of his European mentors who had also been looking at Japanese art, notably Lepère and Rivière. The ingredients for Nordfeldt's *The Long Wave* of 1903 (fig. 167) are a mixture of Hokusai's influential *Manga,* the series of picture books that made his reputation in the West, and Lepère's 1901 *The Rolling Waves, September Tide* (fig. 168), but as Nordfeldt once said, "I have always been interested in the sea and the loneliness of the sea. I was born in Sweden

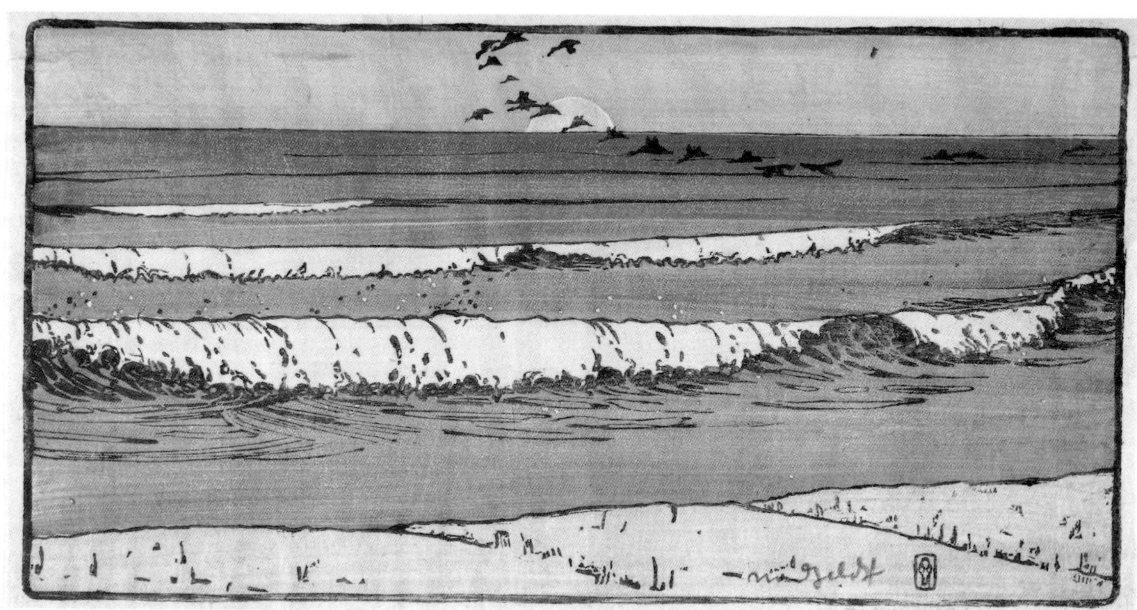

167. B. J. O. Nordfeldt, *The Long Wave,* 1903. Color woodcut. Print Collection, Miriam and Ira D. Wallach Division of Art, Prints and Photographs, The New York Public Library, Astor, Lenox and Tilden Foundations

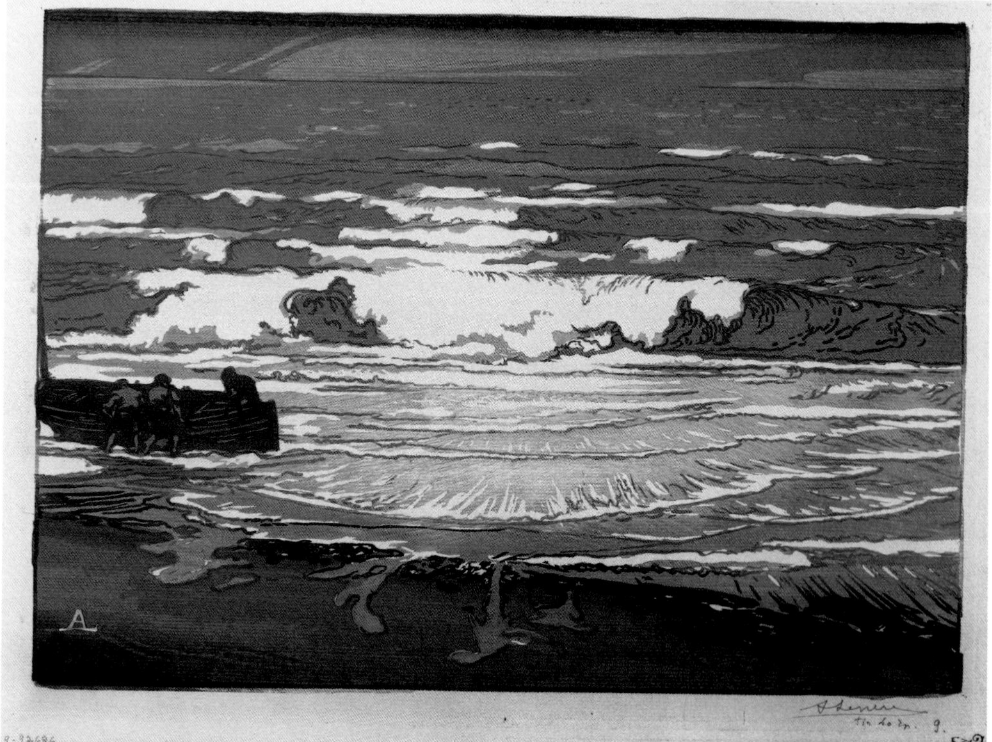

168. Auguste Lepère, *The Rolling Waves, September Tide,* 1901. No. 9. Color woodcut. Boston Public Library, Print Department

and thus I try to create the feeling of loneliness, of depth, of weight and volume and force."[198]

In an interview in January 1908, at the time his woodcuts were on display at the Art Institute, Nordfeldt revealed that he made about two hundred and fifty impressions of each image (they are numbered sequentially within the image).[199] He was proud of the fact that he designed, carved, and printed the images himself, but often they are amateurish, almost crude in technique if compared with their Japanese models. Attracted by the romantic concept of the woodcut, he — like others in the Arts and Crafts movement — walked a fine line between rough craftsmanship and highly sophisticated design. In Nordfeldt's prints a self-conscious primitivizing — a stripping down to essentials — goes hand in hand with a superficial elegance derived from Japanese aesthetics.

Nordfeldt created about fifteen color woodcuts between 1903 and 1907, but the majority of them are dated 1906, the year of Frank Lloyd Wright's Hiroshige exhibition.[200] Japanese parallels for *The Skyrocket* (figs. 169 and 170) and *The Bridge* (figs. 171 and 172) are easy to find. The foreground shoreline in *The Skyrocket* is stylized to resemble the flattened cloud bands often seen in Hiroshige prints, for example, but the bull's-eye centering of the moon and fireworks gives the design a forthright boldness and an almost naïve charm. *The Storm, Skeldervicken* (fig. 173) has strong parallels with Rivière's Japanesque scenes of *Fishing Boats Setting Sail* (fig. 174) from his woodcut series *Breton Landscapes* of about 1893, and Nordfeldt makes his most overt references to Japan here: the asymmetrical composition, slanting rain falling like a curtain in front of the design, diagonal flight of seagulls, and red title cartouche are all obvious references to Hiroshige. Nordfeldt leaves behind the naturalism and anecdotal content that seem to weigh down Rivière; more abstract and concise, he is far advanced on the path to modernism.

The subtle and evocative gray silhouettes and the graduated inking of the block in his Sudbury River scene, *Mist, the Anglers,* calls to mind

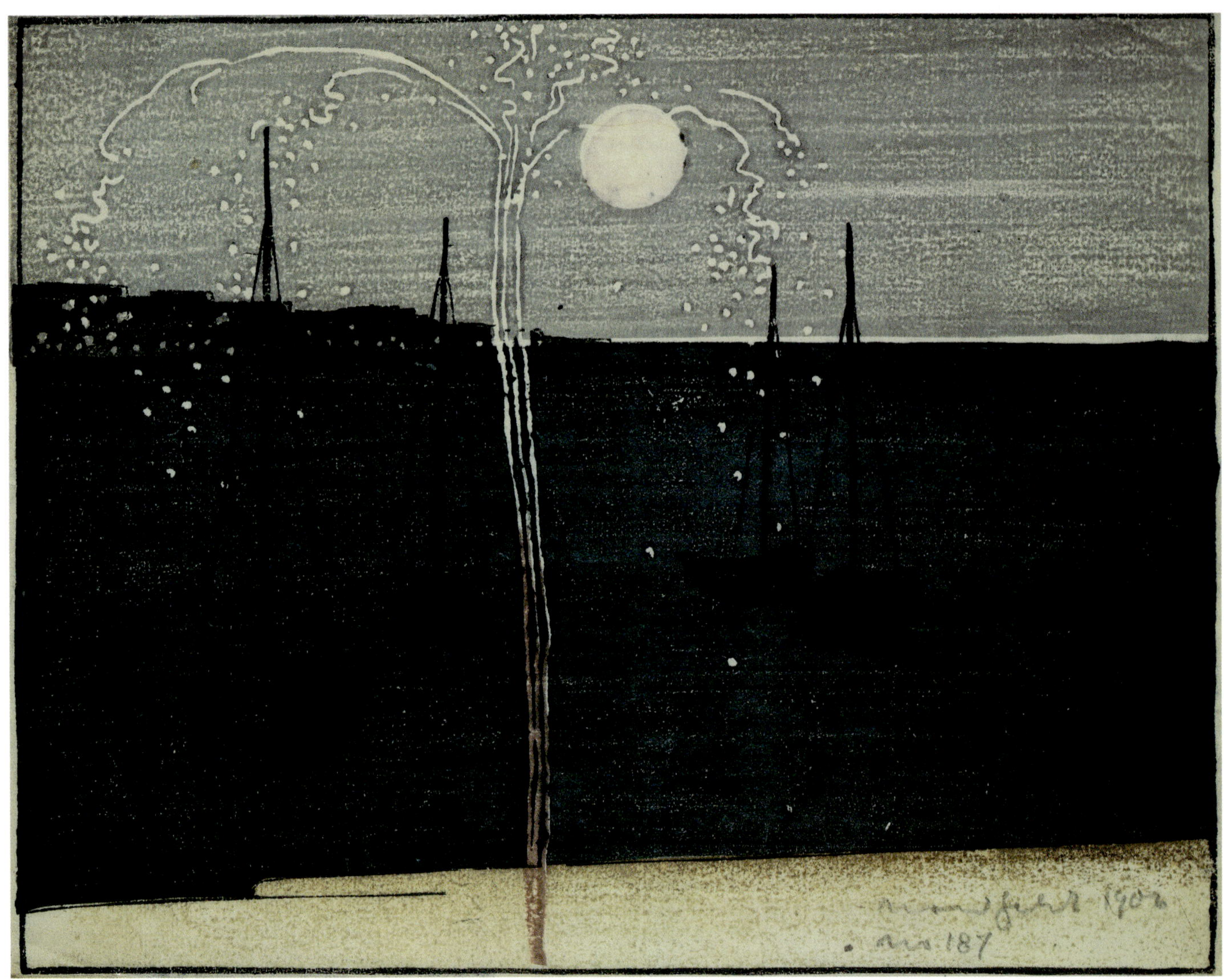

169. B. J. O. Nordfeldt, *The Skyrocket,* 1906. No. 187. Color woodcut. The Metropolitan Museum of Art, New York, Gift of Mrs. B. J. O. Nordfeldt, 1955

170. Utagawa Hiroshige, *Fireworks at Ryōgoku.* From the series *One Hundred Famous Views of Edo,* 1857. Color woodcut. The Metropolitan Museum of Art, New York, Purchase, Joseph Pulitzer Bequest, 1918. Formerly Frank Lloyd Wright Collection

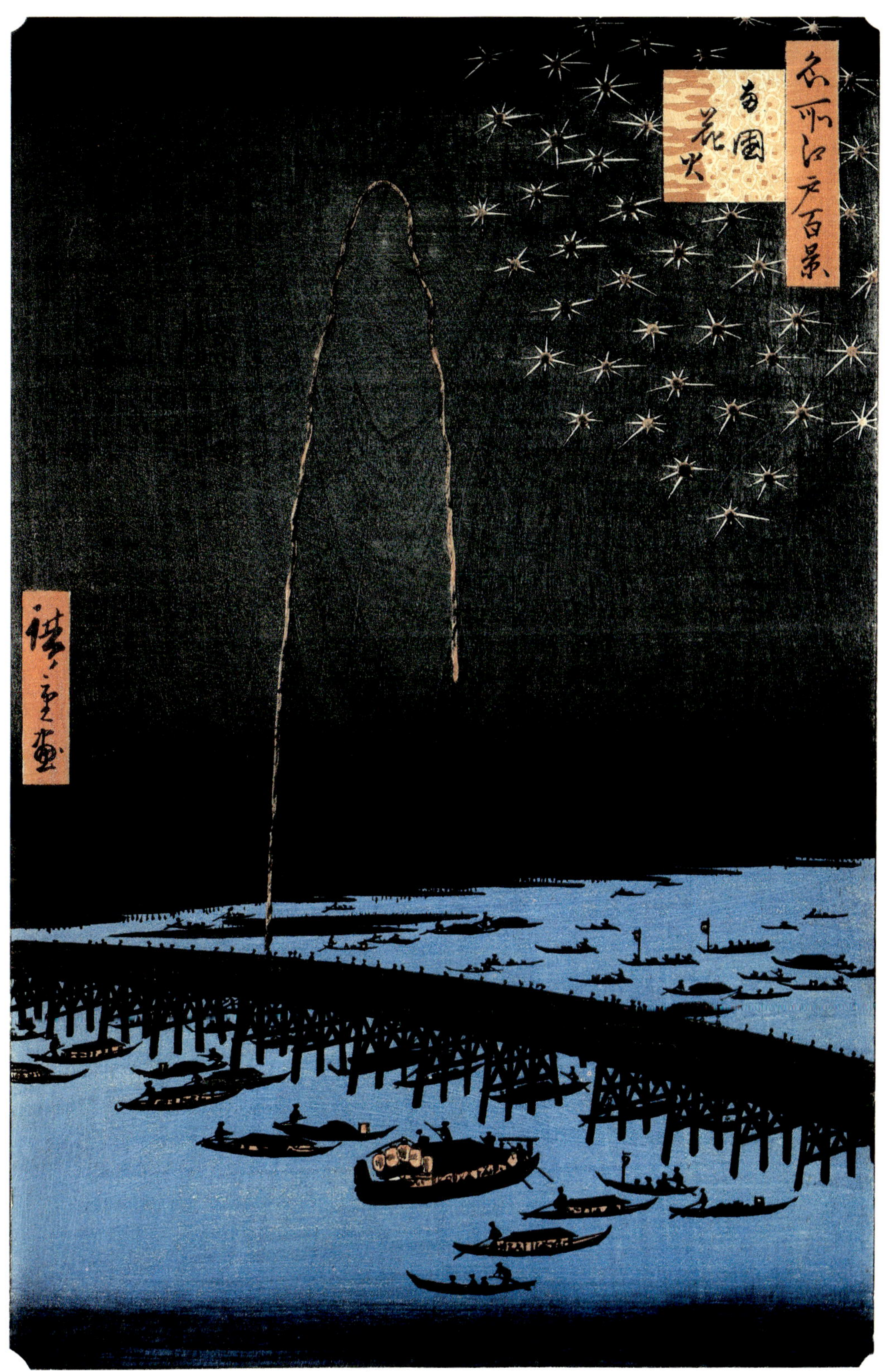
名所江戸百景
両国花火
廣重画

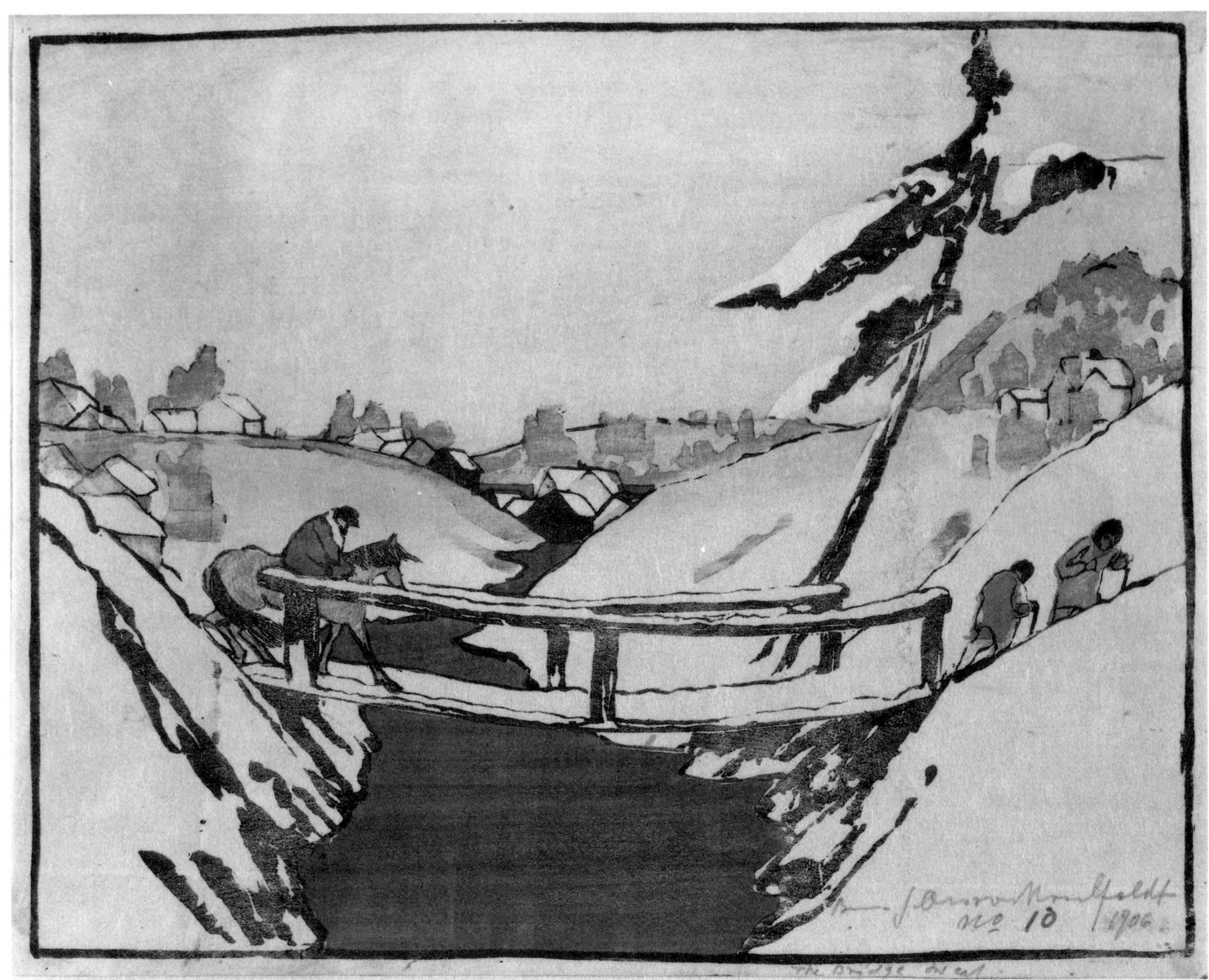

171. B. J. O. Nordfeldt, *The Bridge,* 1906. No. 10. Color woodcut. Print Collection, Miriam and Ira D. Wallach Division of Art, Prints and Photographs, The New York Public Library, Astor, Lenox and Tilden Foundations

172. Utagawa Hiroshige, *Snow Scene with Chinese Verse.* From the series *Japanese and Chinese Poems for Recitation,* c. 1840–41. Color woodcut. The Mann Collection, Highland Park, IL

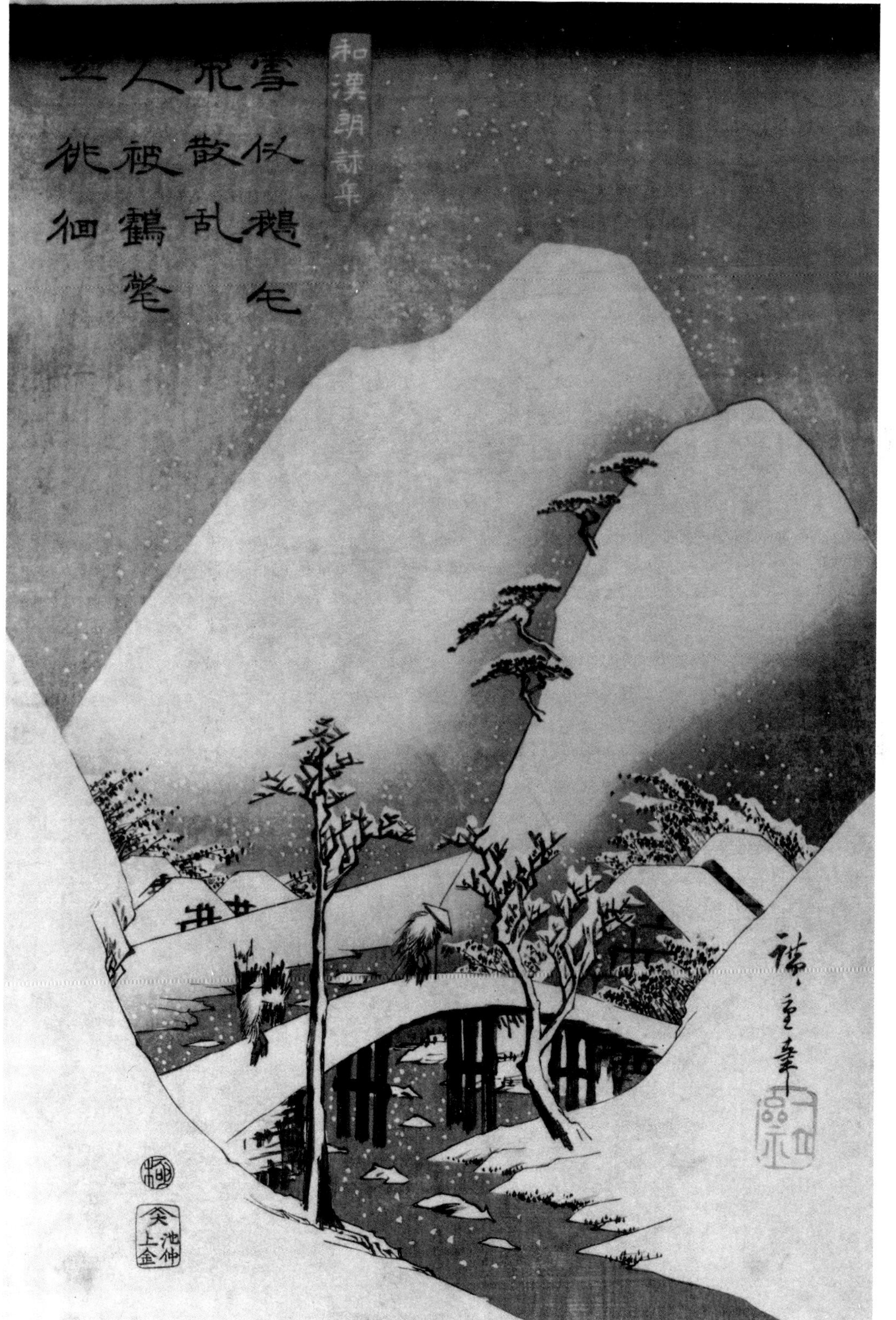
和漢朗詠集
雪似鵝毛
飛散乱
人被鶴氅
立徘徊
廣重筆

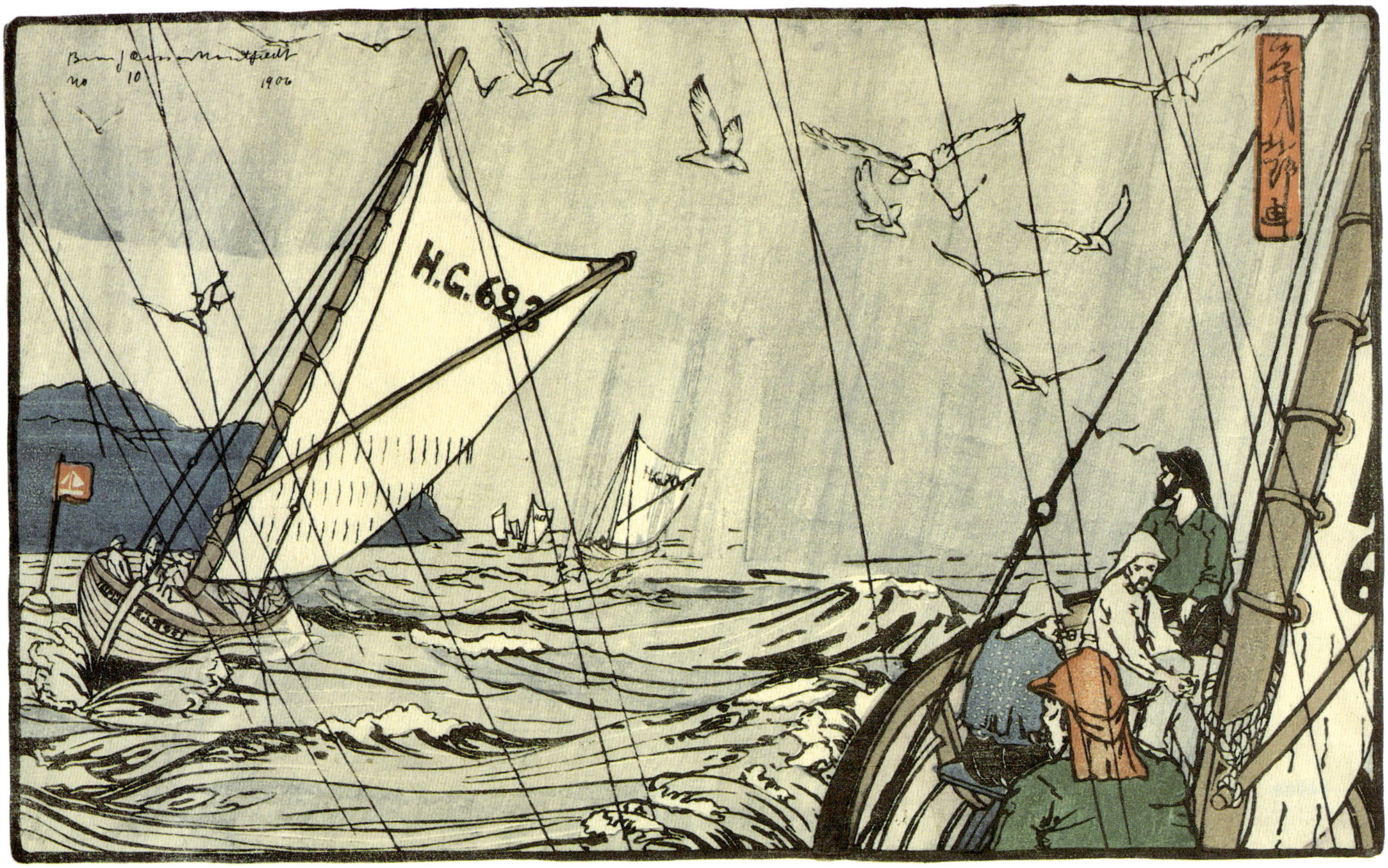

173. B. J. O. Nordfeldt, *The Storm, Skeldervicken,* 1906. No. 10. Color woodcut. Print Collection, Miriam and Ira D. Wallach Division of Art, Prints and Photographs, The New York Public Library, Astor, Lenox and Tilden Foundations

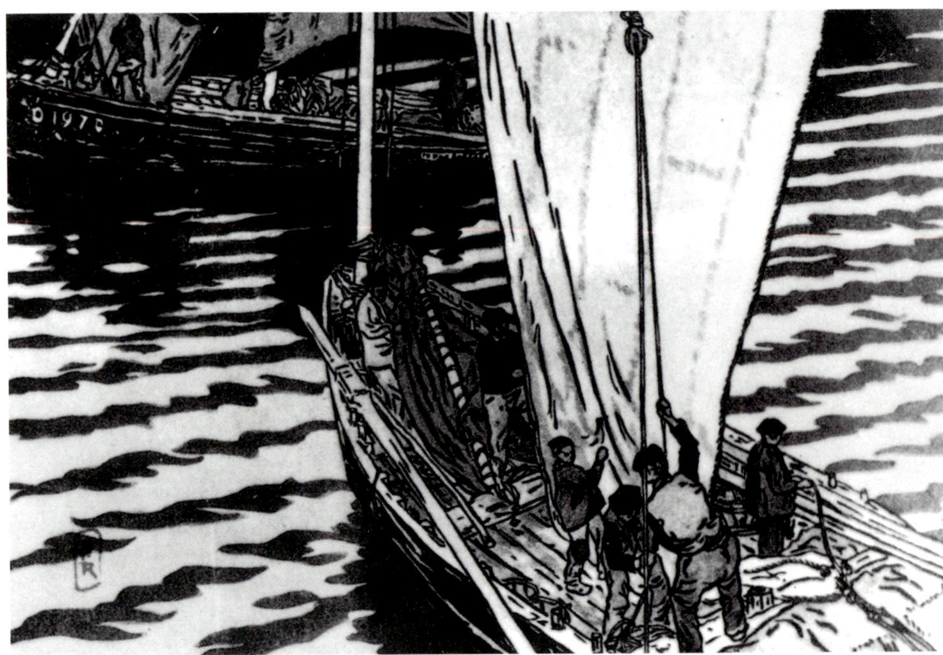

174. Henri Rivière, *Fishing Boats Setting Sail.* From *Breton Landscapes,* c. 1893. Color woodcut. Bibliothèque Nationale, Paris, Cabinet des Estampes

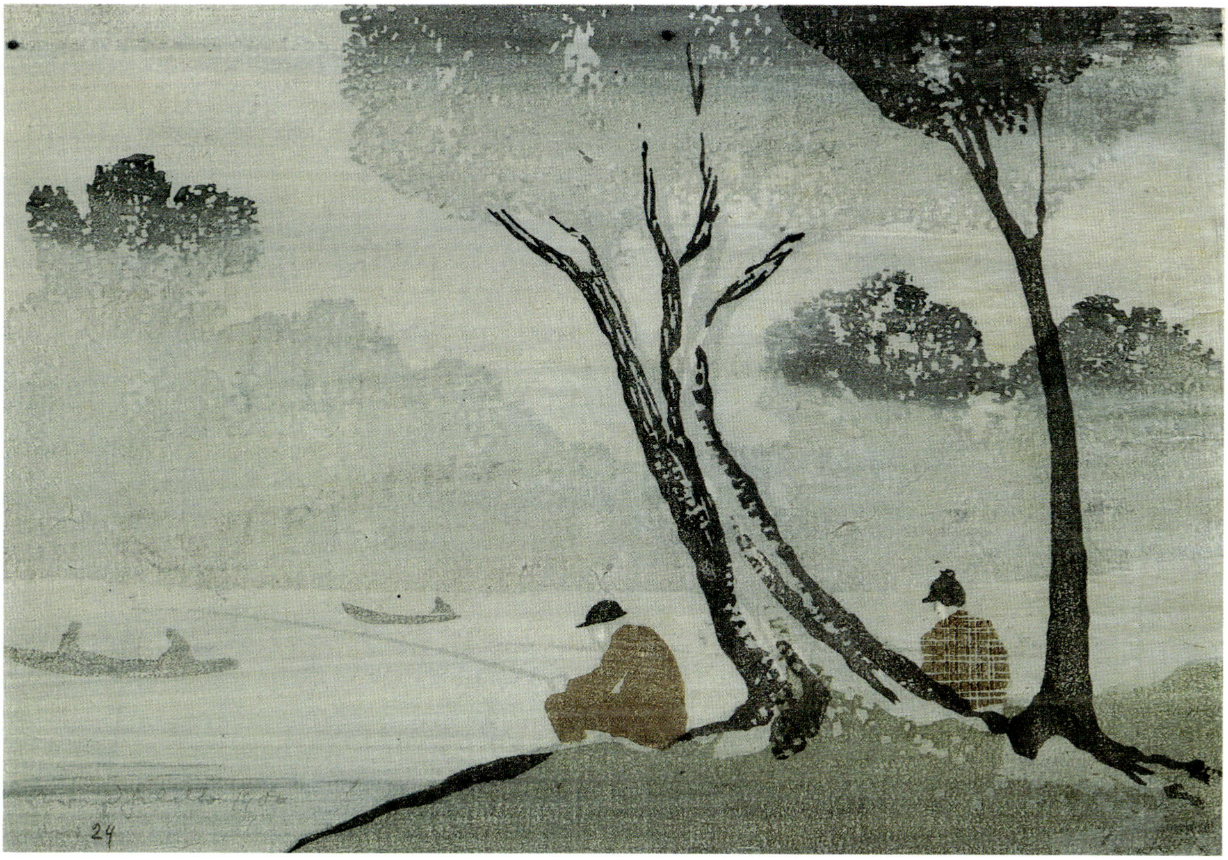

175. B. J. O. Nordfeldt, *Mist, the Anglers,* 1906. No. 24. Color woodcut. Private collection

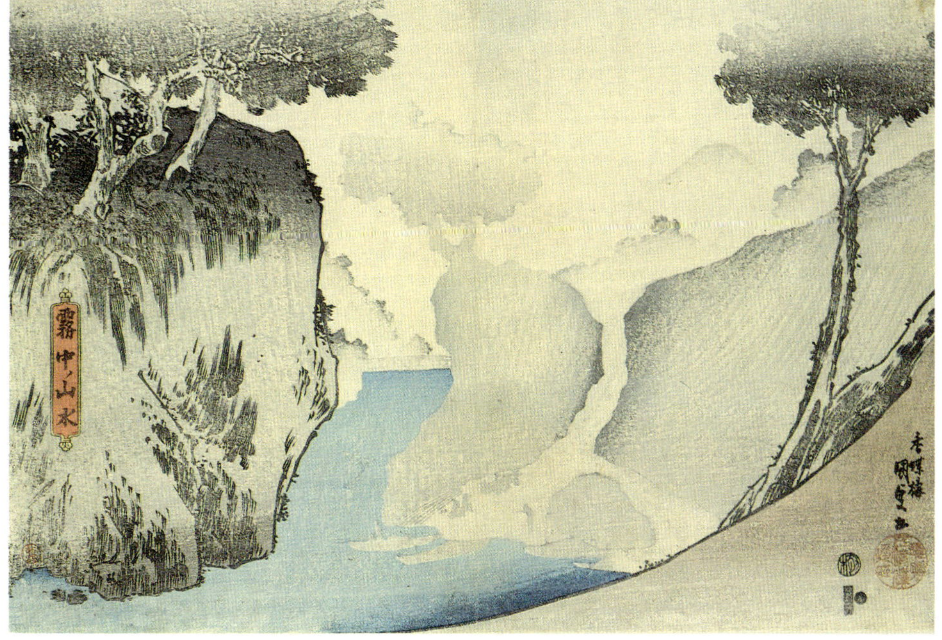

176. Utagawa Kunisada, *Landscape in Mist,* c. 1827–44. Color woodcut. The Metropolitan Museum of Art, New York, The Howard Mansfield Collection, Rogers Fund, 1936

Kunisada's beautiful *Landscape in Mist* (figs. 175 and 176). Distant fishing boats, nearly invisible at first glance, hover like pale shadows in the lower foreground of both prints. Nordfeldt's thin application of washes, brushed on in long, sweeping strokes, closely parallels Kunisada's unusually poetic and painterly image — much more painterly than the bright blocks of flat color typical of Hiroshige. Nordfeldt's figures are mute "types" reminiscent of Seurat's *Sunday Afternoon on the Island of La Grande Jatte.* The dominant gray-black color harmonies and the soft-focus abstraction also place this print in a suggestive relationship with the contemporary pictorialist images of American photographer Alvin Langdon Coburn (see pp. 222–26).

The later oil paintings that made Nordfeldt's reputation have been called "dour" and "strong"; they feature expressive forms, austere and stern in their near abstraction and intellectualized concern with formal composition. They convey a sense of brooding, solitary communion with nature. Remarkably, these qualities of controlled, concentrated expression are already inherent in the early woodcuts, the work of a man described as oppressed by "self-doubt and loneliness" in his early years.[201] In *The Rock, Nahant* (fig. 177) an isolated detail of nature is enlarged to monumental scale, creating a ponderous, dark color mass that is very like the rugged rock forms that dominate his canvases around 1950.[202] Here, again, the language is entirely American, but the original spark of inspiration for Nordfeldt may have been a Rivière lithograph such as *Study of a Wave* of 1893 (fig. 178) or even Seurat's 1885 *Bec du Hoc, Grandcamp.* For those who know Japanese prints, however, Nordfeldt's woodcut speaks immediately of the many variations on this theme (the single enlarged foreground rock jutting up from the sea) by Hiroshige, as in *Mount Fuji Viewed from Futamigaura in Ise* from the 1858 series *Thirty-six Views of Fuji.* Without ever going to Japan, Nordfeldt saw, studied, and assimilated the Japanese aesthetic, extracting elements from this new style and making it his own. This ability to absorb, synthesize, and recreate served him well throughout his life as he moved from one style to the next.

A footnote to Nordfeldt's career as a block printer occurred during his summers in Provincetown between 1914 and 1917. He was a member of the closely knit group of Provincetown printers (including Edna Boies Hopkins) who were attracted to Cape Cod during the war years. In this atmosphere of collective expertise and free exchange of ideas, he developed a modern method of working that represented a complete departure from the time-consuming and physically demanding Japanese process (which he may have abandoned after 1907 for that reason). He

> *became impatient with the mechanical labor of cutting so many blocks of wood (one for each color) before he could express his idea; one day he surprised the others by exhibiting one block, with his complete design on that, instead of parts of it being cut on five or six blocks. He had cut a groove in the wood to separate each color, and in printing this left a white line which emphasized the design.*[203]

With his invention of the so-called "white-line" print, a typically pragmatic American approach, Nordfeldt eliminated much hard work. The color harmonies of his *Putting to Sea* (fig. 179) have changed as well: they are the candy-sweet pastels of the summer colony, applied with thick watercolor pigments that have an opaque, chalky look. Taken together with the much larger scale of the paper, these more aggressive, active images have a bold new "American" look.

Elizabeth Colwell

Among Nordfeldt's students was the Michigan-born Elizabeth Colwell (1881–1954/56), who had, like himself, received instruction at the School of the Art Institute. (They had both studied life drawing with John H. Vanderpoel.) Various explanations have been given as to why the color

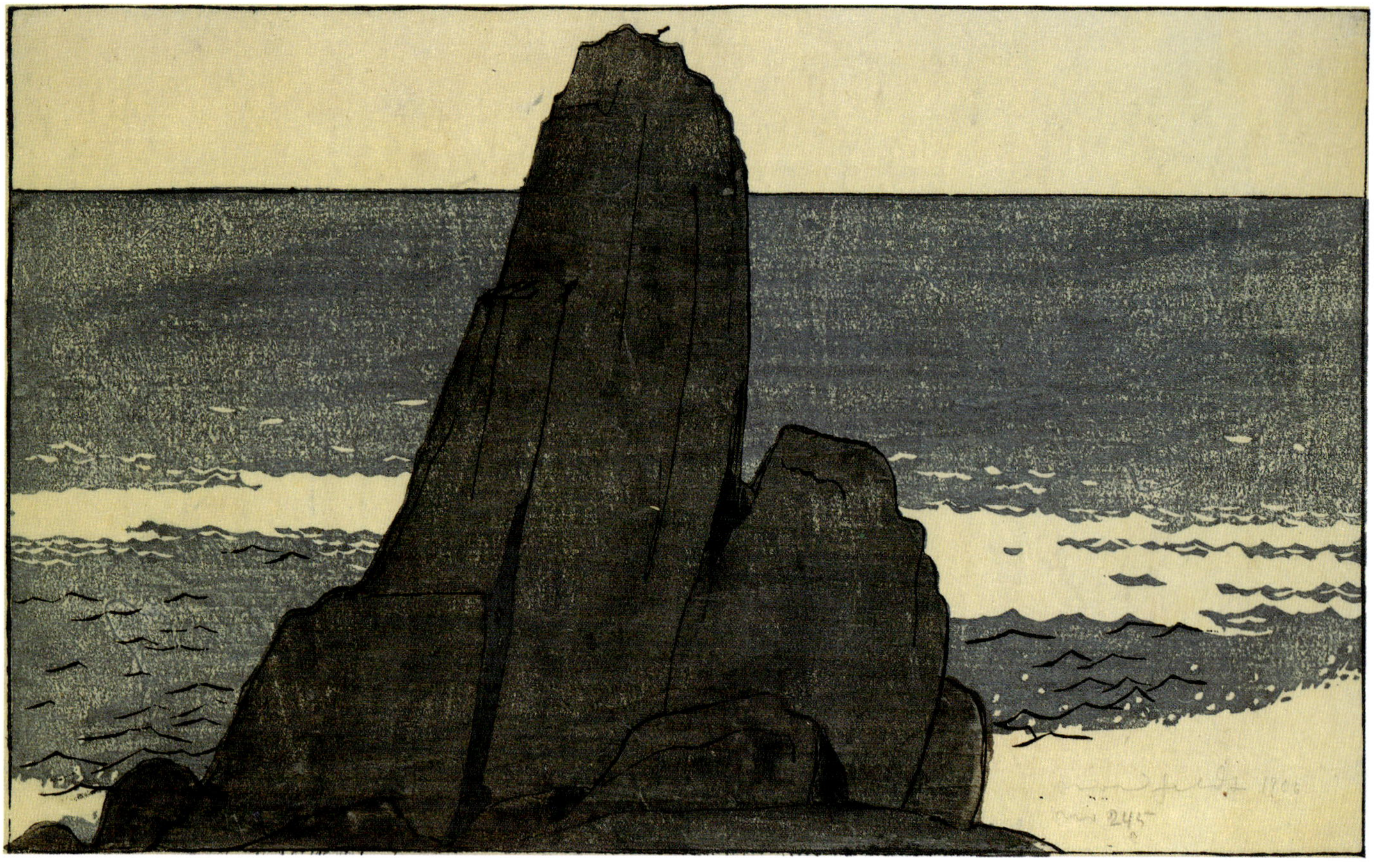

177. B. J. O. Nordfeldt, *The Rock, Nahant,* 1906. No. 245. Color woodcut. The Metropolitan Museum of Art, New York, Gift of Mrs. B. J. O. Nordfeldt, 1955

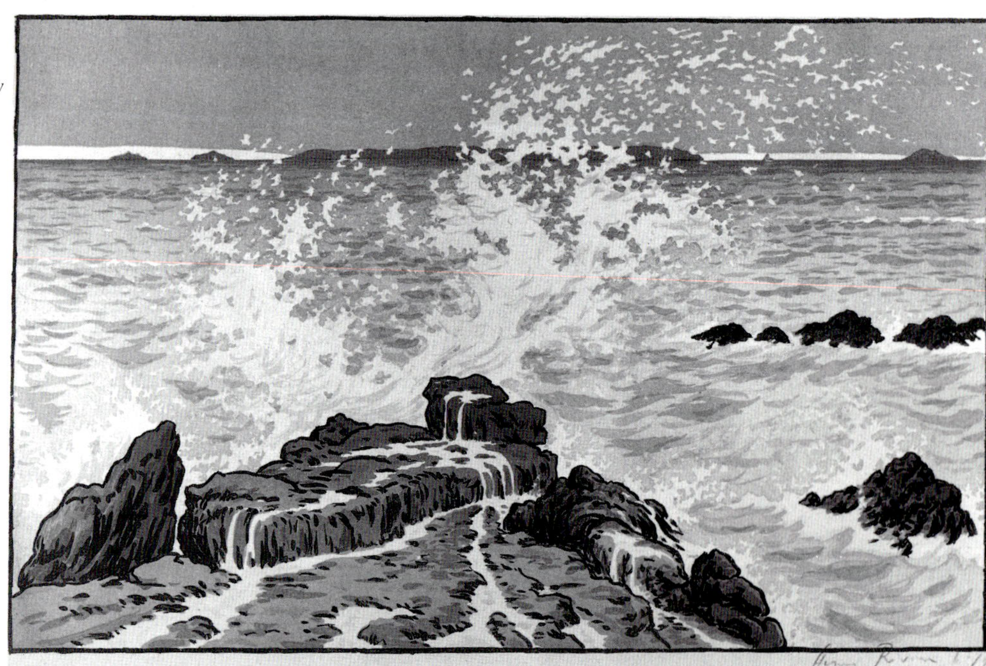

178. Henri Rivière, *Study of a Wave,* 1893. Color lithograph. The Jane Voorhees Zimmerli Art Museum, Rutgers, The State University of New Jersey, Mindy and Ramon Tublitz Purchase Fund

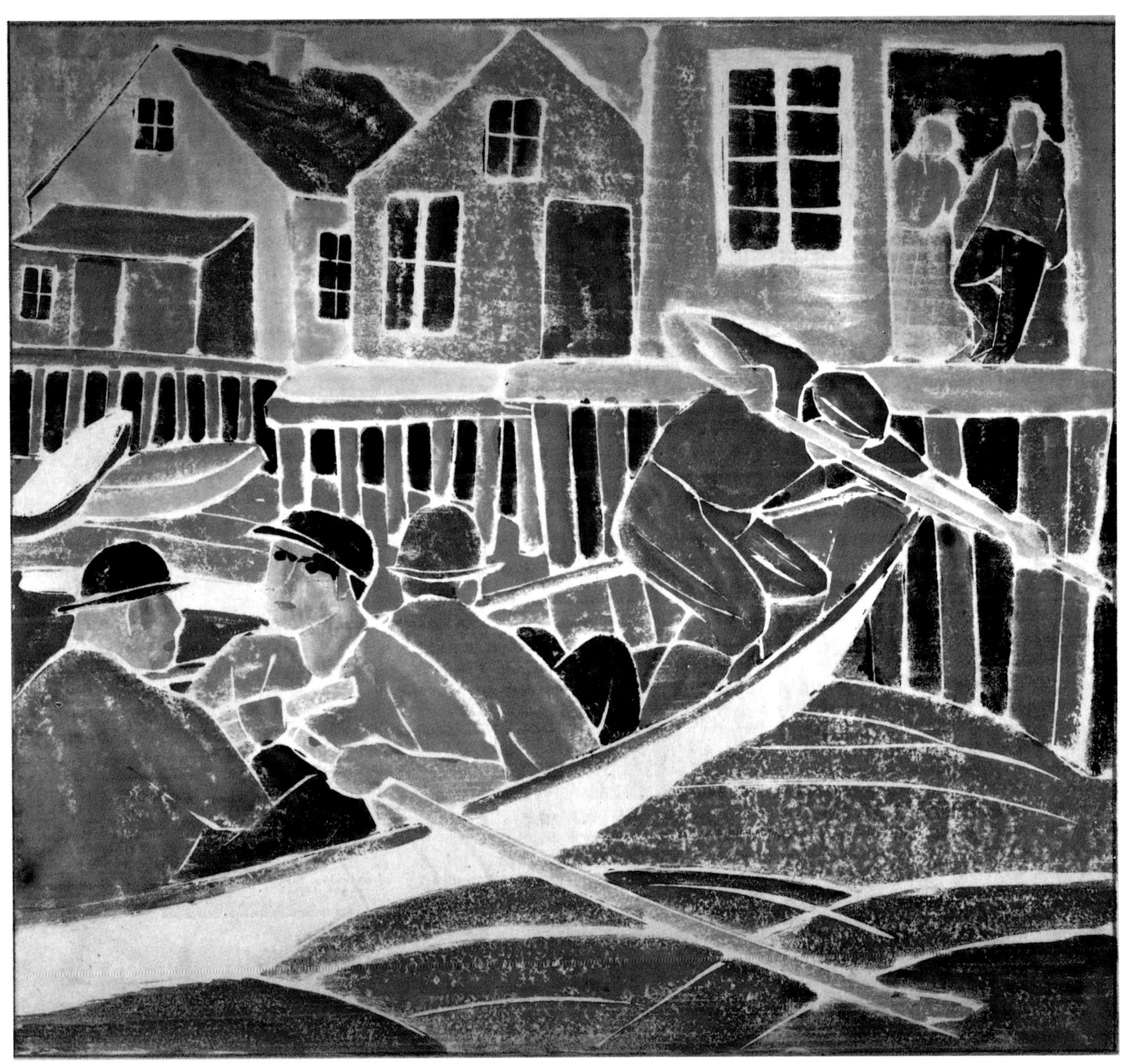

179. B. J. O. Nordfeldt, *Putting to Sea,* c. 1916. Color woodcut. The Metropolitan Museum of Art, New York, Gift of Mrs. B. J. O. Nordfeldt, 1955

woodcut attracted so many women artists. The technique is said to be simpler than that of the etching press; blocks are small and can be cut and stored at home without the expense of a studio; tools likewise are of only moderate expense. These arguments are not convincing. Colwell, like Helen Hyde, was in addition an etcher as well as a painter. Further, the true Japanese process required highly specialized training. Nordfeldt's commercial success rested entirely on his output of etchings; that he abandoned the woodcut suggests it was ultimately too time-consuming and laborious to be a commercially viable medium for him. Many of the women artists were independently wealthy. Further, those who were most serious about their craft insisted on purchasing authentic tools which could even mean the expense of a trip to Japan.

Colwell's woodcuts (some twenty to thirty images in all) were shown regularly in group exhibitions during the teens and early twenties in Chicago, New York, and Boston, but she was known primarily as a designer of bookplates, decorative borders for artistic brochures, and fancy lettering, including initial letters. She practiced hand lettering for years, and is known as the designer of a typeface cut by the American Type Founding Co. called "Colwell Hand Letter."

Birch Tree of 1906, the year of Nordfeldt's "Hiroshige" series, is her earliest dated color woodcut (fig. 180). A full moon is just visible against a very pale lavender sky. The print is quite reminiscent of Nordfeldt in its unadorned simplicity, muted colors, and thin application of color washes, although Colwell's style is more crisp and astringent, with a structural strength deriving from her work as a commercial designer. She, too, cut and printed her own blocks.[204] She shows an understanding of Japanese models in the stark abstraction of the setting and the dramatic cropping of the tree on all four sides. (Hiroshige's *One Hundred Famous Views of Edo* comes to mind at once.) The centering of the crow, however, and the attention to the naturalistic texture of the tree bark is quite definitely Western. This print was a gift to Helen Hyde in 1911, presumably during Hyde's visit to Chicago that year to make arrangements with one of her agents, Roullier's Gallery.

Alice Ravenal Huger Smith

Japanese prints affected even artists who worked in relative isolation far from the major metropolitan centers (figs. 181 and 182). Alice Smith (1876–1958) was born into a well-to-do Charleston family, studied art at the local Carolina Art Association (for the rest, she was largely self-taught), traveled only rarely, and never went abroad. After first working with oils, she began to discover herself as an artist between 1910 and 1920, when she tried her hand at color woodcuts. She eventually devoted herself almost exclusively to watercolors, concentrating on lush and romantic views of her native Low Country coastal area.

Smith had access to an extensive collection of over four hundred ukiyo-e prints assembled by her cousin and mentor, Motte Alston Read (d. 1920), during his years in Boston, where he held the Chair of Physiography at Harvard University, and then in Charleston after his retirement for health reasons. She helped him catalogue the collection, which was subsequently given to the Carolina Art Association, at the Gibbes Art Gallery in Charleston, and she is also known to have experimented with printing directly from the actual Japanese woodblocks that he had acquired. Read's passion for ukiyo-e was stimulated by his longtime friend Frederick Gookin at the Art Institute of Chicago.[205] Gookin also took a personal interest in the woodcuts of Read's cousin, Alice Smith: "Were the old Japanese masters of landscape painting still alive and could see these pictures, they could not fail to be delighted by them as I am," he wrote her. "Your study of the essential quality in Hiroshige's prints has, I feel sure, helped in perhaps more than you realize."[206]

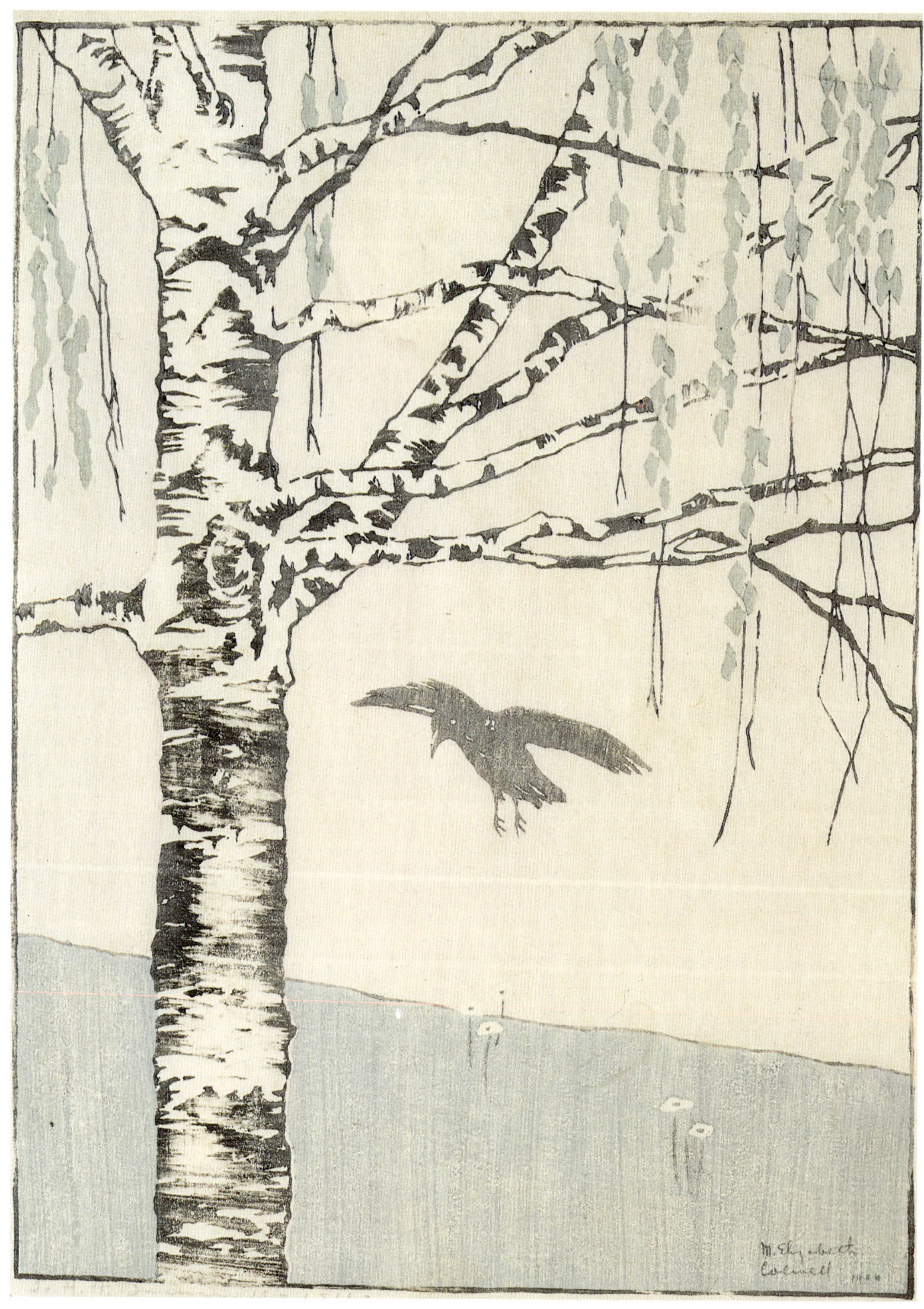

180. Elizabeth Colwell, *Birch Tree,* 1906.
Color woodcut. Private collection

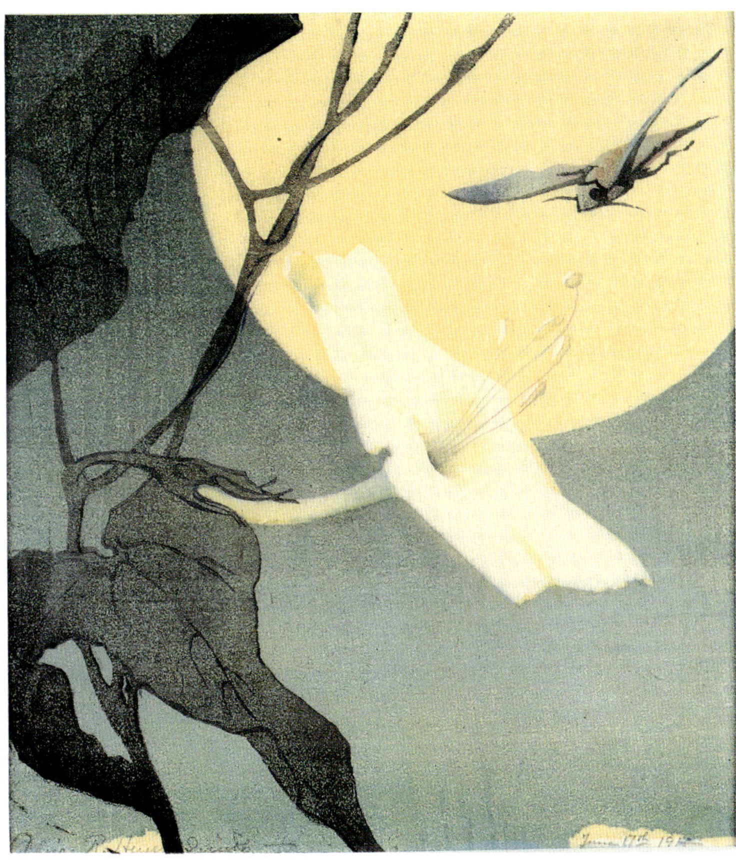

181. Alice Ravenal Huger Smith, *Moon Flower and Hawk Moth,* 1917. Color woodcut. Gibbes Art Gallery, Charleston

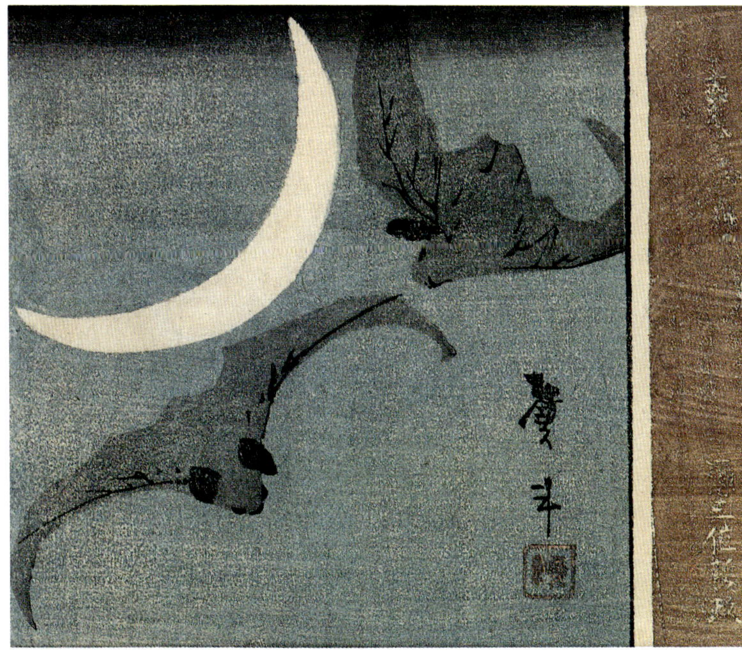

182. Katsushika Hokusai, *Bats and Moon.* Color woodcut. Gibbes Museum of Art Charleston. Formerly Motte Alston Read Collection

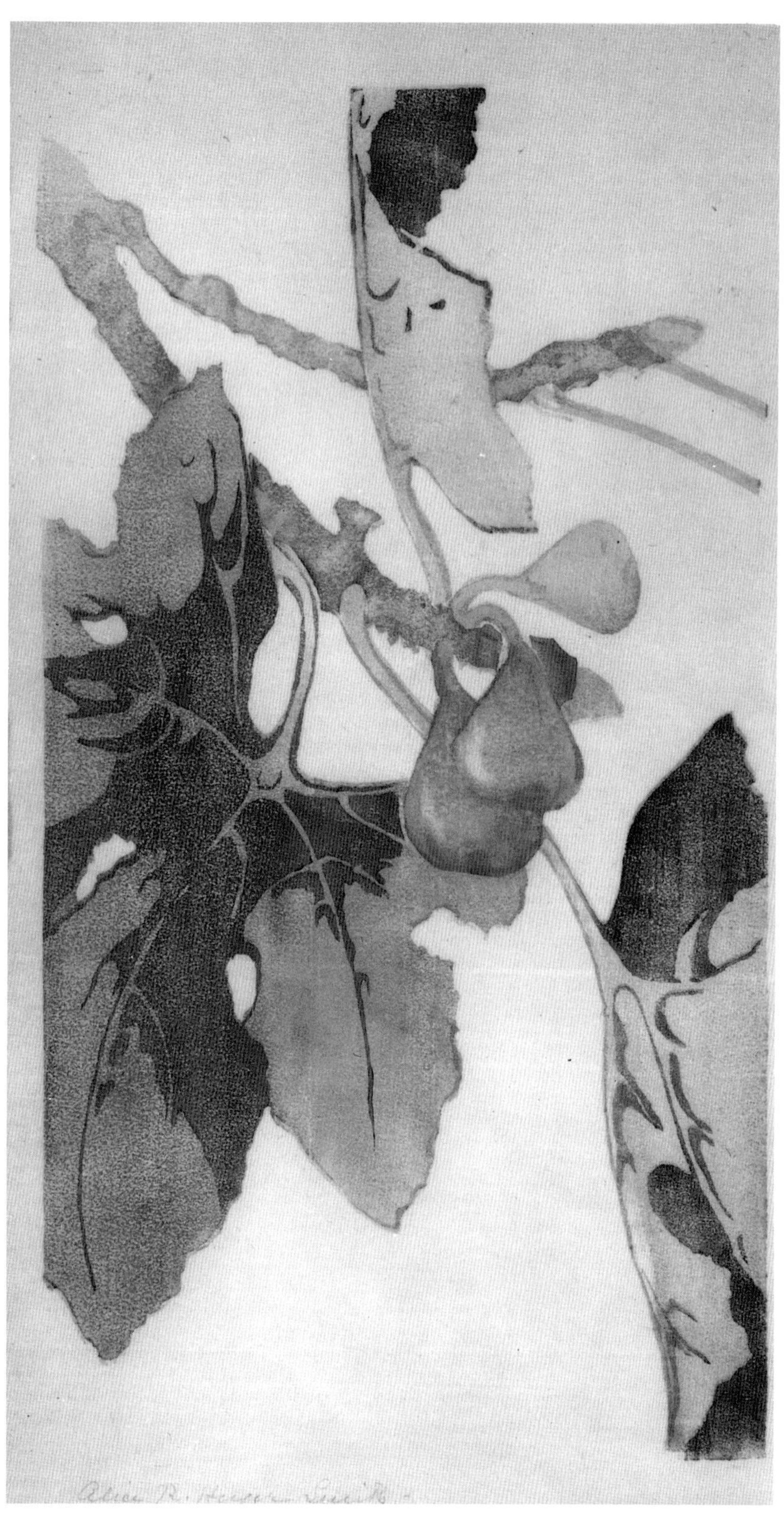

183. Alice Ravenal Huger Smith, *Celestial Figs,* c. 1918. Color woodcut. Gala M. Chamberlain Collection

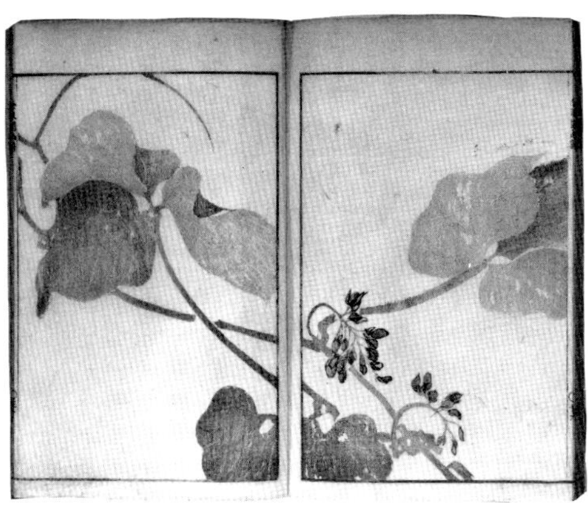

184. Kawamura Bumpō, *Kimpaen gafu* (A Book of Paintings by Kimpaen), 1820. Woodblock printed book. Ravicz Collection

Martha Severens has observed that "the influence of the Japanese print on Smith's work was real and palpable. . . . With the Japanese, Smith shared a sense of simple design, most vividly evident in her vertical compositions."[207] *Celestial Figs* is undated but was exhibited at the Art Institute of Chicago in 1919 (fig. 183).[208] The impression illustrated here came from the collection of Helen Hyde, who spent the winter of 1916 in the Carolinas making a series of sensitive etchings and lithographs of black family life on the old plantations.[209] When Hyde received a package with Smith's woodcut in January 1918 in Chicago she wrote back:

You astound me yes you do! I was so amazed at your print. It is so sure and finished, clean in technique. I am so proud of my pupil — I feel like a pouter pigeon or like one of those conjugal ducks from Japan that swell out their chests in such a ridiculous exhibit they nearly fall over backward. It is absurd to call you my pupil for you have gone far beyond in the printing tone. . . . It looks like a Japanese painting.[210]

Hyde, who had relied on artisan assistants, and had all but abandoned the woodcut medium after resettling in Chicago in 1915, subsequently displayed Smith's work on her mantle. Another fan of Smith's woodcuts was Bertha Jaques (1863–1941), one of the major powers in American printmaking and a founder of the Chicago Society of Etchers. A close friend of both Hyde and Gookin, she helped Smith order cherry and pine printing blocks as well as Japanese paper. Her reaction in 1918 upon seeing Smith's latest print was strong: "We surrender — both Helen Hyde and myself! You have beaten us at our own game!"[211]

A parallel for the tumbling rhythms of Smith's *Figs* can be found in the pages of the 1820 *Kimpaen gafu* by Kawamura Bumpō (1779–1821; fig. 184) or the vertical flower and bird prints by Hiroshige. No doubt she had also absorbed the lessons of Dow's "principles of composition" (see fig. 130). By 1924 she had produced no more than a total of about eight woodcuts; her father urged her to give up printmaking in favor of watercolors, to him a more familiar and serious art form. For Alice Smith, the era of infatuation with the craft of the self-made print had passed.

Photography and Japonisme

American pictorialist photographers at the turn of the century were still struggling to convince a recalcitrant public (not to mention artists and illustrators, who felt threatened by the medium) to accept their work as a legitimate form of fine art. Not surprisingly, they wrestled with the same artistic concerns as printmakers and painters. Many of them (Stieglitz, Steichen, Weston, and White, for example) were touched by the Japanese aesthetic of simplicity, abstraction, evocative empty spaces, even narrow vertical formats.[212] Japanese art helped them to see naturalistic objects in a new light.

Alvin Langdon Coburn

Alvin Langdon Coburn (1882–1966), born into a middle-class family in Boston, responded intuitively to the stimulus of Japanese prints and paintings during his early years of apprenticeship (fig. 185). He received a Kodak at the age of eight and by age eighteen, in 1900, he was participating in an avant-garde group show in London organized by his distant cousin F. Holland Day. Artistically precocious, he had the status of an ambitious infant prodigy and was apparently idolized in London literary circles, where he was nicknamed "the Hustler." Coburn spent most of his life in England, taking British citizenship in 1932, immersed in a search for his own Holy Grail. Whistler and Lafcadio Hearn were among his special objects of veneration, but at the formative stage of his

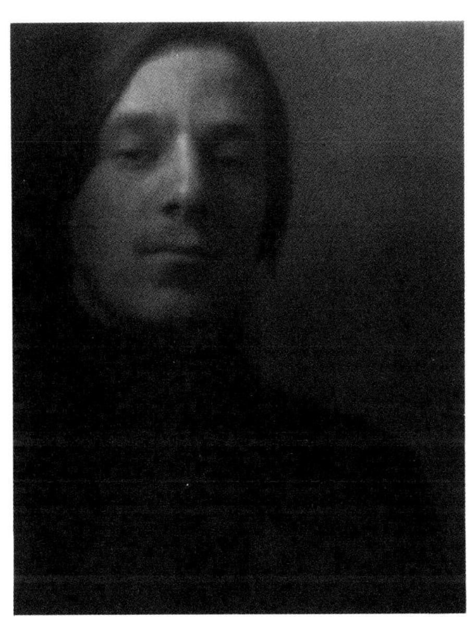

185. Alvin Langdon Coburn, *Self-Portrait*, c. 1905. Platinum print. International Museum of Photography at George Eastman House, Rochester, NY

career he was profoundly influenced by Arthur Wesley Dow.

In 1902, after a year in Paris under the tutelage of Steichen, he opened a studio in New York and studied with Gertrude Käsebier (1852–1934), who probably encouraged his attendance at Dow's summer school in Ipswich. (Käsebier and Dow were on the faculty at Pratt together.) During two summers with Dow, 1902 and 1903 (on the eve of Dow's trip to Japan), Coburn received a firm grounding in the principles of good composition and in the concept of notan. He was also exposed to Japanese art. "I learned many things at [Dow's] school," he wrote, "not the least an appreciation of what the Orient has to offer us in terms of simplicity and directness of composition."[213] His 1903 *The Bridge, Ipswich* (fig. 186) is taken from the same angle as Dow's miniature woodcut of 1895 (fig. 124). Dow was himself a photographer and based some of his Ipswich woodcuts on his own photographic studies.

Coburn was still in his early twenties when he produced some of his best work (fig. 187). British scholar Mike Weaver called attention to the parallels between Hiroshige's *Ferry at Haneda* from *One Hundred Famous Views of Edo* and Coburn's 1904 *Wapping*, from his series of views of London (figs. 188 and 189).[214] Like Hokusai with his *Thirty-six Views of Fuji* followed by his three-volume book *One Hundred Views of Fuji* (1834–c. 1836), Hiroshige, a commercial artist, appealed to a jaded public by stretching for offbeat, amusing, novel angles of vision to enliven his series (he never depicted the same place twice). Hiroshige plays off enlarged foreground objects and the background in diverse and provocative ways, with the foreground typically more active, the background more neutral and passive.[215] Using a bowsprit as a large foreground repoussoir element, Coburn captures the same dramatic effect, and he flattens space in the Japanese manner with a steeply rising ground plane and high horizon. To this end, he pioneered the use of a telephoto lens, which effectively flattens perspective so that near and far elements appear to be on one plane.

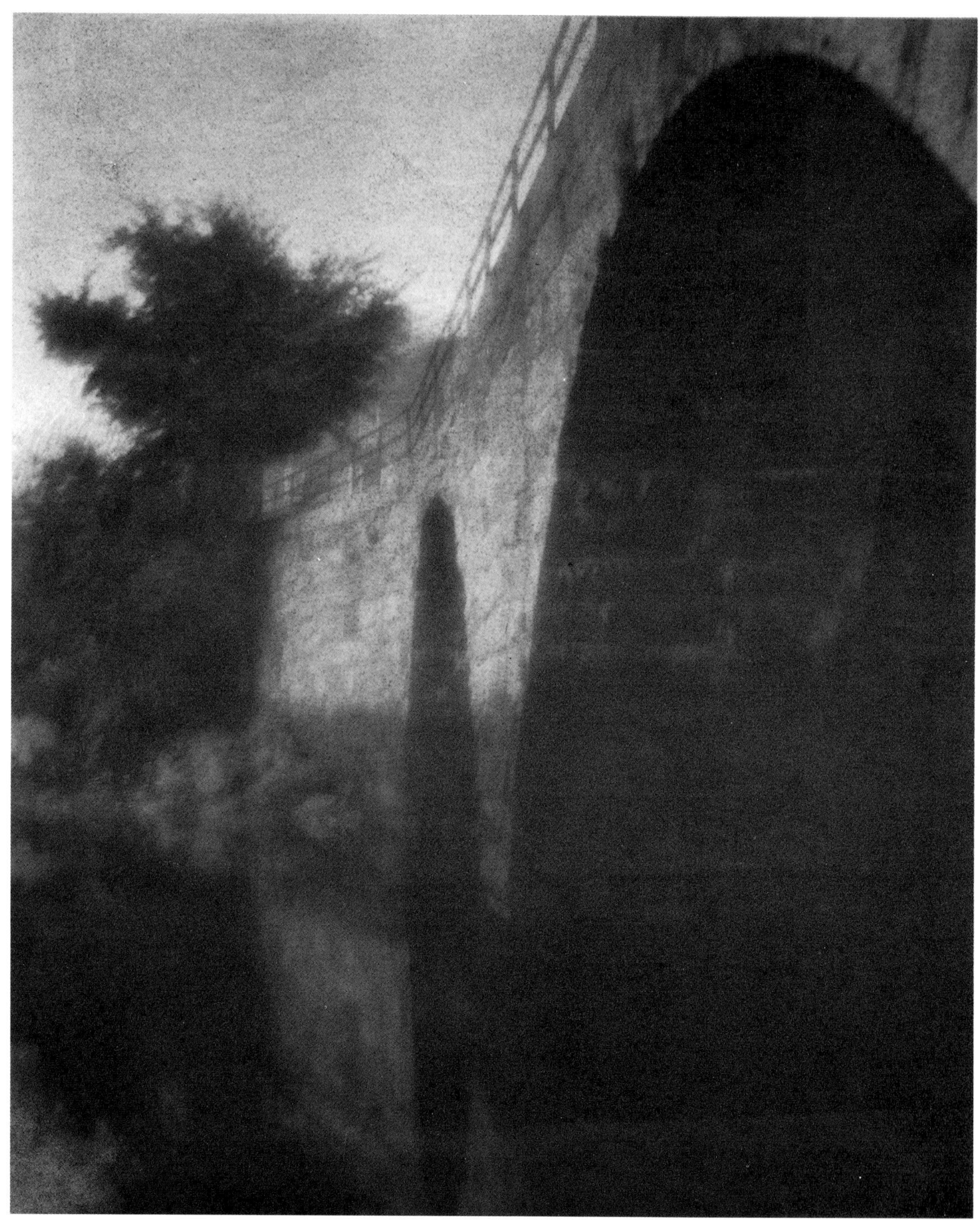

186. Alvin Langdon Coburn, *The Bridge, Ipswich,* 1903. Photograph, blue-gray pigment gum-biochromate over platinum. The Metropolitan Museum of Art, New York, Alfred Stieglitz Collection, 1949

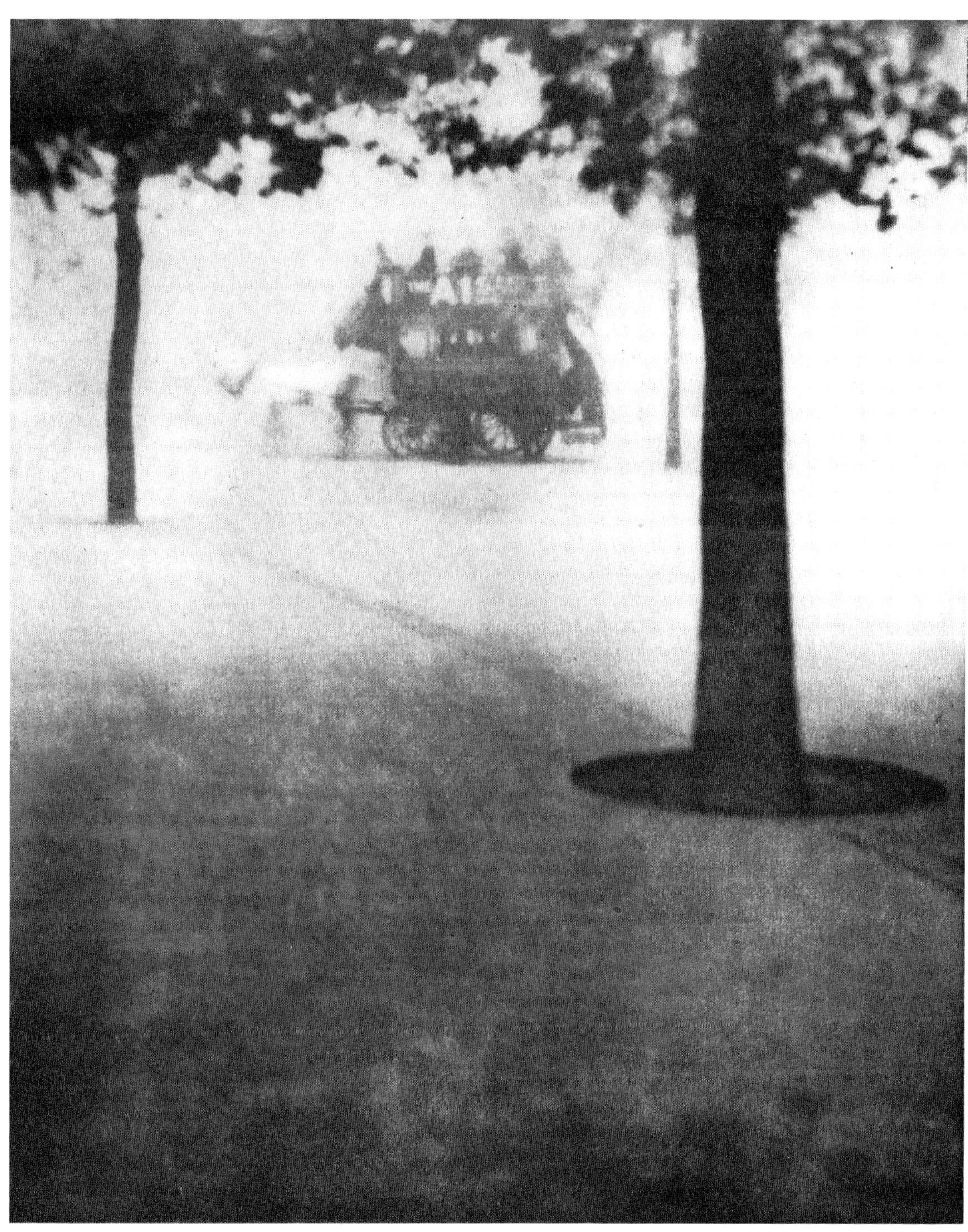

187. Alvin Langdon Coburn, *Hyde Park Corner,* 1905. Plate V from *London,* 1909. Photogravure. Museum of Fine Arts, Boston. Benjamin P. Cheney Fund

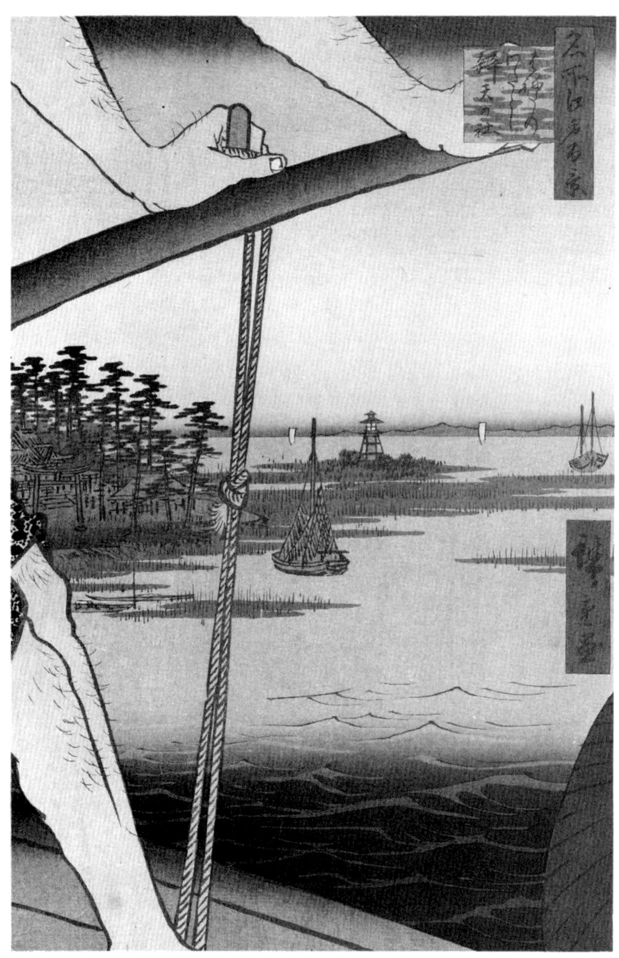

188. Utagawa Hiroshige, *Benten Shrine and Ferry at Haneda.* From the series *One Hundred Famous Views of Edo,* 1857. Color woodcut. Worcester Art Museum, Worcester, MA

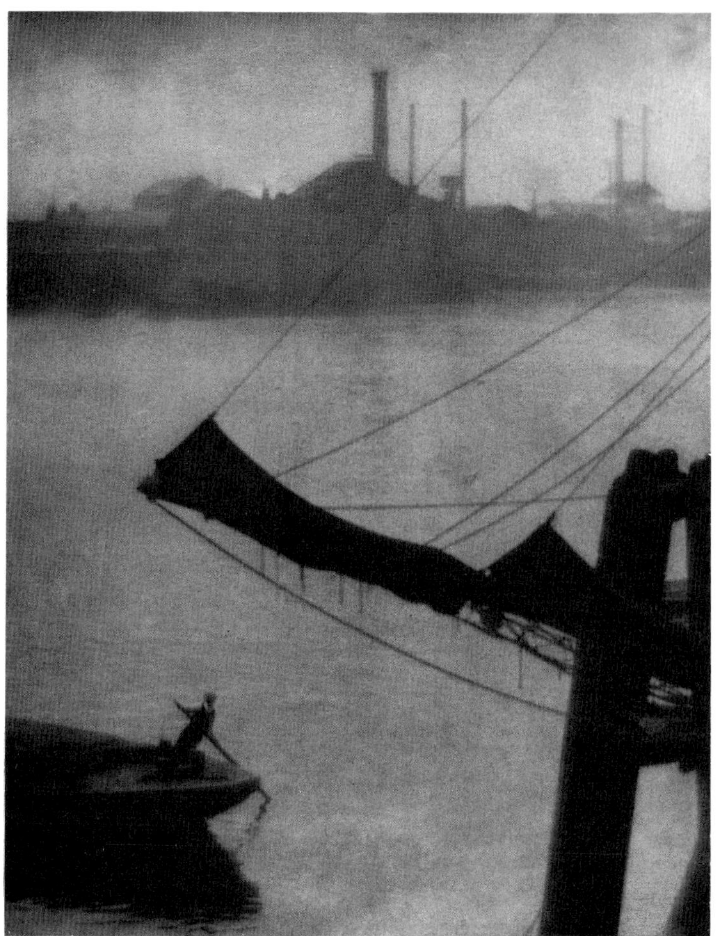

189. Alvin Langdon Coburn, *Wapping,* 1904. Plate X from *London,* 1909. Photogravure. International Museum of Photography at George Eastman House, Rochester, NY

From the beginning Coburn avoided historical and allegorical tableaux, and turned his camera on commonplace locations such as Ipswich rooftops and London bridges to illustrate the theories articulated by Dow, and to recreate the cityscape themes of Hiroshige's "Famous Places" of Edo, most of which include a river, canal, or bay. Dow minimized representation in favor of formal artistic concerns, but for Coburn the spiritual meaning was as significant as the decorative or formal patterns. A student first of the occult, and then strongly attracted to a variety of mystery religions, Coburn wanted to approach the infinite — he was "more Taoist than Dowist" in his beliefs.[216] By the time he became a member of the Universal Order, which dedicated itself to the study of sacred texts ranging from Greek to Chinese and Buddhist, his religious concerns entirely subsumed his creative energies.

Coburn referred to himself as the "Whistler of photography," and he achieved this ideal vision with a combination of the new soft-focus lens and the platinum printing technique, which made possible "clarity without sharpness and softness without fuzziness." With the telephoto and soft-focus lenses he could achieve spatial and luminous simplification, the equivalent of the "elimination of the inessential" that was perceived as a fundamental virtue of Japanese prints.

Arnold Genthe

By coincidence, it was scenes of the neighborhood children of San Francisco's Chinatown, "the Canton of the West," that acted as a "starter" for both Arnold Genthe and Helen Hyde in the mid-1890s.

Born in Germany, Arnold Genthe (1869–1942) grew up in Hamburg in a cultivated, scholarly family. A formidable linguist, he was also given to wandering in museums and was exposed there to Asian art under the tutelage of Dr. Justus Brinckmann, author of *Kunst und Handwerk in Japan*

(1889), the first comprehensive book on the subject in German. Genthe emigrated to San Francisco in 1895 as tutor for the son of a wealthy baron and was soon launched in society. Fascinated by the teeming street life of San Francisco's Chinatown, and especially its children, he taught himself photography. His view is by no means sentimental. His *Children Smoking,* for example, conveys a far different mood from the cuddly cherubs of Helen Hyde's etchings, but the imagery was perceived by his public as "picturesque" at a time when this still meant something fresh and new. In 1909 Genthe and his friend Will Irwin, a prominent California journalist (married to Helen Hyde's youngest sister, Hallie), published *Pictures of Old Chinatown* together. (Most of Chinatown had been destroyed in the earthquake of 1906.)

Genthe became a successful high-society photographer, settling in New York City in 1911. His reputation was that of "a Don Juan, a hermit monk, a Chinese sage, a university professor, all rolled into one."[217] He began collecting Japanese art in San Francisco, crediting an early encounter with Fenollosa for sparking his interest in prints. He haunted the auction houses, and over a period of twenty years accumulated a collection of two thousand ukiyo-e woodcuts. He prided himself on being a discriminating connoisseur whose goal was to eliminate all but the earliest impressions. When he sold four hundred prints at auction in New York in 1917, he was so well versed in the subject that he wrote the catalogue himself. Nearly half the collection consisted of works by Hiroshige, Hokusai, and Utamaro.[218] Genthe devoted a chapter of his memoirs, *As I Remember,* to Japan, where he traveled for six months in 1908. He was a serious and sensitive visitor, who took the trouble to learn some colloquial Japanese and practice calligraphy. He climbed Mount Fuji and spent a few months with the Ainu aborigines. He was also ideally situated to collect Japanese art. His host

would have sent word to the curio dealers of the place that a distinguished collector from America was with them and wanted to see some of their wares. Along they would come

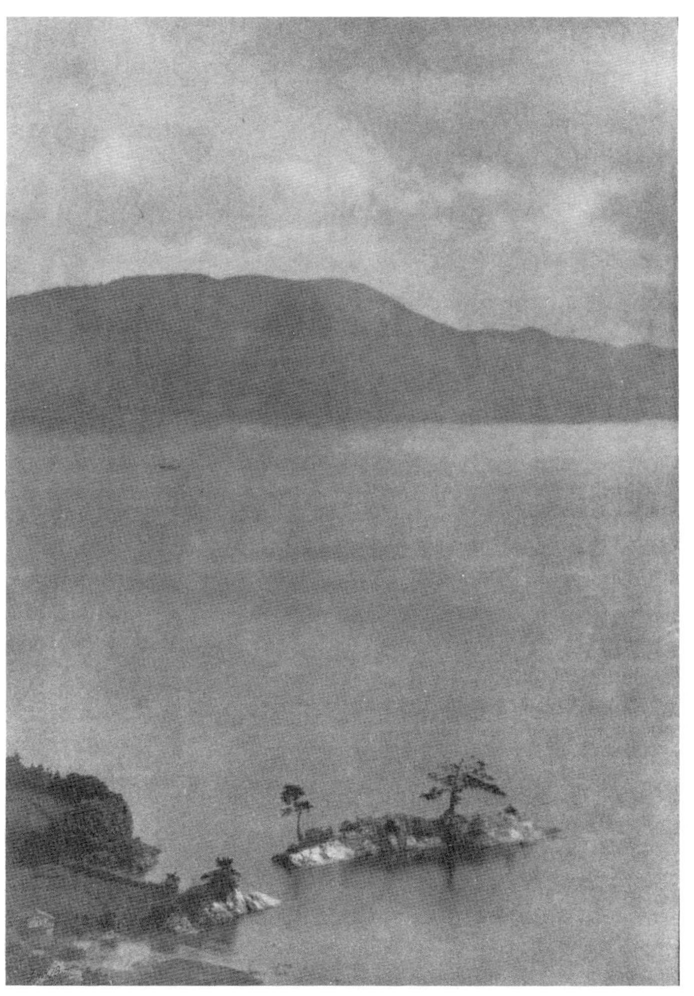

190. Arnold Genthe, *The Inland Sea,* 1908. Gelatin silver print. The Metropolitan Museum of Art, New York, Alfred Stieglitz Collection

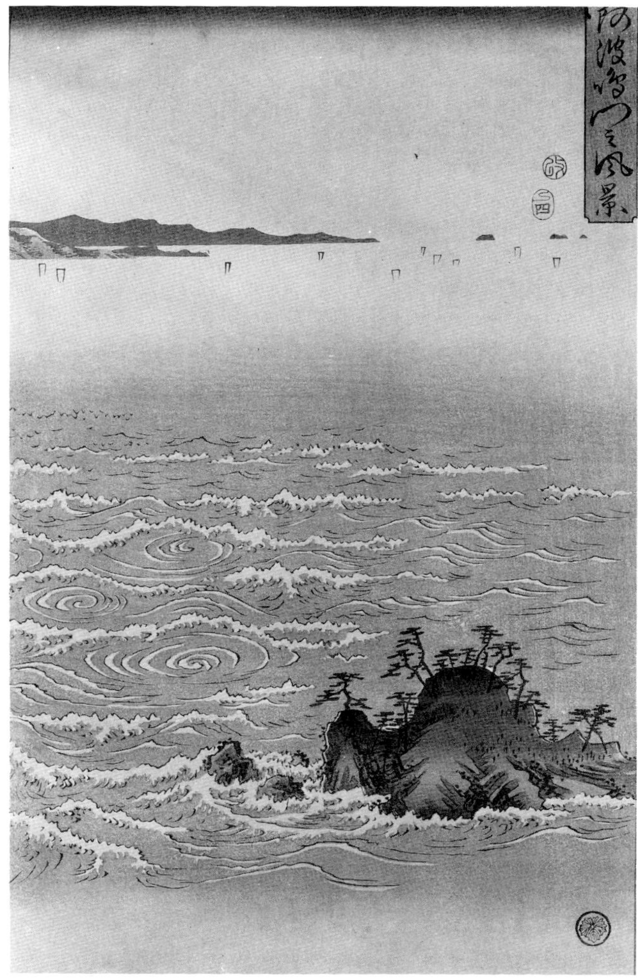

191. Utagawa Hiroshige, *Whirlpools at Awa,* from the series *Snow, Moon, and Flowers,* 1857. Right-hand panel of triptych, color woodcut. The Metropolitan Museum of Art, New York, Bequest of Mrs. H. O. Havemeyer, 1929. H. O. Havemeyer Collection

in the evening with large bundles, and before an audience that included the entire household, the servants in the background at a respectful distance, they spread out a fascinating array of embroideries, hangings, kimonos, netsukes, kakemonos, *prints, illustrated books, ancient swords, etc. There were long sessions with much bargaining and tea drinking in the best Japanese manner. . . .*[219]

A comparison of his 1908 bird's-eye view of the Inland Sea and the right-hand panel of a Hiroshige triptych, *Whirlpools at Awa,* suggests that Genthe was trying to see the world through the eyes of a Japanese artist (figs. 190 and 191). This photograph has been described by his friend Dorothy Neumeyer as

a mood — no deep shadows or highlights — just calmness, the water surrounded by hills and mountains. In the distance there is a small boat in the quiet water. When I asked Genthe where he was when he took the picture, he just looked at me with a wry little smile and said nothing; one would not explain such serenity. This lovely Inland Sea reminds me of Genthe's calmness. Perhaps he had a temper, but he never displayed it.[220]

Viewed in terms of mood, the Hiroshige does appear lively and animated, alive with crisply delineated, swirling whirlpools. Genthe strives rather for the soft-focus, muted look of a painting. His own appraisal of ukiyo-e is of interest in this regard:

A great value of the good examples of these . . . prints, aside from their intrinsic beauty, lies, to my mind, in the fact that they constitute an admirable introduction to an intelligent appreciation of the works of the great Japanese painters. . . . Being easily accessible to everyone, they are the best preparation for our Western eye for understanding the significance of Oriental line and Oriental pictorial conventions.[221]

An archetypal figure of late pictorialism, Genthe was pleased when people mistook his photographs for mezzotints. Although Japonisme was only a brief moment in his career, it seems that prints may have helped to shape his way of composing. For example, his 1908 photograph of the *Great*

192. Arnold Genthe, *The Great Buddha*, 1908. Gelatin silver print. Courtesy James F. Carr

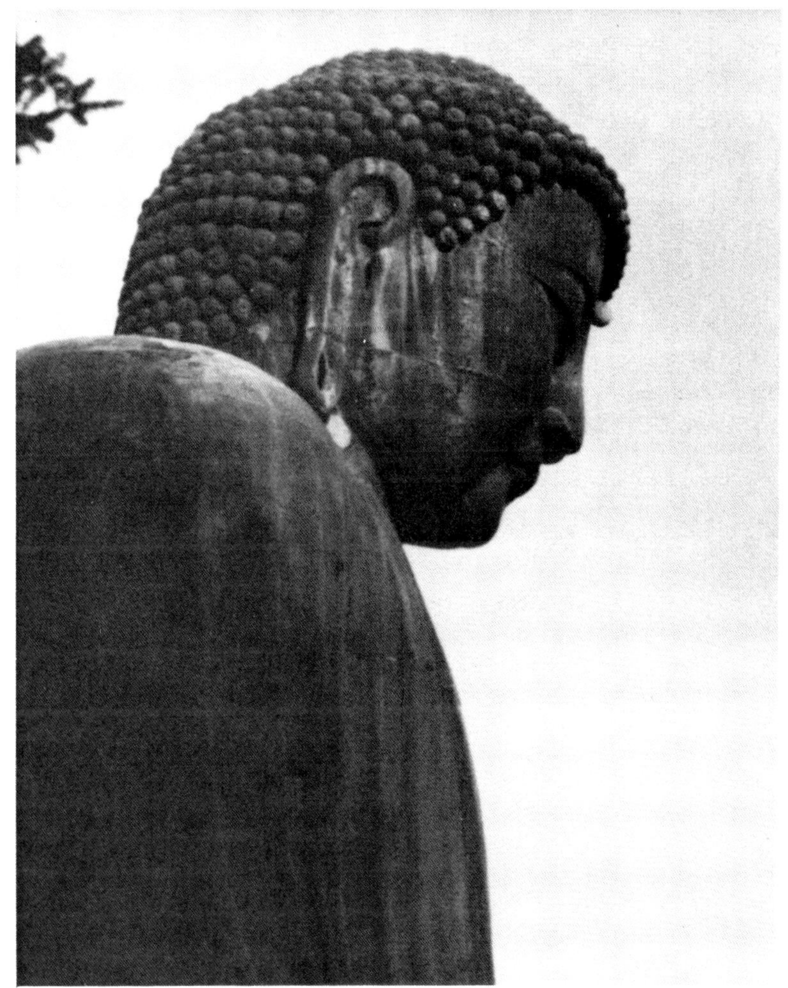

Buddha at Kamakura is quite original and daring in its choice of angle (fig. 192). Almost everyone from Venetian Felice Beato, one of the first Western photographers to work extensively in Japan, to John La Farge had pictured this huge sculpture, a "must" on the tourist circuit, in full frontal view framed by trees. Genthe gives us a tight, close-up profile, eliminating all but the right shoulder, with only the tiniest wisp of foliage retained for scale. The use of the flattened silhouette is very reminiscent of the black shadow picture (*kage-e*) profiles of kabuki actors by mid-nineteenth century printmakers such as Yoshiiku (who may in turn have been influenced by the new art of photography). The technique serves Genthe well in his later field of specialization, commercial portraits of the rich and famous; one might well compare his profile of Eleonora Duse with that of the Great Buddha.

Conclusion

Americans did not invent Japonisme and a recurring theme in our study is the dependence on French and English sources of inspiration. In the 1890s a young American artist was expected to spend at least a year in Paris, usually at the Académie Julian, and perhaps in London as well. Some, like photographer Alvin Langdon Coburn, decided to live abroad. In Europe they were initiated into modern art and its close relative, Japanese art. The influence of French and British Japonisme, as well as the influence of Japanese art itself, is an important factor in this complex story. Further complicating the picture are the effects of East-West interaction: as Japanese artists and illustrators were exposed to Western naturalism, it became increasingly difficult to distinguish national boundaries. Around 1900 a Japanese oil painter such as Kuroda Seiki, trained in Paris, looks Western, whereas Henry Bowie, an American trained in Kyoto, looks Japanese. This total submersion of personality is an extreme at one end of the spectrum. On the other hand, there were some Americans in the late nineteenth century, like Robert Blum and Theodore Wores (1859–1933) (and they were not alone — one could add British, French, and others to the list), who confronted Japan and remained essentially untouched. They simply recorded what they saw.

It remained for a more resourceful and suggestible generation of American artists to make something new out of their encounter with Japan. They seem to fall into two broad categories. First there were the illustrators like Hyde and Lum who created a commercially successful, viable "picturesque" style heavily dependent on Japanese models and craftsmanship. While not on the highest level of art, they attracted a wide popular following. Lum was inadvertently caught up in the movement for the artistic revival of the woodcut in Japan, and in a small way might be said to have had a reverse impact in Japan. Then there are the proponents of modernism like Dow, Hopkins, Nordfeldt, and Wright who found in Japanese art a meaning and structure that acted as a stimulus in their personal drive toward abstraction.

The American encounter with Japan occurred at a moment when there was a great longing both in Japan and in the West for the "other," the distant shore. Japan was mysterious in part because of the language barrier. Few foreigners could be aware of the rich inner life and intellectual heritage of the Japanese. Even those who lived in Japan were often loath to acknowledge evidence of modernization. There was no praise by Westerners for the huge new industrial complexes or the commercial talents and wealth of Meiji entrepreneurs. Boston Brahmins like Bigelow and Morse, and artists such as Blum and Hyde headed East in search of images of Old Japan, the Japan of Hokusai and Hiroshige. At the same time the Japanese themselves were looking for a new "other" culture. Writers like Natsume Sōseki went to England, Mori Ōgai to Germany, and Nagai Kafū to France; the modern Japanese painter also looked to the French. Wealthy young entrepreneurs like Matsukata Kōjirō (1865–1950) enrolled at Rutgers College, joined the football team, and learned the secrets of Western industrialization. The collection of French Impressionists formed by Matsukata as a hobby when he became president of the Kawasaki Dockyard Co. is still one of the finest of its kind and is now housed in the National Museum of Western Art in Tokyo. He was famous in Paris in the 1920s as the rich Japanese who bought art in bulk, pointing to an entire wall of paintings with his cane and saying "I'll take everything." When he visited Monet's studio in Giverny in 1921 he purchased sixteen paintings on the spot and returned five months later to buy another eighteen. The Japanese — then as now — have always had an instinctive affinity for the Impressionists and Post-Impressionists, no doubt because these painters had learned so much from the art of Japan; Monet had more than two hundred Japanese prints hanging on the wall of his home at Giverny. To bring the story full circle, Matsukata was also a pioneer Japanese collector of ukiyo-e prints; he purchased a collection of more than eight thousand in France around 1920 with the hope that by returning them to their native land, he would give Japanese artists and scholars the opportunity to study an aspect of their culture that was still little known to them.[222]

The first wave of influence from Japan to America came during the 1870s and 1880s, with dramatic results in the decorative arts and interior design. By the turn of the century a series of trade fairs, wealthy collectors, and increasing ease of travel to Asia stimulated a second generation of Americans to a more sophisticated understanding of and deeper involvement with Japanese pictorial arts (particularly ukiyo-e). By the mid-twentieth century a different kind of Japanese art served as a source of inspiration for the Action Painters; Mark Tobey, Franz Kline, Robert Motherwell, and others drew on more subtle sources. The spiritual roots of their elitist abstract art come from the simplified, spontaneous black-and-white brushwork of Zen ink painting and calligraphy. Today, American graphic artists such as Helen Frankenthaler are still drawn to the craftsmanship of the Japanese printmaker, and they travel to Japan to supervise the carving and printing of their blocks.

As we have seen, Japonisme reinforced the romantic ideals of numerous artists at the turn of the century. For others it served as a catalyst in the exploration of modernist aesthetics. Such was and is today Japan's ironic enticement to the West.

NOTES

1. "Expedition to Japan," *The Friend, A Religious and Literary Journal,* April 19, 1851, p. 243. The primary reference work on the Japanese impact on the United States remains Clay Lancaster, *The Japanese Influence in America* (New York: Walton H. Rawls, 1963). Although Lancaster concentrates on the influence on American architecture and landscape gardening, he also outlines the influence of the Philadelphia Centennial Exhibition (1876). Similar attention is given to the World's Columbian Exposition, held in Chicago in 1893. On a much smaller scale, Lancaster's emphasis was followed by Sally Mills in her exhibition and catalogue *Japanese Influences in American Art* (Williamstown, MA: Sterling and Francine Clark Art Institute, 1981), and by Carol C. Clark, *American Japonism: Contacts Between America and Japan, 1854–1910* (Cleveland: Cleveland Museum of Art, 1975). A start in another direction was recently made in the book *In Pursuit of Beauty: Americans and the Aesthetic Movement* (New York: Rizzoli/The Metropolitan Museum of Art, 1987), where the Japanese impact on American interiors was accurately discussed (137–39) as part of the fascination with changing home environments. Also see Jane Converse Brown, "'The Japanese Taste': Its Role in the Mission of the American Home and in the Family's Presentation of Itself to the Public as Expressed in Published Sources, 1876–1916" (Ph.D. dissertation, University of Wisconsin, 1987).

2. Mills, *Japanese Influences in American Art,* 111. She cites William L. Neumann, *America Encounters Japan: From Perry to MacArthur* (Baltimore: The Johns Hopkins University Press, 1963), 44. Japanese gifts received by Perry are housed in the Smithsonian Institution, Washington, D.C. These pieces include lacquers and porcelains most likely of contemporary manufacture. For reproductions of a few pieces see Lancaster, *Japanese Influence in America,* 18, fig. 9.

3. Mills, *Japanese Influences in American Art,* 11. The Japanese mission that came to the United States in 1860 elicited great interest from the press. See "Our Japanese Visitors," *Harper's Weekly,* May 19, 1860, p. 316; "The Japanese at Washington," ibid., May 26, 1860, p. 331 (with numerous engravings of their activities); "The Japanese Embassadors," ibid., June 2, 1860, pp. 337–38; "The Japanese Embassy and their Attendants," ibid., June 23, 1860, p. 396, with an engraving after a photograph by Mathew Brady); and "The Japanese Ball at the Metropolitan," ibid., June 30, 1860, pp. 408–10. Additional early awareness of Japan and its objects is evident in reports on the impact Japan was having on contemporary European exhibitions. See "Japanese Manufactures at the Great Exhibition," *The Friend,* October 18, 1862, p. 54. The Alcock collection of Japanese art, amassed in Japan and then shown in London, was emphasized.

4. For reference to objects exhibited in Philadelphia see *Harper's Weekly,* August 12, 1876. An article in *Harper's Weekly* for August 26, 1876, considered the importance of the Japanese bazaar. Americans praised Japan's openness to progress and industry. For this and related issues see Robert W. Rydell, *All the World's a Fair: Visions of Empire at American International Expositions, 1876–1960* (Chicago: University of Chicago Press, 1984), 29–31.

5. Stimulated by the Japanese and in the forefront of this revitalization process was the Haviland Porcelain Manufactory in Limoges. Reference to Haviland pieces in the Japanese taste is found in *Harper's Weekly,* November 25, 1876, pp. 949–50.

6. The Haviland presence at the Philadelphia Centennial was facilitated by the fact that beginning in 1865, Theodore Haviland, the son of David Haviland, had represented the company in the United States. The company's shop at 47 John Street in New York City made it even easier for Haviland to play an important role in the Centennial and to exhibit a number of pieces there. Several letters between Charles and Theodore (now housed in the Haviland Archives in Limoges) document discussions on the Philadelphia Centennial Exhibition. How many members of the Haviland company actually went to the United States in 1876 remains to be examined, although it is probable that several (representing the firm or themselves) were in Philadelphia that summer. Information on the Haviland family and the manufactory's role at the 1876 exhibition was largely provided by Jean d'Albis (Limoges), whose own work on the Haviland firm has greatly clarified the historical picture of its contribution.

7. From the mid-1860s on, Japanese illustrated books, of varying quality, were found at numerous locations in Paris. All types of shops, including the new "department store," sold these objects on a regular

basis. For further reference see Gabriel P. Weisberg, "Japonisme: Early Sources and the French Printmaker, 1854–1882," in *Japonisme: Japanese Influence on French Art, 1854–1910* (Cleveland: Cleveland Museum of Art, 1975), 1–19. Also see Geneviève Lacambre, "Les Milieux japonisants à Paris, 1860–1880," in *Japonisme in Art: An International Symposium,* ed. Chisaburo F. Yamada (Tokyo: Committee for the Year 2000 and Kodansha International, 1980), 43–55.

8. For reference to Bing's early Japonisme see Gabriel P. Weisberg, *Art Nouveau Bing: The Paris Style 1900* (New York: Harry N. Abrams, 1986), 10–43. Bing's shop also attracted the American art agent George A. Lucas, who purchased Japanese pieces for his clients William Walters, whose collection, with that of his son, Henry, formed the basis of the Walters Art Gallery in Baltimore, and Samuel P. Avery, a New York dealer. For further reference see *The Diary of George A. Lucas: American Art Agent in Paris, 1857–1909,* ed. Lillian M. C. Randall (Princeton: Princeton University Press, 1979), 561, where it is noted that in 1883, Bing was paid 6,000 francs on Walters's account. On April 10, 1883, Lucas paid Bing 150 francs for a Japanese birdcage.

9. For a discussion of Bing's ties with America see Gabriel P. Weisberg, "S. Bing in America," in *The Documented Image: Visions in Art History,* ed. Gabriel P. Weisberg and Laurinda S. Dixon (Syracuse: Syracuse University Press, 1987), 51–68. For further reference to Morse see Dorothy G. Wayman, *Edward Sylvester Morse: A Biography* (Cambridge, MA: Harvard University Press, 1942). Wayman, 297, cites Morse's journal in 1883 on his visit to Paris:

After breakfast . . . I started for a Japanese exhibition . . . met M. Bing, the great dealer in Japanese art and M. Louis Gonse, director of the Gazette des Beaux-Arts. *. . . From there to Bing's store and saw the largest stock of Japanese pottery I have yet seen, but such prices! If my collection could be retailed for half what Bing charges I should make Vanderbilt jealous.*

Wayland, 298, notes his having dinner with Bing and Hayashi. On another visit to Paris in November 1887, Morse had further contact with Bing, Hayashi, and Gonse. He also extensively examined pottery in Bing's store.

10. See *Moore's Art Galleries, 290 Fifth Avenue, The Collection of S. Bing of Paris: Chinese Porcelain, Jades, Bronzes, Japanese Pottery, Crystals, Lacquers, Metal Work, Ivories, etc., Exhibition at 220 Fifth Avenue, Sale at Moore's Galleries, New York, April 26–29, 1887,* pp. 1–60. Bing mixed Chinese and Japanese objects in this sale — a practice established in France in the early 1860s. Bing was selling all types of pieces, most of which may have been contemporary, in the United States in order to reach the still untapped market that he thought existed in many of the larger cities. Julia Meech has suggested in discussions with the author that the presentation of Chinese and Japanese objects in one sale might show a breadth of taste in America.

11. Weisberg, "S. Bing in America," 54. The fact that Bing had his own showrooms in New York (even if they were sublets) implies that he was positioning himself for continued exposure in the United States and for close ties with others — some of whom became personal associates — in spreading the taste for all things Japanese.

12. A similar tone was found in the advertisement for *The Evening Post,* April 21, 1887, p. 3. For further review of this sale see "Bric-à-Brac, The Bing 'Opening,'" *The Art Amateur,* November 17, 1887, pp. 124–25. The use of "bric-à-brac" in the review's title also suggests that not everyone was taking these objects seriously, a point undoubtedly reflecting the level of quality of some objects in the exhibition.

13. Montezuma, "My Notebook," *The Art Amateur,* June 17, 1887, p. 3. This article insinuates that there were not, as yet, many trained or knowledgeable collectors in New York who were willing to spend considerable sums on Japanese art objects. Hence, some exquisite pieces could have been secured at low prices.

14. For further reference see *Catalogue of Rare and Valuable Art Objects comprising Chinese and Japanese Porcelains, Faiences . . . including many Specimens for Collectors and Amateurs to be sold by auction under the direction of the firm of S. Bing, 220 Fifth Avenue, New York, at Davis and Harvey's Art Galleries, no. 1212 Chestnut Street, April 16–20, 1888.* The catalogue was prepared by John Getz.

15. *Catalogue of Bronzes and other Works of Art comprising Antique Chinese and Japanese Porcelains . . . to be sold by auction under the direction of the firm of S. Bing at their art rooms, nos. 220 and 222 Fifth Avenue, New York, November 21, 1888.* The sale lasted until November 27.

16. See *Catalogue of Antique Chinese and Japanese Porcelains, Pottery, Enamels . . . to be sold at Public Sale by order of S. Bing, Paris, on Friday, February 23 . . . at The American Art Galleries, Madison Square South, New York, 1894.* Most likely the objects in this sale were of considerably higher quality

than those Bing had sold earlier, a factor emphasized by his close relationship with the prestigious American Art Galleries.

17. On the significance of *Artistic Japan* see Gabriel P. Weisberg, "On Understanding *Artistic Japan*," *The Journal of the Decorative and Propaganda Arts* 1 (Spring 1986): 6–19. Beginning with an article published on June 8, 1889 (p. 538), *The Japan Weekly Mail* continually reported on the value of *Artistic Japan*. This type of attention in an international periodical that was not dedicated to the visual arts further emphasized the role that Bing and others were playing in trying to bridge the differences between Eastern and Western cultures and attitudes. It also marks another way that Bing's importance as a figure in Japonisme was impressed upon Americans.

18. "The Fine Arts, Art Notes," *The Critic*, December 4, 1889, p. 302.

19. Weisberg, "S. Bing in America," 60–61.

20. For reference see *Japanese Engravings: Old Prints in Color Collected by S. Bing, Paris* (New York: The American Art Galleries, 1894).

21. "Art Notes," *The Critic*, March 17, 1894, p. 187.

22. "The Fine Arts," *Boston Herald*, April 8, 1894, p. 13. The reviewer called Bing's traveling collection "magnificent."

23. Reference to Bing and Fenollosa is found in Lawrence W. Chisholm, *Fenollosa: The Far East and American Culture* (New Haven and London: Yale University Press, 1963), 91, where mention is made of Bing visiting Fenollosa in Boston. Fenollosa's interest in arranging traveling exhibitions of high quality ukiyo-e prints was attested to by the fact that in May 1894, he borrowed several hundred from Bing for exhibition purposes (Chisholm, 93).

24. Gozo Tateno, "Foreign Nations at the World's Fair, Japan, by his excellency, the Japanese Minister at Washington," *The North American Review* 156 (1893): 38. Apparently everyone was taking this exposition very seriously as a way to bring nations into closer communication and communion. Consequently, the press made legitimate attempts to present to a broad audience the various attitudes of the involved nations. Japan sought further commercial ties with the United States through heavy visibility at the exhibition. For further discussion see Rydell, *All the World's a Fair*, 49–51, who asserts that Japan was seen to have an "Americanizing" influence on other "backward" Asian countries.

25. Ibid., 39–41. An effort to convey the qualities of various epochs in Japanese architecture spurred the recreation of well-known buildings. For further discussion see "The World's Columbian Exposition, The Japanese Village," *Harper's Weekly*, March 18, 1893, p. 259, with an illustration of Japanese workmen assembling one of the buildings at the Chicago fair (see fig. 6 *infra*).

26. Lucy Monroe, "Chicago Letter," *The Critic*, August 19, 1893, p. 129. Monroe commented on the distinguished, cosmopolitan gathering in the teahouse, where true enthusiasts took off their Western shoes and sat on the floor in the Japanese manner. The teahouse was also constructed to make American visitors fully aware of the ceremonial side of Japanese existence by focusing on the cult of tea drinking. Furthermore, this ceremony showed Americans how Japanese customs influenced attitudes, dress, and architecture.

27. Ibid., 129. This is one of the few references to either the presence or the type of Japanese prints exhibited at the fair. What remains confusing is the use of the term "process prints," since it could suggest different states of a Japanese print or it could refer to a work that was being used for educational purposes.

28. Julia Meech-Pekarik, "Early Collectors of Japanese Prints and The Metropolitan Museum of Art," *Metropolitan Museum Journal* 17 (1984): 96.

29. For further reference to Freer's collecting habits see Helen Tomlinson, "Charles Lang Freer: Pioneer Collector of Oriental Art" (Ph.D. dissertation, Case Western Reserve University, 1979). Ties between Bing and Freer are evident in letters now found in the archives of the Freer Gallery of Art, Washington, D.C.

30. For brief mention of the Havemeyer interest in Japanese art see Meech-Pekarik, "Early Collectors of Japanese Prints," 97–99. Meech has correctly noted that collecting Japanese objects per se was not the Havemeyers' main preoccupation. Nevertheless, when they hired Louis Comfort Tiffany and Samuel Colman to redecorate their home in New York, they were directly exposed to the Japoniste mode. Meech has also discussed the fact that Weir purchased Japanese prints from Bing and Hayashi via the mail. Additional information on the

Havemeyers' interest in Japanese objects is contained in Frances Weitzenhoffer, *The Havemeyers: Impressionism Comes to America* (New York: Harry N. Abrams, 1986).

31. J. Jackson Jarves, "Japanese Art," *The Art Journal* 8 (June 1, 1869): 182–83.

32. J. Jackson Jarves, "A Genuine Artistic Race," *The Art Journal* 33, (March 1–July 1, 1871): 77–79, 100–101, 136–37, 161–62, and 185–86. This approach of using Japanese illustrated books as a source of information on Japanese life, legends, and customs emanated from earlier French critics who wrote in a similar vein in the late 1860s. This practice was also advocated by the noted Japoniste Philippe Burty. For further reference to Burty's Japonisme see Gabriel P. Weisberg, "Philippe Burty and a Critical Assessment of Early Japonisme," in *Japonisme in Art: An International Symposium,* 109–25.

33. For further information see Haga Tōru, "The Diplomatic Background of Japonisme: The Case of Sir Rutherford Alcock," in *Japonisme in Art,* 27–42.

34. Sir Rutherford Alcock, *Art and Industries in Japan* (London, 1878) notes that an "era of Japonism" had overtaken all of Europe. This attitude, expressed in a book that was readily available in the United States, would have increased awareness that Japonisme was a truly international tendency. Significantly, Alcock used the accepted term "Japonisme" rather than develop new terminology.

35. Philippe Burty's early articles, especially those that followed recent developments in Japonisme, were translated into English. For further reference see Burty, "Fine Art—Japonism," *The Academy* 8 (August 7, 1875): 150–51. Again, English editors used the French term in an English version.

36. On Liberty's interest in supporting Japanese art see *Liberty's, 1875–1975* (London: Victoria and Albert Museum, 1975). Liberty maintained associations with Japanese enthusiasts he knew on the Continent, such as Philippe Burty, and he established a lasting relationship with Siegfried Bing. He may have competed with Bing in collecting certain types of Japanese objects, possibly textiles, when they became integral to Liberty's own designs in the 1890s.

37. *Catalogue of and Notes upon the Loan Exhibition of Japanese Art held at the Fine Art Society,* introd. Marcus B. Huish (London, 1888).

38. *Catalogue of a Collection of Drawings and Engravings by Hokusai, exhibited at the Fine Art Society* (London, 1890).

39. See A. Lasenby Liberty, "The Industrial Arts and Manufactures of Japan," *Journal of the Society of Arts,* June 6, 1890, pp. 673–84.

40. The utilization of this term appeared in English dealer catalogues in the mid-1880s, suggesting that it was one way critics and entrepreneurs attached their own inflection to a movement that had gained considerable visibility. The term rapidly spread to the United States, where the periodical *The Art Interchange* used the term "Japanesque" to describe the Japanese-style decoration and design of certain plates. For further reference see *The Art Interchange* 14, no. 6 (March 12, 1885): 63 (design for an oyster plate). This is not the only occasion where the term "Japanesque" was used in this magazine. In discussions with Peyton Skipwith of the Fine Art Society of London, it was noted that the terms "Japanesque" and Japonisme remained in common usage throughout the 1880s. Since "Japanesque" was gradually superseded in literature by "Japonisme," it appears that the infrequent use of the term "Japanesque" led to its gradual replacement.

41. A preliminary version of this essay, focusing on Helen Hyde and Arthur Dow, first appeared in a conference paper submitted for *Perspectives on Japonisme, The Japanese Influence on America,* ed. Phillip Dennis Cate (New Brunswick: Jane Voorhees Zimmerli Art Museum, Rutgers, The State University of New Jersey, 1989).

42. See Meech-Pekarik, "Early Collectors of Japanese Prints," 97–99.

43. Ibid., 108.

44. For a discussion of Morse see Money Hickman and Peter Fetchko, *Japan Day by Day: An Exhibition Honoring Edward Sylvester Morse* (Salem, MA: Peabody Museum of Salem, 1977); also Wayman, *Edward Sylvester Morse.* Morse catalogued his ceramics for the Museum of Fine Arts in *Catalogue of the Morse Collection of Japanese Pottery* (Cambridge, MA: Riverside Press, 1901); see also *Japanese Ceramics from the Morse Collection, Museum of Fine Arts, Boston* (Tokyo: Tokyo Shimbun, 1980).

45. William Anderson, *Descriptive and Historical Catalogue of a Collection of Japanese and Chinese Paintings in the British Museum* (London: Longmans, 1886).

46. Yamaguchi Seiichi, "Kobayashi Bunshichi jiseki" (Kobayashi Bunshichi and His Achievements), *Saitama daigaku kiyō* (Bulletin of Saitama University) 6 (November 1987): 7. For a concise review of Fenollosa's career see S. Miyoshi, "Ernest Fenollosa," *The Japan Magazine* 11 (December 1920): 281–85. The definitive work on Fenollosa is Yamaguchi Seiichi, *Fuenerosa* (Ernest Francisco Fenollosa: A life devoted to the advocacy of Japanese culture), (Tokyo: Sanseidō, 1982), 2 vols. See also Lawrence W. Chisholm, *Fenollosa: The Far East and American Culture* (New Haven: Yale University Press, 1963). For Fenollosa and Hōgai see Hosono Masanobu, *Kano Hōgai — The Man and His Art* (Tokyo: Yamatane Museum of Art, 1988).

47. Fenollosa, *The Masters of Ukioye* (New York: W. H. Ketcham, 1896).

48. Walter Muir Whitehall, *Museum of Fine Arts Boston: A Centennial History*, 2 vols. (Cambridge, MA: The Belknap Press of Harvard University, 1970) 1: 116. For more on Bigelow see T. J. Jackson Lears, *No Place of Grace: Antimodernism and the Transformation of American Culture 1880–1920* (New York: Parthenon Books, 1981), 228.

49. *Exhibition of Posters* (Massachusetts Charitable Mechanic Association: October 2–November 30, 1895). A second poster exhibition, which included "Japanese posters" in the form of battle prints, was held in Chicago in 1897: *Catalogue of an Exhibition of American, French, English, Dutch, and Japanese Posters from the Collection of Mr. Ned Arden Flood* (Chicago: The Quadrangle Club, 1897). The author is indebted to David Kiehl for pointing out these sources. For Matsuki see Murakata Akiko, "Nibi hōshi — Matsuki Bunkio — no koto (Matsuki Bunkio, Priest of Japanese Beauty), *Ukiyo-e geijutsu* 66 (1980): 3–13.

50. Ernest Fenollosa, *An Outline of the History of Ukiyo-ye* (Tokyo: Kobayashi Bunshichi, 1901), 3.

51. Oliver Statler, *Modern Japanese Prints: An Art Reborn*, introd. James A. Michener (Rutland, VT: Charles E. Tuttle Co., 1959), 7.

52. For a discussion of La Farge's early contacts and fascination with Japanese art see Henry Adams, "John La Farge's Discovery of Japanese Art: A New Perspective on the Origins of Japonisme," *The Art Bulletin* 67 (September 1985): 449–85. This lengthy examination of La Farge's interest in Japanese art and his collection of Japanese prints set new parameters to the priority of discovery.

53. Ibid. The literature on La Farge's use of Japanese themes and motifs is extensive. For further reference see Henry Adams, et al., *John La Farge* (New York: Abbeville, 1987).

54. For reference to this attitude see Henry Adams, "The Mind of John La Farge," in *John La Farge*, 48–49. Adams noted that La Farge "overlooked precisely those varieties of Japanese art that seem — at least from our modern perspective — most unique and peculiar to Japan."

55. This attitude is implied in articles by James Yarnall, especially his "John La Farge's *Portrait of the Painter* and the Use of Photography in His Work," *American Art Journal* 18, no. 1 (Winter 1986): 4–20, and "New Insights on John La Farge and Photography," ibid., 19, no. 2 (Spring 1987): 52–79. The use of photography can be considered, as it was in France, one way that an artist or a novelist could compile and store data for future reference. While Yarnall hints at this concept, he does not examine the naturalistic tendencies of the period that would have helped to make La Farge increasingly sensitive to these issues.

56. La Farge's connection to photographs taken in Japan is complicated. There is every suggestion that he used his own photographs for his watercolors. The author is indebted to Dr. Mary Panzer, photographic historian, in trying to piece together La Farge's relationship to photography. In her notes to the author she cites Yarnall, who says "that despite plentiful references very few photographs have survived" (letter from Panzer to the author, May 10, 1989). Since Yarnall is referring to photographs La Farge took, we must accept his archival research as being conclusive. However, Panzer also suggests that there were other sources for potential photographic influences, including Henry Adams, and Bigelow's collection of photographs purchased in Japan, now housed in the Peabody Museum at Harvard. Adams is known to have borrowed Bigelow's camera to take photographs. Aside from the immediate interest of La Farge and his fellow Japonistes in photography, his ties with artists in Newport, who were also evaluating the importance of photography, need further exploration.

57. Adams, "Mind," 49. Adams gave the rather derogatory judgment that "unfortunately most of the Japanese watercolors are far drier in effect, and in appearance rather like picture postcards."

58. Ibid., 53. For reference to ways in which La Farge's travel watercolors can be assessed see *American Traditions in Watercolor: The Worcester Art Museum Collection,* ed. Susan Strickler (Worcester, MA: Worcester Art Museum, 1987), 74, 76.

59. Ibid., 49. In the auction catalogue of the John La Farge Collection at The American Art Galleries, held March 29–31, 1911, the notice appeared that under "Lot 431 — Albums and Books: containing numerous landscapes, houses and customs of the Japanese," there were about twenty-seven volumes of material.

60. For further reference see "Japonica — First Paper — Japan the Country," *Scribner's Magazine* 8, no. 6 (December 1890): 662–82; "Japonica — Second Paper — Japanese People," ibid., 9: no. 1 (January 1891): 17–30; "Japonica — Third Paper — Japanese People (continued)," ibid., 9, no. 2 (February 1891): 165–76; and "Japonica — Fourth Paper — Japanese Ways and Thoughts," ibid., 9, no. 3 (March 1891): 321–40. Illustrations accompanying the text were reproduced after drawings and watercolors that were commissioned from Robert Blum. For further reference see Sir Edwin Arnold, *Japonica* (New York: Charles Scribner's and Sons, 1892).

61. For a discussion of Blum's interest in Whistler see Bruce Weber, "Robert Frederick Blum (1857–1903) and His Milieu" (Ph.D. dissertation, City University of New York, 1985), 97–168. The literature on Whistler's ties with Japonisme is extensive. For further reference see David Park Curry, *James McNeill Whistler at the Freer Gallery of Art* (New York: W. W. Norton, 1984), especially the bibliographic references.

62. Two photographs, mounted on board, that were originally taken at the Philadelphia Centennial Exhibition of 1876 are found in the collection of the Cincinnati Art Museum. Inscribed to Robert Blum and dated Christmas 1877, these photographs were taken by the Centennial Photographic Company of Philadelphia. They record objects that were part of the original Japanese installation, and as such they constitute an early document of the type of photographs Blum collected in relation to all things Japanese.

63. Weber, *Blum,* 334–35. Also see Julia Meech-Pekarik, "Frank Lloyd Wright's Other Passion," in *The Nature of Frank Lloyd Wright,* ed. Carol R. Bolon, Robert S. Nelson, and Linda Seidel (Chicago: The University of Chicago Press, 1988), 139, on Shugio Hiromichi.

64. Weber, *Blum,* 339. Although often seen to be competing with Siegfried Bing, Hayashi and his European counterparts were the primary forces in molding Western reception of the highest quality of ukiyo-e prints by 1900. For a brief introduction to the role of Hayashi see Segi Shinichi, "Hayashi Tadamasa: Bridge Between the Fine Arts of East and West," in *Japonisme in Art,* 167–72.

65. Weber, *Blum,* 339. This author cites the reference in Blum's personal diaries.

66. For a discussion of the complicated issues then surrounding the Japanese art world see Takashina Shūji, "Eastern and Western Dynamics in the Development of Western-Style Oil Paintings During the Meiji Era," in *Paris in Japan: The Japanese Encounter with European Painting* (Saint Louis: Washington University Press, 1987), 21–31, and J. Thomas Rimer, "Tokyo in Paris/Paris in Tokyo," in ibid., 33–79.

67. As quoted in Weber, *Blum,* 340–41, from Robert Blum's Japanese diary of June 1890 to May 1891. Julia Meech has noted that the reference to Fenollosa's collection was to his own personal pieces.

68. Weber, *Blum,* 342. The Robert F. Blum Collection of Japanese prints, albums, and illustrated books entered the Cincinnati Art Museum in 1905 and 1906. The 1905 gift came from his sister, Mrs. Henrietta Haller, and consists of 43 Japanese illustrated books, 14 albums, and Hiroshige's *Eight Views of Lake Biwa* mounted on a scroll; 4 of the albums are *koban* folding albums by single artists; the remaining 9 *ōban* albums contain 409 prints. The 1906 gift of 170 single-sheet prints came from Blum's estate. Later artists predominate in the Blum collection, and the few prints by earlier artists, such as Utamaro and Kiyonaga, are of inferior quality. Artists represented in the 1905 gift include Eisen in his series of the *Keijo Dochu Sugoroku.* The author is indebted to Julia Meech for sharing this information with him.

69. Weber, *Blum,* 341 and 345.

70. For reference see Robert Blum, "An Artist in Japan," *Scribner's Magazine* 13, no. 4 (April 1893): 399–414; ibid., no. 5 (May 1893): 624–36; ibid., no. 6 (June 1893): 729–49.

71. Blum's use of photographs to document his models in his studio or in the apartments of others recalls the way some French naturalist painters insistently recorded their models in photographs, occasionally with themselves actually painting from the model. For reference to this tendency see Gabriel P. Weisberg, "P. A. J. Dagnan-Bouveret and the Illusion of Photographic Naturalism," *Arts Magazine* 56, no. 7 (March 1982): 100–105. In this case, Dagnan-Bouveret, one of the primary figures in the evolution of Salon naturalism in painting, also used other photographs as specific models for forms in his paintings, which further complicates the way naturalists used photographs as part of their creative process.

72. Weber, *Blum,* 345, as quoted from Jessie Jones, "Mr. Blum's Advice to Art Students: Jotted Down by One of his Painting Class at the Art Student's League, New York," 116. Blum's attitude toward photography again echoes the concepts espoused by Dagnan-Bouveret. The French atelier system would have conveyed this approach to students and visitors.

73. For a discussion of the use of composite photographs in the creation of drawings and final paintings in the career of Dagnan-Bouveret see Gabriel P. Weisberg, "Making It Natural: Dagnan-Bouveret's Constructed Compositions for the Paris Salon of the 1880s," *The Scottish Art Review,* special no. 15, no. 4 (1982): 7–15. Dagnan-Bouveret was well known in America, and the working methods he espoused may have been verbally transmitted in artistic circles.

74. For further reference see Edwin Arnold, "Japan Revisited," *The Cosmopolitan* 14, no. 1 (November 1892): 3–11; ibid., no. 2 (December 1892): 132–42; ibid., no. 3 (January 1893): 285–93. *The Cosmopolitan* articles were illustrated with photographs as well as watercolors, which demonstrates that this type of documentary material was being accepted for contemporary periodicals.

75. See Shugio Hiromichi, *Catalogue of an Exhibition of Japanese Colored Prints and Illustrated Books* (New York: [Grolier Club], The De Vinne Press, 1889). For further reference to this show and Shugio Hiromichi see Meech-Pekarik, "Early Collectors," 108.

76. Exhibitions of Japanese art proliferated in America during the 1880s and 1890s. These shows and their catalogues continued to attract collectors and artists in New York, Boston, and Chicago as well as in smaller cities. The regional sponsorship of Japonisme in America is worthy of continued examination.

77. For reference see Shugio Hiromichi, *Catalogue of an Exhibition of Japanese Prints* at the Grolier Club, 29 East 32 Street, New York, April 1896 (see fig. 14 in the present volume for poster). Utamaro was well represented (see catalogue numbers 101–24) as was Hokusai (see catalogue numbers 135–61).

78. See "The Fine Arts: Japanese Prints at the Grolier Club," *The Critic,* April 18, 1896, p. 279.

79. See "Minor Exhibitions," *The Art Amateur,* December 1890, p. 4. Also see *The Critic,* November 15, 1890, for a similar reference to Japanese sources. For reference to the catalogue see *Catalogue of an Exhibition of Illustrated Bill-posters,* at the rooms of the Grolier Club at 29 East 32 Street, New York (November 1890), especially numbers 1–38 (Chéret) and 46–50 (Grasset).

80. See "Modern French Posters," *The Critic,* April 18, 1896, p. 279.

81. See *Salon de l'Art Nouveau, premier catalogue* (Paris, 1895), no. 626, where the names of de Quarqueville [*sic*], Bradley, Penfield, Cox, and others are listed without giving specific references to the individual posters included in the exhibition.

82. See Vittorio Pica, "A travers les affiches illustrées, I Etats Unis," *L'Estampe et l'Affiche* 1 (September 1897): 163–69. Pica placed American posters first in his discussion, affording them prominence in a field that they were helping to revolutionize. Translated from Italian, the article was illustrated with excellent lithographic examples by Rhead, Bradley, and Dow, which gave them even greater exposure to audiences on the Continent and in Paris than would have been possible through exhibitions. The constant juxtaposition of American and European posters in the artistic press was deliberate, for it accentuated the movement's international basis and its similarities of style, purpose, and source.

83. For reference to these qualities in European posters see *The Critic,* November 15, 1890. Mary Cassatt's color prints, her ties with Japanese art, and the availability of some of her prints in the United States are discussed in Nancy Mowll Mathews and Barbara Stern Shapiro, *Mary Cassatt: The Color Prints* (New York: Harry N. Abrams, 1989).

84. For reference to Rivière and ties with the world of the Japonistes see Armond Fields, *Henri Rivière* (Salt Lake City: Peregrine Smith, 1983), especially the chapter on "Color Lithography and Japonisme, 1896–1902."

85. On Toulouse-Lautrec see *Henri de Toulouse-Lautrec: Images of the 1890s,* ed. Riva Castleman and Wolfgang Wittrock (New York: The Museum of Modern Art, 1985).

86. Roberta Waddell Wong, "Will Bradley: Exponent of American Decorative Illustration at the End of the Nineteenth Century" (Ph.D. dissertation, The Johns Hopkins University Press, 1971), 48–49.

87. Lynn Scholz, "Louis John Rhead," in *Rhead Artists and Potters, 1870–1950* (London: Geffrye Museum, 1986), 11. In discussions and in written correspondence, Scholz substantially affected the author's perceptions of Rhead and his work. For further discussion of the poster movement see *American Posters of the Nineties,* introd. Roberta Wong (Boston: Boston Public Library, 1974).

88. "Printers and Engravers: Cover Designs by Louis J. Rhead," *Art Age* 3, no. 35 (June 1886): 192, with reproductions of drawings by Rhead, and 198. Scholz confirmed that the majority of Rhead's drawings for periodicals or books have not been found.

89. For reference to this ceramic table service see Jean Paul Bouillon, Christine Shimizu, and Philippe Theibaut, *Art, Industrie et Japonisme, le service "Rousseau,"* Les Dossiers du Musée d'Orsay (Paris: Musée d'Orsay, 1988).

90. These 1885 designs are unattributed and unsigned. The chance that these designs were completed by Louis Rhead has not been dismissed in discussions with Lynn Scholz. By 1886, Rhead was creating designs for *The Art Interchange.* In a letter to the author, June 8, 1989, Scholz noted that at D. Appleton and Company, "until 1888, his work was unsigned and otherwise unattributed."

91. For further reference see *Rhead Artists,* 11.

92. Ibid. One vase George Wooliscroft Rhead (Louis's father) decorated for Minton's was noted as being adapted from the Japanese. See "Early and Special Family Ceramics," in *Rhead Artists,* repro., 15. George Rhead worked at Minton's from 1870 and then at its Art Pottery Studio in London until it burned down in 1875. Scholz wrote in a letter to the author, June 8, 1989, that "Louis was exposed to a heavy dose of Japonism in the Potteries and at South Kensington—long before coming to America."

93. Scholz, "Rhead," p. 12.

94. Rhead has been considered a proponent of American Art Nouveau. See Diane Chalmers Johnson, *American Art Nouveau* (New York: Harry N. Abrams, 1979), 170–72.

95. For a discussion of the importance of Whistler's Peacock Room and Japanese sources see Curry, *Whistler at the Freer,* 52–69.

96. For a reference to an example see Lancaster, *Japanese Influence in America,* fig. 9.

97. For a discussion of the relationship between Bradley and Beardsley see Wong, "Bradley," 123–25. Beardsley's work acquired an international following through English magazines such as *The Studio* and other periodicals widely known in the United States. Bradley, like Rhead, was quite familiar with the English Arts and Crafts tradition and with popular illustration.

98. Wong, "Bradley," 91. Although tentative in suggesting ties with Japan, Wong does venture that the Japanese mania throughout the Midwest, and specifically at the Chicago fair of 1893, could have sensitized Bradley to appreciate Japanese sources.

99. It is not known when this early poster, apparently never copyrighted, was first made available to the public. As Wong ("Bradley," 158), has noted, the Library of Congress assigned the date of May 1894 to the image, assuming that it was to be used to announce the first issue of the periodical. Other writers have assigned slightly later dates to its initial appearance without firmly documenting their theories. An early criticism of the print appeared in December 1894. For further reference see *American Art Posters of the 1890s in The Metropolitan Museum of Art* (New York: Metropolitan Museum of Art, 1987), 104.

100. For reference to Wright's interest in Japanese prints see Julia Meech-Pekarik, "Frank Lloyd Wright and Japanese Prints," *Metropolitan Museum of Art Bulletin* 40, no. 2 (Fall 1982): 49–56.

101. Wong, "Bradley," 185.

102. Johnson, *American Art Nouveau,* 175–204. The poster movement reigned supreme from 1894 to 1896, just when the international Art Nouveau movement was being established.

103. For reference see John Sloan, "Autobiographical Notes on Etching," reproduced in Peter Morse, *John Sloan's Prints: A Catalogue Raisonné of the Etchings, Lithographs, and Posters* (New Haven and London: Yale University Press, 1969), 383. The notes added to this paper refer to articles published in 1895 or 1896 in newspapers that "confirm predominantly Japan's influence in Sloan's poster style."

104. Ibid., 383.

105. Ibid.

106. Ibid.

107. See *Posters in Miniature, with an Introduction by Edward Penfield* (London: John Lane, 1896), n.p., for two designs by Sloan that display these qualities and Beardsley's impact.

108. For this concept see Raymond Koechlin, *Souvenirs d'un vieil Amateur d'Art de l'Extrême Orient* (Chalon-sur-Saône, 1930), pp. 42–46.

109. Ibid.

110. Ibid., 22ff. For a brief discussion of this group see Glenn D. Lowry with Susan Nemazee, *A Jeweler's Eye: Islamic Arts of the Book from the Vever Collection* (Washington, D.C.: Arthur M. Sackler Gallery, in association with the University of Washington Press, Seattle, 1988), 24. Vever became a member of the Friends in 1892. This group was composed of the leading supporters of Japanese art and culture, although visitors may have been admitted to some gatherings. Early members of the Friends in France included Bing, Hayashi, Raymond Koechlin, Louis Gonse, Gaston Migeon, Claude Monet, and Henri Rivière.

111. This and the immediately following quotes are from Henry P. Bowie, *On the Laws of Japanese Painting* (San Francisco: P. Elder, 1911). Reprint: New York: Dover Publications, 1952. For biography of Bowie see *Kindai Nihonga no yoake* (Dawn of Modern Nihonga), ed. Hosono Masanobu (Tokyo: Nihon bijutsu-in and Asahi shimbunsha, 1989), 137–38.

112. For discussion of Sloan see Morse, *John Sloan's Prints.*

113. Henry Bowie, "Japanese Painting," *The Japan Magazine* 11 (May 1920), p. 33.

114. For a concise biography see Bertha E. Jaques, *Helen Hyde and Her Work: An Appreciation* (Chicago: The Libby Co., 1922), 9–11.

115. William Dinwiddie, "Miss Helen Hyde of Japan," *Harper's Bazar* 40, no. 1 (January 1906): 13.

116. For Guimet and Régamey see Ellen P. Conant, "The French Connection: Emile Guimet's Mission to Japan, A Cultural Context for *Japonisme,*" in *Japan in Transition: Thought and Action in the Meiji Era, 1868–1912,* ed. Hilary Conroy, Sandra T. W. Davis, and Wayne Patterson (Rutherford, NJ: Fairleigh Dickinson Press, 1984), 113–46.

117. Jaques, *Helen Hyde,* 10.

118. The intaglio press is described in a letter from Jaques to Alice Smith dated Chicago, September 6, 1923 (Alice Smith Papers, South Carolina Historical Society, Charleston).

119. The date of her return to America is given in a letter from Hyde to Fritz Weitenkampf dated Tokyo, May 30, 1914 (Print Collection, New York Public Library).

120. Photographs of her house were published in 1906 (Dinwiddie, "Miss Helen Hyde"), and in 1908 by Jaques, "An Artist's Home in Japan: How Helen Hyde has modified an eastern environment to meet western needs in its own way," *The Craftsman* 15 (November 1908): 186–91). A postscript: when the Museum of Art opened at the University of Oregon in Eugene, in 1933, it housed not only the Oriental collection of its benefactor, Gertrude Warner (1863–1951), who had spent some years living and traveling in Asia, but also a room dedicated to Warner's friend Helen Hyde. (Hyde visited Warner in Shanghai for six weeks in 1907, and Warner visited "Nellie" often in both Tokyo and Nikkō.) Included in the Hyde room in Eugene were her prints, watercolors, and, most amazing, a set of hand-carved furniture, replicas of the furnishings in Hyde's home in Tokyo!

121. "San Francisco Women Who Have Achieved Success," *Overland Monthly,* November 4, 1904, p. 517.

122. Norman Springer, "High Tribute to Helen Hyde," *San Francisco Bulletin,* May 26, 1919.

123. Letter from Hyde to her family, dated Tokyo, July 7, 1913 (California Historical Society, San Francisco); see also Yanagi Soetsu, "Introduction: Leach in Japan," in Bernard Leach, *A Potter's Book* (London: Faber and Faber, 1940), xviii.

124. She illustrated *Moon Babies* with verses by G. Orr Clark (R. H. Russell, 1900). Another collaboration with Mabel Hyde was a child's "nonsense" book in the style of Lewis Carroll, said to have been translated into Japanese (MS1085, California Historical Society).

125. Hiraishi Noriko of the University of Tokyo was able to identify the Japanese source for at least sixteen of the songs in Hyde's maquette.

126. Inventory of Hyde collection in the California Historical Society; letter from Helen Hyde to her family dated Tokyo, July 7, 1913 (California Historical Society).

127. Harriet Quimby, "How Helen Hyde Studied Art in Japan," *San Francisco Call,* November 1, 1901, p. 10.

128. Isozaki Yasuhiko and Yoshida Chizuko, *Tokyo bijutsu gakkō no rekishi* (History of the Tokyo School of Fine Arts) (Tokyo: Nihon bunkyō, 1977), 14. Satō Dōshin, "Kangakai ni tsuite" (About the Painting Appreciation Society), *Kindai Nihonga no yoake,* 110–12.

129. *Nihon bijutsu-in daijikkai kaiga kyōshinkai mokuroku* (Catalogue of the Tenth Competitive Exhibition of the Nihon Bijutsu-in), Spring 1901, 16–18. Hyde had a painting of a Buddhist temple guardian, *Ni-ō,* in the Fall 1901 exhibition. I am grateful to Yamanashi Emiko for calling these references to my attention.

130. Letter from Hyde to Fritz Weitenkampf, dated Karuizawa, July 19, 1914 (Print Collection, New York Public Library).

131. Emil Orlik, "Anmerkungen über den Farbenholzschnitt in Japan (1900)," *Die Graphischen Künste* 25 (1902): 31–34; for Bosch Reitz see Meech, "Early Collectors of Japanese Prints," 113.

132. "Studio Notes," *San Francisco Chronicle,* November 4, 1904, p. 7.

133. See Julia Meech-Pekarik, *The World of the Meiji Print* (New York and Tokyo: Weatherhill, 1986), 214ff.

134. Murata was still working for Hyde in 1911. E. J. Blattner, "Helen Hyde, An American Artist in Japan," *The International Studio* 45, no. 177 (1911): 53.

135. Giles, "The Modern Movement of the Colour Print," *The Original Colour Print Magazine,* June 1, 1924: 7.

136. "A Painter of the Japanese," *The New York Times,* April 15, 1906.

137. Dinwiddie, "Miss Helen Hyde," 15.

138. "San Francisco Girl Attains Eminence with Pictures of Japanese Life," *San Francisco Examiner,* August 24, 1910: 7.

139. Elisa Evett, *The Critical Reception of Japanese Art in Late Nineteenth Century Europe* (Ann Arbor, MI: UMI Research Press, 1982), 103.

140. Blattner, "Helen Hyde," 54.

141. This and other biographical data are found in letters from Sir Colin Crowe, Bertha Lum's son-in-law, to Mr. Tim Mason, June 25, 1983, and from Lum's daughter Peter Crowe to "Elise," New York, July 10, 1962. Letters courtesy of Tim Mason and The Fine Arts Museums of San Francisco, Achenbach Foundation for Graphic Arts. Peter Lum's autobiography, *My Own Pair of Wings* (San Francisco: Chinese Materials Center, Inc., 1981), contains a great deal of undocumented data about Bertha Lum. Additional information provided by Tim Mason in conversation with the author in August 1985, and by Robert O. Muller in November 1987.

142. Michael P. Conforti, "Orientalism on the Upper Mississippi: The Work of John S. Bradstreet," *The Minneapolis Institute of Arts Bulletin* 65 (1981–82): 2–35; Wendy Kaplan, *The Art That Is Life: The Arts and Crafts Movement in America, 1875–1920* (Boston: Museum of Fine Arts, 1987), 151.

143. Ethel Bogardus, "Successful Women of San Francisco," San Francisco newspaper clipping, source unknown, 1929. Courtesy Achenbach Foundation for Graphic Arts.

144. "Revives Quaint Art of Woodblock Printing: Local Woman Produces Beautiful Specimens of Old Oriental Craft," *Los Angeles Times,* November 28, 1926, sec. 2, p. 7.

145. H. H. Tolerton, "Bertha Lum," *Exhibition of Original Wood Block Prints in Color by Bertha Lum* (Chicago: Albert Roullier's Art Galleries, November 30–December 21, 1912).

146. Igami Bonkotsu, "Mokuhanga no shinka" (The True Value of Woodblock Prints), *Waseda bungaku* 7 (May 1907): 4–9; Tolerton, "Bertha Lum"; Lum erroneously cites the date of this trip as 1908. For Iwamura Tōru see *Geien zōkō-hoka* (Miscellaneous Manuscripts of Art and Literary Circles), ed. Miyagawa Torao (Tokyo: Heibonsha, 1971), 275–306.

147. "Revives Quaint Art," 7.

148. Igami, "Mokuhanga no shinka," see also Iwakiri Shinichirō, "Igami Bonkotsu," in *Fūshin* 1 (July 1988): 8–33.

149. A note of warning regarding Lum's dating: she redated her prints whenever she reissued them in a new edition, so that the same image may appear with a date ranging from 1908 to 1918, for example, and always preceded by the word "copyright"! For Nishimura see Nishimura Kumakichi, "Surishi Kumakichi mukashibanashi (Reminiscences About Printer Kumakichi)," *Ukiyo-e geijutsu* 2, no. 3 (March 1, 1933): 57–60 and 2, no. 4 (April 1, 1933): 72–74.

150. *Daijikkai taiheiyō gakai katarogu* (Tenth Pacific Painting Society Catalogue) (April 21–May 18, 1912). The author is indebted to Yamanashi Emiko for locating this catalogue.

151. *Exhibition of Japanese Paintings in Water Color by Hiroshi Yoshida, Hachiro Nakagawa, Shinzo Kawai, Takeshiro Kanokogi, Kunishiro Mitsutani, Banka Maruyama* (Boston Art Club: December 5–15 [1900]); *Special Exhibition: Watercolors by Prominent Japanese Artists* (New York: The American Art Galleries, 1901); "Yoshida Brings His Artist Sister," *Boston Herald,* April 1, 1904, p. 5; Gerald D. Bolas, "American Responses to Western-Style Japanese Painting," *Paris in Japan,* 13–19.

152. Letter from Catherine Lum Riva, Genoa, Italy, to Virginia Neal Lum, quoted in a letter from Virgina Lum in Beverly Hills, California, to Judson D. Metzgar dated January 18, 1956 (courtesy Sylvia Ragsdale); see also "Revives Quaint Art."

153. "Studio-Talk: New York," *International Studio* 72 (January 1921): 199–203; Tom Vickerman, "Woman from Iowa Outdoes Orientals at Their Own Game," *Chicago Evening Post,* July 26, 1932, p. 6.

154. Rafael Fernandez, *Eastern Winds: The Imprint of Japan on Nineteenth and Twentieth Century Western Graphics* (Williamstown, MA: Sterling and Francine Clark Art Institute, 1982), 7.

155. For these insights into Hearn, I am indebted to Hirakawa Sukehiro, "Was She Really Reconciled?—Ghost Wife Stories in Chinese, Korean, Japanese and American Literature," in *Modernizing Japan in Comparative Perspective,* reprinted from *Kiyō hikaku bunka kenkyū* 26 (Tokyo University, 1987).

156. "Notes," *Bulletin of the Minneapolis Institute of Arts* 6, no. 6 (June 1917): 47–48. The prints were a gift to the museum in 1916 from Ethel Morrison Van Derlip (1876–1921), a wealthy benefactor and the wife of the president of the Minneapolis Society of Fine Arts. That same year, she and her brother gave the museum $50,000 for the erection of a building for the museum's Art School. Her father had given the land for the museum. Mrs. Van Derlip was presumably a friend of Bertha Lum who is described as still a resident of Minneapolis in the 1917 museum *Bulletin.* The Institute was officially inaugurated in 1915 and the print department opened in 1916. The Lum woodcuts at the museum are still in their original mats. *Bulletin of the Minneapolis Institute of Arts* 10, no. 9 (December 1921): 66–67

157. Bertha Lum, *Gods, Goblins and Ghosts* (New York: Lippincott, 1922), 15.

158. "Notes," *Bulletin of the Minneapolis Institute of Arts* 6, no. 6 (June 1917): 47.

159. Letter from Catherine Lum Riva to Judson D. Metzgar (undated), and letter from Peter Lum Crowe, probably to Metzgar, undated, probably 1950s (courtesy Sylvia Ragsdale). Money Hickman and Satō Yasuhiro, *The Paintings of Jakuchū* (New York: The Asia Society and Harry N. Abrams, 1989), pl. 26.

160. Joseph Coburn Smith, *Charles Hovey Pepper* (Portland, ME: The Southworthe-Anthoensen Press, 1945), 15–16.

161. Alan French, "The Paintings of Charles H. Pepper," *World Today,* December 1905, p. 1274.

162. *Aquarelles de Charles H. Pepper* (Paris: L'Art Nouveau, December 1897).

163. Letter from Charles Hovey Pepper to his parents dated Kyoto, June 3, 1903 (courtesy of Frances Pepper Tarson).

164. Smith, *Pepper,* 17.

165. Ibid., 16.

166. "Beikoku Gaka Peppā-shi no Shirankai-hyō" (American Painter Mr. Pepper's Critique of the Purple Wave Society), *Bijutsu shinpō* (Art News), October 20, 1903, 122.

167. Arthur Wesley Dow, "First Notebook Ipswich to Daitokuji, Kyoto," Arthur and Dana Dow Papers, Archives of American Art, Smithsonian Institution, Gift of Mrs. George N. Wright, 1976. Entry for Thursday, October 8, 1903.

168. Ibid., entries for October 19 and 22. Woodcuts by other Westerners, including Austrian Fritz Capelari, and English artists Charles Bartlett (1860–1940) and Elizabeth Keith (1887–1956), were published in Tokyo beginning in 1915 by one of Japan's leading print dealers and publishers, Watanabe Shōzaburō (1885–1962), who began as a shop assistant to Kobayashi at the time the latter was working with Pepper. See Watanabe Tadasu, ed., *Watanabe Shōzaburō* (Tokyo: Watanabe mokuhanga bijutsu garo, 1974).

169. Charles Hovey Pepper, *Japanese Color Prints* (Boston: Walter Kimball, [1905]).

170. Annotated copies of American Art Association auction catalogues for Japanese print sales: the 1916 Judson Metzgar sale, the 1920 Ficke sale, and the 1921 William and John T. Spaulding sale; see also Smith, *Pepper,* 34–35. A portion of Pepper's collection of Japanese prints was given to the Museum of Fine Arts, Boston, by his daughter Eunice Langenbach, and most of the remainder, which included a representative sampling of landscape and figure prints and some outstanding vertical diptychs by Hiroshige, were recently sold at auction by the family. The Pepper sales were held at Sotheby's, New York, on May 14 and December 8, 1983; also lots 174 and 175 on November 9, 1984.

171. Arthur Wesley Dow to Minnie Eleanor Pearson, February 7, 1893 (Dow Papers, Archives of American Art, Smithsonian Institution, Washington, DC).

172. *The Important Private Collection of the Late Professor Arthur Wesley Dow* (New York: The American Art Galleries, March 27–29, 1923). There is a copy annotated with names of bidders in the library of the Metropolitan Museum of Art.

173. Whitehill, op. cit., 123 and 126.

174. *Special Exhibition of Color Prints Designed, Engraved, and Printed by Arthur W. Dow,* introd. Ernest F. Fenollosa (Boston: Museum of Fine Arts, 1895). Dow began his series of miniature vertical Ipswich prints in 1893, the date printed on a wrapper he made for a set entitled *Along Ipswich River: Ten Color Prints by Arthur W. Dow.* In the end he produced at least fourteen separate designs.

175. Arthur Wesley Dow, "Painting with Wooden Blocks," *Modern Art* 14 (Summer 1896): 90.

176. Nancy Finlay, *Artists of the Book in Boston* (Cambridge, MA: Houghton Library, 1985), 55. For a complete discussion of Dow see Frederick C. Moffatt, *Arthur Wesley Dow (1857–1922)* (Washington, DC: Smithsonian Institution Press, 1977).

177. The prospectus for Dow's 1893 summer class can be found in the files of the Ipswich Historical Society. It states that Japanese paper, brushes, and ink can be procured in Ipswich. For Ipswich prints see Kaplan, *The Art That Is Life,* 319–20.

178. Yamaguchi, "Kobayashi Bunshichi jiseki," 7.

179. "Dao kyōju no Nihon bijutsu kan (Professor Dow's Views on Japanese Art)," *Bijutsu shinpō,* December 20, 1903, p. 5.

180. See entries for October and November in Dow's Japan diary, Dow Papers.

181. See Watanabe Shōzaburō, *Catalogue of Wood-Cut Colour Prints,* (Tokyo: S. Watanabe, 1936), 107.

182. Record card for E. B. Boies in the archives of The Pratt Institute, Brooklyn, NY.

183. Edna Boies Hopkins Scrapbook, November 1903. Archives of American Art, Smithsonian Institution, Washington, DC, Gift of Mary Ryan.

184. In 1908 James Hopkins received the Walter Lippincott prize of the Pennsylvania Academy of the Fine Arts. *The American Art Annual* 7 (Boston: 1909–10), indicates that in 1909–10 the couple had an address on Chestnut Street in Philadelphia. For biographical information about Hopkins, I am indebted to research compiled by Catherine Ryan and made available to me by Mary Ryan. See *Edna Boies Hopkins: Color Woodcuts 1900–1923* (New York: Mary Ryan Gallery, 1986).

185. S. Bing, *Exposition de la gravure japonaise* (Paris, 1890). Many books by Keisai are listed in *The Important Private Collection of the Late Professor Arthur Wesley Dow.*

186. *Special exhibition of Color Prints by Edna Boies Hopkins* (Cincinnati Museum, October 31–November 17, 1914). In *An Exhibition of Wood Block Prints* (Boston Art Club, January 5–21, 1920), featuring Provincetown Printers, we read: "The printing may be done by rubbing [on the back of the paper] or it may be done in a regular printing press. The colors for 'rubbed' prints may be water colors or oil paints. For printing on a press the colors need to be ordinary printer's ink."

187. Janet Altic Flint, *Provincetown Printers: A Woodcut Tradition* (Washington, DC: Smithsonian Institution Press, 1983), 36.

188. Judson Metzgar, *Adventures in Collecting* (San Francisco: The Grabhorn Press, [1930s]), 76.

189. For more on this subject see Meech-Pekarik, "Frank Lloyd Wright's Other Passion," 125–53.

190. Kaplan, *The Art That Is Life,* 197–98; David Hanks, *The Decorative Designs of Frank Lloyd Wright* (New York: E. P. Dutton, 1979), 173–76. According to Wright's son John Lloyd Wright, the architect owned an 8-by-10 plate camera and built a darkroom off the balcony of his studio; Frank Lloyd Wright, *The Frank Lloyd Wright Collection of Japanese Antique Prints* (New York: The Anderson Galleries, 1927), Cat. 244.

191. "The Japanese Print Exhibition," *Bulletin of the Art Institute of Chicago* (April 1908): 36–38.

192. *The Domestic Scene (1897–1927): George M. Niedecken, Interior Architect* (Milwaukee: Milwaukee Art Museum, 1981).

193. Laura Stewart, "The Man, The Work, The Times," *B. J. O. Nordfeldt: An American Expressionist,* introd. Sam Hunter (Pipersville, PA: Richard Stuart Gallery, 1984), 57. For a biography of Nordfeldt see Van Deren Coke, *Nordfeldt the Painter* (Albuquerque: University of New Mexico Press, 1972). The author is grateful to Gabriel Weisberg for pointing out the many similarities between Nordfeldt and French color print artists.

194. *Meadowsweet* pamphlet in the library of the Department of Prints and Drawings, The British Museum, London. Fletcher had previously printed two of Batten's designs, but this was his first original work; Frank Morley Fletcher, "The Woodblock Colour-Print," *The Original Colour Print Magazine,* June 1, 1924, p. 5.

195. John D. Batten, "Woodcut Printing in Water Colours," *The Studio* 3 (1884): 144–48.

196. Frank Morley Fletcher, *Wood-Block Printing* (London: John Hogg, 1916), 3; T. Tokuno, "Japanese Woodcutting and Wood-cut Printing," ed. S. R. Koehler, *Report of the United States National Museum of 1892* (Washington, DC, 1893), 221–44, plates IV–XIII. Reissued as a pamphlet in 1894. Reprinted with commentary by Peter Morse, "Tokuno's Description of Japanese Printmaking," in *Essays on Japanese Art Presented to Jack Hillier,* ed. Matthi Forrer (London: Robert G. Sawers, 1982), 125–34.

197. Joseph Knowles, "Santa Barbara's Historic Link to Color Wood Block Printing," *Noticias* 16, no. 1 (Winter 1970).

198. Stewart, "The Man, The Work, The Times," 50.

199. "Block Printing Japanese Mode: Same Process Used by Mr. Nordfeldt in Making Prints of Western Subjects," *New York Herald,* January 26(?), 1908; *Etchings and Dry Points and Color Prints from Wood*

Blocks by B. J. Olsson-Nordfeldt (Art Institute of Chicago, January 1908). Titles for Nordfeldt prints follow those given in the 1908 Art Institute catalogue and the November 1908 exhibition catalogue (*The Print Collector's Bulletin: An Illustrated Catalogue of Painter-Etchings, B. J. Olsson Nordfeldt*) prepared by the artist's Chicago dealer, Albert Roullier.

200. The key block designs for several of the 1906 prints were published in 1905. See Alice C. Henderson, "Bror J. Olsson-Nordfeldt," *The Sketch Book* 5, no. 1 (December 1905): 187–92. Nordfeldt and a writer friend spent the year 1905 in a borrowed house in Framingham, Massachusetts.

201. Sam Hunter, "Nordfeldt's Modernist Odyssey," in *B. J. O. Nordfeldt: An American Expressionist,* 25.

202. See for example *Sea, Rock, and Fish,* oil on canvas, 1950, in the F. M. Hall Collection, Sheldon Memorial Art Gallery, University of Nebraska, Lincoln. Illustrated in ibid., 43.

203. The artist Ada Gilmore as quoted in Flint, *Provincetown Printers,* 15.

204. "Chicago Artists' Biographies: Colwell," pamphlet file of the Burnham Library, Art Institute of Chicago; Alice Rouillier, "The World of Elizabeth Colwell," *The Graphic Arts* 4 (March 1913): 237–48.

205. Angela D. Mack, "Notes on the Collection," *The Magic of Japanese Woodblock Prints* (Charleston: Gibbes Art Gallery, 1982).

206. Included in a letter from Gookin to Smith dated July 6, 1922, quoted in Martha R. Severens, *Alice Smith and Japonisme* (Charleston: Gibbes Art Gallery, 1989).

207. Severens, *Eight Southern Women* (Greenville, SC: Greenville County Museum of Art, 1986), 36–37; see also Severens, "Lady of the Low Country," *South Carolina Wildlife* (March–April 1979), 16–25.

208. *Catalogue of an Exhibition of Etchings and Block Prints* (The Art Institute of Chicago, April 4–May 1, 1919).

209. Jaques, *Helen Hyde,* 28.

210. Letter from Helen Hyde to Alice Smith dated Chicago, January 7, 1918. The Alice Smith papers, South Carolina Historical Society, Charleston. The author is indebted to Martha Severens for calling attention to this source.

211. Letters from Bertha Jaques to Alice Smith dated Chicago, January 6, 1918, and January 27, 1919. Loc cit.

212. For examples see *Le Japonisme* (Paris: Editions de la Réunion des Musées Nationaux, 1988), figs. 428–41.

213. Helmut and Allison Gernsheim, *Alvin Langdon Coburn* (New York: Frederick A. Praeger, 1966), 22.

214. Mike Weaver, *Alvin Langdon Coburn: Symbolist Photographer* (New York: Aperture/George Eastman House, 1986), 16–19.

215. For a thorough discussion of the Hiroshige series see Henry D. Smith and Amy G. Poster, *Hiroshige: One Hundred Famous Views of Edo* (New York: George Braziller and The Brooklyn Museum, 1986).

216. Weaver, *Alvin Langdon Coburn,* 18.

217. Arnold Genthe, *As I Remember* (New York: Reynal and Hitchcock, 1936), 138 and 144–45; also Jerry E. Patterson and Dorothy Wilcock Neumeyer, *Arnold Genthe 1869–1942: Photographs and Memorabilia from the Collection of James F. Carr* (Staten Island: Staten Island Museum, 1975).

218. *400 Japanese Color Prints Collected by Arnold Genthe* (New York: The Anderson Galleries, 1917). After this sale he focused primarily on Chinese art. There are photos of his Asian art collection in the archives of the Library of Congress.

219. Genthe, *As I Remember,* 225.

220. Patterson and Neumeyer, *Arnold Genthe,* 22.

221. *400,* foreword.

222. Julia Meech, *The Matsukata Collection of Ukiyo-e Prints: Masterpieces from the Tokyo National Museum* (New Brunswick, NJ: The Jane Voorhees Zimmerli Art Museum, Rutgers, The State University of New Jersey, 1989).

INDEX

A number in *italics* refers to the page on which an illustration appears; *cpl.* indicates a colorplate.

LENDERS TO THE EXHIBITION March 20, 1990

Archives of American Art, Smithsonian Institution
The Art Institute of Chicago
Boston Public Library
California Historical Society
Gala Chamberlain
Cincinnati Art Museum
Rare Book and Manuscript Library, Columbia University
Frank J. Dowd, Jr.
The Fine Arts Museums of San Francisco,
 Achenbach Foundation for the Graphic Arts
Gibbes Museum of Art
Grolier Club of New York
Remi Hirano
International Museum of Photography at George Eastman House
Ipswich Historical Society
Andrew Terry Keats
Kelmscott Gallery, Chicago
Mr. and Mrs. Allan Maitlin
The Mann Collection, Highland Park, Illinois
Meilinki Enterprises
The Metropolitan Museum of Art
The Minneapolis Institute of Art
Robert Muller
Museum of Fine Arts, Boston
National Museum of American Art, Smithsonian Institution
New York Public Library, Astor, Lenox and Tilden Foundations
Rose Ann O'Connor
Peabody Museum of Archaeology and Ethnology,
 Harvard University
Peabody Museum of Salem
Roy Pedersen
Private Collections
Prof. Dr. G. Pulverer, Cologne
Ravicz Collection
Rutgers University Libraries
Mary Ryan
Santa Barbara Museum of Art
Sterling and Francine Clark Art Institute
University of Minnesota Library
Museum of Art, University of Oregon
Wolfsonian Foundation
Worcester Art Museum
Mr. and Mrs. George N. Wright
The Jane Voorhees Zimmerli Art Museum, Rutgers University

PHOTOGRAPH CREDITS

Susan Howard Boice, Ipswich, MA: 120, 132, 135; Ron Chamberlain, Occidental, CA: 183; *The Chicago Literary Club,* 1926: 154; Christie's, New York: 144; © 1989 Trustees of Dartmouth College, Hanover, NH: 49; *Descriptive Catalogue of an Important Collection of Japanese and Chinese Pottery, Porcelain, Bronzes, Brocades, Prints, Embroideries, Kakemono, Screens, Ivories and Gold Lacquers selected by Mr. Bunkio Matsuki.* Boston: Leonard and Company's Galleries, April 1898: 18; Arthur Wesley Dow, *Composition: A Series of Exercises Selected from a New System of Art Education.* Boston: J. M. Bowles, 1899: 130; © 1989 The Fine Arts Museums of San Francisco: 77, 80, 94, 108, 113; Ron Forth: 2, 23, 24, 25, 26, 27, 28, 29, 33, 44; Daniel L. Grantham, Jr., Savannah, GA: 181, 182; Grolier Club, New York: 12; Hosono Masanobu: 52; Helen Hyde, *Jingles from Japan.* San Francisco: A. M. Robertson, 1902: 64; *Illustrated Catalogue of Etchings by American Artists.* Chicago: Albert Roullier Art Galleries, 1913: 188; Images 4, Stamford, CT: 10, 79; Jack Liu, Eugene, Oregon: 84, 95, 96; Bertha Lum, *Gods, Goblins and Ghosts.* Philadelphia: Lippincott, 1922: 112; Wayne McCall: 99; Marceau, New York: 11; The Metropolitan Museum of Art, New York: 42, 56, 156, 166; © 1989 Museum of Fine Arts, Boston: 13, 17, 19, 75, 100, 118, 119, 123, 125, 147, 150, 151, 187; Otto E. Nelson: 66, 175, 180; New York Public Library: 92, 164; Otsuka Kogeisha, Tokyo: 53, 54, 55; Patterson and Neumeyer, *Arnold Genthe 1869–1942: Photographs and Memorabilia from the Collection of James F. Carr.* Staten Island, NY: Staten Island Museum, 1975: 192; Plymouth Photo, Rochester, NY: 121, 127, 128, 134, 138; Princeton University Library, Princeton, NJ: 8; Nathan Rabin, New York: 14, 114, 116, 117, 158; Rijksmuseum, Amsterdam: 74; Nick Romanenko, New Brunswick, NJ: 122, 131, 146; Robert D. Rubic, New York: 71, 76, 82, 83, 133, 142, 143, 152, 167, 171, 173; Mary Ryan Gallery, New York: 140; M. Sexton, Salem, MA: 115; *Sketch Book* (December 1905): 164; © 1979 Sterling and Francine Clark Art Institute: 72; Ken Strothman: 155, 159, 161; Jann & John F. Thomson Photography: 64, 112, 184; Tokyo National Research Institute for Cultural Properties: 87, 102; Jay Turkel, PPI, Princeton, NJ: 73, 141, 145; University of Minnesota Library: 90; Victor's Photography, Piscataway, NJ: 16, 34, 40, 41, 43, 57, 58, 65, 78, 85, 111, 124, 149, 178; Yvonne Weisberg: 1, 3, 4, 5, 6, 7, 25, 30, 31, 32, 35, 36; Siegfried Wichmann, *Japonisme.* New York: Harmony Books, 1981: 174; © Worcester Art Museum, Worcester, MA: 137, 188.